SKILLS

*f*or

EFFECTIVE

HUMAN

SERVICES

MANAGEMENT

SKILLS

*f*or

EFFECTIVE

HUMAN

SERVICES

MANAGEMENT

Richard L. Edwards and
John A. Yankey, Editors

NASW PRESS

National Association of Social Workers
Silver Spring, MD

Library of Congress Cataloging-in-Publication Data

Skills for effective human services management / edited by Richard L. Edwards and
    John A. Yankey.
        p.   cm.
   Includes bibliographical references and index.
   ISBN 0-87101-195-6
   1. Human services—Management.   2. Human services—United States—
Management.   I. Edwards, Richard L.   II. Yankey, John A.
HV41.S564   1991
361'.0068—dc20   91-16322
                                                        CIP

Printed in the United States of America

Cover and interior design by Janice Mauroschadt Design

CONTENTS

PART 1

THE ORGANIZING FRAMEWORK

PART 2

BOUNDARY-SPANNING SKILLS

PART 3

HUMAN RELATIONS SKILLS

COORDINATING SKILLS

DIRECTING SKILLS

Foreword

Effective management is of great import to social work for a pragmatic reason: effective managers ensure the delivery of quality human services. Developing effective managers, therefore, is a fundamental concern for the National Association of Social Workers. As the primary organization for professional social workers, NASW is committed to helping social workers enhance their skills and professional standing and to improving the lives of people in our society.

One of NASW's objectives has been to communicate the importance of sound modern management tenets to the provision of human services, but until recently we have had limited vehicles for doing so. I am pleased to say that *Skills for Effective Human Services Management* is the third management book to be published by the NASW Press in the past three years.

The profession has long needed a book like this one that can serve as a basic text for preparing practitioners to become skilled managers. Within these 22 chapters, the reader will find a solid foundation for the management skills needed to head any human services organization. Collectively, the chapters present the careful analysis of individuals who are seasoned administrators, as well as excellent scholars.

The editors, Richard L. Edwards and John A. Yankey, are to be congratulated. In constructing this book, aimed at upper- and mid-level managers, they developed a clear organizing framework—the competing values framework—that will help managers recognize and deal with the complexity of managing a human services organization. Then they guided the authors in delineating the skills required so that each chapter relates directly to the framework, but is free of any artificial shaping to fit it. Chapters can be used together or on their own to work on specific areas. The result is a cohesive book that will challenge the reader and deliver substance that fills in the gaps in their preparation for management.

Skills for Effective Human Services Management happily fills a void in the social work literature. The book will be a superb addition to the texts used in schools of social work to prepare future managers. With its framework and skills-building exercises in each chapter, it also will be an excellent self-guided text for current managers and those who aspire to be upper-level managers.

Many human services organizations are led by social workers; therefore, the profession has a responsibility to prepare its practitioners to fill the roles of chief operating officers and chief executive officers. I am pleased that the NASW Press is bringing this book to the profession.

MARK G. BATTLE, ACSW
NASW Executive Director

Acknowledgments

In any edited book project, there are many individuals who contribute to the final product. We first wish to thank the authors of the individual chapters. Without their efforts, this book would not exist. We also thank Chris Ball for his editorial assistance during the early phases of manuscript preparation and Wendy Almeleh for her efforts in the final editing process. Special appreciation goes to Alma Martin, at Case Western Reserve University's Mandel School of Applied Social Sciences, who cheerfully provided us with word-processing services; our publisher, Linda Beebe, at NASW Press, for her counsel and support throughout all phases of this project; and Nancy Winchester, managing editor at NASW Press, for coordinating the publication process.

Others who deserve special thanks include Mark Litzler, who contributed the original cartoons included in the book, and Professors Robert E. Quinn and John Rohrbaugh, who originally conceived of the competing values approach to organizational effectiveness that was later developed by Quinn into the approach to leadership that serves as the framework for this book.

Finally, we want to thank all of our students, colleagues, and mentors, who have, over the years, taught us so many valuable lessons about management. For our managerial strengths, we give them full credit; for our shortcomings, we take responsibility.

R.L.E. and J.A.Y.

Introduction to the Volume

The world of management in the human services is changing rapidly. Part of the change is related to changing conditions—increased incidences of social problems, reduced governmental appropriations for human services programs, evolving service technologies, and the like. Yet, part of the change is also related to developments in management in the for-profit arena.

In the early 1980s, traditional approaches to American management began to be questioned. The characteristics of successful businesses and managers were identified, and questions were raised about whether management-education programs were really preparing leaders for the realities of contemporary management. A major study of the curricula of schools of business (Porter & McKibbon, 1988) suggested that management-education programs needed to place a greater emphasis on human skills. Quinn, Faerman, Thompson, and McGrath (1990, p. v) noted that

> what is now available in management education is necessary but insufficient. All . . . modern organizations, as never before, and even at the lowest levels, are in need of competent managerial leaders. They want technical ability but they also want more. They want people who can survive and help the organization prosper in a world of constant change and intense competition. This means both technical competence and interpersonal excellence.

The business sector has become inundated with books on what makes for excellence, for high productivity, and for overall success (see, for example, Blake, Mouton, & Allen, 1987; Kanter, 1983; Lawler, 1986; Ouchi, 1981; Peters & Waterman, 1982). To a great extent, the management of human services organizations has been influenced by what is occurring in the for-profit or business sector. There is more stress on excellence, on leadership, and on accountability. Yet, the very things that are now being stressed in the world of business—the human skills—are the things that human services managers have historically been best at. The trick is for human services managers to identify and acquire the technical skills and competencies that are called for in today's human services organizations and to integrate them with the human relations skills and competencies that have always been their forte.

Human services managers often experience some difficulty in using texts and training materials that have been developed for the for-profit sector. This book addresses the particular needs of human services managers. The content is aimed primarily at mid- and upper-level managers, who can benefit directly from it as they strive daily to attain excellence, as well as indirectly, as they help those whom they supervise do a better job of managing. But, even though it is directed mostly to managers, this book will also be useful in social work and other human services programs that include management education and training as part of their curricula.

Organizing Framework

The organizing framework for this book is a metatheoretical model of organizational and managerial effectiveness called the competing values framework (Edwards, 1987, 1990; Edwards, Faerman, & McGrath, 1986; Faerman, Quinn, & Thompson, 1987; Quinn, 1984, 1988; Quinn et al., 1990; Quinn & Rorhbaugh, 1981, 1983). This model, which is described more fully in Chapter 1, serves to integrate four contrasting sets of management skills: boundary-spanning skills, human relations skills, coordinating skills, and directing skills. Each set of skills has two inherent roles that managers must play to be successful in that sphere of organizational activity. The eight roles are those of broker, innovator, facilitator, mentor, monitor, coordinator, producer, and director. The competing values framework helps make explicit the fact that managers must function in a world of competing values, in which their daily activities most often do not represent a choice between something "good" and something "bad," but, rather, a choice between two or more "goods" or values. As used in this book, the competing values framework helps managers to consider the complexity and multiplicity of their roles within their respective organizations and stresses the point that the performance of a role is rarely an "either-or" situation.

The first section of the book provides an introduction to the competing values framework. The remaining chapters are organized in four parts that relate to the four major sets of skills. Each chapter covers the roles associated with the particular set of skills that are addressed in its respective section. Taken as a whole, the eight roles shed considerable light on what is expected of managers and the competencies they must develop to be effective.

The validity and importance of the eight roles have been demonstrated in several empirical studies. One study (Quinn, Denison, & Hooijberg, 1989) of more than 700 managers revealed that the measures of the eight roles met standard validity tests and that the roles appear in the four indicated quadrants. Another study (Pauchant, Nilles, Sawy, & Mohrman, 1989), involving over 900 managers, also found support for the eight roles and indicated that of 36 possible roles, these eight were considered the most important ones to be performed by managers. Still another study (Quinn, 1988) found that managers who did not perform these eight roles well were considered ineffective, whereas managers who did perform them well were considered very effective.

Learning Approach

This book is designed to be used in a number of ways. It can be used as an individualized learning tool, a primary text in a management-training or educational setting, or a supplement to other texts. The chapters are organized in a manner that facilitates the development of competencies that are needed to perform the various managerial roles. The structure of the chapters represents a variation of a learning model developed by Whetten and Cameron (1984), which involves assessment, learning, analysis, practice, and application. The first chapter includes an assessment instrument that will enable managers to gain insight into their relative strengths and weaknesses in relation to the eight roles. The succeeding chapters include a narrative section that provides the reader with information about the particular topic addressed in that chapter, examples particularly relevant to human services managers, and one or more skills-application exercises that provide opportunities to apply the material to realistic situations.

The particular topics addressed in the chapters were identified as a result of the editors' experiences as hands-on human services managers and as trainers and educators. It is believed that the array of topics covers many competencies that are not typically found in a single management book, but that are vitally important in the real world of human services management. In choosing the authors of the various chapters, the editors were intent on including those who have had substantial hands-on experience in human services management and who reflect the diversity of gender, race, and ethnicity in the contemporary human services work force. In addition, the editors believe that effective management requires, along with a range of technical and human skills, a sense of humor. Thus, a number of cartoons have been included in the book.

References

Blake, R., Mouton, J., & Allen, R. (1987). *Spectacular teamwork: What it is, how to recognize it, how to bring it about.* New York: John Wiley & Sons.

Edwards, R. L. (1987). The competing values approach as an integrating framework for the management curriculum. *Administration in Social Work, 11*(1), 1–13.

Edwards, R. L. (1990). Organizational effectiveness. In L. Ginsberg (Ed.), *Encyclopedia of social work: 1990 supplement.* Silver Spring, MD: NASW Press.

Edwards, R. L., Faerman, S. R., & McGrath, M. R. (1986). The competing values approach to organizational effectiveness: A tool for agency administrators. *Administration in Social Work, 10*(4), 1–14.

Faerman, S. R., Quinn, R. E., & Thompson, M. P. (1987). Bridging management practice and theory. *Public Administration Review, 47*(3), 311–319.

Kanter, R. M. (1983). *The change masters: Innovation for productivity in the American corporation.* New York: Simon & Schuster.

Lawler, E. E. III. (1986). *High-involvement management: Participative strategies for improving organizational performance.* San Francisco: Jossey-Bass.

Ouchi, W. G. (1981). *Theory Z: How American business can meet the Japanese challenge.* Reading, MA: Addison-Wesley.

Pauchant, T. C., Nilles, J., Sawy, O. E., & A. M. Mohrman. (1989). *Toward a paradoxical theory of organizational effectiveness: An empirical study of the competing values model* (working paper). Quebec City, Canada: Laval University, Department of Administrative Sciences.

Peters, T. J., & Waterman, R. H., Jr. (1982). *In search of excellence.* New York: Harper & Row.

Porter, L. W., & McKibbon, L. E. (1988). *Management education and development: Drift or thrust into the 21st century?* New York: McGraw-Hill.

Quinn, R. E. (1984). Applying the competing values approach to leadership: Toward an integrative framework. In J. G. Hunt, D. Hosking, C. Schriescheim, & R. Stewart (Eds.), *Leaders and managers: International perspectives on managerial behavior and leadership.* Elmsford, NY: Pergamon Press.

Quinn, R. E. (1988). *Beyond rational management: Mastering the paradoxes and competing demands of high performance.* San Francisco: Jossey-Bass.

Quinn, R. E., Denison, D., & Hooijberg, R. (1989). *An empirical assessment of the competing values leadership instrument* (working paper). Ann Arbor: University of Michigan School of Business.

Quinn, R. E., Faerman, S. R., Thompson, M. P., & McGrath, M. R. (1990). *Becoming a master manager: A competency framework.* New York: John Wiley & Sons.

Quinn, R. E., & Rohrbaugh, J. A. (1981). A competing values approach to organizational effectiveness. *Public Productivity Review, 5,* 122–140.

Quinn, R. E., & Rohrbaugh, J. A. (1983). A spatial model of effectiveness criteria: Toward a competing values approach to organizational analysis. *Management Science, 29*(3), 363–377.

Whetten, D. A., & Cameron, K. S. (1984). *Developing management skills.* Glenview, IL: Scott, Foresman.

PART

1

THE
ORGANIZING FRAMEWORK

This book is organized in accordance with an approach to organizational and leadership effectiveness known as the competing values approach. In this section, Richard L. Edwards and David M. Austin provide an overview of the roles that managers must perform, comparing and contrasting the roles of managers in the for-profit, public administration, and nonprofit sectors. They then identify three broad types of skills that managers must have, suggesting that the desired mix of these skills will vary depending on the level that a manager occupies in the organizational hierarchy.

Edwards and Austin then discuss the competing values framework, which organizes the roles that managers must play within four distinct sets of skills: boundary spanning, human relations, coordinating, and directing. Eight specific roles, two related to each set of skills, are identified and their implications are discussed. The authors suggest that managers must function in an environment of multiple role demands and competing values that they must understand if they are to be effective.

The chapter concludes with a self-assessment instrument that enables individuals to develop a graphic profile of their relative strengths in relation to each of the eight managerial roles identified in the chapter. The graphic profile suggests areas of content included in this book that may be of particular value for building skills.

Managing Effectively in an Environment of Competing Values

Richard L. Edwards and David M. Austin

We live in an era in which organizational life is characterized by shifting priorities, changing patterns in the allocation of resources, and competing demands. Human services managers are often called on to function in a milieu of reduced governmental appropriations for human services, heightened demands for those services, and higher expectations for accountability. It is sometimes suggested that the only constant in management today is change. Contemporary managers must contend almost daily with rapidly changing political, economic, and social conditions. They must be equipped with a broad range of knowledge, skills, and abilities to perform in a competent, effective manner.

The Executive Role

The role that top-level managers in human services organizations must perform is similar to, but distinct from, that of their counterparts in other types of organizations (Austin, 1989). In the for-profit corporate sector, there is what is perhaps the simplest version of the role of chief executive officer (CEO), which combines policymaking and implementation. In the corporate or industry model, the CEO serves as a member of the corporation's board of directors, as well as its senior administrator. With this model, the ultimate yardstick for measuring the effectiveness of the executive's performance is the level of financial return to the shareholders. Another commonly recognized version of the CEO role is that of the generalist public administrator, in which the CEO is believed to be responsible for the implementation of policy, but not for its formulation. This model is predicated on the belief that elected legislative bodies make policy, and administrators or managers have the responsibility for carrying out policy directives (Wilson, 1978).

With the public administration model, several yardsticks are used to measure the effectiveness of the administrator. These include the consistency of implementation with legislative intent; continuity of the governmental organization; and break-even financial management—that is, operating within the limits of available financial resources (Austin, 1989).

Although there is often a tendency to try to fit the characteristics of the CEO role in voluntary nonprofit and governmental human services organizations into either the for-profit corporate or public administration model, the role of the human services manager is actually distinctive and, in many ways, more complex (Austin, 1983). What the human services manager does is shaped both by the organizational characteristics that nonprofit and governmental organizations share with other types of formal organizations and by the distinctive characteristics of human services organizations (Austin, 1988).

Like their counterparts in the corporate world, human services managers are usually active participants in the formation, as well as in the implementation, of policy, even when their positions are formally defined as not including policymaking. In the real world of the human services manager, most policy issues are brought to an agency's policy board as a recommendation of the top-level manager or executive. Like their counterparts in the world of public administration, human services managers are concerned with such issues as the extent to which implementation efforts are congruent with policy, with the ongoing health of their organizations, and with break-even performance. Also like their public administration counterparts, human services managers have no direct personal economic stake in their organizations' financial performance. Their salaries do not increase in proportion to the size of their organizations' budgets, nor do they get year-end bonuses that are based on financial performance.

Despite these similarities, the role of the human services manager is also different from that of either the corporate executive or the traditional public administrator. Perhaps the most significant difference involves the criteria used to determine success. In the human services sector, the most important yardstick for judging the performance of the human services manager is the quality of the services provided by the organization (Patti, 1987). Another important difference is that the position of the human services manager involves dealing with the interface between two distinctive social structures—the service-production organization and the organized professions of human services (Austin, 1989).

Different Managerial Skills

The position of human services manager and the preferred style of executive performance involve an interactive, adaptive "contingency" process between the individual and the structural context. In turn, that process is shaped both by the operational characteristics of a particular organization and by the situation of that organization in its environment. The job of the human services manager is, of necessity, a proactive one. Effective performance in this position requires leadership in the broadest sense. In providing such leadership, the human services manager is invariably confronted by a series of competing values or demands that are likely to pull her or him in many directions at once and thus that require skill in performing several roles more or less simultaneously. This situation was captured, in part, by Perlmutter (1990, p. 5), who pointed out that "not only is it necessary to keep the shop running smoothly and efficiently today to meet current needs, but it is also necessary to have a vision of and anticipate what is possible and necessary for tomorrow." Perlmutter's statement suggests that managers need to be skilled at both tactical and strategic management.

Managerial performance in any type of organization occurs in a context of organizational change. Like human beings, organizations do not remain static, but go through a variety of phases and life cycles. And, different stages in the organizational life cycle may require different types of skills by the manager (Quinn & Cameron, 1983). Likewise, organizations that perform similar work, but in different environments, may require a different mix of elements in the managerial position. Various individuals may shape the specific elements of the managerial positions they occupy in different ways on the basis of their personalities, training, and experience, as well as their perceptions of the needs of their organizations at given points in time. Furthermore, managers may be called on to use different skills at different points during their careers and over the course of the life of their organizations.

Managers, whatever their level in the organizational hierarchy, have a range of responsibilities and are required to exhibit a variety of skills. According to Katz (1974), these skills may be broadly categorized as technical, interpersonal or human relations, and decision-making or conceptual skills. In entry-level managerial positions, technical skills tend to be important. However, their relative importance tends to diminish as managers move up the organizational structure. On the other hand, the need for decision-making or conceptual skills, although generally less important in positions on the lower rungs of the managerial ladder, tend to increase in importance as one moves up the organizational hierarchy. For top-level managers, conceptual skills are essential and, although these managers must be technically competent, the nature of their jobs does not require their use of technical skills to the same extent as does the nature of the jobs held by their counterparts in lower-level managerial positions. Interpersonal or human relations skills, however, are equally important for managers at all levels of the organizational hierarchy (Katz, 1974; Whetten & Cameron, 1984).

The types of skills required of managers will vary depending on the manager's position in the organizational hierarchy (Figure 1). In human services organizations, individuals who are competent direct service practitioners are sometimes promoted to supervisory or managerial positions in which they may perform well. Their effectiveness may be due largely to the fact that the positions they occupy require the incumbents to have good technical and interpersonal skills. However, as these individuals gradually move up the managerial hierarchy into positions in which conceptual skills are more important, they may continue to be successful or they may begin to display deficiencies. When such an individual is not

Figure 1. Management Skills Required at Different Levels

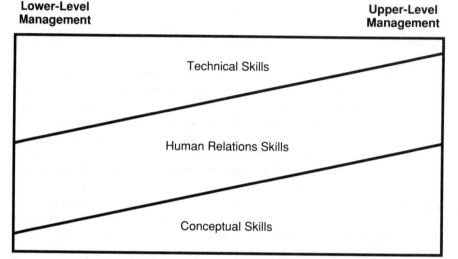

SOURCE: D. A. Whetten and K. S. Cameron, *Developing Management Skills* (Glenview, IL: Scott, Foresman, © 1984). Reprinted by permission of HarperCollins Publishers.

successful in a higher-level position, she or he may be an example of the Peter principle (Peter & Hull, 1969), that is, the individual has been promoted to a position that is beyond his or her level of competence. Of course, some individuals are very successful in attaining the additional competencies necessary for upper levels of management.

The Competing Values Framework

Just as there is no single universal definition of the characteristics of the managerial role, there is no one "best" style of executive performance. However, there is an inclusive, multidimensional model of organizational and management performance, called the competing values approach (Quinn, 1984, 1988), which helps one to understand the criteria that are used to judge the effectiveness of organizations and what managers are called upon to do (Figure 2).

The competing values model is an analytic framework built around two dimensions representing competing orientations or "values" in the organizational context. These dimensions are flexibility-control and internal-external. The combination of these two dimensions distinguishes four sectors of organizational activity, each of which embodies distinctive criteria of organizational effectiveness (Edwards, 1987,

Figure 2. Competing Values Framework: Effectiveness

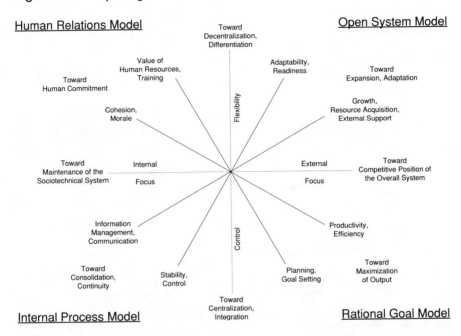

SOURCE: R. E. Quinn, *Beyond Rational Management: Mastering the Paradoxes and Competing Demands of High Performance* (San Francisco: Jossey-Bass, © 1988). Reprinted with permission.

1990; Quinn & Rohrbaugh, 1981, 1983). For an organization to perform well with respect to the various criteria of effectiveness, managers must use the following different and sometimes conflicting sets of skills: boundary-spanning skills, human relations skills, coordinating skills, and directing skills.

The competing values framework has proved to be useful for assessing organizational effectiveness in the human services (Edwards, Faerman, & McGrath, 1986), but because the top-level manager or CEO is ultimately responsible for all aspects of an organization's performance, the framework is also useful as a tool for examining those components that make up the executive or top-level managerial position in human services organizations. In combination, the four sectors identified in the model deal with two major criteria for assessing organizational outcomes—the quality of services provided and the continuity of the organization (Austin, 1989).

Of course, no single managerial position involves an equal emphasis on all four of these sectors. In any given organization, the top-level manager may be involved

Figure 3. Competing Values Framework of Leadership Roles

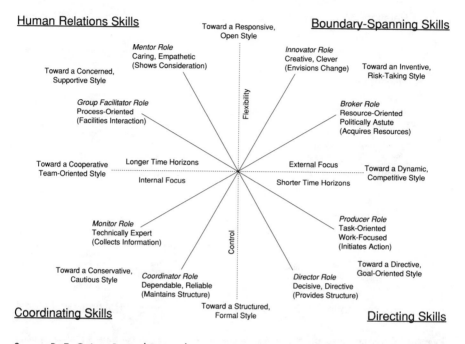

SOURCE: R. E. Quinn, *Beyond Rational Management: Mastering the Paradoxes and Competing Demands of High Performance* (San Francisco: Jossey-Bass, © 1988). Reprinted with permission.

primarily in activities that require the use of certain types of skills, whereas other persons who are part of the executive component, or management team, may carry major responsibilities for activities in other sectors that require other types of skills. Yet, the CEO or top-level manager bears ultimate responsibility for the effectiveness of the organization's performance in all four sectors. The following summarizes some of the key concepts associated with each sector of organizational performance and identifies relevant managerial roles.

Each quadrant depicted in Figure 3 relates to a different set of skills and each set of skills includes managerial traits, behaviors, and patterns of influence inherent within it. In the upper roles in the right-hand quadrant, the manager is called on to use boundary-spanning skills. Since human services organizations, whether voluntary or governmental, are highly dependent on their environments, the manager is constantly involved in activities that cross the formal boundaries of the organization. These activities include obtaining financial resources, establishing and maintaining the organization's legitimacy, adapting organizational programs in response to environmental changes, managing external requirements for reporting and accountability, negotiating formal and informal interorganizational agreements, participating in action coalitions, and positioning the organization to take advantage of new opportunities.

In the competing values model, this sector is defined by the concepts flexibility and external. That is, in the roles in this sector the manager needs to be adaptable and flexible, since she or he will participate in activities that involve dealing with individuals and organizations that are not under her or his direct control and that are external to the formal boundaries of the organization. Quinn (1984, 1988) identified two managerial roles that are relevant to this sector: *innovator* and *broker*.

In effectively performing the role of innovator, the manager needs to be creative and clever. These traits suggest that the manager must have good conceptual skills

"Faced with the two of you, I'm forced to ask, 'Who's holier-than-thou?' "

and be constantly on the lookout for unusual opportunities. The behavior associated with the performance of this role is directed toward envisioning and facilitating change. Managers who perform this role well tend to be individuals who seek new opportunities, encourage and consider new ideas, and are tolerant of ambiguity and risk (Quinn, 1984, 1988).

To perform the role of broker effectively, the manager needs to be resource oriented and politically astute. These traits suggest that the manager must be aware of and sensitive to external conditions, especially those related to the organization's legitimacy, influence, and acquisition of resources. The behavior associated with the performance of the broker role is directed toward acquiring resources, and managers who are engaged in this behavior need to be skilled in developing interpersonal contacts, monitoring the organization's environment, amassing power and influence, maintaining the external image of the organization, and obtaining resources (Quinn, 1984, 1988).

The boundary-spanning-skills sector involves, in particular, the political or "open-system" dimension of organizational performance that is least subject to technical rationalization or computerization. Managerial performance in this sector involves political or negotiating skills and an understanding of the nature of power relationships in the task environment—the arena in which management skills are practiced. It may also require individual short-term "contingency" decision making, in contrast to the systematic and long-term participatory internal decision-making processes that may be important in the mobilization and motivation of the human resources—the people involved. This sector of activity is perhaps the least likely to be fully delegated to other members of an executive team. However, it may also be the sector that policymakers, both volunteer and legislative, define as their particular area of activity and in which explicit limits are placed on the scope of the manager's activities.

The effectiveness of the process of contingency decision making, or strategic adaptation, whether carried out by policymakers, the manager, or both, may be severely constrained by considerations involving other sectors in which policymakers and managers perform. For example, successful "opportunity-seizing" initiatives involving responses to short-term funding opportunities may be inconsistent with the organization's overall goals, may require substantial expenditures for the development of new technical production procedures, and may disrupt the cohesiveness and morale of the staff.

The second major sector of executive responsibility, shown in the upper left-hand quadrant of Figure 3, involves the use of human relations skills. In the roles in this sector, managers are responsible for assuring that the organization has a work force that is competent to perform the work of the organization adequately. Since most of the services provided by human services organizations are produced and delivered through person-to-person interactions, these organizations can be said to be "labor intensive." As a consequence, human relations activities constitute a particularly important component in the life of such organizations.

In the competing values model, this sector is defined by the concepts internal and flexibility. The focus is on the role of the manager in dealing with those individuals and groups who are internal to the organization and who, as autonomous individuals or groups with the skills required in the production of services, represent decentralized centers of authority and influence that cannot be directly controlled by the manager. Quinn (1984, 1988) identified two specific managerial roles in this sector: *mentor* and *group facilitator*.

Managers who are adept at performing the role of mentor are likely to be caring and empathic individuals. Those who possess these traits tend to view organizational members as valued resources and are alert to the members' individual problems and needs. Such managers operate in a manner that is perceived as fair and objective. They are skilled listeners and try to facilitate the development of individuals (Quinn, 1984, 1988). The behavior associated with these traits and activities is directed toward showing concern about and support for staff members.

Effective performance of the role of group facilitator requires the manager to be process oriented, diplomatic, and tactful. Managers who have these traits tend to have excellent interpersonal skills and to be good at facilitating interaction among individuals and groups in the workplace. They are adept at fostering cohesion, building consensus, and bringing about compromises. The behavior associated with these traits and activities is directed toward the creation of a cooperative, team-oriented style.

In performing the roles of mentor and group facilitator, the manager aims to recruit, retain, and motivate a qualified, competent, committed work force. The human resources of the organization should have the knowledge, skills, and abilities to perform their jobs effectively. However, achieving the goal of a well-qualified, competent work force in human services organizations is not easy because the staff often includes members of one or more professions, as well as a variety of volunteer personnel who are involved in both the delivery of services and policymaking. In addition, the work force increasingly includes both men and women, as well as people from a variety of racial and ethnic groups. Furthermore, users of services may be a critical element in the mobilization and motivation of the human resources. Because of the composition of the human-resource component of the organization, managers need to be concerned with the "organizational culture," which includes symbols and traditions, the use of special events, and the definition of organizational values, all of which may be significantly related to motivation (Austin, 1989).

The lower left-hand quadrant of Figure 3 identifies the coordinating-skills sector. Quinn (1984, 1988) identified the roles of *monitor* and *coordinator* in this sector, which is defined by the concepts internal and control. The activities related to this sector are focused primarily on matters that are internal to the organization and that are involved in maintaining the organizational structure. The technical areas in this sector include budgeting and fiscal controls, scheduling procedures, information and communication systems, personnel administration systems, technical training programs, reporting systems, evaluation and quality-control measures, and management of technical equipment and physical facilities (Austin, 1989).

To perform the role of monitor effectively, the manager needs to be technically competent and well prepared. These traits suggest that the manager needs to be well informed and knowledgeable about the work of the people in the organization and have a high degree of technical expertise. The behavior associated with these traits is directed toward collecting and distributing information that is necessary for the smooth functioning of the organization, as well as for the orderly flow of work.

Managers who perform well in the role of coordinator tend to be individuals who are dependable and reliable. Those who have such traits are likely to be consistent, predictable people who seek to maintain continuity and equilibrium in their work units (Quinn, 1984, 1988). The behavior associated with these traits is directed toward maintaining structure, and managers who are engaged in this behavior maintain the organizational stability and work flow through their competence in scheduling, coordinating, problem solving, and ensuring that rules and standards are understood and met.

Because human services organizations are typically so labor intensive, the systematic organization of personnel activities and the monitoring of service-production activities assume great importance and become major elements in the managerial or executive position. In a small organization, it may be possible for the manager to carry out many of these tasks directly, but in larger organizations these types of managerial tasks, especially personnel administration and financial management, are most likely to involve technical staff specialists and sometimes whole staffing units. This is also the sector of organizational life in which systematic and rational procedures often have their widest application (Austin, 1989).

In recent years, the use of computers in all kinds of organizations, including those that provide human services, has become widespread. It is in this sector that computers are particularly valuable because the activities involved often represent structured decision-making choices among known alternatives. For example, issues such as the impact of different combinations of direct salary and fringe benefits on the compensation of the staff, the effects of different combinations of work schedules of staff members and the patterns of use of services by clients, procedures for handling organizational funds, and the tracking of clients all lend themselves to the use of computers. And these activities and others like them are areas in which consistent, centrally controlled decisions seem to be highly correlated with efficiency and effectiveness. These are areas in which the techniques of command and control, developed in industries involved in the production of goods, have most often been used in human services organizations.

The lower right-hand quadrant of Figure 3 identifies the directing-skills sector. This sector is defined by the concepts external and control. Thus, the focus in this sector tends to be on activities that are external to the organization and that are relatively structured and formalized. Managers who are involved in activities related to this sector are dealing with the interface between the products or output of their organizations and the external environment. The technical activities involved include both tactical and strategic planning, setting goals, and monitoring activities. Quinn (1984, 1988) identified the roles of *producer* and *director* in this sector.

The thrust of the manager's activity in this sector is the goal-oriented process, which is aimed at improving the organization's efficiency and effectiveness, as well as enhancing the organization's relative position within its environment. This sector involves activities in which the manager plays a pivotal role, such as the improvement of productivity and goal setting (Austin, 1989).

In performing the role of director effectively, managers must be decisive and comfortable in guiding the work of others. Those who have these traits tend to be conclusive individuals who can plan work appropriately and provide direction. The particular behaviors associated with these traits include setting goals and objectives, clarifying roles, monitoring progress, providing feedback, and establishing clear expectations (Quinn, 1984, 1988).

To perform the role of producer well, the manager must be task oriented and work focused. Those who exhibit these traits tend to be action-oriented individuals who are highly generative. They invest large amounts of energy and derive a great deal of satisfaction from productive work. The behaviors associated with these traits are directed toward stimulating the appropriate performance of members of the organization.

When executives use directing skills, they need to know how to stimulate individual and collective achievement. They also must be comfortable with the use of authority and skilled at delegation, planning, and goal-setting technologies (Faerman, Quinn, & Thompson, 1987).

Because human services organizations are established to accomplish particular societal objectives, the process of defining goals is essential. These organizations are dependent, to a great extent, on their external environments; thus, managers must be cognizant of environmental developments and trends, including those that affect their organization's users or clients, financial and personnel resources, technology, and, ultimately, legitimacy in political terms. Furthermore, organizational continuity assumes relatively great importance for human services organizations, since the costs involved in setting up such an organization and the "good will" represented in its legitimation by the community cannot be turned into financial resources that can be used for other purposes (Austin, 1989).

The reality confronting those who occupy managerial positions is that they must have and appropriately use many different types of skills and must perform many roles. The demands of their roles may shift over time as the organization moves through different phases in its life cycle. In the small organization, the top-level manager may, at one time or another, be required to perform nearly all the roles identified in Figure 3, whereas in the large organization, the manager may delegate the performance of certain roles to others on the management team.

The Nature of Managerial Decision Making

Because organizational life is characterized by an environment of competing values, the decision-making requirements in the position of manager are complex. The choices that confront managers daily are rarely choices between something that is good and something that is bad. If this were the case, then the job of the manager would be relatively easy. Instead, the job of the manager most often involves choosing between two or more things that are good, positive, or valued. This type of choice makes the job of the manager much more difficult.

For example, a manager may be confronted with shrinking resources and thus not able to hire additional staff or provide opportunities for staff development. At the same time, the manager may be confronted with a growing demand for services from clients. Because the size of the work force cannot be enlarged, the increased demand for services may cause the manager to take steps to increase the caseloads of the existing staff. Such an approach may result in greater efficiency, that is, more clients seen without an increase in staff. However, the approach may also have a negative impact on the morale of the staff, which could ultimately lead to increased burnout and turnover. Thus, the organization may lose some of its experienced staff, which will cause it to incur added expenses for recruiting, hiring, and orienting new staff.

Understanding that they are likely to experience pulls from many directions may help managers to identify the possible consequences of their decisions and enable them to take appropriate steps to minimize negative consequences. Viewing organizations from the competing values perspective can assist managers in assessing their particular areas of strength. No one individual will be equally adept at performing all the roles identified in Figure 3. Managers who are secure about their abilities are likely to surround themselves with subordinates whose strengths compliment their own, whereas managers who are less secure tend to surround themselves with individuals whose strengths mirror their own, which may result in some of the organization's needs being inadequately addressed.

Summary

Human services managers must possess a range of knowledge, skills, and abilities and must perform many roles at various times. The particular balance of technical, interpersonal or human relations, and conceptual or decision-making skills required of a manager will vary, depending on the manager's position in the managerial structure. Upper-level managers are called on to use conceptual skills to a greater extent than are lower-level managers. However, all managers, regardless of their location in the hierarchy, need to have good interpersonal skills. The specific types of skills required of managers include boundary-spanning, human relations, internal process, and directing skills. Each category of skills involves the performance of different managerial roles, which are related to different criteria of organizational effectiveness and create an environment of competing values. In this environment, managerial decisions most often represent a tradeoff between two "values" or "goods," rather than a choice between something that is "good" versus something that is "bad." By understanding the multiple role demands and competing values of their jobs, managers may be better able to guide their organizations toward effective performance.

SKILLS-ASSESSMENT EXERCISE

The following instrument will enable you to develop a profile of how you rate on each of the managerial roles identified in the competing values framework. Please complete the Competing Values Management Practices Survey and then transfer your ratings to the Computational Worksheet. Place the score or rating you give each item on the survey next to the number of that item on the worksheet. Note that where the symbol (R) appears on the worksheet, you should reverse your score; thus, if you rated the item 2, then you will reverse your score and record it as 6—1 becomes 7, 2 becomes 6, and 3 becomes 5. If your rating was 4, then place 4 on the worksheet. Next, total your scores in each category and then divide the total by the number of items in that category. This sum will give you a score that you can then enter on the Competing Values Skills-Assessment Leadership Role Profile. When transferring your scores to the role profile, place a dot at the point on the spoke that reflects your score for that role, keeping in mind that the center of the figure is 0 and the hash mark farthest from the center is 7. When you have entered your scores on all eight spokes of the diagram, then draw lines to connect them. The result will be a profile that will help you to identify your areas of relative strength, as well as those in which you may not be as strong. This information may be useful to you as you review subsequent chapters.

continued

Competing Values Management Practices Survey

Listed below are some statements that describe managerial practices. Indicate how often you engage in the behaviors, using the scale below to respond to each statement. Please place a number from 1 to 7 in the space beside each question.

| Almost never | 1 | 2 | 3 | 4 | 5 | 6 | 7 | Almost always |

As a manager, how often would you

_____ 1. Come up with inventive ideas.
_____ 2. Exert upward influence in the organization.
_____ 3. Ignore the need to achieve unit goals.
_____ 4. Continually clarify the unit's purpose.
_____ 5. Search for innovations and potential improvements.
_____ 6. Make the unit's role very clear.

_____ 7. Maintain tight logistical control.
_____ 8. Keep track of what goes on inside the unit.
_____ 9. Develop consensual resolution of openly expressed differences.
_____ 10. Listen to the personal problems of subordinates.
_____ 11. Maintain a highly coordinated, well-organized unit.
_____ 12. Hold open discussion of conflicting opinions in groups.

_____ 13. Push the unit to meet objectives.
_____ 14. Surface key differences among group members, then work participatively to resolve them.
_____ 15. Monitor compliance with the rules.
_____ 16. Treat each individual in a sensitive, caring way.
_____ 17. Experiment with new concepts and procedures.
_____ 18. Show empathy and concern in dealing with subordinates.

_____ 19. Seek to improve the workgroup's technical capacity.
_____ 20. Get access to people at higher levels.
_____ 21. Encourage participative decision making in the group.
_____ 22. Compare records, reports, and so on to detect discrepancies.
_____ 23. Solve scheduling problems in the unit.
_____ 24. Get the unit to meet expected goals.

_____ 25. Do problem solving in creative, clear ways.
_____ 26. Anticipate workflow problems, avoid crises.
_____ 27. Check for errors and mistakes.
_____ 28. Persuasively sell new ideas to higher ups.
_____ 29. See that the unit delivers on stated goals.
_____ 30. Facilitate consensus building in the work unit.

_____ 31. Clarify the unit's priorities and direction.
_____ 32. Show concern for the needs of subordinates.
_____ 33. Maintain a "results" orientation in the unit.
_____ 34. Influence decisions made at higher levels.
_____ 35. Regularly clarify the objectives of the unit.
_____ 36. Bring a sense of order and coordination into the unit.

continued

Computational Worksheet for Self-Assessment

The Facilitator

9 ____

12 ____

14 ____

21 ____

30 ____

Total ____ ÷ 5 = ____

The Mentor

10 ____

16 ____

18 ____

32 ____

Total ____ ÷ 4 = ____

The Innovator

1 ____

5 ____

17 ____

25 ____

Total ____ ÷ 4 = ____

The Broker

2 ____

20 ____

28 ____

34 ____

Total ____ ÷ 4 = ____

The Producer

3 ____ (R)

13 ____

19 ____

29 ____

33 ____

Total ____ ÷ 5 = ____

The Director

4 ____

6 ____

24 ____

31 ____

35 ____

Total ____ ÷ 5 = ____

The Coordinator

7 ____

11 ____

23 ____

26 ____

36 ____

Total ____ ÷ 5 = ____

The Monitor

8 ____

15 ____

22 ____

27 ____

Total ____ ÷ 4 = ____

continued

The Competing Values Skills-Assessment Leadership Role Profile

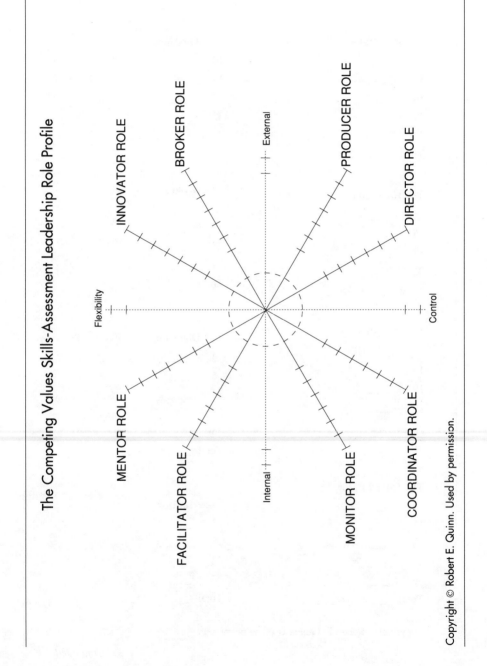

Discussion Questions

The following questions may assist you in developing your managerial skills.

1. What is your reaction to the personal-skills profile revealed on the role profile diagram? Do the results meet with your expectations? Were there any surprises?
2. On the basis of your profile, what areas of managerial skills appear to be the highest priority for further development? What strategies can you use to assist you in developing your skills?
3. Identify where your organization is in terms of its life cycle. What managerial skills are primarily needed at this point in your organization's history? What skills are likely to be needed in the next year? In the next three years?

References

Austin, D. M. (1983). Administrative practice in human services: Future directions for curriculum development. *Journal of Applied Behavioral Science, 19*(2), 143–151.

Austin, D. M. (1988). *The political economy of human service programs.* Greenwich, CT: JAI Press.

Austin, D. M. (1989). The human service executive. *Administration in Social Work, 13*(3/4), 13–36.

Edwards, R. L. (1987). The competing values approach as an integrating framework for the management curriculum. *Administration in Social Work, 11*(1), 1–13.

Edwards, R. L. (1990). Organizational effectiveness. In L. Ginsberg (Ed.), *Encyclopedia of Social Work: 1990 Supplement.* Silver Spring, MD: NASW Press.

Edwards, R. L., Faerman, S. R., & McGrath, M. R. (1986). The competing values approach to organizational effectiveness: A tool for agency administrators. *Administration in Social Work, 10*(4), 1–14.

Faerman, S. R., Quinn, R. E., & Thompson, M. P. (1987). Bridging management practice and theory: New York State's public service training program. *Public Administration Review, 47*(3), 311–319.

Katz, R. L. (1974). Skills of an effective administrator. *Harvard Business Review, 51,* 90–102.

Patti, R. J. (1987). Managing for service effectiveness in social welfare: Toward a performance model. *Administration in Social Work, 11*(3/4), 25–37.

Perlmutter, F. D. (1990). *Changing hats: From social work practice to administration.* Silver Spring, MD: NASW Press.

Peter, L., & Hull, R. (1969). *The Peter principle: Why things go wrong.* New York: William Morrow.

Quinn, R. E. (1984). Applying the competing values approach to leadership: Toward an integrative framework. In J. G. Hunt, D. Hosking, C. Schreisheim, & R. Stewart (Eds.), *Leaders and managers: International perspectives on managerial behavior and leadership.* Elmsford, NY: Pergamon Press.

Quinn, R. E. (1988). *Beyond rational management: Mastering the paradoxes and competing demands of high performance.* San Francisco: Jossey-Bass.

Quinn, R. E., & Cameron, K. S. (1983). Organizational life cycles and shifting criteria of effectiveness: Some preliminary evidence. *Management Science, 29,* 33–51.

Quinn, R. E., & Rohrbaugh, J. A. (1981). A competing values approach to organizational effectiveness. *Public Productivity Review, 5,* 122–140.

Quinn, R. E., & Rohrbaugh, J. A. (1983). A spatial model of effectiveness criteria: Toward a competing values approach to organizational analysis. *Management Science, 29*(3), 363–377.

Whetten, D. A., & Cameron, K. S. (1984). *Developing management skills.* Glenview, IL: Scott, Foresman.

Wilson, W. (1978). The study of administration. In J. M. Shafritz & A. C. Hyde (Eds.), *Classics of public administration.* Oak Park, IL: Moore Publishing.

BOUNDARY-SPANNING SKILLS

*M*anagerial boundary-spanning skills encompass two major roles—broker and innovator. Competencies for the broker role include building and maintaining a power base, negotiating agreement and commitment, and presenting ideas. Competencies for the innovator role include living with change, managing change, and creative thinking. The chapters in this section discuss these competencies and roles in portraying the challenges confronting and opportunities afforded human services managers.

David M. Austin presents a conceptual framework for analyzing organizational networks, suggesting that these networks can be evaluated on four systemic levels: as a part of community "supra-system," as part of service delivery networks, as service organizations, and at the level of program components. This conceptual framework emphasizes the open-system thinking that is critical to effective managerial functioning. Austin offers a number of methods for organizational expansion and adaptation while stressing certain additional management functions, such as assuring accessibility, integrating networks, and maintaining accountability.

Ralph Brody, in his chapter, focuses on the resource-acquisition skills required of human services managers. He presents a detailed approach to obtaining grants, including the important managerial responsibility for first assessing the likelihood of obtaining funding. He pays special attention to the government, foundations, and corporations as potential sources of funding, offering valuable insights into how to gain access to information about sources of funding. In presenting his definitive guidelines for the sections that can be incorporated in a proposal submitted to external funding sources, Brody emphasizes the importance of creative thinking and innovation. Furthermore, he stresses that the effective presentation of ideas is central to the success of human services managers in acquiring resources for their organizations.

Dennis R. Young discusses the importance of entrepreneurship to the boundary-spanning functions of human services managers. To Young, entrepreneurship means more than just developing for-profit ventures; rather, it includes building "new businesses" and establishing new initiatives. He emphasizes the skills of developing a sense of mission, problem solving, applying creativity and ingenuity, exploiting timing and opportunity, and analyzing and taking risks. The mobilization of resources, for Young, requires human services managers to use consensus and team-building strategies, which involve the skills of negotiating agreement and obtaining commitment. These skills necessitate the use of an innovative and risk-taking style. Envisioning, living with, and managing change are key ingredients of this managerial style.

Elliott Davis Moore offers a series of keen insights on the acquisition of resources through the legislative and executive branches of government. The competencies of building and maintaining power bases are viewed as being at the heart of this area of managerial functioning. While emphasizing the usefulness of the traditional problem-solving approach, Moore stresses the importance of the ability of human services managers to present ideas, negotiate agreement and commitment, and be creative in their approach to solving problems. She notes the flexibility required to function effectively in the political arena and the "good manners" required to be successful in negotiating for change. Presenting a series of "do's" and "don't's" for lobbying, Moore underscores the value of political astuteness as part of boundary-spanning responsibilities.

Chauncey A. Alexander presents another area of vital importance to human services managers: participation in coalitions. He identifies different kinds of coalitions, why organizations may choose to join or not join coalitions, and key issues that must be addressed in making coalitions work. The points that are consistently stressed include being flexible, building and maintaining power bases, thinking creatively, and presenting ideas. Alexander emphasizes the importance of negotiating agreement about and commitment to the purpose, structure, and ongoing functioning of coalitions. He views creativity and risk taking as important competencies for human services managers and points out the necessity for human services managers and organizations to adapt continuously to new situations, including the need, on occasion, for quick decision making by a coalition. Central to his view of the successful functioning of coalitions is a common vision or set of shared values by their members.

Clarence Jones offers valuable hints for developing relationships with the mass media, which he believes are crucial for the favorable positioning of human services organizations in the public eye. He recognizes the difficult challenge that the development of such relationships frequently presents, including the contradictory advice presented to human services managers by their legal counsel and their media experts. In a straightforward fashion, Jones presents a number of examples of how human services managers can respond to reporters' questions and his "Ten Commandments" for effective media relationships. Implicit in Jones's view is the ongoing need for human services managers to take risks, in this case by assuming a more proactive and assertive posture with media representatives. Creativity, cleverness, and adaptability are especially essential for effective managerial performance in this regard. Jones considers effective media relationships so critical that human services managers must assume leadership in this area and not fully delegate the function. He strongly encourages human services managers to conduct drills to prepare for crises with the media, just as they conduct drills to deal with other crises.

Understanding the Service Delivery System

David M. Austin

The management of any organization involves dealing with its external environment, as well as with its internal processes (Austin, 1989). In the instance of human services organizations, a significant element in the external environment is the service delivery network, that is, the interrelated group of organizations that are involved in providing a particular type of service within a particular community. The effectiveness of the service outputs of any single organization and, to a large degree, the pattern of development of any single service organization, are determined by the characteristics of the service delivery networks to which the organization belongs.

Service delivery networks develop around a socially recognized problem or around the needs of a population group for particular services. These networks are an increasingly important element in the provision of essential community services. For example, an individual with a severe psychotic episode may go from the family home to the sheriff's mental health deputies to a halfway house run by a community mental health center and then to a community case-management program, through which the person may be involved with a public housing authority, a subsidized job-training opportunity, and a supervised apartment complex. Other examples of service delivery networks include those for juvenile justice–delinquency, teenage pregnancy, mental retardation and developmental disability, child welfare–child protection, and older adults.

These and similar networks in other service areas are found in some form in every community. The functional characteristics of key organizations in each network are often similar from community to community. Moreover, these networks persist over time even as the characteristics of specific organizations and their services change and as organizations disappear and new ones appear.

This chapter is designed to increase the understanding of the external activities of the human services manager. It also provides a conceptual framework for understanding a particular set of elements in the external environment of the human services organization. The emphasis is on the cognitive processes of interorganizational analysis and assessment, rather than on practice skills for intervention.

This chapter includes the following elements:

▶ A conceptual framework for analyzing interorganizational networks
▶ Theoretical concepts involved in interorganizational analysis
▶ Important elements in a fully developed interorganizational service delivery network
▶ An outline that can be used in the analysis of a community service delivery network.

Conceptual Framework

The framework for analyzing interorganizational processes involves four systemic levels. Level 1 is the inclusive community suprasystem that includes the organizational, political, governmental, and association elements that together make up the operational framework, or "task environment," of the human services organizations in a given geographic area. Level 2 consists of the specific service delivery networks, or "implementation structures," through which a particular type of service is made available to the general population within the community. This is the level of primary attention in this chapter. Level 3 comprises the service organizations that are involved with a particular service delivery network: governmental, nongovernmental voluntary, and for-profit service organizations, as well as a wide variety of membership associations. Level 4 includes the components of the programs in individual service organizations. Nearly all contemporary service organizations are, in a limited sense, organizational "conglomerates," administering a series of components, each of which involves a distinct service technology or serves a distinct population. Examples include the family service agency, which has both a preventive mental health–family life education program and an individual and family counseling service, and the community mental health and mental retardation center and the county social services department, both of whose programs may have a dozen or more distinct components. A component of a program generally has an identifiable budget; a unit administrator; direct service personnel assigned specifically to the particular program; and, in most instances, a distinct physical location, ranging from an office to a separate building.

Although the descriptive concept of service delivery networks has been widely used, a more formal, analytic definition of these networks and an analysis of their significance have been set forth by Hjern and Porter (1981). Hjern and Porter's analysis of the actual processes of the provision of services in a community context leads to a community matrix model (Figure 1). In this model, the "service production" elements in service organizations are viewed as components of programs that are linked vertically by the administrative structure of the formal organization and by such organization-centered functions as personnel management and the accountability for and control of funding. These same components are linked horizontally, across a series of organizations, through interorganizational

Figure 1. Community Matrix of Administrative and Program Structures

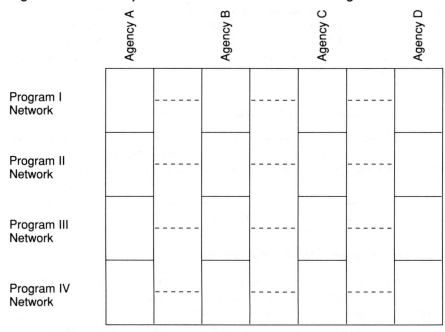

exchanges, in what Hjern and Porter described as "program implementation structures," or, the term used in this chapter, *service delivery networks*.

At the level of the community suprasystem, it is thus possible to identify both a series of vertically structured individual service organizations that are the primary channels for funding allocations and for formal authority and accountability and a series of horizontally structured, interdependent, exchange-linked service delivery networks. These networks may vary markedly from time to time in the mix of program components involved, but they also have basic identifiable characteristics that persist over time.

One of the most important distinctions between the analysis of service delivery networks and the analysis of individual service organizations is that the networks are not "managed" from a clearly defined central location of power and authority. Though there are nodes of influence and power within specific networks, there is no systematic structure of management and control. Indeed, the recurrent cry for more "coordination" among programmatically linked organizations is a reflection of the limited level of control and management that typically exists within such networks. Moreover, although service organizations have relatively explicit organizational boundaries, these networks have identifiable core organizational elements but open, undefined boundaries. That is, the definition of which elements are part of a particular network depends on when and why the definition is being made and by whom.

Interorganizational Structure and Processes

A significant part of this chapter deals with analytic concepts that apply to the complex interactions and transactions that take place among the organizational elements involved in service delivery networks. In addition to articles cited in the following sections, *The Organization of Mental Health Services* (Scott & Black, 1986) contains articles that deal with a theoretical analysis of the service delivery networks related to mental health and mental illness.

Structure of Service Delivery Networks

Following the concepts of Hjern and Porter (1981), a service delivery network can be defined as consisting of the following elements: pool of organizations, core organizations, and network-maintenance structures.

Pool of organizations. The pool of organizations includes all the organizations and associations that are involved, in any way, with the provision of services that are relevant to a particular population group (such as older adults) or to a particular problem condition (such as chronic mental illness).

Core organizations. Within the pool of organizations, the core organizations are the ones that are involved in the greatest frequency of relevant exchanges, control major sources of economic or other resources, or have a formal coordinating or controlling role in the network. Interviews with key informants in network organizations usually result in a high degree of agreement about the three to five organizations that are the core organizations in a given network.

Network-maintenance structures. Many networks have organizational structures that are involved primarily in the maintenance and development of the networks, rather than in the direct production of services. These structures may include informal interorganizational committees, formally structured interorganizational councils, planning bodies, or jointly created organizations that provide support services for individual service agencies.

The Political Economy of Interorganizational Service Networks

The term *political economy* was originally applied to macrolevel societal processes involving interactions between political and economic processes in nation-states.

More recently, however, it has been used as a general framework for examining interactions between governance and authority systems and systems for the allocation of resources, both at the community level and at the intraorganizational level (Austin, 1988; Benson, 1975). The allocation of resources primarily involves financial resources and legitimation. Both elements are essential for the survival of the organization, as well as for its ability to produce the services for which it is organized.

Governance systems include the official processes of governmental decision making, in this instance mainly at the state, county, and city levels; the decision-making processes involved in a variety of special-purpose temporary community structures, such as task forces and study commissions; and the decision-making processes in the nongovernmental voluntary community sector. An example of the latter is the budget-allocation process in United Way organizations. Emphasis is placed on issues of power and organizational and interorganizational "politics." Actual decision making within networks is viewed as being shaped both by the basic requirements of organizational maintenance and survival and by political processes in the inclusive community and the larger society. Those political processes are shaped, in part, by the collective community purposes around which individual service agencies are organized and legitimated.

Interorganizational Exchange Processes

A major part of interorganizational activities involves transactions or exchanges. Although such activities are diverse, widespread, and persistent, from a theoretical perspective the question is why such transactions exist and what determines their pattern.

In the study of organizational exchange relationships, the focal organization is one that is the point of departure in identifying and analyzing exchanges; the organizational set includes the exchange relationships between the focal organization and each of the other organizations and associations with which there are exchanges; and the network includes all exchanges among all organizations in the organizational set, whether or not the focal organization is involved.

The basic concept of interorganizational exchange was set forth by Levine and White (1961). Hall, Clark, Giordano, Johnson, and Van Roekel (1977) explored interorganizational exchanges under three types of exchange conditions: voluntary, contractual, and mandated. Jacobs (1974) dealt with exchange relationships among organizations with unequal power and authority. In turn, Aiken and Hage (1968) explored the impact of interorganizational exchanges on intraorganizational structures within the service organization.

Boundary Spanning

Given the existence of interorganizational transactions, one of the major tasks carried out by organizational personnel is that of "boundary spanning," that is, managing such exchange processes. Boundary-spanning activities range from telephone calls to obtain information from another organization to the negotiation of a major contract for funding a service with a governmental funding organization. Aldrich and Herker (1977) were among the first to examine the forces that affect boundary-spanning behavior.

Case management is a particular form of boundary spanning that has recently received substantial attention. Although its tasks have various definitions, case management primarily involves gaining access to and negotiating service resources, from a variety of organizational and nonorganizational sources, on behalf of a particular individual or household in need of services. The growth of case management reflects the fact that individuals and families who are affected by chronic and persistent problem conditions and disabilities require various services over time, compared to the treatment of acute conditions that often may be handled within a single service program in a limited time. Many persons with these chronic conditions were cared for in institutions until recently; moreover, persons with chronic disabilities now not only live in the community, but live longer. These developments increase the importance of effective service delivery networks.

Stakeholders

A critical aspect of the analysis of networks is the identification of those sets of individuals (and related households) that are directly affected by the processes in the service delivery network. The relationships among these stakeholder groups and the distribution of benefits from the operation of the services in the network often reflect relationships among critical constituencies in the larger society. In particular, the examination of the roles of stakeholders provides an opportunity to examine the position of women and members of ethnic minority groups in the service delivery network.

Users of Services

Individual users of governmental and nonprofit services have relatively limited power within the political economy of the service delivery network (Hasenfeld, 1987). Policy bodies, managers, and professional specialists establish regulations governing service programs, including definitions of eligibility and diagnostic procedures. The users of most human services programs include a disproportionately high number of low-income individuals and families, persons from disadvantaged ethnic populations, and women, all of whom tend to occupy low positions of power in the society at large. Many users of services are children and older adults, who also occupy low positions of power in the society. An important issue in the analysis of a service delivery network is the existence of advocacy groups and specific organizational procedures that are intended to increase the relative power of users of services in the network.

Professionals

The actual production of services in most human services programs is the responsibility of professionals: social workers, teachers, nurses, physicians, lawyers, and others. Relations among professional specialists and among professionals, users, and policymakers are a critical aspect of the analysis of service delivery networks. The structures of organized professions overlap the structures of service organizations. Professional specialists are accountable to both employers and professional associations. Participation in professional associations may provide important supports for professionals against organizational controls over their professional activities.

Professional career development competes with organizational advancement as a source of incentives for individual professionals. Independent professional

"For your convenience we've consolidated all of our forms into one, which I'll ask you to take a few minutes now to fill out."

practitioners are important elements in many service delivery networks. The dynamics of organizational growth and competition among organized professions often complicate staff relationships within and among service organizations. However, informal linkages among professional colleagues across organizational boundaries are frequently an essential element in the functioning of a service delivery network. Although a commitment to provide professional service to users of services is a critical dynamic in the behavior of individual professionals, professionalism is also used to enforce professional judgments on the users.

Gender is an important element in relationships among professionals. The largest groups of professional service providers in human services programs come from professions that are predominantly female, while the professions that control positions of power and authority are predominantly male. Gender also plays an important role in the relations between female professionals and the predominantly male structure of organizational administration and of community policymaking bodies.

Policymakers

Within any service delivery network, there are a variety of policymaking bodies and individuals with policymaking authority, including elected governmental bodies, governmental administrators, boards of directors and executives of nonprofit organizations, and boards of directors of United Way organizations and foundations. Collectively, these policy bodies are predominantly male, from business and professional backgrounds. Policymakers deal primarily with individual service organizations, rather than with service delivery networks. They are mainly involved in issues related to the acquisition and allocation of resources and to organizational accountability. Policymakers in general have different priorities for themselves and for service programs than do either professional staff members or users of services.

Coordination and Planning in Networks

As was already noted, a frequent complaint about service delivery networks is the lack of "coordination" among programs in them. This perception reflects the absence of a central authority with the power to define and enforce interorganizational exchange relationships and to resolve conflicts within the networks. Most networks are also marked by the absence of any systemic approach to planning for development and adaptation, although ad hoc, time-limited approaches to such planning are relatively frequent. Any planning activities usually are marked by a high level of information gathering and report writing and a low level of action, given the lack of a central authority. Since the creation of a strong implementing authority threatens the organizational autonomy of the service organizations in the network, it is usually resisted, even when leaders call attention to the need for planning.

Both operational coordination and network-level planning depend primarily on interorganizational consensus, except when external sources that control financial resources or legitimation or both mandate the coordination of cases or the development of programs. O'Brien and Bushnell (1980) described a variety of patterns of coordination that may be found and the conditions under which each pattern is likely to appear. There is no universal model for managing the coordination and planning of a network; problems are, in general, addressed as unique issues within each service delivery network in each community.

Normative Characteristics of the Fully Developed Network

Much attention is given in the literature on management to the characteristics of an effective organization. Although opinions vary greatly as to the most effective style of management, some assumptions are widely accepted about the need for systematic personnel procedures, financial management procedures, quality-control procedures, and communication systems. Less attention has been given to a normative model of an effective service delivery network than to the deficiencies and inefficiencies of existing networks.

The following elements are suggested as important structural and functional components of a fully developed service network. They can be used by managers to assess the overall adequacy of a particular network.

Accessibility

Access. The most critical element of any service agency or network is access by the community. It is also one of the most frequent sources of complaints. Access may involve a single organizational point, such as a child-abuse hotline for services dealing with child abuse and neglect, or multiple points of access, including various private physicians' offices and public clinics for primary health care. Information about the location of access points should be easily available, and the criteria and procedures for gaining access to services should be consistent.

Information and referral. An important element of access is the existence of a telephone information and referral service, either specific to a particular service network or, more likely, in the form of a community-wide service. An information and referral system may be either a component of a program within a service organization or a freestanding, independent service.

Integration of the Network

Responsibility for maintenance, development, and evaluation. Many networks have no recognized locus of responsibility for oversight and guidance or provisions for evaluating their performance. Responsibility for maintenance and guidance functions may be assigned to a core organization or to several organizations by consensus, legislation, or regulation, or to an interagency council or similar structure. These functions include monitoring and preparing summaries of the network's performance; evaluating the performance of specific components of programs and of the network; environmental scanning for information about changes in the availability of resources and the need for services, legislation, and technological developments; and strategic planning for adaptive changes within the network.

Linkage agreements. Linkage agreements may include written financial contracts, referral and intake agreements, and agreements on the allocation of responsibility and authority, as well as informal verbal agreements among executives or program unit administrators from two or more organizations. Critical areas for such agreements include collaborative case assessment, case planning, and case management, in which the issues of the confidentiality of records and the right of users of services to participate in such planning are central.

Common program-data system. Among the sources of difficulty in networks is the absence of common data elements. The absence of such elements creates communication problems among components in different organizations and makes it difficult to describe the composite activities of the total network, both of which contribute to problems in gaining public support and funding for components that are not highly visible to the public. Common data elements include common definitions of work activities and units of service and a common vocabulary for descriptive information about users of services.

Programmatic linkages. The effective functioning of service delivery networks can also be facilitated through activities that provide visibility for the service network and that support information sharing among staff and volunteers along programmatic lines. These activities may include newsletters, interagency task forces related to specific programs, program-area staff associations, and shared training activities for staff and volunteers.

Public-visibility events. Public-awareness activities are traditionally agency centered. Special efforts are needed to develop the public's awareness of the activities of the total network and to recognize those who contribute to its effectiveness. Such activities may include a jointly sponsored community-education conference, annual conferences of the network at which outstanding staff members and volunteers are publicly recognized, and special media events that focus on the network, rather than on single agencies.

Conflict-resolution mechanisms. One of the differences between a service network and a formal organization is the absence of a hierarchical system of authority to resolve conflicts among units of a program. Unresolved conflicts often disrupt interagency relationships for long periods. An effective network requires specific provisions for the systematic resolution of conflicts, both among organizations and between users of services organizations. Hearings at which the problems of users of services are presented and mediation or arbitration services for interagency conflicts are possible alternatives.

Accountability of the Network

Mechanisms for complaints and advocacy. For many individuals and families who have difficulty finding the services they need, the problems are in the arrangements of the network, not in a single organization. Just as clearly visible procedures for gaining access to the service network are important, so are visible procedures for registering complaints and for seeking help in resolving network-level problems. The absence of a complaint or feedback system for the network is one reason why problems in service networks often persist indefinitely.

Public input channels. In addition to complaint and advocacy resources for individual users of services, there should be regular procedures for obtaining suggestions and criticism from the general public, as well as from the personnel working in the network. Public hearings, focus groups, issue-oriented conferences, media call-in shows, and formal surveys are possible channels.

Summary

Managers and service delivery personnel need to have an in-depth understanding not only of their particular agency or organization, but of the service delivery network of which they are a part. A service delivery network includes a pool of organizations, a set of core organizations, and network-maintenance structures. The various components of the delivery system are involved in interorganizational exchange processes and boundary-spanning activities that affect the users of services, professionals, and policymakers. One of the major complaints about service delivery networks is their lack of coordination, which is related to the absence of a central authority to define and enforce interorganizational exchange relationships and to resolve conflicts. Thus, network-coordination and planning activities are needed to maximize the effectiveness of the network as a service delivery mechanism. Special attention should be given to making services accessible to users, integrating the delivery and evaluation of services, and strengthening the accountability of the network.

SKILLS-APPLICATION EXERCISE

The following outline can form the basis for analyzing the network elements that have been described and for understanding a local service delivery network. This outline may be particularly useful for the manager who is new to a particular agency or community. More experienced managers may find it to be helpful in orienting new staff.

In a classroom or training setting, the outline could be used with teams of students or participants; each two- or three-person team would identify the problem area or population group that would be their focus. The teams would then compile an initial list of a pool of organizations from which they would identify core agencies that would become the primary focus of the analysis. Agency executives or directors of components of programs would be interviewed as key informants. Because time may not allow for the study of the entire network, the outline calls for the team to explore only one component and one interagency exchange relationship in detail. Each team could be asked to make a class or workshop presentation and to prepare a composite written report. Teams would be expected to use computer database and graphic programs to prepare charts and diagrams and to use visual presentations and handouts as extensively as possible in their presentations. Because the assignment is meant to be a learning exercise, it is likely that gaps in information and unanswered questions would remain at the end of the exercise.

Guide for Mapping a Service Delivery Network

I. Overview: Sequential steps in defining a service delivery network
   A. Define a program area: service population or problem condition and geographic service area.
   B. List the pool of organizations: all governmental and nonprofit administrative organizations that are identified with this program area by name, location, and administrator.
   C. Identify examples of for-profit or private practice structures that are related to this pool of organizations.
   D. Identify core service-production organizations: those organizations from among the pool of organizations that are recognized by other organizations as being "key" in the service delivery system (normally three to five organizations).
   E. Identify core program components: the components within each core organization that are specifically involved in this program area.
II. Structure of Service Delivery Network
   A. Structure of program components. *For each component identified in I-E*, provide the following information:
      1. Administrator
      2. Legislative base or source of legitimation

continued

        3. Primary funding source and other significant funding sources
        4. Level of funding for the most recent program year
        5. Number of individuals-households served in a year
        6. Number and type of employed personnel
        7. Program activities
        8. Specific services-benefits provided to users

   B. Identify significant groups or associations related to this program area that are not primarily service-production organizations (advocacy groups, user groups, professional associations, labor unions).

   C. Prepare a *diagram* of the exchange relationships among core components and other significant groups and associations. The diagram should include exchange relationships involving

        1. Users of the service
        2. Financial resources
        3. Records of services and users
        4. Legitimation, licensing, standard setting, planning, technical assistance, and quality control
        5. Advocacy

III. Core Program Component

Select *one* component in *one* service-production organization. For that component, provide the following information:

   A. List the information on this component that is included in II-A.

   B. Discuss the characteristics of the funding pattern, including major limitations-opportunities associated with it. Identify potential changes in funding.

   C. Describe the relation of the component's administrator to the administrative structure of the inclusive organization. Describe the authority of the component's administrator in relation to (1) the budget, (2) personnel, (3) the program, and (4) characteristics of the users.

   D. Describe the organizational structure of service production in this component, including

        1. Outreach functions
        2. Access-facilitating provisions
        3. Intake procedures
        4. Diagnosis, assessment, and analysis procedures
        5. Development of service-program plan
        6. Specific service-production procedures
        7. Coordinating and monitoring services
        8. Termination process
        9. Follow-up and evaluation procedures

   E. List the criteria for eligibility for services:

        1. Economic criteria
        2. Other criteria

   F. Describe the characteristics of users of the program:

        1. Intended users
        2. Actual users

continued

      3. Flow of users: number of different persons served per time unit (day, week, month)
      4. Relation of actual service production to service-production capacity (level of utilization of the program)
      5. Characteristics of eligible and potentially eligible persons who do not use this service and reasons for their nonuse
   G. Describe special issues related to the use of this program by (1) women and (2) persons from disadvantaged ethnic groups.
   H. Discuss the coproduction elements in the service-production process.
   I. Describe any sources of power that users have in the service-production process. Special organizational provisions? Advocacy groups?
   J. Discuss the relation of special-interest advocacy organizations or quality-control procedures or both to this specific component.
   K. Identify the professional-occupational specializations that are involved in service production in this component. Discuss power relationships among these occupational groups within this component.

IV. Analysis of One Interorganizational Linkage

Select one interorganizational exchange relationship involving core components in two organizations, one of which is the component analyzed in Section III. Analyze the exchange relationship from the perspective of each of the two components, indicating the following:
   A. Content of the exchanges: What is being exchanged?
   B. Frequency of exchange transactions
   C. Quantity of the exchanges
   D. Which persons are most directly involved in the exchange relationship? What are their roles in their respective organizations?
   E. Voluntary, contractual-mandatory characteristics of the exchange relationship
   F. Power-dependence characteristics of the exchange relationship
   G. Cooperation-conflict characteristics of the exchange relationship
   H. Degree of consensus-disagreement between the two components on
      1. Definitions of their domain
      2. Ideological definitions
      3. Assessment of the effectiveness of each organization's program and that of the other program
   I. The role played by advocacy groups or special-interest groups of users in this exchange relationship
   J. Problems in this exchange relationship and the source of such problems

V. Analysis of the Service Delivery Network as a Whole
   A. Describe the characteristics of the external political economy of this network (focusing primarily on the cluster of core components), including the following:
      1. Pattern of legitimation for the network: issues affecting legitimation of the network
      2. Adequacy of funding for the network: changes in funding patterns for the network
      3. Adequacy of personnel resources—quantity and quality— changes in personnel-resource patterns

continued

4. Major groups-interests—national, state, and local—affecting the determination of policy for the network
5. Role of users, user groups, and user advocacy groups in the political economy of the network
6. The relation of women and women's advocacy groups to this network
7. The relation of advocacy groups representing persons of disadvantaged ethnic backgrounds to this network
8. Conflicts in the external political economy: ideological, competition over resources, competition among interest groups for the control of policy, among professional specializations, among other interest groups

B. Describe the characteristics of users in the network.
   1. The gender, ethnic, economic, and locational characteristics of eligible persons
   2. The differences between the characteristics of the eligible population and the characteristics of those who actually use this network
   3. The reasons for the differences described in B-2
   4. The special factors that affect the use of this network by women or by persons of disadvantaged ethnic backgrounds or both

C. Describe the coordination-guidance mechanisms.
   1. What is the dominant core organization? What is its role in coordinating the network, planning, allocating resources, controlling referrals, and monitoring and evaluating the program's effectiveness within the network?
   2. Are there any specialized organizational structures for any of the functions identified in B-1, separate from the service-production organization? If yes, describe the organization (or organizations) and the functions it performs.
   3. Is there any provision for coordination at the case-service level? If yes, through what organization? What is the scope of the case management activities?
   4. Are there informal patterns of coordination, planning, and guidance? Do they exist in the absence of formal organizational structures or as an alternative to existing organizational structures?

D. Discuss the role of professional linkages and of formal professional associations in policymaking, planning, and standard setting in this network.

E. Describe the general characteristics of policymakers in this network:
   1. Their primary concerns
   2. The types of conflicts that exist among policymakers, professionals, and service users

F. List the forces for change in this network:
   1. Societal forces creating change
   2. Changes in professional practice
   3. Technological changes
   4. Organizations-groups outside of the network that are seeking to make changes
   5. Organizations-groups within the network seeking to make changes

continued

VI. Evaluating the Service Delivery Network
   A. Assess the network in terms of the following elements.
      1. Accessibility of services: Can persons who need services find them and gain access to them?
      2. Information and referral services for users and potential users
      3. Identification of a "core agency" with responsibilities for planning and developing the program, monitoring the network's performance, coordinating cases, evaluating, and environmental scanning
      4. Common data systems, including common definitions of services and procedures for tracking the provision of services to users
      5. Formal linkage arrangements, including contracts, written referral agreements, and explicit verbal agreements
      6. Programmatic linkages, including task forces on interorganizational programs, staff associations, newsletters, and shared training activities
      7. Public interpretation and visibility mechanisms for the service delivery network
      8. Interorganizational procedures for mediation and conflict resolution
      9. Channels for public input on policy and procedures, including budgets
      10. Independent mechanisms for complaints and advocacy by the public and users of services
   B. Identify positive aspects of this network from the perspective of
      1. Users
      2. The community
   C. Identify service-production *gaps* in the network.
   D. Identify *barriers* in linkages among components of the program.
   E. Identify inefficiencies in the utilization of resources within the network.
   F. Identify any detrimental consequences of the present arrangements in the network for
      1. Users
      2. Service personnel
      3. The community
VII. Recommendations
   Each member of the team should prepare an individual two-page statement identifying issues that are priorities for action within the service delivery network and the reasons for selecting these issues. These should be issues that could be addressed by participants in the network and that could result in improved services for users. The recommendations are to be based on an individual assessment of the information gathered by the team.

References

Aiken, M., & Hage, J. (1968). Organizational interdependence and intraorganizational structure. *American Sociological Review, 33,* 912–930.

Aldrich, H., & Herker, D. (1977). Boundary spanning roles and organization structure. *Academy of Management Review, 2,* 217–228.

Austin, D. M. (1988). *The political economy of human service programs.* Greenwich, CT: JAI Press.

Austin, D. M. (1989). The human service executive. *Administration in Social Work, 13*(3/4), 13–36.

Benson, J. K. (1975). The interorganizational network as a political economy. *Administrative Science Quarterly, 20,* 229–249.

Hall, R. H., Clark, J. P., Giordano, P. C., Johnson, P. V., & Van Roekel, M. (1977). Patterns of interorganizational relationships. *Administrative Science Quarterly, 22,* 457–474.

Hasenfeld, Y. (1987). Power in social work practice. *Social Service Review, 61,* 469–483.

Hjern, B., & Porter, D. O. (1981). Implementation structures: A new unit of administrative analysis. *Organization Studies, 2,* 311–327.

Jacobs, D. (1974). Dependency and vulnerability: An exchange approach to the control of organizations. *Administrative Science Quarterly, 19,* 45–58.

Levine, S., & White, P. E. (1961). Exchange as a conceptual framework for the study of interorganizational relationships. *Administrative Science Quarterly, 5,* 583–601.

O'Brien, G. St. L., & Bushnell, J. (1980). Interorganizational behavior. In S. Feldman (Ed.), *The administration of mental health services.* Springfield, IL: Charles C Thomas.

Scott, W. R., & Black, B. L. (1986). *The organization of mental health services: Societal and community systems.* Beverly Hills, CA: Sage.

Preparing Effective Proposals

Ralph Brody

The process of obtaining funding for important projects or programs can be both enriching and overwhelming. Preparing proposals disciplines thinking and stimulates more purposeful fund-seeking endeavors. But the process can also be awesome because of the many details involved and the many decisions that have to be made. The purpose of this chapter is to identify those aspects of the proposal-preparing process that will make grant-seeking activity more effective.

Conducting a Preliminary Assessment

Because developing a proposal requires the investment of considerable time, energy, and organizational resources, a preliminary assessment should be conducted. During this preproposal phase, one should review the following questions (Brody, 1974, pp. 3–6; Brody, 1982, pp. 170–172; Hall, 1988, pp. 15–20):

▶ Is the idea for the project desirable and feasible? Conduct a preliminary review of the literature and contact persons locally or elsewhere who have undertaken similar projects. Judge whether the problem to be addressed is truly solvable. Clarify during this exploratory period whether the idea is unique or, if a similar project has been done elsewhere, why there are compelling reasons to duplicate it. Assess the urgency of embarking on the problem at this time. Determine who the target population will be. Identify who may support the project. Make a preliminary assessment about the feasibility of the project, given anticipated difficulties in its implementation.

▶ Is your organization able to carry the project forward? Analyze the project in relation to the current mission and goals of the organization. Review whether there is sufficient organizational will and staff capability to take on a new endeavor. Consider the agency's competitive position in relation to other potential applicants. Assess the agency's ability to take on the demands of the project in light of other pressing priorities. If the agency does not have tax-exempt status—501[c][3]—with the Internal Revenue Service (IRS), arrange to have an organization that is exempt serve as the fiscal agent.

▶ Would some funding groups be interested in the idea? Determine through preliminary direct contacts or descriptions of funding sources whether their priorities match the idea for the proposal.

▶ Finally, what are the potential financial consequences of obtaining funding? Examine whether the likelihood of new funding will limit autonomy and curb decision making regarding people to be served or ways of functioning. Consider the impact of discontinued funding at the end of the grant period. Review whether funding is likely to be sufficient to carry out the program adequately.

These questions contain cautions that must be weighed against the almost irresistible attraction of seeking funding for new projects. The clear message: Anticipate as much as possible before you formally prepare the proposal. Do your homework.

Searching for Funding Sources

Having decided to obtain special funding, how does one identify funding sources? First, explore whether funding can best be obtained from the private sector—corporations and foundations—or from the governmental sector. Private-sector funders may allow you considerable freedom to develop your own project, but it may not be possible to receive as much funding as needed. The governmental sector may provide a sizable grant, but there may be more strings attached, that is, recipients may have to abide by specific conditions of the grant. Furthermore, there is often considerable competition for governmental funding.

Identifying Sources of Funding in the Private Sector

With so many foundations in most urban communities, it is necessary to determine which ones are the most appropriate. To avoid a time-consuming, scattered, and often futile approach, it is best to identify initially a core of foundations that match your interests. Although word processing is so easy that it invites one to send "boilerplate" proposals, the indiscriminate distribution of proposals is generally ineffective. Through research, you can pinpoint those foundations whose patterns of giving over the past several years reflect an interest in your problem area.

The best approach to learning about private foundations is to write to the Foundation Center (79 Fifth Avenue, New York, NY 10003). The center will send you a publications catalog that describes major sources of information about foundations. These sources, which include summary statements of each foundation's requirements, are available for purchase or through the facilities of the center in New York or its offices in Washington, DC, Cleveland, or San Francisco. The center also has a cooperating network of library reference collections in all 50 states and some foreign countries (for information, phone 1-800-424-9836).

Among major publications and computer services of the Foundation Center are the following: the *Foundation Directory, Foundation Grants Index, Foundation Center National Data Book,* Comsearch printout, and Sourcebook profiles. To narrow the list further, obtain information directly from foundations. Also, to obtain information on smaller foundations, contact the local office of the IRS or nearest Foundation Center Library for the latest Form 990 PF. This is a form that small foundations must submit annually to the IRS on which they list all their grantees, details on their finances, their funding interests and restrictions, and their application procedures and deadlines.

In summary, the process of searching for appropriate foundations involves these major steps:

▶ Through the *Foundation Directory,* Comsearch printout, the *Foundation Grants Index,* and other specialized directories (including, in some instances, directories of foundations by states), identify foundations that make grants in particular subject areas.

▶ Research the foundations you have identified by checking their sourcebook profiles, published annual reports, and tax returns.

To systematize the search process, prepare a summary worksheet containing the following information on each foundation you explored (Hall, 1988, p. 43):

▶ Names and titles of staff who decide on grant proposals
▶ Geographic restrictions on awarding grants
▶ Types of organizations that are eligible to apply
▶ Purposes of the foundation
▶ Subject area with which it deals and current priorities
▶ Amount of its principal and the total amount allotted for grants
▶ Maximum or minimum amounts of grants
▶ Whether it considers the total cost of the project or only a specific portion
▶ Whether its grant covers indirect costs
▶ Its criteria for selecting proposals and its application process
▶ Whether a letter of inquiry is desired
▶ Deadlines for submission
▶ Policy on renewal.

Approaching Foundations for Funding

After identifying the foundations whose interests, on the basis of past grants, appear to match your concerns, the next step is to determine how to approach them. Although there is no universal rule—each foundation has its own preference and style of operation—in general, small, private foundations require a brief (two- to three-page) letter telling who you are, what your concern is, what you propose to do, and how much funding you seek. A letter to small, private foundations suffices because they rarely have full-time staff and have limited funds and scope; therefore, they can readily indicate whether the proposal is within their area of interest (Kiritz, 1980; Beasley & Saasta, 1978).

This same procedure can be used when approaching corporate-sponsored foundations, which are also listed in materials available in the library reference collections mentioned earlier. After sending a letter, it is important to telephone the person who is responsible for the corporate foundation (sometimes the president of the company, sometimes a person in public relations, and sometimes a specifically designated program officer).

In considering corporate support, ask the following questions:

▶ Does the firm have significant business or employees in the community?

▶ Is the business related in any way to the type of project you are attempting?

▶ Does your organization deal with issues that are of unique importance to the firm?

▶ Would the firm gain a special benefit from being associated with the project, including publicity or visibility with key customers?

▶ Does the firm sell substantial products or services to your primary constituents?

Positive answers to these questions will enhance your chances of obtaining funding (Hall, 1988, p. 49).

In addition to providing grants, corporations can provide other valuable resources, including the expertise of their personnel, gifts from their inventory, company facilities, and released time of their employees (Shakley, 1977).

The approach to a community foundation is different from that used with a corporate or private foundation. A community foundation has such a broad charge—it has to be concerned with the charitable needs of the local community in which it is located—that almost anything fits within that charge. Because community foundations are primarily concerned with local needs, the indiscriminate mailing of requests for funding to such foundations throughout the country is usually a waste of time.

Some community foundations prefer first receiving a proposal and then arranging for an appointment to discuss it. Others encourage you to discuss the proposal with their program officers before you invest considerable time and energy in it. If you can manage to submit a proposal several weeks ahead of the deadline, you may have the opportunity to meet with a foundation's program officer enough in advance to be able to make revisions. Meeting with staff members is crucial because although not everything they recommend to the board of the foundation passes, their opinions and recommendations are highly regarded.

Identifying and Approaching Governmental Sources

Tracking governmental funds may be even more challenging than searching for grants from foundations. The payoff may be greater but, then, so are the restrictions. To be chosen over competitors, one must conduct careful research and have tremendous perseverance. Despite a general decline in support, the federal government is still the largest resource for external funding. Information on governmental funding may be obtained from the following major sources (Borden, 1978):

▶ *Federal Register* (Superintendent of Documents, U.S. Government Printing Office, Washington, DC 20402)

▶ *Catalog of Federal Domestic Assistance* (many libraries have the catalog, or write to the U.S. Government Printing Office)

▶ Federal Assistance Programs Retrieval System (write or phone *Federal Domestic Assistance Catalog,* Staff, General Services Administration, 300 7th Street, SW, Washington, DC 20407; phone (202) 708-5126)

▶ *Commerce Business Daily* (U.S. Government Printing Office)

In addition to these regular sources, every federal agency periodically announces funds that are available for specific projects. Called Requests for Proposals (RFP), these announcements provide detailed guidelines. It is useful to contact the appropriate federal agency to get on its mailing list for an application packet.

On the basis of reading and general contacts with officials, it is possible to determine what is being funded. The next step, then, is to make alterations in the framing of the original issue or problem area to fit the government's priorities. To obtain federal funding, one must conform to the federal requirements, rather than expect that the federal government will make changes to meet an agency's particular needs. Federal agency priorities, as published in the *Federal Register,* usually include the specific population to be served, the application deadline, and the type of proposal document to be submitted.

Call the program officer who is responsible for the grant in your regional office or in Washington, DC, through the name and number listed in the *Federal Register.* The program officer will be able to provide you with criteria for selection and an application packet for the grant program, which includes forms, rules and regulations, and guidelines. If the program officer cannot supply you with this year's criteria because of delays, then ask for last year's. These criteria are vital because they indicate the basis on which the proposal will be judged by impartial readers. Because the procedure generally is for reviewers of a proposal to subtract points when a proposal does not measure up to the criteria for selection, your proposal should be as responsive to these criteria as possible. The RFP application kit contains details of the grant, the average award, the possibility of renewal, requirements for eligibility, the required format, restrictions, and the role of the local or state government. This information should serve as your guideline for preparing the proposal.

Writing the Proposal

The format and length of proposals may vary, depending on the requirements of funders. Governmental proposals have a highly structured format. Proposals for foundations are not usually as structured, but generally they should include what you intend to accomplish and how you propose to do so. The following format is offered as a guide, to be modified if the funder requests a different outline:

1. Summary statement
2. Statement of need

3. Goals and objectives
4. Components of the program: activities and tasks
5. Evaluation
6. Capability of the organization
7. Continuation of the program
8. Budget
9. Appendixes

Summary Statement

Normally a summary statement should appear first because readers need an overview to orient them to the project and to prepare them for the details that are to follow (Jacquette & Jacquette, 1977). The summary should not exceed one page and should contain the following elements: what the need is, what will be accomplished, who you are and why you are qualified, what activities you will perform, what the project will cost, and how long it will take. The summary should be prepared after the full proposal is written because it should accurately reflect the proposal's major elements.

Statement of Need

The purpose of this section of the proposal is to define precisely what condition your organization wants to change. Focusing on local conditions would likely appeal to a local foundation. Dealing with a problem or issue that has implications beyond the local community may be appealing to a large national foundation or a federal agency. Whether the approach is to a local or a national foundation, focus on the people who will be served, not on how funding will be used to benefit the organization (Gooch, 1987, p. 8).

Specify who the target population is, what specific problem will be addressed, where the problem is located, what its origin is, and why it continues to exist. If the problem is multifaceted, then all the significant aspects need to be identified. For example, a problem statement about out-of-school, unemployed, adolescent ex-offenders living in poverty would need to describe their life-style, educational lags, and need for income.

Distinguish the difference between risk, target, and impact populations (Brody, 1982, pp. 41–42). The *risk* population is the total group that needs help or is at risk, for example, 800 ex-offenders in the community. The *target* population is that subset toward whom the program is aimed, such as 70 ex-offenders to be served. The *impact* population is the subset that is likely to benefit from the program, for instance, 45 of those served who will obtain jobs.

If possible, the theoretical basis for the problem should also be discussed. Briefly review the literature on the target population's needs to develop a conceptual understanding of the factors that are causing the problem. Avoid circular reasoning. It is not enough, for example, to say that the problem is the lack of the service that the proposed project is intended to provide (Kiritz, 1980, p. 15).

To demonstrate a grasp of the problem, it is desirable to provide prospective funders with data from a variety of sources: national studies and their local applications, testimony from congressional records, surveys, or quotations from authorities. Give special attention to providing local data on the issue. Unless a funding group requests detailed information in the narrative, do not inundate it with pages of statistics; summarize the data and place detailed, statistical tables in an appendix.

Because many problems are chronic, the statement of need should convey why there is a special urgency to seek funding now. What new crisis has arisen? For example, are the kinds of crimes being committed by adolescents more serious than before? Does new state legislation place a special burden on the local community to deal with delinquency? Are local institutions more prepared now than before to deal with delinquency? A description of the special circumstances makes the importance of funding the project more compelling. The potential funders must see the problem as both timely and critical.

When feasible, indicate how the constituency in the community or the client group has been involved in defining the problem. Such involvement is obviously desirable if the proposal relates to improvement of the community, for the clients are in the best position to comment on what their special needs are. Even those who normally do not participate, such as mentally retarded offenders or recently released mentally ill patients, can be consulted. Their participation in the problem-defining process conveys the message that those who are preparing the proposal have a profound depth of understanding.

Although the statement of need is presented before the section on goals and objectives, it should be written with the objectives clearly in mind. Because needs and objectives must be consistent, it may even be desirable to write the latter section first. Doing so is especially necessary if the prospective funding group has specified what the proposal should accomplish, which is usually the case with federal agencies (Brody, 1982, p. 179).

Goals and Objectives

Organizational or program goals represent broad statements of what the organization wants to accomplish. They provide a general direction for commitment to action. They are global descriptions of a long-term condition toward which the organization's efforts will be directed. Goals are ideals; they are timeless, and they are rarely achieved. Examples of statements of goals are the following: "reduce crime in the community," "upgrade housing," "improve interracial relations," "provide information to low-income clients," "prevent illegitimate births by teenagers," "eliminate child abuse and neglect." Although such statements are inspiring, they are not amenable to clear definition and measurement.

Objectives, in contrast, represent relevant, attainable, measurable, and time-limited ends to be achieved. They are relevant because they fit within the general mission and goals of the organization and because they relate to problems identified in the proposal; they are attainable because they are capable of being realized. They are measurable because achievement is, it is hoped, based on tangible, concrete, and quantifiable results. They are time limited because the proposal specifies the time frame within which results can be achieved. Objectives provide the funding group with clear-cut targets for organizational accountability. Be aware that although objectives are intended to be realistic and achievable, their accomplishment may not necessarily result in the elimination of a problem described earlier in the proposal. Obtaining jobs for 45 ex-offenders will not solve the high rate of recidivism in the community.

Four types of objectives can be prepared (Brody & Krailo, 1978; Drucker, 1976, p. 18; Elkin & Vorwaller, 1972, pp. 104–111; Raia, 1974, p. 24). They are operating, process or activity, product, and impact objectives.

Operating objectives convey the intent to improve the general operation of the organization. Two examples are to sponsor four in-service training workshops in the next three months for 40 staff members and to increase the size of the membership by 150 within the coming year (and thereby put the organization in sound financial shape). Operating objectives enhance the functioning and survivability of the organization. Achieving them puts the organization in a better position to help its target populations.

Activity objectives (sometimes called process objectives) are based on the organization's quantifying the units of services it intends to render. Examples include the following: to serve 300 clients in the program year, to conduct 680 interviews, to hold 17 neighborhood assemblies, and to refer 125 clients to agencies in a year.

Product objectives relate to a tangible piece of work that will be delivered at the end of the funded period. Some examples are to produce a resource directory, to create a case management system, and to produce a videotape that will provide clients with information about the agency's services.

Impact objectives specify outcomes to be achieved as a result of the process activities. Whereas activity objectives reflect the amount of effort to be expended, impact objectives detail the return expected on the investment of time, personnel, and resources. Impact objectives focus on results. The following are three examples: to place 50 percent of the youths enrolled in the vocational training program in full-time jobs within 18 months; to increase the educational attainment of a school's 200 entering students, 80 percent of whom will complete one full year of school; and to obtain a commitment from the board of education and the youth commission to incorporate the program, by the end of the third year, into the regular school program.

The advantage of each of these objectives is that they alert the funders to expect a clear-cut outcome from the project. Stating the objectives in quantifiable terms disciplines an organization to determine what can reasonably be achieved, not only the ideal it would like to achieve. Furthermore, although the format presented here separates goals and objectives from the program's components (see the next section), they may be combined so that specific activities and tasks are listed under each objective.

Components of the Program: Activities and Tasks

This part of the proposal presents a work plan for how the organization intends to accomplish its objectives. To convey the logic and continuity of the project, the proposal should describe, in relation to each objective, what will be done, by whom, and when it will be done. To discipline thinking about planning the work that needs to be accomplished, undertake reverse-order and forward-order sequence planning.

In reverse-order planning, one anticipates what the end point is likely to be for each major activity and then considers the specific tasks under each activity by asking, "What must we do just before we reach our final results and what needs to be done before that and before that and so forth" until one arrives at the beginning point (MacDicken, Trankel, Peterson, & Callahan, 1975, pp. 76, 77). For a project designed for ex-delinquents, one of whose objectives is to obtain jobs, a simplified work plan would be formatted as follows:

Objective: to place 50 percent of previously delinquent youths in the vocational training program for full-time jobs within 18 months

Activity: develop a pool of not less than 40 potential jobs

Tasks: sign contractual agreements with employers, send follow-up letters to personal contacts, mail letters of inquiry, devise contractual forms, train job recruiters, and hire job recruiters

Activity: provide orientation for youths

Tasks: prepare training materials, obtain a facility, train staff, and recruit staff.

In forward-order sequence planning one begins with the first set of tasks and then sequentially plans each step. The exercise of doing both reverse-order and forward-order sequence planning allows you to determine if any important task has been omitted.

The proposal itself should show the results of the detailed planning process through the use of a timeline chart. At the top of the chart, place the period, divided into weeks or months. Along the side, identify major activities and tasks. Horizontal bar lines in the chart reflect the beginning and ending points for each task.

In addition to a visual timeline chart, one should describe in more detail how the program would actually function. When relevant, state in the narrative, for example, how the proposed work program has been successfully used elsewhere, how it will relate to existing programs in the community, and what current resources of the organization will be used.

The determination of activities and tasks will typically involve a group process because knowledge is usually not concentrated in one person, and a consensus may need to emerge if organizational members are to be involved in implementing the proposal. But the actual proposal writing itself cannot be done by a committee; one or two people have to take primary responsibility. The committee members can react to a draft, and their suggestions can then be incorporated.

Evaluation

Evaluation is the process of examining the extent to which an organization has been effective, that is, whether it has achieved its stated objectives. Providing for evaluation is essential because it requires the proposal writer to examine the measurability of objectives and therefore enhances the accountability of the program. Building in evaluation must be part of the early proposal-planning process because it will convey to funders that results will be documented and that information will be available upon which corrective action can be based. Give careful attention to evaluation because it is of growing importance to funders. The questions you want the evaluation to answer for the agency and the funding group and the likelihood of having the resources with which to conduct the evaluation will determine the type of evaluation that is feasible. Impact (or outcome) and process are two forms of evaluations that are typically used in proposals.

To carry out impact evaluation, you may consider three designs (experimental, quasi-experimental, and survey).

An experimental design utilizes sampling techniques, the random assignment of subjects to control and experimental groups, and the control of exposure to treatment or intervention variables. The use of experimental methods presumably eliminates competing explanations for observed results and permits the generalization of findings. With an experimental design, the organization and the funding group can be confident that it was the particular program and not other factors that made the difference in reducing such problems as delinquency, unemployment, or unwed pregnancy. This design seeks to establish a cause-and-effect relationship by precisely identifying those factors that contribute to the success or failure of the program (Rossi & Freeman, 1989, pp. 253–256).

The chief drawbacks of an experimental design—extensive research costs, the requirements of sophisticated techniques, restrictive time delays, ethical questions about assigning individuals to experimental or control groups, and often inconclusive results unless conducted on a massive scale—do not make it a feasible approach for many organizations or for their funders (Weiss, 1972, p. 5). However, organizations that want to claim unequivocally that their interventions have significantly reduced a problem should undertake an experimental research design.

An outcome evaluation involving a quasi-experimental design usually seeks to measure the same group against itself in a before-and-after analysis. Or it may compare a group receiving the intervention with a comparison group without randomly assigning subjects to groups (Rossi & Freeman, 1989, pp. 256–259). Measurement indicators can be devised for each objective and can take on several forms (such as psychological tests or analyses of before-and-after records of behavior). Proposals using this form of evaluation will have to live with the uncertainty that the particular intervention alone may not account for achievements.

A third form of outcome evaluation is surveys involving clients' satisfaction with the service or intervention. For example, you can report whether people think they are safer after a special campaign is mounted. Or clients can be asked if they see a change in the way they are being treated by a particular governmental agency. The difficulty, of course, is that the survey captures a response only at a point in time (Rossi & Freeman, 1989, p. 260).

"You know, I think we had that grant request approved right up to the point when she counted the zeros on the funding amount."

Process evaluation (sometimes referred to as monitoring) examines the internal processes and structure of the program to determine whether it is functioning as planned. Is it achieving its objectives in a timely manner? Is it keeping an accurate record of who is being served and under what conditions? Are clients being processed as expected? What administrative problems are being encountered? The major value of process evaluation is that it helps the program staff review whether they are going off course and allows them to take corrective action before the end of the funding period (Rossi & Freeman, 1989, pp. 170–180). Process evaluation assures funders that proper feedback is being built into the project to help manage it better.

To carry out process evaluation, a local advisory committee may be appointed to judge the effectiveness of the effort and report back to the funder. Another possibility is to identify an expert in the field to visit the project periodically and to furnish reports to the funder. A third possibility is for the project staff to report on its monitoring of the results of the project, particularly when objectives are measurable.

Regardless of the model of the design, the proposal should spell out the questions to be answered and the details of the evaluation plan. These details should include who will perform the evaluation, how they are to be chosen, and what instruments are to be used.

Capability of the Organization

Funders want to know that the organization is capable of implementing the project (Steiner, 1988, pp. 121–122). Because they must be convinced of the staff's competence to achieve what is being promised, one needs to demonstrate credibility for undertaking the project. Describe briefly how and why the organization or agency was formed, past and current activities, the support received from other organizations, and significant accomplishments. Especially if the agency is unknown to funders, provide evidence of involvement and competence in the area in which funds are being requested. Indicate what financial or other resources are available. Letters of endorsement are desirable, but letters that indicate the commitment of actual resources (staff, equipment, and funding) are even more impressive. (Note: Some use the option of discussing the organization's capability as part of a general introduction or in a separate section after discussing the program evaluation. Review the guidelines of the funding source for the specific format.)

Because the proposal itself must be concise, refer to the competence of staff in the appendixes and provide a list of positions, titles, qualifications, the chain of accountability, salary levels, and responsibilities. If appropriate, describe the process of selecting key personnel. Funders appreciate knowing that the agency's board of trustees is actively involved in making decisions and fully supports the proposal. List the trustees and their identifying information in an appendix.

Testimony from key figures in the community is also useful if their endorsement letters are sincere and reflect genuine support. Indicate the roles and names of members of an advisory committee, if appropriate. If requested, include in the appendix an annual report, documentation of the agency's IRS nonprofit status, the latest audit statement, and a copy of the agency's affirmative action policy.

Continuation of the Program

In this section indicate the feasibility of the organization continuing the program beyond the grant period. Foundations that give time-limited funding want assurances that the project will be sustained. Among the options for continued revenue are the organization's operating budget; revenue from clients' fees; third-party payments, such as insurance; special fundraising drives; application for membership or special funding in a United Way or other federated fundraising program; and an assumption of costs by a voluntary organization or governmental agency.

Although it may be difficult to anticipate sources of funding two or three years hence, it is of such crucial importance to funders that a concerted effort should be made to explore options as part of preparing the proposal. At the end of the grant period, a scaled-down version of the program may be absorbed by the existing community institutions. If this is the intent, indicate how it would occur.

The Budget

The budget is important, but unless it reveals major weaknesses or is obviously overinflated, it will not be the primary reason for the rejection or acceptance of a proposal. If your idea is sound, the budget is usually negotiable. This section presents some general guidelines for preparing the budget (see also Brody, 1982, pp. 185–187).

Different funding groups will require various degrees of detail in the budget. Most governmental agencies require a great deal of detail and usually provide budgetary forms and instructions for their completion. Foundations and corporations are less structured in their requirements, but will want a budget that is well thought out and complete.

Some governmental agencies have special instructions for preparing the budget that are separate from program guidelines or regulations. These instructions are continually being revised. Use the most recent instructions available, rather than delay the preparation of the budget. Allow time to make necessary changes if it is found that a new set of instructions is to be issued shortly before the final application is due. Instructions for applying for grants generally include information regarding budgetary forms; examples of how to calculate specific budgetary items; an agency formula for determining the maximum allowance in major budgetary categories; and allowable rates for consulting fees, per diem expenses, and travel. Be prepared to document needs when costs exceed the agency formula.

As an aid to developing the budget, prepare worksheets, which will provide a structure for planning the budget, so that no type of expense is overlooked. Make detailed records of each budgeted item, computed so that you are prepared to present the case and to discuss the potential impact of cuts proposed during negotiations. The worksheets will provide a plan for use in the actual operation of the project.

A good budget will relate directly to the objectives and activities. Each budgetary item should be justified on the basis of its contribution to the potential accomplishments of the project. To prepare a budget, review each major activity and estimate its expense. There should be a clear connection between activities and budgetary items.

The budget is an estimate of what the costs will be. Generally, there will be a degree of flexibility in spending, as long as spending does not exceed the total amount of the grant. Requests for additional changes may be authorized by the funding source. Such requests should be made in writing. The response, also in writing, becomes a formal modification of the budget and changes the conditions of the grant or contract. Adequate planning of the budget will reduce the number of changes required and will establish a degree of credibility that is necessary to obtain permission for needed modifications. Usually, if the grant is to cover more than one year, funding bodies want a breakdown of the year-by-year budget and then a total amount. Also, if more than one funding group is being asked to contribute to the costs, indicate the expected income from multiple sources in the budget. If the organization can make in-kind donations, such as staff time and building space, to the project, then the budget should reflect these contributions.

In the narrative that accompanies the budget, be as specific as possible about unusual costs. It is particularly necessary to do so if the funder is not familiar with the nature of the project. Be able to document the exact costs of each major item. When it is necessary to create new positions, survey other agencies with similar jobs to justify salary scales. If items are included in the budget that cannot be fully supported, the integrity of the project may be open to question.

In regard to salaries, provide a detailed breakdown of each position and the percentage of time that would be allocated. Include fringe benefits—worker's compensation, state unemployment insurance, social security, retirement, and other such items—as a separate category in the budget.

Other direct costs include the following: space; the rental, lease, or purchase of equipment; supplies; travel in and out of town; telephone, including installation; copying; and printing. Add other categories if expenditures are significant. Give details for the basis of cost estimates.

Indirect costs are more difficult to determine than are direct costs but they are important to the financial well-being of the organization. Indirect expenses may include estimated portions of time spent on the project by other staff members, such as the director, the accountant, and maintenance personnel. Such costs may also encompass expenditures that are difficult to account for with precision, such as the depreciation of office equipment. Indirect expenses may or may not include office rental or office equipment and other like items, depending on whether they can be isolated or are an integral part of the administration of the organization.

Indirect costs may be included in the grant request (if they are allowable) by adding a certain percentage for indirect expenses to the direct costs of the grant. That percentage is usually determined by an analysis of the overall financial operations, which is done by an experienced accountant. Many organizations that carry on extensive grant activity with federal agencies negotiate an acceptable percentage with one governmental agency and then are able to use the same rate in contracts with other governmental agencies. The federal government will allow indirect expenses that are arrived at either as a percentage of the total salaries involved in the project or as a percentage (much lower) of the total direct cost of the grant. Some foundations are becoming more accepting about including indirect costs, but depending upon the policies of a particular foundation, it may be necessary to absorb indirect costs in other parts of the budget. Check with your funder about its policies on indirect costs.

If a proposal suggests that a certain number of people will be served, divide the number into the costs to see if the cost of service per client is reasonable. Even if this figure is not made explicit in the proposal, funders often calculate it. Be prepared to defend the per capita cost.

Do not accept less money than is needed for a successful effort just to get the grant. One receives no credit for good intentions if they are not accomplished. Accepting the accountability for a project without having the essential resources to follow through is irresponsible. If fewer dollars are offered, revise the anticipated achievements.

Appendixes

The appendixes to the proposal provide information that is not essential to making the case but that lends reliability and understanding to the organization and its request (Burns, 1989, p. 18). Include the following items: a list of the board of trustees, documentation of the agency's tax-exempt status—501[c][3]—from the IRS, audit, affirmative action policy, statistical charts, letters of support or agreement, evaluation instruments, and other items that bolster your proposal or that may be required by the funder.

Summary

Funders are looking for a proposal that reflects the following:
▶ A match between the funder's priorities and the grantee agency's purpose
▶ A competent staff and a good track record
▶ A committed board of trustees

- A compelling need that will be met in a creative and resourceful manner
- A program that is neither too grandiose nor too limited
- A clear, measurable set of objectives
- A capacity to continue beyond the grant period
- The potential for the funded activity being replicated or expanded upon
- A clearly written document that is free of professional jargon
- An appropriate evaluation.

Following these guidelines can both enhance your competitiveness and provide the basis for a well-thought-out plan that can be implemented effectively to achieve your objectives.

SKILLS-APPLICATION EXERCISE

Funders obviously will vary in the criteria they use for judging a proposal. As was indicated previously, governmental agencies will have specific and unique criteria for each grant. Foundation and corporate funders will tend to be more flexible in using criteria to judge proposals. Using the general criteria identified next, analyze a proposal that has been submitted from the perspective of a funding source (Gooch, 1987; Jacquette & Jacquette, 1977; Mastrine, 1976; Mayer, 1972).

Competence of the Individuals Involved

- Are those who have prepared the proposal considered highly competent?
- Are they dedicated to making their ideas a reality?
- Do they have a successful track record?
- Do they demonstrate a depth of knowledge about what is happening in their community and across the country?
- Are they sufficiently aware of the complexity of the problem?

Participation of the Organization

- Are board members familiar with the proposal? Have they approved it?
- Is the board composed of the best possible combination of representatives of the community, clients, and outside people who can be resources to the organization?
- Is the board willing to provide some of the organization's own resources?
- If applicable, has provision been made for the participation of clients or consumers in the design and implementation of the project?

continued

Desirability of the Proposed Project

► Does the proposal make a strong case for the urgency of funding?
► Is it clearly a high priority for the requesting organization and for the community?
► If similar programs already exist, does the proposal acknowledge their existence and strongly convey why, nevertheless, one more program is necessary?
► Are the results likely to be transferable to other programs and other committees?
► Will the results have a significant impact on the community?
► Is the project creative in proposing an innovative approach to dealing with a community problem?
► If the proposal is asking for the renewal of a grant, has the project adequately demonstrated its accomplishments?
► If the project has fallen short of its accomplishments, does the proposal adequately explain why and what the organization intends to do about it?
► Is the proposal in keeping with the funder's priorities?

Feasibility of the Proposed Project

► Does the proposal illustrate how the project will adequately cope with the problem it has identified, being neither too limited in its objectives nor too grandiose in its claims?
► If the project proposes to meet a long-standing problem, does the proposal have a well-conceived rationale for how it expects to succeed?
► What specific ingredients and talents can the project bring to bear on the problem?
► If the project is to continue, what assurances are there for ongoing funding?
► If funds are being requested for a start-up project, what assurance is there that the requesting organization or another group will continue it?
► If the proposal purports to make institutional changes, what assurance can it offer that it will be able to do so?

References

Beasley, S., & Saasta, T. (1978). Anatomy of a grants process: Federal funding for health. *Grantsmanship Center News, 4,* 20–28.

Borden, K. (1978). *Dear uncle: Please send money—A guide for proposal writers.* Pocatello, ID: Auger Associates.

Brody, R. (1974). *Guide for applying for federal funds for human services.* Cleveland: School of Applied Social Sciences, Case Western Reserve University.

Brody, R. (1982). *Problem solving: Concepts and methods for community organization*. New York: Human Sciences Press.

Brody, R., & Krailo, H. (1978). An approach for reviewing program effectiveness. *Social Work, 23*, 226–232.

Burns, M. E. (1989). *Proposal writer's guide*, Hartford, CT: Development & Technical Assistance Center.

Cleveland Foundation. (1978). Guidelines for grant getting. *Grantsmanship Center News* (reprint), 14.

Drucker, P. F. (1976). What results should you expect? A user's guide to MBO. *Public Administration Review, 36*, 12–39.

Elkin, R., & Vorwaller, D. J. (1972, May). Evaluating the effectiveness of social services. *Management Controls*, pp. 104–111.

Gooch, J. M. (1987). *Writing winning proposals*. Washington, DC: Council for the Advancement and Support of Education.

Hall, M. S. (1988). *Getting funded: A complete guide to proposal writing*. Portland, OR: Portland State University.

Jacquette, L. F., & Jacquette, B. I. (1977). *What makes a good proposal?* (pp. 1–7). Washington, DC: Foundation Center.

Kiritz, N. J. (1980). Program planning and proposal writing. *Grantsmanship Center News* (reprint), 1–8.

MacDicken, R., Trankel, J., Peterson, M., & Callahan, W. (1975). *Toward more effective management*. Washington, DC: U.S. Department of Health, Education, & Welfare, Administration on Aging.

Mastrine, B. (1976). How to effectively plan programs. *Grantsmanship Center News, 3*, 1–12.

Mayer, R. A. (1972). What will a foundation look for when you submit a grant proposal? *Foundation Center Information Quarterly* (reprint).

Raia, A. P. (1974). *Managing by objectives*. Glenview, IL: Scott, Foresman.

Rossi, P. H., & Freeman, H. E. (1989). *Evaluation: A systematic approach*. Newbury Park, CA: Sage.

Shakley, J. (1977). Exploring the elusive world of corporate giving. *Grantsmanship Center News, 3*, 35–58.

Steiner, R. (1988). *Total proposal building*, Albany, NY: Trestletree Publications.

Weiss, C. (1972). *Evaluative research*. Englewood Cliffs, NJ: Prentice Hall.

Providing Entrepreneurial Leadership

Dennis R. Young

The world of human services does not stand still. The problems now faced by distressed groups in our society—homelessness, substance abuse, grinding poverty, AIDS, faltering educational achievement, teenage pregnancy, single-parent families, the tribulations associated with an aging population—differ in scope and character from 10 years ago, and they continue to evolve and become more serious. The economic conditions under which human services agencies operate also have changed rapidly. Governmental funding for human services has been cut substantially, the growth in charitable contributions has been limited, and the reliance on market-based financial support has increased considerably (Salamon, 1984). Human services agencies now depend heavily on fees for service and increasingly on commercial, for-profit ventures (Hodgkinson & Weitzman, 1988). Many agencies have developed highly innovative techniques for soliciting donations and volunteer labor.

Such a world of rapid change requires a dynamic brand of management. Managers, especially chief executives and their top lieutenants, cannot afford simply to be caretaker administrators who oversee the smooth running of steady-state operations. Rather, they must stay abreast or ahead of change, by providing leadership that is "entrepreneurial."

In its generic characterization, entrepreneurship is a process of putting new ideas into practice. Entrepreneurs bring together and catalyze the ingredients—people, financial resources, organizational arrangements, and the like—that are necessary to implement a new concept. That new concept—economist Schumpeter (1949) called it a "new combination of the means of production"—can take many forms. It may be a new kind of service, a new way of providing an existing service, a service provided to a new clientele, new financing or organizational arrangements for providing a given service, or even the revitalization of a program within an existing organizational framework. The point is that the entrepreneurial leader takes an idea or an "invention" off the drawing board and into practice, thereby achieving "innovation."

This broad definition of entrepreneurship goes beyond the conventional notion of developing ventures for profit (see also, Bird, 1989, for broad definitions of entrepreneurship). Those who build new businesses or establish new initiatives within profit-making corporations are indeed "classic" entrepreneurs, but they are by no means the dominant or most important group of entrepreneurial leaders in the human services. Personal financial reward is not the dominant motive for entrepreneurial activity in the human services. Strongly held beliefs, the need for personal achievement, and other motivating factors are at least as important as money (Young, 1983). Moreover, although commercial ventures have become increasingly significant within the nonprofit human services, these ventures represent only a small proportion of the innovative activities fostered by entrepreneurial leaders in this field.

Given the importance of entrepreneurial leadership in the human services, it is appropriate to ask, "What are the skills of entrepreneurship, and can they be taught?" It is not clear that everyone can learn to be an entrepreneurial leader. Such persons are part of a special breed who inspire others and exhibit tenacity, energy, and creativity at extraordinary levels. Nonetheless, three considerations make the "teaching" of entrepreneurial leadership worthwhile: (1) the value of entrepreneurial leadership should be supported and recognized by everyone in the human services, (2) at some stage in many careers, opportunities or circumstances call for entrepreneurial leadership, and (3) formal study can hone and sharpen the skills of people who may be natural entrepreneurial leaders. The remainder of this chapter is intended to assist both occasional entrepreneurs and those who would make a career of entrepreneurial leadership.

Skills of Entrepreneurial Leaders

There is no such thing as a routine venture. However, a wide variety of ventures exhibit remarkable similarity in the skills they require of those leading the charge. In this section, these skills are identified and briefly explained. In the next section, the skills are illustrated through the story of a particular venture. Eight interrelated sets of skills are discussed: developing a sense of mission, problem solving, applying creativity and ingenuity, identifying opportunities and good timing, analyzing risks, consensus and team building, the mobilization of resources, and persistence.

Developing a Sense of Mission

All ventures should start with a sense of purpose. Entrepreneurs who start new organizations or programs must internalize that purpose and use it as a touchstone for setting goals, as well as strategies to meet those goals. They must also inculcate that mission or purpose in those they enlist to develop and carry out the venture. In short, clarity about the mission helps answer the question, "Why undertake this venture?"

In the case of establishing a new organization, clarity about the mission is required to win the support of collaborators, funders, and other providers of resources; governmental officials whose approval may be needed; and other constituents and potential stakeholders. For ventures that are carried out within the framework of an existing organization, the entrepreneur must be clear about how the venture contributes to achieving the organization's mission. Or, if the venture is intended to alter the traditional mission of the organization, the entrepreneur must be lucid about this intention and work to achieve support within the organization for that change.

Problem Solving

Virtually all ventures are intended to solve a problem or exploit a perceived opportunity of some kind (see Bird, 1989). The most obvious level of problem solving may be called "programmatic" or "systemic." At this level, a venture focuses on some need that is inadequately addressed by the existing array of services. For example, the Harlem-Dowling Children's Service, New York City (Young, 1985), was established to provide heretofore unavailable foster care services to older, black children in their own community.

Ventures also address problems at the organizational level. The Harlem-Dowling agency was a spinoff of Spence-Chapin Adoption Services. Its development as a separate agency removed from Spence-Chapin a growing local foster care operation that threatened to divert the agency from pursuing its principle mission as a national adoption service.

A third manifestation of problem solving is often found at the personal level. In the case of the Harlem-Dowling agency, a newly installed first black chief executive was under pressure both to prove herself as a worthy successor to the previous, highly esteemed director and to demonstrate responsiveness to the needs of the local black community. The Harlem-Dowling venture helped solve these problems.

The challenge of problem solving is to recognize the character of the problems that exist at each level and then to analyze how well-formulated ventures can serve as solutions. The better the fit, the easier it will be for the entrepreneurial leader to generate enthusiasm and support for the venture from external constituents, from factions within an organization, and from his or her own reservoir of energy.

Applying Creativity and Ingenuity

Identifying the problems that ventures may address is half the battle. An equally important step is to identify a workable solution, which often requires considerable creativity. In the case of the Group-Live-In-Experience (GLIE), funding a shelter program for runaway youths depended on approval of the new agency by the New York City government (Young, 1985). But the city government was concerned about the new organization's lack of a track record and its viability in the hostile environment of the South Bronx. GLIE was caught in a Catch-22 situation that required some new ideas. A city official suggested that GLIE be taken under the administrative wing of an established agency. It was not a comfortable solution for the entrepreneurial leader of GLIE, but it worked.

Creativity in generating potential solutions to problems is not easily learned from a textbook. The first step is to recognize the need for ingenuity. When all avenues appear to be blocked, one needs to "think around" the constraints to come up with new ideas that diverge from past practices. Consulting extensively with various parties, brainstorming, and obtaining information on how particular problems have been approached in similar circumstances elsewhere are all ways of dealing with this task.

Identifying Opportunities and Good Timing

Good ideas are a dime a dozen. Implementing them is another story. Often the ability to put a new idea into practice depends on identifying a frequently narrow window of opportunity. The merger of the Jewish Board of Guardians (JBG) and the Jewish Family Service (JFS) to form the Jewish Board of Family and Children's Services (JBFCS) is a good illustration (Young, 1985). For many years, the merger had been on the agenda of the Federation of Jewish Philanthropies of New York City, the major private funder of JBG and JFS, to increase efficiency and to provide more comprehensive services. But such mergers were always resisted by constituent agencies. However, the retirement of the chief executive of the JFS and that executive's willingness to talk merger with the head of the JGB presented a special opportunity to start the process.

As with creativity, good timing is difficult to teach in any conventional way. Again, the first step is to recognize that timing is a critical issue for successful venturing. Windows of opportunity open and close. One must be ready to move ahead with ideas and strategies when they open, and one must move with measured haste before they close again. Seasoned entrepreneurial leaders maintain an inventory of "pet projects," in their minds at least. With experience, they gain a sense of when the time is right to move ahead with any of them.

Analyzing Risks

Change is rarely accomplished without taking chances. Successful entrepreneurial leaders are not reckless gamblers, but they do take calculated risks (Bird, 1989). These risks may jeopardize their financial or professional standing and sometimes the stability and well-being of their organizations. For example, the enterprising founders of Melville House in Suffolk County on Long Island, New York gave up financially secure positions in a state agency for the tenuous circumstances of a fledgling private home for teenage boys (Young, 1985). The founder of an outpatient clinic at Sagamore Children's Hospital, also in Suffolk County, risked destabilizing the equilibrium of her organization by moving from an inpatient to an outpatient model (Young, 1985). The executive of Harlem-Dowling risked professional ridicule in proposing that a new agency could sustain itself in the harsh soil of the Harlem community (Young, 1985).

The analysis of risk has been well studied and is even highly technical. But the formal analytic procedures for decision making under risk hinge substantially on the subjective judgments of the decision makers (see, for example, Behn & Vaupel, 1982). Thus, it is the entrepreneurial leader and his or her advisers who must identify the best, worst, and intermediate scenarios that are associated with potential ventures and estimate the likelihood and consequences of each scenario. Once such information is attained, analytic techniques for decision making may be usefully applied. However, this last step is the easiest: The real challenge is to mobilize the information on alternatives, consequences, and probabilities, so the entrepreneurial leader can think through decisions as clearly as possible.

One more point about risk: In the face of impending problems, the alternative of "doing nothing" may be the riskiest. In the case of Harlem-Dowling, for example, continuing the status quo would eventually have led to an organizational crisis that might have forced Spence-Chapin into a less desirable and more costly course of action (Young, 1985).

Consensus and Team Building

Our imagination is still captured by Cinderella stories of small-business entrepreneurs who perfect new products or inventions in their garages and obtain venture capital to market and build companies. But even in business, these "solo" ventures are becoming increasingly rare, as large corporations have come to dominate the processes of technical innovation, financing, and the marketing of new products. In the human services, group processes are much more critical to the success of entrepreneurial leadership, on at least two levels: team building within the organization and consensus building outside the organization. These processes, in turn, require that the entrepreneurial leader be adept in negotiation and other skills for managing human resources.

The case of JBFCS is classic with respect to the necessity for and application of such skills. The merger process was not simply a negotiation between executive directors or board presidents. It involved joint committees at the staff and board levels, which were needed to hammer out agreements over a range of program, organizational, and governance issues. It involved skillful negotiation with federation and governmental officials to ensure adequate resources for the new agency to deal with the transition and to operate effectively thereafter. It involved the delicate handling of appointments to key positions on the board and staff of the merged agency and the smoothing of the ruffled feathers of those who were not appointed to their desired posts.

There is, of course, a substantial literature on negotiating skills (see Fisher & Ury, 1981, for example) and on the management of human resources (see Fombrun, Tichy, & Devanna, 1984), but no adequate way to boil this knowledge down to a few simple principles for entrepreneurial leadership. Several overriding themes may be identified, however:

▶ Find the common interests around which consensus can be developed and teams can be mobilized. In the case of JBFCS, everyone wanted the newly structured agency to be successful and the treatment of constituents from both the original agencies to be fair. Stressing these themes helped find ways to overcome differences and move toward mutually agreeable solutions.

▶ Find the right people for each position of responsibility. A venture's success depends on the delegation of responsibilities to individuals who are skilled and able enough to carry them out effectively and with sensitivity. Do not solve political problems by turning responsibilities over to individuals who will botch the job or make people unnecessarily angry.

▶ Complement your weaknesses with the strengths of others, and vice versa. For example, an entrepreneurial leader who is adept at negotiating for resources and professional opportunities in the organization's external environment should look to complement this strength with the appointment of team leaders who are skilled in the organization's internal procedures and politics.

▶ Reward good performance and find ways to ameliorate potential detractors. The most serious problems of morale and dissension arise when good workers go unrecognized while "squeaky wheels" or those who are thought capable of inflicting damage are rewarded to "avoid trouble." Successful entrepreneurial leaders engender loyalty from their supporters by giving them fair and honest rewards. Respect also is gained from detractors by being candid and consistent and by searching for ways to bring detractors "on board" in a manner that is attractive to them but not counterproductive to the venture at hand.

Mobilization of Resources

New ventures almost inevitably require new resources. For example, commercial ventures require start-up capital, and even such ventures as mergers, designed to save money in the long run, require transitional funding.

Strategies for developing resources in the human services are multifaceted; they require grant seeking from foundations and governmental agencies, the solicitation of contributions from individuals, gaining entry into governmental funding systems, and selling services and goods in the marketplace for profit. The skills associated with raising money these ways are also diverse. In some areas, such as grant seeking and charitable fundraising through techniques of mass appeal, there is an extensive literature on "how to do it" (see, for example, Seltzer, 1987). In other areas, such as the solicitation of large donations from individuals or the amassing of capital through commercial activity, experience is less extensive and less well documented (but see Odendahl, 1987, & Skloot, 1988, respectively).

A review of case studies suggests that the following special techniques are particularly important for entrepreneurial leaders who are attempting to obtain funding for their projects (Young, 1985):

▶ Write proposals for grants from foundations, corporations, and the government.

▶ Use interpersonal skills associated with approaching large donors and convincing (and empowering) wealthy individuals to solicit funds from their colleagues. For example, in the case of Greer-Woodycrest Children's Services, a pledge in the form of a challenge grant by one leading donor precipitated a series of additional pledges to build on-campus residences.

▶ Personalize the impact of individual contributions. For example, in the case of the Florida Sheriff Youth Fund, everything, from buildings to road signs, was marketed to donors, and a variety of other devices (such as "honorary sheriff" certificates) were used to recognize donors.

▶ Develop endowment and capital funds derived, in part, from operating profits from commercially viable services to amass the required capital for new ventures.

▶ Use political savvy and influence to spur the passage of new legislation to fund projects or to help gain entry into established funding streams.

▶ Cultivate long-term personal relationships with funders to smooth the solicitation of resources for future projects.

Circumstances often narrow the choice among alternative funding strategies to one or two obvious alternatives. For example, in the cases of GLIE or Harlem-Dowling, entry into the New York City foster-care-reimbursement system was the only major viable alternative long-term source of operating funds. However, successful entrepreneurial leaders are also careful about the funds they seek. GLIE, for example, shunned funding associated with juvenile delinquency or substance abuse for fear of having its clientele of runaway youths inappropriately "labeled." In other cases, the strings attached to various funding possibilities had to be weighed against the benefits of obtaining the desired resources.

Persistence

As millions of parents know, patience is not easily inculcated in children. For highly energetic entrepreneurial leaders, patience seems equally difficult to maintain. Indeed, it is a special combination of impatience and persistence that helps account for success among members of this group. Entrepreneurial leaders keep pushing their initiatives and are rarely satisfied with the pace of change. But they come back time and again, eventually overcoming the many obstacles and constraints that litter their paths. The founders of Melville House, for example, took in stride every delay in governmental approval, however absurd or upsetting, and strengthened their resolve with each setback. The Harlem-Dowling initiative took 12 years from conception to full operation. The founder of the Brookhaven Town Youth Bureau on Long Island, New York, persisted through five years and two political administrations to see his initiative enacted into law (Young, 1985).

Entrepreneurial leaders are sometimes said to have a short attention span, losing interest once their programs are implemented and have entered a stable state of development (see, for example, Kimberly, Miles, & Associates, 1980). Nevertheless, the tenacity and persistence of successful entrepreneurial leaders in seeing their projects through to implementation is perhaps their most important and universal characteristic.

"I say we add an NCAA Division I football program."

Case Study

Every entrepreneurial project is different. Hence, the particular combination of skills illustrated by any given case will not be typical of all others. The following case, however, does touch all the bases that were explicated earlier.[1]

Thumbnail Sketch

The Pleasantville Diagnostic Center is a unit on the Pleasantville campus of the Jewish Child Care Association (JCCA) of New York City. It operates as a short-term residential facility for referrals by the New York City Family Court or Bureau of Child Welfare of boys who are judged "hard to place." The center provides intensive diagnostic evaluations for formulating appropriate child care plans, including possible long-term placement and treatment. It was established in 1973 on the initiative of Jacob Trobe, then chief executive of JCCA, and Paul Steinfeld, then director of the Pleasantville campus.

What did it take to implement the Pleasantville Diagnostic Center? The following analysis of skills indicates many of the important ingredients.

Analysis of Skills

Developing a Sense of Mission

Historically, JCCA was part of a system of welfare agencies in New York City serving the social service needs of the local Jewish community. But since the 1960s, this agency and others like it have been financed more and more heavily by governmental funds for foster care. In the 1960s and 1970s, the population of children who were in need of services in the city became increasingly non-Jewish and nonwhite and had more difficult emotional and behavioral problems. Although JCCA's population followed these trends as well, it did so too slowly to satisfy critics who cited the needs and the public funding.

In the confusion between historical roots and contemporary circumstances, the leaders of JCCA needed to be clear about the agency's future direction. Trobe had little trouble reconciling the present and future: "This city and this nation have served the Jews well, and we owe it to give something back" (Young, 1985). The underlying purpose of the Pleasantville Diagnostic Center was to help JCCA become more responsive to society at large, while respecting JCCA's roots in service to, and support from, the Jewish community.

Problem Solving

At the programmatic level, the center was supposed to help address a problem of growing seriousness in New York City: The population of children requiring

---

[1]For a full analysis of the case, see D. R. Young, Casebook of Management for Nonprofit Organizations (New York: Haworth Press, 1985).

out-of-home placement was becoming older, behaviorally more difficult and violent, more handicapped, and more dominated by minority groups. The voluntary, nonprofit agencies that served some 85 percent of the children in foster care were coming under severe criticism for not changing their admissions policies and programs fast enough to meet the new needs. A commissioned report issued by the family court criticized the voluntary agencies for being too timid in serving behaviorally difficult children known as Persons in Need of Supervision, and a class-action suit charging discrimination against older nonwhite children would soon be brought against New York City's foster care system by the American Civil Liberties Union. Against this background, the center promised a way to examine the needs of difficult children more efficiently and precisely, thus facilitating their placement in appropriate programs. Presumably, the center would also make it easier for JCCA to accept more difficult children.

At the organizational level, JCCA's problem stemmed from being one of the largest, most prominent voluntary child care agencies serving the city. As such, it was a particular target for critics. Nonetheless, internal factors militated against a rapid response to the city's changing needs. For example, professional staff were apprehensive about bringing more difficult, diverse children into a mix of clientele they thought was already a substantial challenge. Moreover, they feared that accepting more violence-prone children could jeopardize the safety of their existing population.

The center was designed to ameliorate these problems in two ways. First, it would provide a precise analysis of each child's problems and needs. Thus, if a child was recommended for placement in a JCCA facility, the recommendation would be based on reliable information that the child would fit the placement and not introduce undue risk. Second, the fact that the center would be placed physically on the Pleasantville campus meant that a certain amount of acclimation would occur. JCCA staff would become accustomed to having some of the more difficult children on campus and would thus become more comfortable about some of them ultimately being placed in Pleasantville's mainline program.

At the personal level, Trobe was, of course, sensitive to having his agency singled out as being unresponsive to the city's needs. Trobe was a social pioneer with a long history of developing progressive and innovative programs. He needed a way to take action without alienating his colleagues in the agency. The center was a responsible and deliberate way to bring about internal change and to respond to the city's needs.

In Steinfeld, Trobe found a lieutenant of similar mind. Steinfeld was a JCCA careerist who had risen from social worker to campus director during a 20-year period. For Steinfeld, the center was an opportunity for his campus to stand out and for him to excel personally within the JCCA system. Soon after the center succeeded, Steinfeld was promoted to associate executive director of JCCA.

Applying Creativity and Ingenuity

The center was an ingenious concept in itself, an innovative way of introducing deliberate change into a reluctant organization in a manner that could be widely accepted. But new programs always have snags, and this one was no exception. The trustees of JCCA were fearful that the center would become a financial drain on the organization because the normal reimbursement rates for foster care were not adequate to cover this more expensive type of service and because they could not predict if the facility would be used to capacity. The financial concern proved to be a sticking point in negotiations with New York City until an official, Henry Rosner, suggested that JCCA's provision of mental health services in another program context could be used to justify piggybacking a Medicaid per diem rate on top of the foster care rate. This creative thinking around the conventional channels in which the problem was cast proved to be the clincher in reaching agreement to undertake the project.

Identifying Opportunities and Good Timing

The 1972–1973 period was a particular window of opportunity for the Pleasantville Diagnostic Center project. The family court issued its critical report in 1972, and the city's Office of Special Services for Children drew up a list of priorities later in the year, including diagnostic services to facilitate the placement of older, behaviorally difficult children. Inside JCCA, the trustees had recently completed a $6 million building fund campaign to renovate JCCA's facilities; some of these funds could be used to renovate a building for the center. In place were both the sense of urgency and external support and the internal resources to do something. It remained only to exploit this opportunity with timely action.

Analyzing Risks

Undertaking the project was an exercise in calculated risk taking. Introducing a new population to the Pleasantville campus could conceivably lead to instability or violence on the campus and hence upset existing programs. The costs might exceed the projections or the facility might be undersubscribed, which would lead to a financial drain on the agency. But the costs of standing still seemed even higher. A major child care agency, most of whose revenues are derived from public funding, could not be seen as unresponsive and resistant to change. And the benefits of helping to lead that change were more compelling than was defending against the criticisms indefinitely or building up to a crisis at some later date. In the end, the gamble paid off. The center was well subscribed, operated smoothly, and helped introduce measured change into JCCA.

Consensus and Team Building

Even as strong a leader as Trobe could not implement the project by himself. His staff and trustees had to be on board. Indeed, having Steinfeld, the director of Pleasantville, assume a sense of "ownership" of the project was essential to its success, particularly with respect to mobilizing campus personnel behind it. Also essential was the consensus achieved by the trustees of the JCCA, who were largely concerned with the financial implications. Although the trustees were willing to consider some level of subsidy, they had to be convinced that a near break-even plan was achievable. And, of course, the trustees' support was especially important to permit the use of the building fund to carry out the renovations needed for the new center.

Mobilization of Resources

As was mentioned, two key issues needed to be resolved before the center could proceed. The existence of a new building fund was fortuitous; in other circumstances, Trobe would have had to seek alternative funds for the capital improvements that were required. Of greater concern were the operating funds. Negotiations with New York City officials proved critical to obtaining a per diem reimbursement rate through foster care and Medicaid that would permit the center to operate without becoming a financial liability. The excellent relationships that Trobe had cultivated with city officials established the foundation on which those officials worked actively with the JCCA to solve the problem of reimbursement.

Persistence

In retrospect, the project was conceived and implemented within a relatively compact time frame and through a fairly smooth process without major setbacks. Nonetheless, the energy devoted to the project during this period was intense, and the persistence of Trobe and Steinfeld in the midst of conflicting pressures largely accounted for its success.

In some sense, too, the center was part of the mental inventory of Trobe as he sought constantly to exploit opportunities to implement new programs that could respond to the changing social needs of his community. A few such centers had been developed elsewhere, and Trobe was particularly enamored of the analogy of a "Mayo-type clinic" that would look into the emotional makeup of a child, much as a medical clinic would determine a child's physical problems. When the window of opportunity opened, Trobe was ready to move into it.

Summary

Each human services venture has its own flavor and may be found to illustrate some of the key skills more than others, as well as certain variations of techniques and strategies within areas of skills. In the Pleasantville case, implementation within an existing system required substantial organizational and political savvy and somewhat less emphasis on marketing and fundraising than other cases might illustrate. Nonetheless, the full array of capabilities was brought to bear, and none was irrelevant to the success of the project.

In general, as has been observed in this chapter, as many as eight different sets of skills are required for the successful leadership of entrepreneurial ventures in human services organizations. These skills include developing a sense of mission for the venture; formulating the venture so it solves systemic, organizational, and personal problems; applying creativity and ingenuity to work around difficult constraints; attending to the timing of initiatives to take advantage of windows of opportunity; analyzing the risks associated with alternative actions; building consensus among relevant constituencies and assembling strong teams to carry out plans for ventures; mobilizing the necessary financial and other material resources; and persisting in the face of discouragement and resistance. The mastery of such skills is what sets apart the entrepreneurial leader from the run-of-the-mill manager in the human services.

SKILLS-APPLICATION EXERCISE

One can gain further appreciation of the ingredients of successful entrepreneurial leadership in human services by trying to think through in advance the skills that will be required by a new, worthwhile project. First, describe the project in some detail, then try to answer the following questions:

▶ What purpose does the venture serve? Does it fit the mission of the organization within which it will take place? If not, how will the organizational mission be adapted? Or will the venture require a new organization?

▶ What problems does the venture solve? What programmatic needs does it serve in society? What problems does it solve within the context of the organization in which it will take place? What problems does it solve for the entrepreneur?

▶ What roadblocks and constraints may be anticipated in implementing the venture? What creative ways can be thought of to circumvent these difficulties? Are some of these difficulties insurmountable?

▶ What is the window of opportunity for the new venture? Can the venture be undertaken now? What circumstances need to change before one goes ahead? How long can one wait before the opportunity disappears?

▶ What risks are associated with the venture? What are the potential damages that could be incurred by the entrepreneur, by the organization, and by other stakeholders if the venture fails? How likely is the venture

continued

to fail? What are the risks of not undertaking the venture? Do these risks outweigh the risks of going ahead?

▶ Who must agree before the venture can be undertaken and be successful? How can the support of key groups be mobilized behind the proposed venture? What common interest can mobilize these groups? What does each group bring to the table, and how does each benefit from the project? What can the entrepreneur do to garner the support of each key group or individual?

▶ What resources, financial and otherwise, will be needed to get the project started? How and from whom will these resources be obtained? How will the project support itself in the long run?

▶ How long will it take to gain support for the project and see it through to implementation? Does the entrepreneur have the required tenacity, sufficient interest, and dedication to stick with the project?

A successful entrepreneurial leader will consider these questions carefully and perhaps decide to alter the venture or not proceed with it. But he or she will also be energized by the challenges reflected in these questions and motivated to go ahead in the appropriate circumstances with a promising strategy and concept of the venture.

References

Behn, R. D., & Vaupel, J. W. (1982). *Quick analysis for busy decisionmakers*. New York: Basic Books.

Bird, B. (1989). *Entrepreneurial behavior*. Glenview, IL: Scott, Foresman.

Fisher, R., & Ury, W. (1981). *Getting to yes*. Boston: Houghton Mifflin.

Fombrun, C., Tichy, N. M., & Devanna, M. A. (1984). *Strategic human resource management*. New York: John Wiley & Sons.

Hodgkinson, C., & Weitzman, M. (1988). *Dimensions of the independent sector: A statistical profile*. Washington, DC: Independent Sector.

Kimberly, J. R., Miles, R. H., & Associates. (1980). *The organizational life cycle*. San Francisco: Jossey Bass.

Odendahl, T. (Ed.). (1987). *America's wealthy and the future of foundations*. New York: Foundation Center.

Salamon, L. (1984). Nonprofit organizations: The lost opportunity. In J. L. Palmer & I. V. Sawhill (Eds.), *The Reagan record* (pp. 261–285). Cambridge, MA: Ballinger.

Schumpeter, J. (1949). *The theory of economic development*. Cambridge, MA: Harvard University Press.

Seltzer, M. (1987). *Securing your organization's future*. New York: Foundation Center.

Skloot, E. (1988). *The nonprofit entrepreneur*. New York: Foundation Center.

Young, D. R. (1983). *If not for profit, for what?* Lexington, MA: D. C. Heath.

Young, D. R. (1985). *Casebook of management for nonprofit organizations*. New York: Haworth Press.

5

Influencing Legislation for the Human Services

Elliott Davis Moore

Envisioning and enacting change is the hallmark of human services professionals. Clinical social workers help clients make positive changes in their internal and external worlds. Human services managers change organizations to adapt, maintain, and improve services. Because of the increasing dissonance between human need and societal response, more professionals are cautiously expanding their role as change agents to include the political environment. Political action is a legitimate function for those who are involved in the system for delivering human services; after all, the political arena is where society's response to human needs is determined. As Wade (1966, p. 65) noted:

> Those who do not believe it is important to seek leverage, and those who do not place political action toward the attainment of social welfare goals as a top priority item in the agenda of our profession, are suggesting that social work should disengage itself from life.

Wade challenged human services professionals to break through inhibitions and move into the political arena. He and many others emphasized the professional obligation of social workers to act politically on behalf of their clients (see Wolk, 1981). Some professionals have been moved to action, and many others will soon join the ranks of advocates, reformers, lobbyists, and even officeholders. Managers are spanning their boundaries into the political environment (Quinn, 1984), but are they expanding their roles with the skills they need to be effective?

The purpose of this chapter is to assist human services professionals in identifying and developing the skills necessary to be effective change agents in the political environment. The skills that will be discussed, analyzed, and applied are relevant to influencing the political process in either the legislative or executive branch of government. The examples given primarily describe events in the state legislature from which relevance to other political areas can be extrapolated.

A manager who becomes involved in influencing legislation and regulations for the human services will do so to various degrees. The manager's roles may range from serving as a member of a coalition to being the lead lobbyist for the issue. Regardless of the intensity and level of involvement, the political action skills set forth in this chapter should promote effective interaction with the political environment.

Problem-Solving Skills

The skills that managers need to interact with the political system are analogous to those used in casework. Problem-solving skills are crucial to establishing and implementing an effective plan of action. Mahaffey (1972), who was one of the first to relate traditional social work practice skills to political action, identified the following areas of skills: defining the problem; surveying the setting and participants' roles; assessing the forces concerned, including contradictory and countervailing forces; determining goals; implementing plans; and feeding back information. A modified version of the problem-solving approach is used as the framework of this chapter.

Defining the Problem

Many social policy issues are of concern to human services managers. Among them are low welfare payments, the lack of public housing, inadequate access to health care, child abuse, alcohol and other drug abuse, AIDS, illiteracy, and homelessness. The diversity and importance of all these issues can drive reform efforts in a hundred different directions. Political campaigns without direction and focus, however, do not produce winners. Therefore, it is imperative to establish a few viable priorities.

Case in Point: NASW's Experience

The National Association of Social Workers (NASW) is a membership association that represents every practice specialization of the profession. Members' interests are numerous and diverse. No organization can address concurrently all the concerns and special interests of its constituents; therefore, a rational, realistic method of setting priorities is needed. NASW (1988, p. II-2) established the following criteria in developing its national legislative agenda.

▶ The agenda must be *consistent with NASW policy.*

▶ The agenda must attempt to achieve an *overall balance of issues that is representative of the membership.* In doing this, we weigh and choose issues that reflect professional, as well as societal needs, and we try to select at least one issue that directly relates to each major field of social work practice.

▶ The agenda must be *"do-able"*—that is, it must contain realistic legislative objectives and must be managed within available resources.

▶ The agenda must reflect those *issues in which NASW's involvement will make a difference in the legislative outcome.* We deliberately avoid setting a high priority on certain issues for which other organizations have a historical and successful legislative track record. (In such cases, our action may be limited to specific, targeted aspects of the legislation or to a more limited, supportive role.) We try to select issues that will directly affect NASW's membership and directly utilize the members' specific expertise.

▶ The agenda must include a balance of issues which reflects *varying levels of priority* and, consequently, *varying levels of legislative intervention.*

Managers who are responsible for establishing political action goals must be skilled in developing viable frameworks for decision making.

Assessing the Forces

Which way is the wind blowing? Forecasting political currents and shifts in direction can propel a legislative agenda toward its goals. Managers who accurately assess the interrelationships of political subsystems and understand how they affect political outcomes are able to use this insight to achieve their goals. Opposing forces are intrinsic in the political environment, and those that prevail change over time. Assessing the ebb and flow of the tide gives a reliable indication of how to proceed with a political agenda.

Case in Point: Changes in the Wind

In fall 1988, several months before the Tennessee legislative session opened, a small group of statewide organizations began to coalesce informally around a sensitive political issue: legislation to prohibit discrimination against persons with AIDS. In its formative stage, the coalition began to assess the probability of passing protective legislation in Tennessee.

The outlook was not good. Although the members of the coalition were committed to the cause, the coalition did not have the political power needed to be a match for the countervailing forces. The opposition included both organized business and insurance lobbies—two of the most powerful special-interest groups in the state. Nevertheless, the coalition decided to introduce the legislation; the severity of the problem was the compelling force.

After one year and many scrimmages in committees, the opposition was prevailing. There was no chance that the legislation would pass unless political forces began to shift. The next year the shift occurred. While the coalition assessed whether it should try for yet another year to gain passage, the opposition began to retreat. The business lobby was distracted by a bombardment of controversial legislative initiatives by its staunch rival—organized labor. The coalition saw the shift in political forces as a significant opportunity to move the legislation forward. Its members moved quickly before the decoy collapsed. This strategy worked. The AIDS antidiscrimination legislation was passed after a two-year struggle.

Most remedies for social ills are difficult to implement because they threaten the status quo, are complex, and usually cost money. Human services professionals have a propensity for addressing issues that agitate negative forces. "It costs too much, and how do you know it will work?" are resounding and repetitious objections to the development of new programs. Patience and tenacity are prerequisites for success.

Choosing the Solution

For every unmet human services need, there are numerous options for addressing it. Rely on experts, research, and experiences in other states in reaching a consensus on how to address a problem. The chosen solution becomes the proposed bill or regulation that, if enacted by either the legislative or executive branch, becomes public policy.

In considering a solution, one must evaluate the political climate of the time. Is there money in the state or national coffers? If the answer is no and the solution requires new funds, consider proposing a funding mechanism as part of the solution. Such a proposal can make the difference between success and defeat. Is the political climate conservative or liberal? Emphasize those elements of the solution that are more likely to win the broad-based support. Do not be deceitful; simply emphasize the strengths instead of the weaknesses.

Case in Point: Can You Make the Shoe Fit?

Teenage pregnancy is a national epidemic, and many states are developing programs to help teenage mothers and their children break the cycle of poverty. In Tennessee, two women's groups—the Nashville Women's Political Caucus and the League of Women Voters—decided to work in partnership to pass legislation and to obtain funding for an innovative approach to this problem.

The proposed legislation would establish model learning centers for teenagers in counties with the highest rates of teenage pregnancy. These centers would provide school-based care and parenting training services for teenage parents who are enrolled as students and would offer elective courses in parenting and child development for interested students.

The leadership of the groups that were promoting the program began to refer to the proposal as the TLC, the acronym for teen learning center. TLC, also widely recognized as the acronym for "tender loving care," conveyed the appropriate connotation for a program that would address the special needs of teenagers and their babies.

The TLC program was drafted into a bill and circulated to other groups, policymakers, experts on the problem, and legislators. During this review process, the "politically astute" suggested that the name should be changed. Their primary reasons for reaching this conclusion were as follows:

▶ TLC connotes "taking care of" and, unfortunately, might create the image of teenagers enjoying the pleasures of nursery time with their adorable little babies. The concern was that some of the "bizarre" political minds might question whether this program would encourage the very thing it was attempting to stop—teenage pregnancy.

▶ Although the governor's office and some legislators were sensitive to the problems surrounding teenage pregnancy, it was apparent that this issue was not a priority. The governor was intent on focusing on the school dropout problem and was ready to propose several legislative initiatives related to this issue.

On the basis of these two political observations, TLC would be combatting strong negative forces. How could funding be obtained for the program when minuscule revenues existed and the program was not a top priority? This analysis, put into the problem-solving mode, clearly said: Refocus! Reemphasize! But could a change of name eliminate the negative connotation and continue to represent accurately the original intent of the project? The answer was yes. Exit TLC and enter the Dropout Prevention Act of 1990. More than half of all pregnant teenagers drop out of school. One of the main reasons they drop out is that affordable high-quality day care is not available. Surely, the governor would embrace this program as an extension of his school dropout initiatives.

It worked! The Dropout Prevention Act of 1990 won the governor's approval, passed both the Tennessee House and Senate, and received full funding. The change of name had a significant, positive impact; it demonstrated that the issue of teenage pregnancy was convergent with the state's high-ranked political goal. By emphasizing the compatibility of this proposal with that goal and minimizing the negative distortions, the movers of this legislation synchronized the need, the solution, and the political environment.

Developing a Strategy

The problem is defined and a solution chosen. Now a strategy is needed to achieve the end. A strategy is an organized plan of action that is carefully developed and implemented to obtain a desired outcome in the political process. A viable strategy is designed to correlate with the nature of the problem to be addressed, the solution, and the political climate.

Is the issue public or nonpublic? According to Meredith and Myer (1982), a public issue, such as education, taxes, highways, or gambling laws, is of interest to almost everyone. "Almost everybody knows about these problems and has strong opinions about the proposed solutions" (Meredith & Myer, 1982, p. 6). Few measures that are resolved in state legislatures are public issues. Most are nonpublic, since they are of special interest to only a few people. Changes in licensure laws, private acts, and local road projects are examples of nonpublic issues.

If the issue to be addressed is a controversial public issue, the strategy may require broad-based coalitions, wide-ranging press coverage, many "hired-gun" lobbyists, and a well-financed campaign that may take several years. At the other extreme are the highly specialized issues that are of significance to few. These issues are often easily passed; they receive little scrutiny because few legislators take time to "nitpick" such matters. The strategy for their passage is low key, behind-the-scenes contacts.

The strategy developed should relate directly to the scope and difficulty of the issue at hand. Do not form extensive coalitions if no one is going to oppose the legislation. Do not inundate legislators with hundreds of letters and telephone calls if the voice of the opposition is just a whisper. Overly zealous efforts can cause negative reactions and hostility.

"We could obliterate homelessness with just what it costs to retain good public relations and lobbying counsel. Of course, dropping them would mean not getting invited to any more Capitol Hill parties."

Once the severity of the fight has been forecast, the "who," "what," and "when" questions may be determined. Who and how many allies are needed? Does the issue warrant enlisting the support of the elite power brokers, or should the power brokers be saved for a more difficult future challenge? Should the initiative begin early as an all-out surprise attack or be delayed until the end of a legislative session when tiredness and frenzy create opportunities to slide something by? Should support be gained publicly or quietly behind the scenes? The accuracy of these analyses predetermines your success or failure in the statehouse halls.

Implementing the Strategy

Innovative thinking and careful analysis provide the groundwork for a sound strategy to enact change. Cognitive skills have transformed a perceived need into a verifiable supposition that now must be sanctioned by the political system. The administrator who has been involved in developing the proposed policy initiative must now actuate its implementation. A different set of skills is needed to gain access to the system and to influence political outcomes.

The human services professional must now leave the role of innovator (Quinn, 1988) and assume the responsibilities of broker. The manager will be involved in "short-term contingency decision making or strategic adaptation" (Austin, 1989, p. 23) as the proposed policy initiative moves through the political environment.

Lobbying is the art of influencing the political process for desired outcomes. Yes, the manager who has the responsibility for implementing the strategy will be lobbying and must come to terms with any negative connotation of the term *lobbyist*. Learning to be comfortable with power relationships is the first step to gaining a solid footing on political turf. The comfort level is high for those who have an in-depth knowledge of the political process and its procedures, the power structure and its players, and their interrelationships. Being comfortable with confronting and embracing power is an essential trait for managers in the broker-lobbyist role.

Case in Point: First Time Out!

For 10 years, social workers in Tennessee had been organized around and collectively working on the passage of the first social work licensure law in the state. In 1984, a shift in political forces brought optimism that this could be the year for success. The Board of Healing Arts (an overall regulatory board) had been "sunsetted" out of existence and all groups of allied health professionals under its jurisdiction were being shuffled under new board structures. No new groups had been licensed by the state in 10 years, but perhaps social workers could seize this opportunity to slip their agenda into the political frenzy of restructuring.

The manager-lobbyist who led this charge had never brokered a piece of legislation through the Tennessee General Assembly. There was little time to learn, many mistakes to make, and a determination to succeed in spite of the obstacles. The roller-coaster path of this legislation experienced the following ups and downs:

▶ The novice lobbyist assumed that the sponsors (a House member and a Senate member) of the legislation would take an active role in securing votes for passage by the State Government Operations Committee and on the floor.

Of course, since professional issues are nonpublic issues, legislators are not likely to be actively involved; they are genuinely interested in many of these issues, but rely on the experts to broker the legislation. The sponsors assumed that the lobbyist had all the "ducks in a row" for the committee vote. They were wrong.

The bill failed in the committee; somehow, no one took the time to count the yeas and nays—an unfortunate illustration of the counterproductiveness of ill-matched expectations.

▶ The lobbyist then assumed it was over. What a humiliating experience; the effort seemed to end before it ever got started. The bill was lost forever in that "deep hole." Then a seasoned lobbyist came to the rescue and informed the novice of procedures by which bills can be reconsidered: The Senate rules outline every step of this process. The importance of mentorship cannot be overstated.

Ignorance of procedures came close to being a death sentence for the bill. The lobbyist, however, now took time to read the rules, to lobby each committee member intensely, and to count the yes and no votes. The bill passed out of committee a few weeks later with votes to spare.

▶ Because of this close call, the novice manager-lobbyist decided it was time to go all out. As the bill moved toward a Senate vote, she arranged for every senator to be inundated with numerous telephone calls and letters asking for his or her support of social work licensure. The lobbyist was confident that all was well.

But again, the strategy was inappropriate. A nonpublic issue that no longer has any organized opposition does not warrant extreme political pressure. The senators were becoming irritated by an overly zealous grass-roots effort.

The lobbyist redirected her efforts once more and called the troops home. The phone calls and letters subsided in time to soothe the senators' end-of-session jitters. The bill passed both the Senate and House with no dissenting votes. The novice lobbyist responded first with shock and then with celebration. She regained her composure before informing her constituents of the bill's passage.

The Seasoned Lobbyist Would Say. . .

Making sound decisions requires the ability to monitor the environment (to assess accurately the levels of support and opposition) and to understand and interact with the political process and the power structure that drives it. Many times, the forces moving a piece of legislation must adapt to detours, manipulate curves, hold on during roller-coaster ups and downs, and tolerate frustrating "stops" and "go's."

A consistent analysis of the political environment and a strategy that is adaptable to its inherent changes in direction should be able to keep the issue on track. Those who are engineering the campaign must be skilled at short-term decision making to deal with contingencies, be comfortable with power relationships, and be tenacious in efforts to obtain support and resources to keep moving (Austin, 1989).

Necessary Skills

Power of Communication

Those who influence regulations and legislation must have good communication skills that are adaptable to many different audiences. Both written and vocal communication skills are important tools for the manager/lobbyist:

Written Skills	Verbal Skills
Drafts of legislation	Testimony—special hearings
Drafts of amendments	Testimony—committees
Summaries of bills	Legislative groups
Testimony	Office visits
Documentation of need	In the "halls"
"Pro and con" questions and answers	Outside the chambers
Letters of support/opposition	Social situations
Legislative reports	Board presentations
Legislative alerts	Civic groups
Press releases	Television and radio interviews

Communication in the political arena has two purposes: to educate and to influence. Being explicitly aware of the purpose and tailoring the message to the receiver are essential elements of good communication skills. The proposal can be a tour de force and not win approval if the need is not substantiated and communicated. Facts are crucial to educating officials and legitimating the need for an initiative. Accounts of personal experiences motivate public officials to take action. Producing and communicating evidence that creates the appropriate balance between academic and emotional appeal is essential to building support for the issue. And what should you say?

▶ *Do not* inundate legislators and bureaucrats with too much information. Too much information will not be read or listened to and can give the perception that the issue is too complex to be addressed at the present time.

▶ *Do* synthesize technical information in an easily communicable fashion. Present supporting evidence that is understandable and believable.

▶ *Do not* create sensationalism. Too many tearjerking stories can create a perception of absurdity, disbelief, and nonprofessionalism.

▶ *Do* include examples of how the present policy is not getting the job done. Well-presented personal accounts humanize the rhetoric and the theoretical.

▶ *Do not* present supporting evidence that cannot be defended if its validity is questioned. *Credibility is essential to success.*

Interviewing Skills

The human services manager who is actively pursuing a legislative or regulatory goal will spend most of the time influencing decision makers on a one-to-one basis. The office visit offers the opportunity, it is hoped, to discuss without distraction the merits or concerns of an issue. The executive-lobbyist who initiates the conversation has a purpose in mind (to influence) and has the responsibility to move the conversation toward the desired goal. This "verbal exchange" meets the criteria of an interview as defined by De Schweinitz and De Schweinitz (1962) in their classic, *Interviewing in the Social Services.* In most situations, the lobbyist and public official will alternate between interviewer and interviewee as the process moves them toward the decision to agree or disagree.

If agreement is reached, the lobbyist has used interviewing skills to reach a desired outcome. If no agreement is reached, interviewing skills can assuage hostility and promote mutual respect among individuals with different points of view. Even in the face of adversity, the lobbyist who knows how to listen (another interviewing skill) will leave the office knowing much more about the decision maker. The decision maker's likes and dislikes, philosophies, personal styles, and personality traits all communicate to the lobbyist the likelihood of future alliances on a different issue.

Interviewing in a state legislature has one distinct advantage over interviewing in a human service agency. The executive-lobbyist can actively research the public official before the first meeting, thereby reducing the elements of the unknown. Knowing something about the person is a tactical advantage in making the initial approach.

"Blue book," voting and legislative records, place of residence, occupation, and input from other lobbyists and public officials are all available sources of information on individual legislators and members of the executive branch. Experienced lobbyists who know the decision makers well can usually predict a yes or no response before the question is asked. But as in human services interviews, *the professional should assume nothing.* Explicitly stating the "want"; providing supporting data for the "why"; and leaving with an explicit response of yes, maybe, or no are the purposes of the interview.

But the process does not end here. If the answer is "yes, I will support, . . . " thank the person profusely, continue to check back with him or her, and reinforce the support with news of your progress. If the answer is "maybe," provide more information, keep going back, and enlist the assistance of others. If the answer is "no, I will not support, . . . " assess how firm that decision is, check back to reaffirm it, and consider negotiation.

Negotiation

During the life cycle of a bill becoming law, negotiation occurs at some level all along the way. Cohen (1980, p. 16) defined *negotiation* as "the use of information and power to affect behavior within a web of tension." Each time a legislator or member of a regulatory body is resistant to a change agent's point of view, negotiation is the next method of intervention. A skilled negotiator is someone who has the knowledge, sense of timing, and power to persuade the "right" people to do the "right" thing.

Those who sit at the bargaining table should participate only if they bring with them information that can change the legislators' or regulators' perception that "the proposal is a new idea so we must be cautious" to "this proposal is no longer a new idea and it sounds OK" (Cohen, 1980). Human services professionals who negotiate for social change should remember the importance of exchanging information and should rely on research and practice to assuage the legislators' or regulators' fear of trying something new.

The message should be clear: The desired change in legislation or regulation has valid historical, empirical, and practical bases. There is no need to be reluctant; embrace the change.

When should negotiations be initiated? Certainly, when an impasse to achieving desired outcomes occurs, negotiation should be considered a viable option. Most times, it is the only option.

When the Governor Objects

The words of a powerful, majority-party governor decide the fate of many pieces of legislation. When a bill stalls in committee because the governor opposes its passage, negotiation is the only option left; the lobbyist quickly knocks on the governor's door, asking for the opportunity to talk about it—to negotiate. The main objective at this point is to use the power of information and persuasion to press for reconsideration of the governor's position on the legislation. Much is gained if agreement is reached to begin negotiating. What can be accomplished at this point?

▶ The lobbyist has the opportunity to offer additional persuasive information on the importance of the state responding to the human needs addressed by the legislation.

▶ The lobbyist also gains additional information on the governor's needs. Why did the governor oppose the legislation? Does the governor agree with the target but not with the line of approach?

▶ The exchange of information may illuminate that shared objectives do exist and all parties can avoid a win-lose situation by involving themselves in collaborative problem solving (Berryman-Fink, 1989).

Do Not Forget Why You Are There!

For human services professionals who are involved in the business of influence, beware of gaining passage of the bill merely for the sake of "winning." The environment in which legislative advocacy occurs is highly competitive, and the issue of win-lose can become a personalized internal battle. Professional values and ethics require ongoing assessment as changes occur through negotiation:

▶ Is the client group still the primary interest? Or has the need to avoid personal defeat become paramount?

▶ Does the legislation or the regulation in its amended version still maintain the integrity of the profession? Peer review is needed to assure that the values, ethics, knowledge, and mission of the profession are being advanced in the intent and design of the policy initiatives (see NASW, 1990).

When the going gets tough, review the original purpose of the legislation. Social workers and other human services professionals are involved in political action to promote the general welfare of society, not to promote their own needs to win.

Conclusion

Those who wish to be active participants in social reform will likely find themselves on the front lines, both on the offensive and in reactive situations. An important arena for influencing social reform is through legislative systems. Human services managers can, and must, take leadership roles in influencing legislation that will benefit both the clients who are being served and the social work profession.

Unfortunately, some human services managers perceive that all power is owned by someone else. This perception of their profession's powerlessness can be a significant impediment to their developing a leadership position in the external environment. It is not possible for all human services professionals to understand and work effectively in the legislative arena. For a human services manager, however, it is imperative. The examples of success are plentiful. The skills can be mastered. And, they must be used.

Summary

This chapter has emphasized the relevance and importance of applying problem-solving skills in forging political outcomes. These skills are applied at all levels in the delivery of human services where needs, solutions, and environments converge to create positive changes. At the social policy level, the change agent identifies the problem and develops a plan of action that requires careful navigating to avoid political undertows. Analytical and decision-making skills are needed in choosing appropriate issues and strategies.

Human services managers in the political world use their role of innovator to envision what change is needed to improve the quality of life. The role of broker is crucial to the enactment of the targeted change. Communication, tactical, and negotiating skills are necessary competencies to win passage of legislation that addresses human needs.

S K I L L S - A P P L I C A T I O N   E X E R C I S E

You are the top human services manager in an area office on aging. A number of the elderly clients of the agency are living on fixed incomes. Many of them are greatly concerned about their increasing health care needs for which they may not have the necessary health insurance coverage. A bill has been introduced into the state legislature to provide health insurance coverage for all state residents. It is a bill that, although not as comprehensive as would be desired, is essential. You have been asked by several of your managerial peers to take the leadership in developing a legislative game plan aimed at passing this bill. Your board of trustees has strongly endorsed your doing so as an appropriate leadership role.

- ▶ What information do you need to develop this legislative game plan?
- ▶ What information on the bill itself may already exist? How would you obtain this information?
- ▶ How would you involve and influence your own legislator (even if he or she was not on the committee dealing with the bill)?
- ▶ Would you involve your professional association in your efforts? How?
- ▶ Who is likely to be opposed to this bill?
- ▶ Who can be anticipated to be in favor of the bill?
- ▶ In presenting testimony, what would you see as some of the key strategic issues?
- ▶ What options exist for coalition building?
- ▶ What specific legislative strategies would you consider using at different points in the legislative life of the bill?
- ▶ Would you use your clientele (and other elderly persons) in your efforts? How?

References

Austin, D. M. (1989). The human service executive. In *Administrative leadership in the social services* (pp. 13–35). New York: Haworth Press.

Berryman-Fink, C. (1989). *The manager's desk reference*. New York: AMACOM.

Cohen, H. (1980). *You can negotiate anything*. New York: Bantam Books.

De Schweinitz, E., & De Schweinitz, K. (1962). *Interviewing in the social services*. London, England: Latimer, Trend.

Mahaffey, M. (1972). Lobbying and social work. *Social Work, 17,* 3–11.

Meredith, J., & Myer, L. (1982). *Lobbying on a shoestring: How to win in Massachusetts . . . and other places, too.* Boston: Massachusetts Poverty Law Center.

National Association of Social Workers. (1990). *Code of ethics.* Silver Spring, MD: Author.

National Association of Social Workers. (1988). *Legislative/political handbook.* Silver Spring, MD: Author.

Quinn, R. E. (1984). Applying the competing values approach to leadership: Toward an integrative framework. In J. G. Hunt, D. Hosking, C. Schreishman, & R. Stewart (Eds.), *Leaders and managers: International perspectives on managerial behavior and leadership.* Elmsford, NY: Pergamon Press.

Quinn, R. E. (1988). *Beyond rational management: Mastering the paradoxes and competing demands of high performance.* San Francisco: Jossey-Bass.

Wade, A. P. (1966). The social worker in the political process. *Social Welfare Forum, 1966* (pp. 52–67). New York: Columbia University Press.

Wolk, J. L. (1981). Are social workers politically active? *Social Work, 26,* 283–288.

CHAPTER
6

Creating and Using Coalitions

Chauncey A. Alexander

The courtship and nurturance of, and often the eventual separation from, the organizational creature named *coalition* can be invigorating, frustrating, and fatiguing. The coalition, a product of multiple cohabitations, parallels in some ways a teenage pregnancy. It may be aborted or delivered. It may face a precarious future with many foster parents, or it may survive its trials to gain its own identity, stronger than its progenitors. Regardless of what scenario unfolds, the coalition challenges the basic knowledge and skills of the human services manager with its range of demands for successful performance.

Coalitions: Genesis and Gambit

Coalitions are loosely woven alliances of two or more individuals, groups, or organizations that are formed for the purpose of limited cooperative activity. Coalitions usually are ad hoc arrangements, frequently single issue focused, and may remain in existence for various periods (Whitaker, 1983). The strengths and the weaknesses of coalitions often relate to their diversity.

There are numerous reasons for individuals, groups, and organizations to become members of coalitions. These reasons, often related to the diversity of coalitions, are as follows:

- ▶ To gain some objective not achievable through individual action
- ▶ To share resources, such as information, money, people, and power
- ▶ To increase the perceived power being directed toward a specific purpose or cause
- ▶ To increase the visibility of a purpose or cause
- ▶ To increase access to media representatives
- ▶ To gain access to bipartisan legislators
- ▶ To provide a "buffer" in relation to controversial issues.

Despite these important reasons for forming coalitions, there are some barriers that militate against or make it difficult to do so. First, the degree of philosophical differences among organizations, though coalitions are the instrument for accommodating diversity, may prevent participation or may serve as a brake on the completion of a joint mission. Withholding participation in a coalition is also a statement of opposition to the defined mission, or a secondary means of control. Second, there is a fear that credibility will be lost if the coalition acts in some way that is inconsistent with the modus operandi of a particular individual, group, or organization or if a participant brings, by previous or current actions, disrepute to the group. Third, the loss of visibility and identity will be significant for the stronger members of a coalition, whereas it may be considered a gain for smaller or weaker members. Finally, the willingness to relinquish some controls to the ultimate decisions of the group requires calculations and decisions that are based on the degree of trust of the coalition members and of the process.

Organizing and Implementing the Coalition

The initiation of a coalition can be guided by a series of questions, the answers to which will determine the future working relationships and the likelihood of success. The questions include these:

▶ What are the precipitating problems or issues that suggest the need for a coalition? Which of them seems to be paramount?

▶ How is the problem or issue to be defined? What is the common understanding shared by those who may be interested in coalescing?

▶ What are the common interests among potential coalition members? Who is likely to share such interests? Should these stakeholders (individuals, groups, or organizations) be asked to join the coalition?

▶ Are there existing networks that have a legitimate stake in the problem or issue and that have the right and capacity to participate in the coalition?

▶ From what groups or individuals is there apt to be opposition or resistance?

▶ What is the commitment of these potential members to collaborate?

▶ What resources will each of the potential members bring to the coalition?

▶ Who is the most appropriate individual to convene these potential members? These questions may require several meetings to arrive at adequate answers and to gain the initial understanding and commitments that are necessary to move successfully into the second phase of coalition building: setting directions for the coalition.

A series of issues must be dealt with in organizing and determining the direction for the coalition. Chief among these are the following:

▶ The objectives the coalition desires to achieve must be defined, refined, or both. These objectives must be clearly articulated and agreed to by the members. If some members cannot agree to all the objectives, their differences should be openly discussed and decisions should be made about whether they should continue or whether accommodations should be made in the definition of the coalition's mission.

▶ The target or targets of the coalition's activities should be determined. Will the focus be the government? If so, what branches and levels? Professional organizations? Public opinion? Are there key influential persons who strategically should be targeted to achieve the identified objectives? Answers to these questions will suggest the level and scope of the coalition, as well as the structure required to achieve the objectives.

▶ A steering committee should be established to plan and coordinate the coalition's activities. This committee should be empowered by the members to take action on behalf of the coalition when time constraints preclude involving all members. A major challenge is to establish only that level of structure required to achieve the objectives. Too much structure could result in the coalition becoming an end in itself, thereby diverting the resources needed to work toward achieving the objectives.

▶ There must be clarity in regard to funding and expenditures. Some agreements must be reached about the sources of funding and about the processes of obtaining funds and controlling expenditures.

▶ Decision making will present ongoing challenges. To the extent possible, all members of the coalition should be involved. Decision-making processes should be negotiated, taking into account the responsibilities of members' relationships with their respective constituencies. Furthermore, it is critical to determine the degree to which members will need to involve a "higher authority" in finalizing decisions, especially in areas in which there are differences among members.

"The first meeting of the coalition 'Groups Organized to Conserve Humorous Acronyms (GOTCHA)' will now come to order."

▶ Communication is a vital consideration for coalitions. Attention must be paid to how the steering committee will communicate with other members of the coalition, as well as how members will communicate among themselves and with their constituents. Examples of communication include statements of understanding, monthly meetings, minutes of meetings, special mailings, newsletters, and reports.

▶ An analysis of the respective positions of supporters, sympathizers, nonsupporters, and opponents of the coalition's points of view will be necessary. Plans for dealing with these "fors" and "againsts" should be made and reviewed periodically.

▶ A well-defined plan of action should be developed for achieving the coalition's objectives. This plan should assign specific tasks, time frames, and responsibilities. It becomes the overall framework within which the coalition will pursue its objectives. The steering committee will modify the plan as situations and assumptions change.

Case Study: Health Care Task Force

Many agencies that come before United Way allocation panels are experiencing heavy deficits. Although political leaders perceive this country to be wealthy and to have a minimum of social problems, the mass media portray a different story. These media inform us of sick and homeless people in the 26 cities in the county; of the large number of elderly persons who need assistance in their own communities; of the poor who are "flooding" voluntary health clinics; and of low-paying service industries that are supplying the majority of new job opportunities for young people and women, while manufacturing companies are relocated or eliminated through mergers or acquisitions. Indeed, there is trouble in Paradise!

Initial Tasks

Bill Jackson, executive director of a community health agency, is asked to chair a health care task force to address the most critical issues of health care services and financing issues. Where does he begin? Is this task force to be a short-term committee, a network of services, or a coalition? If the latter, is it what Roberts-DeGennaro (1987) described as an *organization-set* (organizations that provide essential resources or services to a focal group)? Or a *network* (the totality of all units connected by a certain type of relationship)? Or an *action-set* (a group of organizations that form an alliance for a limited purpose)?

Not to worry! Jackson simply asks himself, "Where does a social worker begin with a problem?" He answers, "Where the client is." Thus, interviewing and listening skills are needed when one talks with worried United Way officials, pressured agency directors, and bureaucrats of health care services. What written reports or studies can provide background information on the community's needs; service programs; and private, volunteer, or public relationships?

How will this diverse information be processed, so different views are sorted and the vested interests of each person and agency are assessed? Is this not where the scientific method begins, with the search for information (Berger & Patchner, 1988)? And will notes be made on the information and data systems that are not available (often a purposeful way to avoid confronting social problems) because such a development may be part of the coalition's eventual demands?

In the face of different views of the social problem of health care, each with a certain amount of validity, their importance intensified by the growing underclass of indigents, how are these arguments sorted out, and against what are they tested (Kormorita & Chertkoff, 1973)?

The social work profession approaches all problems of people—individual, group, community, or societal—with the underpinnings of a social work value system. The most universal principles are those adopted by the International Federation of Social Workers (1976, p. 2) as follows:

- Every human being has a unique value, irrespective of origin, ethnicity, sex, age, beliefs, social and economic status or contribution to society;
- Each individual has the right of self-fulfillment to the degree that it does not encroach upon the same right of others;
- Each society, regardless of its form, should function to provide the maximum benefits for all of its members;
- The professional social worker has the responsibility to devote objective and disciplined knowledge and skill to aid individuals, groups, communities, and societies in their development and resolution of personal or societal conflicts and their consequences;
- The professional social worker has the primary obligation to the objective of service, which must take precedence above self-interest, aims or views.

Can these values be held to in the face of equally strong different values? How are these basic values implemented within a conflicting value structure, such as described by Edwards (1987)? The task thus becomes how to help various interests find areas of agreement that will lead to a consensus and to support of an approach to solve the puzzle of the financing of health care services for indigent people.

A Meeting of Interested Parties

At the meeting of interested parties, a variety of views are presented. The representative of the hospital council asks for pressure to increase Medicaid rates, citing regulated payments of only 60 percent of the costs. The spokesperson of the medical association claims $200 million a year in uncompensated care by physicians. The representatives of the Visiting Nurses Association, the home health agency, and others, all United Way beneficiaries, complain about hospitals and physicians dumping nonpaying and sicker patients on them.

"The state keeps cutting our budget," explains the spokesperson from the county health care agency, presenting examples of the reductions in federal funds. Some desperately declare that hospital and physicians' costs are out of control. The representative of a solitary, voluntary community clinic tells about having to refer clients without funds or transportation to the social service department to apply for Medicaid. Fingers point everywhere but at home. Amid this maelstrom of complaints, human services manager Bill Jackson is introduced as United Way's choice for a future chair.

But never fear, help is near! Previous contacts and analyses are about to pay off. Acknowledgment of the feelings that people express is important, possibly by a restatement of examples of trouble they gave previously in individual interviews. (Is this not meeting feeling with feeling—the basis for making connections with people with problems?)

Recognition of the representatives' verbalization of their unique interests; their frustrations; and, above all, the need of people for decent health services makes the meeting all the more important and productive. (Is their self-determination obtaining expression?)

Although there may be no immediate solution, a possible plan may be drawn up from the valuable information. The situation is complex and will take some time, since problems have been building for years. More facts are needed. Responsible officials must be cultivated. The community should be informed and support should be obtained for whatever measures everyone can agree on. (Is this not devoting disciplined knowledge and skills to this volunteer effort?)

That is the secret. Everyone has different views. However, they are just being asked to work together, to investigate the various health services and to try to determine the forces involved and the need. All actions of the task force will be determined by consensus and will require eventual approval of the board of United Way. Is that agreeable?

Oh, yes, there is an additional proposal. Because the understanding and support of the community are so important, should the task force not be broadened to include additional supporters? The employers who are saddled with a 30 percent increase in their annual health insurance premiums for employees may be eager for some relief, as may the unions representing those employees. Other overworked providers, such as nurses and social workers, may be concerned. Various civic groups, the League of Women Voters, minority groups, the committee for the homeless, and churches have expressed concern about health care problems and are crucial links to the people in need.

Bill Jackson also proposes an important rule for participating in the task force on the basis of his familiarity with Alexander's (1976) clarification of types of representation. Questions such as the following must be addressed:

▶ Will observers be welcomed?

▶ Is each participant in the task force to be designated by an organization?

▶ Will each participant have responsibility to a constituency and not just be voicing his or her own opinions?

▶ Will there be a role for technical experts?

▶ How will information be provided to organizations, their members, and leaders about the task force's findings and actions?

▶ How will their support be sought?

These questions will need attention, and a consensus will have to be achieved on the answers. Such answers will be especially important for the future success of the task force.

An agenda for the "official" first meeting of the task force could be similar to the one presented in Exhibit 1.

Where is the skill in such monthly meetings? The ability to obtain and share information is a valuable asset to most organizations. A formidable coalition is both educated and welded by probing key issues through expert presentations, working on subcommittees to deal with special problems, reaching a consensus, and beginning to question public officials. That's strategic management for human services workers!

Exhibit 1. Preliminary Agenda, Health Care Task Force Meeting

1. Welcome and introductions
2. Minutes of the previous meeting: presentation, corrections, approval
3. Information exchange. An important function of the task force is to keep its members apprised of important health care matters and to provide opportunities to share programs, opinions, and actions. Each organization can supply copies of information to be distributed to the task force members. Some examples are these:
   A. Hispanic Education Forum on Health Needs
   B. Report on Hospital Council Beds Occupancy Study
   C. Others
4. Mental Health Services Crisis. Representatives of the Mental Health Association, Alliance for the Mentally Ill, County Mental Health Agency. What are the key problems and service issues? Which should be the task force's priorities for action? Questions, discussion, and action as indicated.
5. Information and Referral (I & R) Subcommittee Report. The I & R Subcommittee is working on the priority of establishing a countywide I & R service to help people reach the most effective services for their problems (see attached).
6. Legislative Review Committee Analysis. Recommended action to be presented to state legislators and the county Board of Supervisors (see attached).
7. Other Business
8. Next Meeting: date and anticipated program

Report of the Task Force

Nine months later, the following story breaks in the local newspapers:

HEALTH CRISIS ENDANGERS OUR COUNTY RESIDENTS

Twenty percent of our county residents, some 400,000 men, women, and children, are "health care deprived," according to the report of the Health Care Task Force of the United Way released today.

Every resident is in danger from the problems of the health care system, the report advises.

Five categories of deprived are noted:

▶ Insured seniors: Medicare covers only 38 percent of the health care costs of senior citizens.

▶ Financially assisted: Only half of those eligible for Medicaid assistance are receiving services.

▶ Medically indigent adults: Only a third of those not qualifying for financial assistance programs are able to obtain health services.

▶ Medical marginals: Those who are economically marginal are turned away from services because of overcrowding.

▶ Great uncounted: Thousands of persons without access to services, such as the homeless and the mentally ill, go uncounted.

The United Way report warned that the deterioration of public services and key components of the health care system—trauma centers, well-baby clinics, immunization programs, and others—posed dangers for the life of every resident.

The report pointed to key problems that have led to the crisis: cost shifting from the federal to the state to the county governments to the individual consumer; reductions in services instead of cost controls; the reduced quality of services; lack of planning, data collection, and research on services; and the lack of fixed responsibility by public officials.

Copies of the report are available from the United Way office at 3333 Service Boulevard.

Media Blitz

After this first news release to the media, the two major newspapers use the task force's report for a three-day series on health care conditions. The television stations present one-minute news bites and a panel discussion show. Public officials are cautiously complimentary on the revelations, pointing to the responsibility of the next highest jurisdiction. Some compliments come in with requests for the report from frustrated residents who see their problems identified. The task force members are proud of their work and product.

Then everything goes quiet. The task force is a victim of the "Sudden Glory, Early Obscurity" syndrome. How can Bill Jackson make this social problem a priority for the community? What is next? Back to basics to get back to the future! When clients reach one level in dealing with a problem, what is next? How can members of the task force deal with this step?

It will not be easy. The task force has been working to put a simple issue, health care for indigents, into perspective. It succeeded. But the issue has "trails" running everywhere. Few members of the coalition are interested in every trail. So how will Jackson help people find and focus on the problem of most concern? With some insights from Gentry (1987) and March (1987) and a bow in the direction of planning, the task force may be able to select one or more priorities, short or long term, on which to work.

But wait! The task force's prophecies of disaster prove to be true. The university medical center makes headlines with the announcement that it has to turn away pregnant women from its obstetric service because of overloading by indigent patients. The center even has guards at the emergency entrance to warn women that they will be in danger from using the service and should go elsewhere. Even the center's provider colleagues are indignant at that action. Is it not unethical or immoral?

More Buck Passing

The task force schedules an emergency meeting on this issue at which representatives of the medical center, the medical association, the county health care agency, and the social service agency present their views. The medical center's case is straightforward. The center is licensed for 250 obstetric beds and is deluged with an average of 500 patients daily. Most other hospitals are dumping indigent patients on the center; its personnel work 70 to 80 hours a week, 12 to 15 hours a day; and one of the physicians fell asleep last week while driving home and had a serious accident. The center now has a $13 million deficit from last year's overload and nonpayment of fees. It appealed to the state Medicaid system without success. Now "the community" must take more responsibility.

What can the two county agencies do?, their representatives ask. It is up to the state, since obstetric care for indigents is paid for by Medicaid. The spokesperson for the medical association declares that although it may be up to the state, the county has abdicated its responsibility because, by policy, it does not allocate money to primary health care and it is not taking leadership in lobbying the state. Overloaded obstetricians in the community cannot continue to carry Medicaid and nonpaying patients, pay liability insurance, and stay in business. Many of the representatives of organizations at the meeting express indignation and demand action.

Is There a Solution?

What action can be taken, and how? With all the different positions, the sub rosa guilt, and overt anger, will the group not fly apart on this issue? Or is this issue typical of the reasons why the task force has worked to understand the crisis in health care services? Clearly, this emergency again has focused attention on the issue and provides an opportunity to inform the community and offer recommendations for addressing the problems. The task force's statement can be prepared for widespread dissemination:

United Way Health Care Task Force
Statement on Obstetrical Diversion at University Medical Center

Our county's health care crisis, as predicted in the June 1988 report, is reaching a catastrophe, as demonstrated by the problems of the obstetrical service at the university medical center. Impending failures of service also confront our county residents in the operation of trauma centers, emergency rooms, community clinics, and other health services.

Every resident, regardless of income or position, faces problems of access to health care services and the reduced quality of health care from the consistent pattern of cost shifting, financial reductions, and the lack of communitywide planning.

The "obstetrical diversion" policy of the medical center represents an act of desperation, demonstrating conflicting values and actions created by the lack of community support and responsibility from the proper authorities.

In effect, the problems of the obstetrical service are a 3.5 Richter-scale precursor to an 8.5 health-care earthquake, a symptom of the inadequate and fragmented health care system.

The United Way Health Care Task Force, consisting of 45 representatives of public, private, and voluntary organizations, recommends the following short-term actions to deal with the immediate problems, while working within a two-year time limit to obtain longer-range solutions:

▶ The university medical center, in conjunction with appropriate agencies, should immediately develop a mechanism to guarantee that any obstetrical patient it cannot serve will be helped to reach appropriate service rapidly and humanely.

▶ The county board of supervisors should direct the county health care agency to take responsibility for convening provider organizations to develop immediate emergency arrangements for obstetrical patients and a plan for continuous service to pregnant women from prenatal care through birth and follow-up.

▶ The county board of supervisors should allocate emergency funds for these actions and take aggressive steps to obtain increased budgetary allocations from the state.

Making the Coalition Work

What happened between finger pointing and this statement of action adopted by the task force? What methods, techniques, and skills are necessary to help people define and focus on the issues? What process must be involved to recognize both the university medical center's legitimate economic problem and its culpability for its inappropriate action?

How does one deal with avoidance techniques that appear along the way (Alexander, 1987)? What are the problems in obtaining approval for action from a diversified, though essentially conservative, United Way board of directors? (Does this process not have a familiar ring and parallel the casework, or the misnamed "direct practice," process?)

Since the coalition's behavior varies from fragility to frigidity, the role of each organization is to build a component of the ultimate position and action of the group. Welding those components by finding the central concern that all can support is not just an accident. It takes hard work and disciplined effort, as evidenced in this follow-up report from the task force to the United Way's board of directors.

Memorandum

To: County United Way Board of Directors
From: Health Care Task Force
Subject: Summary Report and Request

The endorsement and support by the board of the task force statement on "obstetric diversion" at the university medical center was most helpful. It is encouraging to report that the county board of supervisors allocated money to serve an additional 500 women and established a county perinatal task force on which United Way is represented.

The individual meetings of 12 to 22 task force members with individual supervisors were productive. Along with the task force's requests, individual organizations presented their reasons for support, together with statements of the problems and the importance and cost-effectiveness of prevention. In several instances, we know that the contacts by individual board members, as we had requested, were influential.

At the supervisor's hearing on the matter, the lead statement by the chair of the task force was followed by supporting statements by 23 of the member organizations of the task force. At least two of the supervisors spoke favorably of the public, private, and voluntary partnership reflected in this action.

Unfortunately, another of the task force's prophecies has come true with the potential demise of one of the four trauma centers in the county. We are working on this problem and will bring our recommendations to the board of directors as soon as possible.

Meanwhile, we ask your approval of the proposal to obtain a professional staff person to support the task force's operations. Participation in the task force has grown from the original 12 provider groups to 48 organizations representing all sectors of the county. The responsibility of the volunteer chair, aided by some United Way clerical service, has grown to a full-time effort that cannot be sustained.

Two foundations are interested in aiding the work of the task force. We believe it is in the interests of the United Way to demonstrate its tangible collaboration with the foundations by allocating $20,000.

What policy questions are raised by this memorandum? The United Way seems to have a successful community effort on its hands, so why question it? But with more involvement, potential conflict, and increasingly complex power relationships to come, can and should the organization, which was established principally for community-wide fundraising, continue on the coalition-building path? Will it inevitably offend certain forces in the community? Or does this commitment demonstrate its broad concern for social needs that may get it increased financial support (Brilliant, 1986)?

These frequently are the questions with which successful coalitions must grapple. At the broader policy level, questions emerge as to whether the coalition is the illegitimate offspring of an immature social relationship, a mistaken conception, a foundling for temporary placement, or a full-fledged member of the organizational family.

Summary

Coalitions present a strategic approach to bringing about change, or they keep change from occurring. Success in coalition building requires special attention to the organizational, and often personal, interests of the coalition's members, as well as recognition of the significant strengths and weaknesses of the diversity of its membership.

Gaining knowledge of the unique elements and methodology of coalition building—the careful planning, development of consensus and compromise, continual communications, sharing of funding and decision making, and learning how to handle victory and defeat—is a continual process.

And, finally a commitment to democratic values is needed, keeping in mind the warning of Saul David Alinsky (as quoted in Bradley, Daniels, & Jones, 1969, p. 200): "There can be no democracy unless it is a dynamic democracy. When our people cease to participate—to have a place in the sun—then all of us will wither in the darkness of decadence. All of us will become mute, demoralized, lost souls."

SKILLS-APPLICATION EXERCISE

You are the director of a metropolitan, public human services department, as well as the president of the state's association of human services directors. In your state, the Aid to Families with Dependent Children (AFDC) program provides benefits equivalent to 65 percent of the determined level of need. The state's association of human services directors has taken a formal position supporting an increase in AFDC benefits to 100 percent of the level of need. You have decided that the association cannot accomplish this goal alone—that help is required. Forming a coalition appears to be a strategic approach to achieving the goal.

In moving ahead with the establishment of such a coalition, do the following:

▶ Identify the goal or mission of the coalition in a single paragraph.
▶ Determine some major targets for the coalition's activity.
▶ Delineate potential members for the coalition.
▶ Identify some preliminary objectives for possible consideration by the coalition.

continued

> ▶ Given the potential members, list the possible assets and liabilities that each brings to the coalition.
> ▶ Identify the "fors" and "againsts," the likely points of view of those who are most apt to be affected by the coalition's efforts.
> ▶ Develop a strategy and tactics for pursuing the coalition's mission.

References

Alexander, C. (1976). What does a representative represent? *Social Work, 21*, 5–9.

Alexander, C. (1987). Techniques for organizational inertia: Barriers to the future. *NMA Annual Conference Proceedings*, 1–12.

Berger, R., & Patchner, M. (1988). Sources of data. *Implementing the research plan* (pp. 15–39). Beverly Hills, CA: Sage.

Bradley, J., Daniels, L., & Jones, T. (1969). *International dictionary of thoughts* (p. 200). Chicago: J. G. Ferguson.

Brilliant, E. (1986). Community planning and community problem solving: Past, present, and future. *Social Service Review, 60*, 568–589.

Edwards, R. (1987). The competing values approach as an integrating framework for management curriculum. *Administration in Social Work, 11*, 1–13.

Gentry, M. (1987). Coalition formation and processes. *Social Work with Groups, 10*, 39–54.

International Federation of Social Workers. (1976). *International code of ethics for the professional social worker*. Geneva, Switzerland: Author.

Kormorita, S., & Chertkoff, K. (1973). A bargaining theory of coalition formation. *Psychological Review, 80*, 149–162.

March, J. G. (1987). Theories of choice and making decisions. In F. M. Cox, J. Erlich, J. Rothman, & J. Tropman (Eds.), *Strategies of community organization: Macro practice* (pp. 279–297). Itasca, IL: F. E. Peacock.

Roberts-DeGennaro, M. (1987). Patterns of exchange relationships in building a coalition. *Administration in Social Work, 11*, 59–67.

Whitaker, W. (1983). Organizing social action coalitions: WIC comes to Wyoming. In M. Mahaffey & J. Hanks (Eds.), *Practical politics: Social work and political responsibility* (pp. 136–158). Silver Spring, MD: National Association of Social Workers.

7

Developing Strategic Media Relationships

Clarence Jones

Talk about competing values! The confidentiality of clients is sacred. It is part of the social worker's honor and heritage. It is enforced in most states by statutes that carry criminal penalties. Violating the ethic of confidentiality may be grounds for instant dismissal. But failing to talk to the media—to tell them precisely what happened in the case that is currently in the media spotlight—may also be disastrous. If you clam up, the media will make you appear insensitive, incompetent, and evil.

A zealous prosecutor, playing to the media, will portray the human services manager as a villain and charge him or her with a crime. In the media firestorm, the manager may be burned at the stake.

It is a tough balancing act. Few human services managers are good at walking this precarious tightrope. Their training, their experience, and the advice of their lawyers often take them into media disasters that do immeasurable damage to their agencies, their employees, their clients, and their careers. But human services managers can learn how to use the media to bring about change; to get what they want; and to protect their clients, their agencies, and themselves.

Survival Skills

The news media have become the most powerful force in this society. Name a group or institution more powerful. Congress? The courts? The president? The church? The news media can create, almost overnight. They can destroy with one story. They are the agents of change. They set the agenda for us as a people. Nothing is even considered until the media—by writing or talking about it—tell us that the time has come.

The people who control the budget, the current project, and the future of human services are creatures of the media. These political creatures live or die by what the media write or say about them. They dance to the media's tune.

The ancient ritual of human sacrifice is still practiced in America. When a child dies in foster care; when budgets go crazy as a result of events that could never be predicted; when parents wage savage battles, using their children as weapons in a custody war; when a dedicated, conscientious social worker makes a simple mistake and a client dies or is badly injured—then the "high priests" of politics and the media select a victim to sacrifice—usually a manager in human services. There is a perfunctory trial—either a public hearing or a media exposé—and the manager's head is lopped off. The politicians and the journalists wipe their hands and pat themselves on the back for a job well done, and business goes on as usual.

Americans seem to believe that the sacrifice will appease the gods: that no more children will die; that spending will be kept under control; that parents in crisis will be civil; that old people will stay healthy and independent; that other social workers will be deterred from making the same mistake. Nothing changes, you see. In some spiritual, mysterious fashion, there has been retribution and justice and that makes everything OK. The problem is not solved. The politicians and the journalists have simply put another bureaucrat's head on their pikes. The mob is appeased—until the next time.

Part of being a manager is constantly to make choices: to put competing values on the scale and decide which outweighs the other—which way the organization should tilt, in which direction it should go now, what should be changed, and when and where and how. No matter how talented and dedicated, if the human services manager is caught in a crossfire and does not know media survival skills, he or she is apt to be the next human sacrifice.

Turning the Tables

Many managers wince at the suggestion that they should adopt aggressive, proactive tactics to deal with the media. They have been conditioned to accept public humiliation or termination. If it becomes their turn, they will go quietly. They find it hard even to consider any other scenario. That is just the way it is, always has been, and always will be. It is better to take chances in the political mine fields, for at least they know the players and the rules. They have some basic political savvy or they would not have gotten this far.

In today's world, managers owe clients, staff, and agencies more than that. They owe them their best effort to improve the delivery of human services in this country. They should be solving problems, not burying them. They should be telling the public how the system fails and what it would take for it to succeed. That is the only way the system will change.

The human services arena has changed dramatically in the past 25 years, but too many managers do not seem to notice. Hardening of the arteries has set in. Their reactions are rigid and predictable:

▶ "The confidentiality law and ethic will not let me comment."

▶ "It is my job to keep society's failures out of sight. If the public sees my clients, the politicians will be blamed for their pain and suffering. The politicians, in turn, will take retribution on my staff and me."

▶ "We're going to be sued on this one. Anything we say to the media will come back to haunt us in court. Put a clamp on the staff."

▶ "We're outnumbered and outgunned on this one. We'll have to lay low. If nothing else works, play dead. We'll take some casualties, but eventually they'll go away and leave us alone."

▶ "Don't rock the boat. Better to put your head down and take your beating. Keep the long-term objectives in mind, so you won't scream each time the lash cuts into your back."

These responses are wrong. Human services managers avoid nasty fights. In a barroom brawl, they would be conscientious objectors. They are sensitive caregivers, cerebral diplomats. They believe an ounce of mediation is worth a pound of brute force. Years of working their way up the bureaucratic ladder have convinced them that whistle-blowers have a death wish. He or she who ducks and runs away lives to fight another day.

Most managers in human services consider the news media a threat—trouble-makers who neither understand nor care about the clients or the agency, headhunters who are looking for another story that will win awards and increase ratings and circulation, people who know virtually nothing about social work and have little time or interest to learn. In many places, at many times, this perception may be correct.

Like most people with a social work orientation, you wish the news media would change. That is highly unlikely. The current economic and competitive forces within the news media will probably make these traits and behaviors even more dominant and widespread. If you continue to use old responses and tactics, you will continue to lose on an even grander scale. You have the option, however, to stop and see the world as it really is and to learn to play the media game a new way. You can win the media game, without sacrificing your confidentiality ethic, to accomplish dramatic changes in human services with little risk in pending civil suits and with little political or job risk.

Take this hypothetical example. Erma Engraight lives with her three children in an abandoned bus. The family is poorly clothed and fed. Their sanitary conditions are horrible. They beg on the street for their hand-to-mouth existence. Erma has applied for assistance. The agency social worker immediately found her an apartment. "Not good enough," she said. "I want a nicer place." A second apartment was found. "Still not good enough," she said. "Find me a really nice place, or I'll go to Captain Airwaves and tell him you won't help me."

The social worker begins the process of taking custody of the children and placing them in protective care. Erma carries out her threat and tells Captain Airwaves she repeatedly has asked for help, but the agency has denied it to her and her children. When Captain Airwaves shows up at the agency office, unannounced, camera rolling, what should he be told?

When this hypothetical question is asked of human services managers, there is great unanimity. Tell the reporter, "No comment." That response is suicidal. It seems to confirm Erma's false charges. This strategy will be terribly damaging to your agency. It will discourage the staff and lower their morale. The manager's image will be further tarnished. The agency will be less likely to get what it needs from the legislature or board. "No comment" reinforces the public's stereotypical view that the "system" is a disaster, filled with bungling bureaucrats who care more about saving themselves and red tape than about the people they are supposed to serve.

A number of options would serve the clients, the agency, and the human services managers better. Some of them are as follows:

▶ "I can't talk about specific cases, Captain Airwaves. As you know, our clients must have absolute confidentiality. The law requires it. Our ethic requires it. But let me show you how we handle requests for assistance. Let me show you the housing we have on standby for clients with problems like those you've recited."

▶ Repeat the first option and add, "I have a written waiver form here. If a client signs this form in our presence, she waives her right to confidentiality, within any boundaries she sets. If you take this form to someone who has a complaint and she signs it, we'll be glad to talk to you about her case."

▶ Repeat the first two options and add, "If there is someone out there, living in the squalor you've described, we'll not only talk to you about her case, we'll let you videotape how we handle her application for assistance. I think I can guarantee that she and her children will be in clean, warm housing before dark."

▶ If the reporter is someone you trust, say: "I'd like to talk to you in confidence." When the reporter asks what you mean, you can respond: "I will answer your questions if you pledge that nobody—absolutely nobody—will ever know I discussed this case with you." If the reporter agrees to your conditions, you can state: "What you've been told is absolutely untrue. We've offered Erma two different places to live. She said she wanted a really fancy place and would use you to hurt us if we didn't put her up in the Taj Mahal. If you check the court records and your sources, you'll find that we've scheduled a protective custody hearing for her children tomorrow."

▶ Repeat the first option and add, "A client who goes public can open the confidentiality door. If you will let me see your videotape or read an accurate transcript of what a client said about her dealing with this agency, I can respond—but only in those areas that she has publicly discussed."

Lawyers who tell human services managers not to talk to reporters often do so in good conscience. They, too, have a long history and ethic. The old ethic said they must do their best to protect their clients' interests in a pending litigation. The legal ethic is also changing because the damage that will be done by unfavorable coverage by the news media often far outweighs the damage inflicted by a court trial. Once the case is on television or the front page, lawyers have an ethical responsibility to help their clients in the media trial as well as in the court trial. Telling clients to stonewall arguably amounts to malpractice.

Lawyers also must begin to weigh these competing values when they advise their clients. The landscape is littered with corporations and individuals who followed their lawyers' advice and were destroyed by the media. In some cases, the companies died before they got to court. Negative media coverage drives corporations into bankruptcy as customers and stockholders abandon them. It sometimes kills individuals, too. Suicides, mental breakdowns, and the inability to find jobs can be the result of a media disaster.

A Better Way

Some bright spots exist and can be helpful to human services managers. When someone put cyanide in Tylenol capsules and killed seven people, the lawyers at Johnson & Johnson urged company officials to say nothing to the media. James Burke, the chief executive officer, heard their advice and decided to play it another way. He quickly expanded the corporation's capacity for answering reporters' questions. The reporters were briefed frequently. Mike Wallace and a "60 Minutes" camera crew were allowed to videotape an executive meeting at the height of the crisis. Burke went on "Donahue" and took questions from the audience.

Burke's courage in deciding to open the doors to the media is universally cited as the public relations coup of this generation. It was perhaps the most outstanding public relations victory of the century. If Burke had followed his lawyers' advice, many contend, the company would have failed. Tylenol made up about a third of the corporation's gross revenue. As a result of Burke's media strategy, Tylenol rebounded stronger than ever.

Absolute guidelines cannot be drawn on when and how to talk to the media, but as a human services manager, you have a number of options. You should not decide how to deal with the media on the basis of out-of-date reflexes. Choices should be reviewed and possibly explored with trusted, experienced staff. The world has changed. In a media crisis, conventional wisdom, traditional responses, and a lawyer's advice are often wrong. The following points offer some guidance.

The Ten Commandments of Media Relations

The Ten Commandments of Media Relations[1] were developed to help managers cope. Some are just basic common sense. But fear of the media often leads you to do strange things. These commandments should help you develop some regular routines and policies for coping with reporters, editors, and photographers on a regular basis.

1. *Always appear open and cooperative; never lie.* When you close a door in the face of a reporter or refuse to provide a document, it triggers a violent visceral

---

[1]*For more information the reader is referred to C. Jones,* How to Speak TV, Print, and Radio *(Tampa, FL: Video Consultants, 1991).*

reaction, particularly if the reporter has a legal right to enter that door or see that document. Lying, on the "Media Morality Scale," is often worse than the sin it covers. In the past, people who lied to reporters were able to claim they were misquoted. No longer. With audio- and videotapes, the words are preserved forever. The lie plays on the 6 o'clock news, the 11 o'clock news, the morning show, and again at noon. The lie will be used to discredit the agency at every opportunity. Do not lie.

2. *Personalize the organization.* To be successful with the media, you have to be creative at showing real people in the organization doing what they do best. All public relations boils down to one simple concept: Who are you? What do you do?

3. *Develop media contacts.* Personal relationships with reporters and editors will result in better coverage. This fact is never stated out loud. It is a strange game in

"Your crisis management plan should include more than 'four Hail Marys and two Our Fathers.' "

which you collect poker chips that will someday be cashed in. How are contacts developed? Invite reporters to lunch. At lunch, make it clear that you are available when they need a resource. Emphasize the first commandment: "Just want you to know we have an open door to reporters and photographers at our place. Call. We'll do our best to help you." Good reporters have many contacts. They depend on them. Contacts call with tips on stories. They volunteer inside information they know will help with today's major story. And when it is time for a story about the profession or organization, the contact will be quoted. These quotes enhance the positive image of the organization, and they will not hurt the manager's career.

Remember, all stories are not clear-cut. Reporters have tremendous power in deciding which stories will be written and which will be thrown away. Stories take a slant or tone in the choice of a word or a phrase. When the agency is having problems, the reporter who knows you personally and respects your competence and integrity will write a different story from the reporter who is a stranger.

After you develop contacts, reporters will call when they get tips suggesting that something is wrong at the agency. Rumors, and the stories they generate, die when the reporter-contact is assured that the rumors are false. When the rumors are true, you, the manager, must never suggest to the reporter that you are owed a break. If you do, the game is over. You lose all your chips and a good media contact. You go directly to the front page; you do not pass Go.

4. *Take good stories to the reporters.* The bad news almost always leaks out. So you assume that good news leaks, too. It does not. Gossips inside the agency take bad news to the media. It is a natural phenomenon. There is no natural counterpart for leaking good stories. A system must be created in the organization so everyone is sensitive to good stories. There must be a way for those ideas to reach the person who is responsible for public relations. It is that person's job to try to sell the good story. Thousands of good stories die every day simply because the media never heard about them.

5. *Respond quickly.* If you or your organization is under attack, you must respond immediately. Once you are cast as the villain in a story, it is difficult—often impossible—to change that image, no matter what is done. A good media policy requires a response to all reporters' telephone calls within 15 minutes. If the person the reporter is trying to reach is out of touch, someone else should return the call. Returning telephone calls helps prevent surprises on tomorrow's front page. It is important to know what the reporter is pursuing. The agency would not have been called unless the story involves the staff, the profession, or a client. Every story about you and the agency should include your viewpoint. Sometimes, the reporter simply needs information. In this case, you become a resource, your image is enhanced, and you are viewed as an expert.

6. *Never say, "No comment."* Why? It violates the first commandment (appear cooperative). The public hears something else. You must be hiding something—evading. If nothing is wrong, why not talk?

In reality, however, reporters cannot be told everything in all situations. If detectives tell too much about a kidnapping, the victim may die. If the CEO discusses a proposed merger, the negotiations may fall apart. The grand jury witness who tells reporters what happened in the jury room will be held in contempt and jailed. If the human services caseworker discloses anything about a client, he or she can be prosecuted, lose his or her job, and be sued for invasion of privacy. The lawyer, banker, accountant, or physician who tells reporters about conversations with a patient or client violates a sacred trust.

So what can you say when reporters ask questions that you should not answer? Assuming a cooperative posture (the first commandment) is essential. Then, explain carefully why the details cannot be given. Promise that if, or when, these conditions change, the reporter will be contacted immediately. In real life, managers who are successful at the media game also learn how to talk to reporters in confidence.

7. *It is okay to say, "I don't know."* Do not try to fake it. Do not assume that employees did what they were trained to do. Do not use statistics unless you are absolutely certain of the numbers. Reporters do not expect managers to have the Library of Congress in their heads. But reporters do expect managers to know where the information is and to be able to retrieve it quickly. It is frequently helpful to include a staff member in any complicated interview or news conference. The staff member's job is to answer difficult technical questions or to obtain the records you need to answer the reporter's question. "I can't remember the exact figure," the reporter is told. "But, Bill, if you'll get the 1987 committee report, that'll have it. We'll have those numbers before you leave the building." In this way, you appear helpful, open, and cooperative. "I don't know. But I'll find out and get what you need."

8. *If you make a mistake, confess and repent.* This is another basic in the American character. We respect people who admit they made a mistake *if* they do whatever they can to make it right. How different our tribal character would be if George Washington had said to his father, "Cherry tree? What cherry tree?" In the new Media Morality, the lie, the cover-up, and insensitivity are greater sins than the crime itself. In public life, however, you cannot confess the same sin too often.

9. *Use the big dump.* When there is bad news to dump, dump it all at once. Do not let it dribble out. Doing so will prolong the stories and multiply the damage. Once you decide to confess and repent, you may be tempted to confess only part of the sin. That is human nature. But two months after the first story, some relatively insignificant piece of information will be discovered by an enterprising reporter. *"Look what we found!"* the headline will scream. *"Exclusive investigative report!"* The new finding is actually so insignificant that it would not have been considered news if it had been dumped the first day. But when follow-up stories repeating the original allegations add tiny bits of new information, the damage increases with each new story.

Once again, it is far better to dump everything the media will probably find. There will not be time on the air or space in print to disclose it all. And then it will be old news. You can move on past the problem. "Dirt" that you disclose is always less newsworthy than "dirt" that reporters dig up by themselves. As long as the news media believe there is more to be mined, they will continue to dig. That is their job. When they believe the mine is exhausted, they will move on to more fertile subjects.

10. *Prepare.* Most organizations have carefully prepared disaster plans. They conduct fire drills, tornado drills, earthquake drills, hurricane drills. They buy insurance and prepare for the worst. It is much more likely that the manager and the agency will experience a media disaster before a fire, earthquake, or tornado. Yet few organizations or agencies prepare for this more likely hazard.

As a part of the preparation, a manager should develop a written policy on the media. Key spokespeople ought to be trained to deal with the media. And they need to practice what they've learned often. Otherwise, they get rusty. Their reflexes are dulled. Hypothetical media incidents should be studied. For example, what if an agency suddenly discovered a major internal theft? What would a hospital say to the media if a major slip-up occurred in the operating room and a famous patient died? How would a bank explain an employee who helped a drug smuggler launder millions of dollars? What would be the position of the human services agency if it returned a battered child to the parents and the parents killed the child? What would a judge say when he released a career criminal and that criminal murdered a little girl within a week?

All these things happen with some regularity. We are human. We make mistakes. Our systems are imperfect. If we do not prepare for the media disaster, it can easily destroy us, our organizations, or both.

Summary

Human services managers often dislike reporters, especially investigative reporters and editors. Establishing good media relationships is one of the most challenging managerial skills. It requires constant attention and refinement. Human services managers may need to significantly alter their attitudes and behavior to respond effectively in conflicting situations.

The Ten Commandments of Media Relations offer instructive guidelines for changing attitudes and behavior. It has become increasingly important for human services managers to prepare a workable media relations plan and to practice its implementation regularly. Although a human services manager may never be totally comfortable dealing with the news media, following the guidelines will lead to increased effectiveness and fairer treatment for the manager and the agency.

SKILLS - APPLICATION EXERCISE

Sam Smith is a foster parent for teenage boys. Everything in his past indicates that he is an excellent foster parent. He takes a personal interest in the boys and has had remarkable success. Some of the foster children he encouraged to go to college have become successful professionals and businessmen. Last year, Smith was named Foster Parent of the Year.

Smith calls you (the human services manager whose agency has custody of the foster children in Smith's home), extremely shaken. An investigative reporter for a local television station has just barged into his home, unannounced. The reporter—Molly Muckraker—claims to have sworn affidavits and on-camera interviews with three boys at Smith's home. These boys contend that Smith paid them to engage in sexual acts. Furthermore, they claim he has now filed "trumped up" charges against them in juvenile court because they no longer are willing to submit to him.

Smith says he became so angry at the allegations that he lost his temper, shouted an obscene word at Muckraker, and threw her and the camera crew out of his home. All of this was videotaped. From what Muckraker said to him, her story likely will be on the air today or tomorrow.

Smith says the charge is absolutely untrue. He is willing to take a lie-detector test. He contends that the boys are trying to "frame" him because he caught them smoking marijuana (after earlier catching them and getting their agreement not to do it again) and has filed a juvenile delinquency proceeding against them.

As the manager of the agency with custody of the youths placed in Smith's home, what do you do now? What advice is offered by the Ten Commandments of Media Relations?

HUMAN RELATIONS SKILLS

Managerial human relations skills encompass the roles of mentor and group facilitator. Competencies for the mentor role include an understanding of self and others, interpersonal communication skills, and development of subordinates. Competencies for the group facilitator role include team building, participatory decision making, and conflict management. The chapters in this section give attention to these competencies and roles in effective managerial performance.

Peter J. Pecora offers a comprehensive approach to recruiting and selecting employees in which he suggests steps and guidelines for implementing a system that is consistent with affirmative action and equal employment opportunities. He pays considerable attention to the processes involved in recruiting, selecting, and placing employees. In a wide-ranging discussion of job descriptions, the public relations aspects of recruitment, and job-application forms and tests, he emphasizes the importance of objectivity and fairness. Pecora presents especially useful information about conducting screening interviews and describes two interviewing strategies—the Patterned Behavior Description Interview and the Situational Interview. Implicit in this chapter are the incorporation of the characteristics of caring and the demonstration of consideration into the recruitment and selection of personnel. These characteristics are required to affirm that an organizational climate fosters commitment, a team orientation, and the personal development of its employees.

Darlyne Bailey provides an overview of past, present, and future approaches to the design and maintenance of effective organizational teams. She presents a developmental theoretical framework through which to look at stages of team development and the behavior that is frequently associated with each stage. The stages—forming, storming, norming, performing, and adjourning—serve as an instructive framework for looking at the internally focused flexibility of the human relations approach. Bailey emphasizes the importance of understanding self and others, participatory decision making, and the management of conflict as pivotal competencies in the effective performance of managers in the human services. The achievement of a high degree of commitment, cohesion, and morale among employees may require human services managers to become the ultimate team leaders. Consensus building and the involvement of employees are viewed as critical aspects of the process orientation that is uniquely important in the human relations approach.

Regina Nixon and Margaret Spearmon present an insightful discussion of managing in a multicultural environment. Suggesting that it is a strategic, as well as moral, issue, they define "pluralistic management" as leadership that aggressively pursues the creation of a workplace in which the values, interests, and contributions of diverse cultural groups represent an integral part of the organization's mission, culture, politics, and procedures and in which these groups share power at every level. Nixon and Spearmon present a typology for human services managers to assess their organizations' standards with respect to diversity and pluralism. In addition, they underscore the awareness skills that are required for effective performance, including the self-analysis of the "I" and the cultural literacy of the "we and they." The emphasis on understanding self and others is continued through attention to organizational assessment skills via the evaluation of cultural and institutional arrangements. The authors view employee-empowerment skills through participation-oriented styles and an emphasis on career development as key ingredients in effective management.

Dixie L. Benshoff, in an incisive, witty style, contributes her thinking about women as managers. She questions whether women are considered for managerial positions in the same way men are, identifies the factors that women can control to increase their probability of being promoted, and suggests how women can enhance their value once they are in key managerial positions. Using results from numerous studies, Benshoff pinpoints special issues and challenges that women encounter in pursuing managerial positions and performing effectively as managers. To be most effective, Benshoff suggests, women need to acquire and manipulate power (and to feel comfortable about doing so) and to work on their need for recognition; they should not become complacent and just tend to their jobs. She views support groups as important for women and the support of such groups by human services managers and organizations as consistent with and indicative of a positive human relations approach. Benshoff concludes with a series of "need to's" that are instructive for both the personal and the professional development of women in the workplace. Of special value in this chapter are the insights into the sometimes different views and approaches of women and men in mentoring and facilitating roles in organizations.

Robert F. Rivas contends that the dismissal of problem employees is a managerial prerogative, but recognizes that unions influence the process. He provides an overview of the phenomenon of "separating" employees and underscores the importance of supervision in arriving at such a conclusion. Offering a typology of supervision, Rivas underscores the relationship of supervision to performance. In addition, he strongly emphasizes the importance of performance evaluation and feedback for the effective management of the dismissal processes. He urges human services organizations and managers to assume a proactive approach. To this end, he offers guidelines to prepare for and conduct dismissal interviews.

Richard L. Edwards and John A. Yankey conclude this section with Chapter 13, on managing the decline of organizations. As resources diminish, many managers are confronted with the need to restructure their organizations and reduce their work force. The authors present managerial processes for making decisions—many of them difficult—about downsizing human services organizations. Attention is given to focusing on the "health" of the organization, assessing its strengths and weaknesses, and exploring the psychological postures related to cutbacks and to reactive and proactive ways of responding to organizational decline.

Recruiting and Selecting
Effective Employees

Peter J. Pecora

In the human services, line staff and supervisors constitute one of the most important resources for maximizing the productivity and effectiveness of agencies. In terms of the mobilization of resources, the recruitment and screening of potential staff members is an essential skill. This chapter presents an overview of some of the important principles for recruiting, screening, and selecting employees, including two exercises that will enable readers to test and practice their skills in this area.

The employee-selection process requires both analytical and interpersonal skills, as well as knowledge of affirmative action (AA) guidelines and of the rules of the Equal Employment Opportunity Commission (EEOC). For example, in terms of analytical skills, the position for which you are recruiting must be defined in task-specific ways. Task-based job descriptions must be developed, and essential "competencies" of workers (knowledge, skills, abilities, and attitudes) must be identified. Interpersonal skills are required for interviewing job candidates in a courteous and professional manner.

In this chapter, the necessary steps and guidelines for the recruitment and selection of employees are described, including the ways in which AA and EEOC guidelines affect the processes of recruitment, selection, and placement. *Recruitment* involves assigning new employees to positions and orienting them properly so they can begin working. *Selection* is concerned with reviewing the qualifications of job applicants to decide who should be offered the positions. *Placement* involves assigning new employees to the positions and orienting them properly so that they can begin working (Shafritz, Hyde, & Rosenbloom, 1986). In this chapter, the first two components are emphasized.

Portions of this chapter were adapted from P. J. Pecora and M. J. Austin, Managing Human Services Personnel. *Copyright © 1987 by Sage Publications, Inc. Used by permission of Sage Publications, Inc.*

Steps and Guidelines for Recruiting, Screening, and Selecting Staff

The major steps involved in recruitment and selection are these:

▶ Develop a job description that contains information regarding the minimum prerequisite qualifications for the position in terms of education, experience, and skills.

▶ Recruit employees through posting announcements of positions and through advertising.

▶ Screen applicants using application forms, reviews of résumés, and tests (if appropriate).

▶ Conduct screening interviews.

▶ Select the person and notify other applicants that a decision has been made.

The necessary interpersonal skills include the ability to work collaboratively with agency staff to develop common expectations for the position and a common set of interview questions. Supervisory and other administrative personnel must also be able to interview job applicants in a professional and courteous manner.

The employee-selection process should be considered an important investment of an administrator's time. If this process is not carried out properly, supervisory staff and managers will spend valuable time and energy unnecessarily—through additional supervision—to overcome the employee's marginal performance, the increased organizational conflict, and the stress involved in transferring or firing the person.

Developing a Job Description and Minimum Qualifications

The first step in the employee-selection process is to define the job and the types of knowledge, skills, and abilities that are necessary for effective performance (see McCormick, 1979; Pecora & Austin, 1987, pp.18–33). A task-based job description helps administrators develop a clear definition of the job and the type of qualifications necessary to perform it. Agencies use such job descriptions in preparing employee-recruitment materials, the next step in the process.

In preparing job descriptions for recruitment purposes, be sure they contain clear and specific statements of the essential duties of the positions. In addition, the knowledge, skills, abilities, educational degrees (if any), and years of related job experience required need to be specified. For ethical and legal reasons, the required minimum qualifications for a job should match the work to be performed. In other words, can you substantiate the connection between the education and experience required and the tasks of the job?

Recruiting Employees

The next step is to prepare announcements of the position to (1) publicize officially the availability of the position, (2) describe the tasks of the job, (3) attract a wide range of qualified candidates to improve the pool of candidates and maximize compliance with the legislative intent of both the EEOC and AA, and (4) inform interested persons of the minimum qualifications and the process involved in applying for the position.

The recruitment and selection of employees is a form of *public relations*. The quality of recruitment materials and the respect and professionalism displayed to applicants shape the image of your agency—especially to the many applicants who were *not* selected. How the recruitment and screening process is handled either improves or damages the reputation of your agency. For example, if you receive applications from 45 persons, interview eight, but select only one, the 44 persons not selected are then left with a positive, neutral, or negative impression of the agency. If unsuccessful applicants are treated fairly in a demanding, well-organized professional screening process, they may be disappointed, but their level of respect for the organization will probably increase. Thus, future case referrals or community image may depend on the people *not* hired.

This "public relations" aspect of recruitment has implications for how the other steps in the process are carried out. For example, the announcement of the position should be as detailed as possible to allow potential applicants to determine early whether the position would fit their qualifications, current interests, and career goals. Communication with job applicants and screening interviews should be handled carefully. To meet AA laws and regulations, the job announcement must include the following information:

▶ Job title, classification, and salary range (although salary ranges in some organizations are listed as "open" and "negotiable")

▶ Location of job (geographic and organizational unit)

▶ Description of duties

▶ Minimum qualifications

▶ Starting date for the position

▶ Application procedures (what materials should be sent to whom?)

▶ Closing date for the receipt of applications (Klingner & Nalbandian, 1985, pp. 88–89).

A typical announcement of a position is shown in Figure 1 (although most newspaper advertisements are shorter because of their cost). Various forms of this basic announcement can be distributed to a variety of organizations, placed as newspaper advertisements, listed in professional newsletters, and given directly to potential applicants. Many organizations make special efforts to recruit women or minorities by contacting certain community organizations, churches, departments and placement centers of universities, minority newspapers, radio shows, and other community groups. These special efforts may also be necessary because of economic or other factors that may be affecting the labor market and the availability of qualified applicants.

Check to see that the announcement contains the necessary details of the position and is clearly worded. Make sure that the application deadline is realistic, given the

Figure 1. Sample Position Announcement

POSITION ANNOUNCEMENT
Family Preservation Service Specialist
Children's Services Society
Seattle, Washington

Function and Location
Provides intensive in-home services to families considering out-of-home placement for one or more members. Is on call 24 hours per day to provide crisis
intervention and other family services and problem resolution. Will work out of the
Wallingford social services office.

Duties and Responsibilities (Partial List)
1. Provides in-home crisis-oriented treatment and support to families in which
   one or more family members are at risk of being placed outside the home in
   foster, group, or institutional care to prevent child placement.
2. Works a 40-hour nonstructured workweek (including evenings and weekends)
   to be responsive to the needs of families.
3. Provides family education and skills training as part of a goal-oriented
   treatment plan to prevent the recurrence of or to reduce the harmful effects of
   the maltreatment of children.
4. Advocates for family members with schools, courts, and other social service
   agencies to help family members obtain financial assistance, housing, medical
   care, and other services.

Qualifications
Master's degree in social work, psychology, educational psychology, or psychosocial nursing is required. Graduate degree in social work preferred. Experience
in counseling families and children is required. Knowledge of crisis intervention,
social casework, communication skills, and family therapy techniques is required.
Knowledge of cognitive-behavioral interventions, group work, and functional
family therapy is desirable. Must have reliable transportation. Required to live in
county served. Salary range: $23,000–29,000.

Application Procedures and Deadline
An agency application form, résumé, and cover letter describing related education
and experience must be submitted. Position closes April 15, 1991. Starting date is
tentatively scheduled for May 10, 1991. Please send application materials to—
   Annette Jandre
   Program Supervisor
   Children's Services Society
   4601 15th Avenue, NW
   Seattle, WA 98103
   (206) 263-5857

AN EQUAL OPPORTUNITY EMPLOYER
ALL QUALIFIED INDIVIDUALS ARE ENCOURAGED TO APPLY

usual delays in the dissemination of announcements and the response of applicants (for example, does the deadline allow the applicant sufficient time to respond to the announcement?). Consider also whether the announcement has been distributed to enough community, professional, or other groups. Both formal and informal networks are useful for publicizing the position. Finally, keep a record of how and where the position was advertised or posted and include your personal recruitment efforts.

Screening Applicants

Application Form

If properly designed, the application form can provide a significant amount of information about the applicant's qualifications. It should gather objective data about the applicant's previous work history. Other aspects of the screening process (reference letters and calls to former employers) focus on *how well* the applicant performed in his or her preceding jobs.

Application forms typically require the following information:

▶ Name, address, and phone number or numbers

▶ Educational degrees and related course work

▶ Employment history (positions, places of employment, major duties, dates of employment, reason for leaving, supervisor's name)

▶ Veteran status (this information may be required—some agencies give "points" for employment tests or special consideration to veterans)

▶ References

▶ Any disabilities that would interfere with performing the particular job

▶ Adult convictions for a Class-A misdemeanor or felony

▶ AA information, such as ethnic group, sex, age, and any disability (this information is detached from the application and is kept on file for AA analysis).

In addition, some agencies require applicants to complete a questionnaire in which they indicate their level of knowledge and skills for major tasks of the job and provide references of supervisors or instructors who can verify the information. The agency's application should not contain questions that violate AA guidelines, such as those on marital status or number of children.

Tests

The use of tests to screen and select candidates in social welfare organizations is limited because of the lack of adequately validated and appropriate employment tests, the need to validate tests, and the recent controversy surrounding the fairness of such tests (American Psychological Association, 1980). Opponents of testing argue that tests are rarely powerful predictors of job performance and tend to discriminate against certain groups, typically ethnic minorities (Howell & Dipboye, 1982; Zedeck & Cascio, 1984). But given the lack of alternatives for screening a large number of applicants, tests may continue to be used in certain social welfare agencies.

It should be pointed out that tests are being used increasingly as screening devices. For example, some states are using licensing examinations, developed by the American Association of State Social Work Boards, that attempt to test qualifications at both the BSW and MSW levels (Teare, Higgs, Gauthier, & Feild, 1984). These examinations may encourage the development of tests for screening applicants for social service jobs nationwide. In addition, recent research on psychological testing has shown that certain types of tests (such as those testing cognitive ability) are valid predictors of successful job performance across jobs and settings (see Zedeck & Cascio, 1984, pp. 484–485). Finally, Mufson (1986) reported that scores on certain scales of the California Psychological Inventory were successful in discriminating between the most and least desirable child welfare workers.

Beach (1975) offered the following guidelines for using tests as devices to select employees: (1) tests should be used only as a supplement to other selection devices, not as a substitute for them, (2) tests are more accurate at predicting failure than success, (3) tests are more useful in picking a select group of people who are most likely to succeed on the job from among a much larger group, (4) tests should be validated on one's own organization, (5) tests can make their greatest contribution in situations in which it is difficult to obtain satisfactory employees through other selection methods, (6) test scores should *not* be viewed as precise and exact measures of the characteristic being tested, and (7) high test scores are not necessarily better predictors of satisfactory job performance than are slightly lower scores.

Preliminary Screening

Once the application forms and test scores (if any) have been received, a preliminary screening of applications should be conducted by a small committee of administrators, supervisors, and staff to eliminate applications that clearly do not meet the minimum standards and to help select a group of applicants to be interviewed. To facilitate this process, a "screening grid" may be used (see Figure 2). Each application is reviewed in relation to the minimum qualifications and the applicant's competencies or experience in certain areas (such as the amount of training in protective services, the number of years of direct practice experience in child welfare, and the number of years of supervisory experience). Be sure to include ample space on the screening grid for the section labeled "special charac-teristics." This section allows reviewers to note the applicant's abilities, experi-ences, or training that may be of special relevance to the position.

Figure 2. Grid for Screening Applicants for a Child Protective Services Supervisor Position

Applicant's Name	MSW or MA in One of the Social Sciences (Yes/No)	Years of Experience in Social Services	Years of Experience in Child Protective Services	Specialized Training in Child Protection	Years of Supervisory Experience	Unusual Characteristics or Qualifications

The usefulness of the screening grid and the application-review process depends, to some extent, on the amount of information provided by the applicant. Clearly the committee's ability to assess the applicant's qualifications, beyond adherence to minimum qualifications, is dependent upon the application form, résumé, and any other information that is gathered. Therefore, some agencies also ask applicants to supply a detailed cover letter describing how their education, training, and experience qualify them for a particular job. Detailed cover letters and screening grids facilitate the initial screening process, especially when the screening committee may have to consider 10 or more applicants.

In screening applicants, double-check to ensure that the job-application form provides information that helps you determine whether the applicant has related education, training, and experience. In addition, check that the application form does not contain questions that are illegal according to EEO laws. The following information cannot be requested in either an application form or a job interview: maiden name, type of residence, proof of age, verification of birthplace and citizenship, language and national origin, photographs, physical condition, religion, criminal record, military service, organizational affiliations, and references (Jensen, 1981). But be prepared to encounter many fellow staff members who are not aware of what questions are illegal or improper to use in application forms and interviews. Many staff wonder where these guidelines originate. The next section on AA and EEO regulations summarizes some of the most important guidelines.

AA and EEO

Legislation for EEO and AA continues to affect the recruitment, screening, and selection of employees in both business and social welfare organizations. The distinctive components of EEO laws are based on Title VII of the 1964 Civil Rights Act and other laws, including the Age Discrimination Employment Act of 1967; Sections 503 and 504 of the Rehabilitation Act of 1973, as amended; the Vietnam Era Veterans Readjustment Assistance Act of 1974; and the Equal Pay Act of 1963. As Klingner and Nalbandian (1985, p. 64) noted:

> With few exceptions, Title VII (EEO) prohibits employers, labor organizations, and employment agencies from making employee or applicant personnel decisions based on race, color, religion, sex, or national origin. Although it originally applied only to private employers, the concern of EEO was extended to local and state governments by 1972 amendments to the 1964 Civil Rights Act.

Equal opportunity laws reflect a management approach to reducing discrimination against employees by ensuring that equal opportunity is implemented in all employment actions. Executive Order No. 11246 and other laws require nondiscrimination, which involves the elimination of all existing discriminatory conditions, whether purposeful or inadvertent. Agencies and governmental contractors must carefully and systematically examine all their employment policies to be sure that they do not operate to the detriment of any persons on the grounds of race, color, religion, national origin, sex, age, or status as a handicapped individual, disabled veteran, or veteran of the Vietnam era. Administrators must also ensure that the practices of those who are responsible for matters of employment, including all supervisors, are nondiscriminatory (personal communication with S. Radley, Office of Equal Opportunity, University of Utah, 1986).

In contrast, AA requires that most organizations take steps to ensure the proportional recruitment, selection, and promotion of qualified members of groups,

"I'd say our recruiters did an exceptional job identifying you."

such as ethnic minorities and women, who were formerly excluded. Most employers, unions, and employment agencies are required to plan and document, through written affirmative action programs (AAPs), the steps they are taking to reduce the underrepresentation of various groups. Most public and private organizations that provide goods and services to the federal government and their subcontractors must comply with the AA provisions described in Executive Order No. 11246; guidelines for handling AAPs are found in Title 41, Part 60-2 (known as "Revised Order No. 4") of the Office of Federal Contract Compliance.

Although both EEO and AA seek to eliminate discrimination in employment, the safeguards and improvements mandated by these guidelines in relation to specific practices for recruiting, screening, selecting, and promoting employees vary. For example, a mental health agency may develop a specific campaign to recruit and hire more female supervisors to increase the proportion of female administrators in the agency as part of its plan to comply with AA regulations. In contrast, EEO agency guidelines cover such areas as the type of questions that can be asked on an employment application or in an interview and emphasize the use of screening or interviewing committees that are composed of a mix of men, women, and ethnic minorities.

Knowledge of EEO and AA guidelines is essential for designing employment application forms and interviewing protocols that avoid the use of illegal questions. However, recent and ongoing court cases may alter what is permissible under EEO and AA guidelines. Governmental updates and legal consultations are important resources for assessing the adequacy of procedures. Other sources of information are the *Labor Law Journal* and the following manuals, which are regularly updated: *Employment Practices, Equal Employment Opportunity Commission Compliance Manual*, and *Office of Federal Contract Compliance Program Manual* (Commerce Clearing House); *Affirmative Action Compliance Manual for Federal Contractors* (Bureau of National Affairs); *Equal Employment Opportunity Compliance Manual* (Prentice Hall); and *Handicapped Requirements Handbook* (Federal Programs Advisory Service).

EEO, AA, and the Classification of Jobs

In addition to banning certain types of questions on applications or in interviews, the EEO guidelines forbid any selection process for candidates that has an "adverse impact" on any social, ethnic, or gender group, unless the procedure is validated through the analysis of jobs or research on the selection of employees (Equal Employment Opportunity Commission, 1978). Descriptions and notices of positions that delineate knowledge, skill, ability, education, or other prerequisites require a determination of whether the prerequisites are genuinely appropriate for the job. Some requirements (such as years of experience, certificates, diplomas, and educational degrees) may be considered unlawful on the basis of previous court decisions for a particular position. Proscriptions against discrimination in employ-ment demand that any requirement (education or experience) that is used as a standard for decisions about employment must have a manifest relationship to the job in question (Meritt-Haston & Weyley, 1983; Pecora & Austin, 1983).

The use of standards that disqualify women, minorities, or other groups at a substantially higher rate than white (Caucasian) male applicants would be unlawful, unless they could be shown to be significantly related to the successful performance of a job and otherwise necessary to the safe and efficient operation of the job for which they are used. (Educational requirements are defined as a test by the federal government [EEO regulations 29CFR §1607.2, 1975] and must be validated in accordance with EEO's testing guidelines [29CFR §1607 et seq., 1975].) In addition, if an agency validates its selection criteria, the EEO guidelines require that it demonstrate that no suitable alternative with a lesser adverse impact is available (personal communication with S. Radley, Office of Equal Opportunity, University of Utah, 1986).

When an adverse impact can be demonstrated with regard to a screening instrument or process (a test or structured interview, for example), employers should use alternative measures that are equally valid but produce a less adverse impact. Unfortunately, little progress has been made in identifying and using valid screening procedures as alternatives to educational and experience qualifications (Zedeck & Cascio, 1984). Nevertheless, an agency should carefully analyze its jobs and clearly define their tasks and requisite knowledge, skills, and abilities. This information is essential for establishing minimum qualifications for various posi-tions, so qualified individuals can be recruited and selected. Figure 3 provides a concise summary of what is acceptable and unacceptable to use in application forms and as interview questions. It is based on EEO and AA regulations. Note that the guidelines for people who have physical disabilities are being revised, and questions must be carefully considered. To check your knowledge of these guidelines, test yourself using the Skills-Application Exercise 1 at the end of this chapter.

Conducting the Screening Interview

Because of the problems associated with testing, many social welfare agencies have traditionally relied on the employment interview as a screening device. During the interview, you should address four major questions. First, does the applicant have the necessary knowledge, skills, and abilities? Second, does the person have the motivation and initiative to do the job well? Third, will the individual be compatible with the other employees in that unit and the agency as a whole? (This question requires learning about the applicant's work style and personality, to some degree, through the interview process and later through a check of references). Fourth, can desirable candidates be convinced to leave their jobs to come to work for you (Attard, 1984, p. 17)?

Figure 3. Guide to Fair Employment Regulations on Preemployment Inquiries

Acceptable	Subject	Unacceptable
Name "Have you ever used another name?" /or/ "Is any additional information relative to change of name, use of an assumed name, or nickname necessary to enable a check on your work and education record? If yes, please explain."	Name	Maiden name
Place of residence	Residence	"Do you own or rent your home?"
Statement that hiring is subject to verification that applicant meets legal age requirements. "If hired can you show proof of age?" "Are you over 18?" "If under 18, can you, after employment, submit a work permit?"	Age	Age Birthdate Dates of attendance or completion of elementary or high school. Questions that tend to identify applicants over 40.
Language applicant speaks, reads, or writes.	National Origin	Questions as to nationality, lineage, ancestry, national origin, descent or parentage of applicant, applicant's parents or spouse. "What is your mother tongue?" /or/ Language commonly used by applicant. How applicant acquired ability to read, write, or speak a foreign language.
Names and addresses of parent or guardian if applicant is a minor. Statement of company policy regarding work assignment of employees who are related.	Sex, Marital Status, Family	Questions that indicate applicant's sex. Questions that indicate marital status. Number or ages of children or dependents. Provisions for child care. Questions regarding pregnancy, child bearing, or birth control. Name or address of relative, spouse, or children of adult applicant. "With whom do you reside?" /or/ "Do you live with your parents?"
	Race, Color	Questions as to applicant's race or color. Questions regarding applicant's complexion or color of skin, eyes, hair.
Statement that photograph may be required after employment.	Physical Description, Photograph	Questions about applicant's height and weight. Require applicant to affix a photograph to application. Request applicant, at his or her option, to submit to photograph. Require a photograph after interview but before employment.
Statement by employer of regular days, hours, or shifts to be worked.	Religion	Questions regarding applicant's religion. Religious days observed /or/ "Does your religion prevent you from working weekends or holidays?"

continued

Figure 3. Continued

Acceptable	Subject	Unacceptable
"Have you ever been convicted of a felony, or (within specified time period) a misdemeanor that resulted in imprisonment?" (Such a question must be accompanied by a statement that a conviction will not necessarily disqualify the applicant from the job applied for.)	Arrest, Criminal Record	Arrest record /or/ "Have you ever been arrested?"
Statement that bonding is a condition of hire.	Bonding	Questions regarding refusal or cancellation of bonding.
Questions regarding relevant skills acquired during applicant's U.S. military service.	Military Service	General questions regarding military service such as dates and type of discharge. Questions regarding service in a foreign military.
	Economic Status	Questions regarding applicant's current or past assets, liabilities, or credit rating, including bankruptcy or garnishment.
"Please list job-related organizations, clubs, professional societies, or other associations to which you belong—you may omit those that indicate your race, religious creed, color, national origin, ancestry, sex, or age."	Organizations, Activities	"List all organizations, clubs, societies, and lodges to which you belong."
"By whom were you referred for a position here?" Names of persons willing to provide professional or character references for applicant.	References	Questions of applicant's former employers or acquaintances that elicit information specifying the applicant's race, color, religious creed, national origin, ancestry, physical handicap, medical condition, marital status, age, or sex.
Name and address of person to be notified in case of accident or emergency.	Notification in Case of Emergency	Name and address of relative to be notified in case of accident or emergency.

SOURCE: Adapted from J. Jensen, "How to Hire the Right Person for the Job," *Grantsmanship Center News,* 9(3) (1981), pp. 28–29. Copyright © 1981, The Grantsmanship Center. Reprinted with permission. For a schedule of Grantsmanship Center workshops and for information on how to order Grantsmanship Center publications, write to The Grantsmanship Center, Dept. DD, 650 S. Spring St., #507, P.O. Box 6210, Los Angeles, CA 90014 and request a free copy of the Center's Whole Nonprofit Catalog.

Purposes of the Interview

Staff members should also be aware of the purposes of the interview:

To aid in screening and selecting applicants who best meet the position requirements. Data on the application are examined for gaps in time, missing information, and apparent inconsistencies, and any irregularities should be discussed and corrected. Additional information that is not contained in the application is gathered.

To develop good public relations. An agency may have over 20 applicants for a position. Whether each applicant is interviewed, the primary contact with the agency for many is through the interviewer. The interviewer, therefore, is the agency's representative to the professional community and must promote good public relations. Good public relations include prompt action. A hiring decision should be made as quickly as possible so that all applicants, whether interviewed or not, can be told of their status.

To educate applicants. The interviewer must be able to explain aspects of the position that are not readily apparent from the description of the position. Explanations requested may cover anything from a more detailed description of the position to the agency's overall policies (Glueck, 1978, p. 226).

Predictive Value of Interviews

Many researchers argue that interviews, as typically conducted, are of limited predictive value (Campion & Arvey, 1989; Howell & Dipboye, 1982). Despite the lack of conclusive empirical evidence in this regard, interviews are the most widely used means of selecting personnel. And there is some evidence that properly conducted interviews may yield information that is valid for predicting an applicant's performance of a job (Eder & Ferris, 1989; Mayfield, Brown, & Hamstra, 1980). Ross and Hoeltke's (1985) study of a residential child welfare program, in which a structured interview was used to rate applicants in relation to 10 competencies associated with "excellent" staff, tested the ability of the interview to select superior workers by correlating the scores on the interview with four measures of the performance of workers and found this method to be beneficial. Although this method requires further validation, the results are encouraging.

Furthermore, there is a growing body of practice wisdom (see Campbell, 1983) and some research (Eder & Ferris, 1989) that provide useful guidelines for interviewing applicants for jobs. For example, a number of studies have documented the usefulness of training interviewers in the steps in the selection process, interviewing techniques, and methods for combining various sources of information to evaluate applicants (Carlson, Thayer, Mayfield, & Peterson, 1971).

Preparation for Interviewing

The successful interviewing of applicants also involves preparation in a number of areas. Clearly, each member of the selection committee should be familiar with the duties, responsibilities, and qualifications of the job. Interviewers should know the applicant by carefully reading the application form, résumé, cover letter, and letters of reference before the interview. They should be prepared to check out any inconsistencies or gaps in the interview and possibly later when calling references. Finally, to standardize the areas covered in the interview, the staff should monitor each member of the screening committee to make sure that the same job-related questions are asked of each applicant because applicants may respond differently to the same questions when asked by different interviewers (Robertson, 1982).

Interviewers need to gather information to answer the following two basic questions:

1. *Can the applicants do the job?* To assess the applicants' potential to assume specific responsibilities, the interviewers should examine their previous work and nonwork experience, training and education, and actual behavior during the interview.

2. *Will the applicants do the job?* Interviewers may overlook the applicants' willingness to perform. This part of the information collecting involves the examination of applicants' preferences for and interest in the nature of the work to be done, their preferences for conditions of employment (such as salary, hours, and travel), and the compatibility between their career goals and the organization's career opportunities (Goodale, 1989, p. 316).

In general, select open-ended questions that cannot be answered with a simple yes or no, but require information or explanations. In other words, interviewers should start their questions with what, why, where, when, and how; *not* can, did, or have. Do not hesitate to ask the applicant to provide more details. It is also important to establish a comfortable, confidential, supportive, and nonthreatening atmosphere to reduce the applicant's nervousness or hesitancy to talk. In this regard, you should divert or hold all calls and visitors, avoid interviewing from behind a desk that is stacked high with books and papers, have all the necessary materials (applicant's résumé, application form, note-taking equipment, description of the position) ready, and set aside adequate time for the interview and between interviews (Robertson, 1982).

Phases of the Interview

These guidelines are designed to maximize the effectiveness and fairness of selection committees. But preparation alone is not sufficient: the interview itself should be conducted in a smooth, directed, professional manner and be led by one spokesperson for the group. There are essentially three phases in an effective interview: opening, information gathering, and closing. Each phase is critical for gathering the proper information or for providing applicants with the necessary details of the screening process (Robertson, 1982).

During the opening, or introductory, phase, the interviewer uses small talk to relax the applicant and to help him or her settle into the interview setting. This phase may last anywhere from two to 10 minutes, depending on the overall length of the interview. The transition from this phase to the information-gathering phase is usually accomplished by an introductory statement that may take the following form:

> We're glad you could meet with us today. We will have the next 45 minutes to discuss the position and your qualifications. Members of our committee will be asking you questions and possibly taking some notes. After that, you will have an opportunity to ask questions about the position and our agency.

The lead interviewer may then *briefly* review the agency and the nature of the position. In the information-gathering phase, the interviewers provide direction without talking too much (certainly no more than 30 percent of the time). Job-related questions and follow-up questions should help the applicant describe his or her qualifications more clearly. It is also important to assess the degree of match between the applicant's career goals and the agency's mission.

To signal the end of this phase, the lead interviewer may say, "Now that we have had the opportunity to discuss your experience, do you have any questions for us before we discuss the procedures and time lines for filling the position?" This statement invites the applicant to ask any questions he or she may have other than "What happens next?" This is an important part of the interview because superior candidates often have thoughtful or challenging questions about the agency. If questions arise that you cannot answer at that time, offer to phone the applicant with the answer (Robertson, 1982).

Before closing the interview, the lead interviewer should describe the time line for the final selection, along with any further steps that must be taken (telephoning references, a possible follow-up interview, the date when the decision will be made, and how the applicant will be notified). Finally, thank the applicant for his or her interest in the position and summarize the timetable for hiring. During the interview, try to avoid the following mistakes discussed by Jensen (1981):

▶ One serious mistake is to fail to establish rapport through a hurried interview, allowing frequent interruptions, not using "active listening" techniques, or making sarcastic or critical remarks. These problems impede communication by making candidates more uncomfortable. The absence of an interview strategy with preplanned questions can produce incomplete or nonsystematic information about the applicant.

▶ A common mistake of many novice interviewers is to dominate the interview with details about the organization, to jump in to fill a pause in the conversation, and not to allow the applicant to present his or her qualifications. A more problematic technique is to put the candidate under significant stress. Deliberate or inadvertent stress destroys rapport, causes resentment, inhibits the open disclosure of information, and is not equivalent to stress on the job. However, the use of realistic job-related role-play simulations, although slightly stressful, *is* a bona fide method for assessing an applicant's skills and abilities. The Homebuilders program of the Behavioral Sciences Institute has used such an approach successfully for many years.

► Finally, another common mistake is to form a premature judgment about an applicant (based on the applicant's unusual physical appearance, mannerisms, or speech) that biases the interviewer's acceptance of important information given later in the interview.

An exercise to practice interviewing skills appears in Skills-Application Exercise 2.

At the close of the interview, some organizations conduct a tour of the agency to familiarize applicants with the organization. These tours provide applicants with a more complete picture of the nature of the organization and the job. The tours may also lead to additional questions or comments from the applicant that are useful for selecting the appropriate employee.

Two Practical Interviewing Strategies

Two techniques may help you maximize the validity, reliability, and usefulness of the interview process. One technique is the Patterned Behavior Description Interview (PBDI), in which a special set of questions is incorporated into the interview. This process allows the interviewers to move beyond asking general questions to focus on what applicants have actually done in the past regarding certain situations. "The PBDI zeros in on what applicants have accomplished (or failed to accomplish) and how they went about doing it, in situations similar to ones they will face on the job" (Janz, 1989, p. 159). For example, an interviewer might ask an applicant how he or she responded to a hostile client, what circumstances were involved, and how the applicant handled the situation. The answers to this question reveal the specific choices the applicant has made in the past. Long-standing patterns of behavior are highly predictive of future behavior.

A second related technique is the situational interview, which poses hypothetical questions to applicants such as "What would you do if . . . ?" and is one of the few approaches to interviewing that are based on any type of theory (in this case, goal-setting theory). Goal-setting theory states that intentions or goals are the immediate precursors of a person's behavior (Locke & Latham, 1984). "The purpose of the situational interview is to identify a potential employee's intentions by presenting that person with a series of job-related incidents, and asking what he or she would do in that situation" (Latham, 1989, p. 171). The technique uses job analysis and performance-appraisal analyses to devise ways of scoring an applicant's response to a "what if" question in relation to what interviewers think would result in effective job performance. Interviewers then use the scoring criteria to rate each applicant. Results from a number of recent studies have shown relatively high levels of reliability and validity (see Latham, 1989, for specific guidelines on how to use this technique).

To summarize, during the interview phase, train your interviewers in the basic phases and principles of the selection process. Develop a list of standard questions to be asked of each applicant by the same interviewer (interviewers, of course, can ask nonstandardized follow-up questions, but all applicants should be asked the same "core" set of questions). The committee should set aside a quiet place for the interview in which there are no interruptions. Choose a person to lead the interview through the opening, information gathering, and closing phases. Finally, establish a realistic time line for the selection process and inform all applicants of how and when they will be notified.

Selecting the Person and Notifying the Other Applicants

Once the final candidates have been interviewed, their references may be called to clarify questions or issues that have arisen during the interview. Reference checks can be important for obtaining information on how the applicant interacted with his or her fellow employees; exploring questions left unanswered during the interview; and determining work habits, attendance, and other criteria of performance. The most cost-effective approach is to phone references, especially if you use open-ended and nondirective questions that seek to confirm the facts of the person's position (such as the date of hire, job responsibilities, relationships with colleagues, rapport with clients). Experienced interviewers keep their approach on the phone businesslike, and they avoid sounding too eager to hire the person. One of the most important questions to ask is whether the reference would hire this person again ("the rehire question"). This question may elicit information that is valuable for screening candidates. Do not reveal information obtained in reference checks to the candidate. If the person is not hired, state that the person who was selected more nearly met the qualifications of the position. Divulging information from references is a violation of confidentiality, and many organizations are therefore becoming wary of releasing information (Jensen, 1981). In fact, some human services and other agencies are being advised to provide only information regarding the duration of the former employee's employment unless the screening agency can provide a signed release of information from the applicant or unless the employee, upon leaving that agency, had signed a form authorizing the release of performance-related and other reference information.

After contacting the references of the highly rated candidates, the selection committee chooses one candidate by assessing the information collected about his or her job-related qualifications and the degree to which that candidate's career goals, practice skills, and philosophy of work fit the agency and the position. The person selected is usually offered the position over the phone, and if he or she accepts, is sent a written letter of confirmation (or asked to visit the agency to confirm his or her acceptance of the offer). Once the acceptance is received, the other applicants should be promptly notified and thanked for their interest in the position and the agency.

In carrying out this step in the selection process, administrators should be careful to contact a sufficient number of the applicant's references. The committee members should be encouraged to take their time to weigh carefully all the information that has been gathered to determine the most qualified and committed applicant. They also should consider whether the agency has a firm commitment from the primary candidate before notifying the other applicants. Finally, the letter notifying the other applicants should be worded sensitively to ease their disappointment and to thank them for their interest in the position.

Summary

This chapter has reviewed the steps and guidelines necessary for recruiting, screening, and selecting staff for human services agencies. These steps and guidelines are summarized in Figure 4, which follows on page 136. Organizational excellence is determined, in large part, by the staff's compatibility with and commitment to the program's mission. Sound recruitment and screening practices help ensure that effective staff are hired and that a minimum number of people are released during the probationary period. Although this process requires organizational, analytical, and interpersonal skills, it is critical for obtaining high-quality personnel.

Figure 4. Summary Checklist for Recruiting, Screening, and Selecting Employees

Step 1: Developing a Job Description and Minimum Qualifications

A. Does the job description contain clear and specific task statements that describe the essential duties of this position?
B. Are the knowledge, skills, abilities, educational degrees (if any), and years of related job experience specified anywhere?
C. Do the required minimum qualifications for the job match the work to be performed; that is, can you substantiate the connections between the education and experience required and the tasks of the job?

Step 2: Employee Recruitment

A. Do the job announcements include the necessary details of the position?
B. Are the announcements clearly worded?
C. Is the application deadline realistic, given the usual delays in dissemination and publication; that is, does the deadline allow the applicant sufficient time to respond to the announcement?
D. Have you distributed the announcement to enough community, professional, or other groups? Have you used both formal and informal networks in publicizing the position?
E. Is a record being kept of how and where the position was advertised or posted, including personal recruitment efforts?

Step 3: Screening Job Applicants Using Application Forms and Tests (if Appropriate)

A. Does the application form provide information that helps you determine whether the applicant has related education, training, and experience?
B. Does the application form contain questions that are illegal according to EEO laws?
C. Can you structure the application form and process so applicants are asked to submit a cover letter or other summary statements to highlight how their training and experience qualify them for the position?

Step 4: Conducting the Screening Interview

A. Have you trained the interviewers in the basic phases and principles of the selection process?
B. Have you developed a list of standard questions to be asked of each applicant by the same interviewer?
C. Has a quiet place been set aside for the interview, and phone or other interruptions prevented?
D. Have you chosen a person to lead the interview through the opening, information-gathering, and closing phases?
E. Have you established a time line for the selection process and informed each applicant of how and when he or she will be notified?

Step 5: Selecting the Person and Notifying the Other Applicants

A. Have you contacted a sufficient number of applicants' references?
B. Has the committee weighed carefully all the information gathered to determine the most qualified and committed applicant?
C. Do you have a firm commitment from the primary candidate before notifying the other applicants?
D. Is your letter notifying the other applicants worded sensitively to ease their disappointment and thank them for their interest in the position?

SKILLS-APPLICATION EXERCISE 1

Equal Employment Opportunity Exercise

According to current law and/or EEOC policy:

1. You may keep on file information concerning your employee's race, color, religion, sex, or national origin.
    T_____   F_____   Don't know_____

2. If your department is charged with one form of discrimination and the EEOC's investigation finds the charge to be untrue, the EEOC may find you guilty of another form of discrimination even if you were not charged with it.
    T_____   F_____   Don't know_____

3. You may use the fact that a job applicant has a long arrest record as a reason for not hiring him or her.
    T_____   F_____   Don't know_____

4. You may require a pregnant woman to take a leave of absence at a specified time before her delivery date.
    T_____   F_____   Don't know_____

5. An employer must give a woman who has been on maternity leave her *same* job and salary and guarantee no loss of seniority when she is ready to return to work.
    T_____   F_____   Don't know_____

6. If a job applicant's religious faith requires that he or she not work on a normal workday, you may refuse to hire him or her.
    T_____   F_____   Don't know_____

7. Even if your department has few or no staff members who are from racial minorities, it is permissible for you to refuse to hire a person from a racial minority because he or she failed an employment test.
    T_____   F_____   Don't know_____

8. This decision is permissible: John is 60. Bill is 38. You choose Bill because he is younger and, therefore, will be able to devote more years to the department before retirement.
    T_____   F_____   Don't know_____

9. You may terminate or refuse to hire a white man because of a record of convictions for crimes.
    T_____   F_____   Don't know_____

10. You may discharge a man for refusing to cut his long hair.
    T_____   F_____   Don't know_____

11. You may refuse to hire an applicant because of a poor credit rating.
    T_____   F_____   Don't know_____

12. It is permissible to refuse employment to someone without a car.
    T_____   F_____   Don't know_____

continued

13. General questions about a high school or college degree may be asked during an interview even though that educational degree is not necessary to perform the job.
   T_____ F_____ Don't know_____
14. You may ask an applicant's age or date of birth.
   T_____ F_____ Don't know_____
15. You may ask an applicant if he or she is a citizen or ask his or her place of birth so as not to violate immigration laws.
   T_____ F_____ Don't know_____
16. You may ask applicants if they have any mental or physical handicaps that relate to their fitness to perform a particular job.
   T_____ F_____ Don't know_____
17. You may ask an applicant whether he or she is married.
   T_____ F_____ Don't know_____

SOURCE: Abstracted from materials developed by Gloria J. Rendon, Training Section, Personnel Administration, University of Utah, Salt Lake City. Used with permission.

Answers to Equal Opportunity Exercise

NOTE: These answers must be viewed with some caution because EEO regulations are periodically revised and the decisions of local court cases may have implications for employment practices in your agency.

1. T On application forms, this information is separated before the application is screened.
2. T
3. F The person has to be *convicted* and the crime job-related.
4. F This decision is generally made by a woman and her physician except if the woman is ignoring her physician's orders. In corrections and other fields, the employer can require a leave of absence if there is a possibility of physical assault.
5. F The employer may reinstate her in a comparable job.
6. T But the employer is required to make a good-faith effort to adjust the schedule before refusing to hire or terminating the candidate or employee.
7. T Provided that the employment test is objective, valid, and job-related.
8. F Age discrimination is illegal.
9. T The issue is conviction—not merely arrest, and it depends on the job. If the conviction is not job-related or if you hired other convicts who were not of ethnic minorities, you may be violating EEO policy.
10. F Generally the length of hair is not a condition for firing an employee. But the decision depends on the job because a hair net may be required, especially in restaurants and institutional food services. In addition, a police department was upheld in a recent Supreme Court case for mandating short hairstyles because of special circumstances, such as safety.

continued

11. T It applies only in certain cases, however, because the poor credit rating has to be job-related. (For example, to work at certain bank jobs, you have to be bonded with a bonding company, and bonding is contingent upon a good credit rating.)

12. F Not owning a car does not mean being without transportation— except in areas without mass transportation where the job requires a personal mode of transportation.

13. F An educational degree is not necessary for the job.

14. T Possibly, but only for work in a liquor store or other positions for which the age requirement is clearly related.

15. T But this question is controversial and varies according to the way it is asked. Use questions such as the following: Are you a citizen? (Yes or no). If not, do you have a visa? Do you have a "green card"? This is a difficult situation because the personnel department sometimes checks visas or green cards before applicants are interviewed, but the interviewer does not have this information. Check with your state employment office to ensure that your practices conform to the latest set of regulations.

16. T But how the question is asked is important. One appropriate question is this: Do you have a physical disability or mental or physical condition that would prevent you from performing this job?

17. F

SKILLS-APPLICATION EXERCISE 2

Interviewing Skills

Members of a selection committee or graduate students can practice these interviewing skills by dividing into separate groups to develop a set of interview questions for a position. One member of each group becomes an "applicant" for the other group, while the other members choose who will lead the interview and which persons will ask what questions. The "applicants" from each group switch and are then interviewed by the other group. After the interview, the applicant and the group members debrief by discussing what went well and what aspects of the process could be improved. This interviewing simulation allows members of a selection committee to pilot-test a set of interview questions and practice interviewing skills.

References

American Psychological Association. (1980). *Principles for the validation and use of personnel selection procedures* (2nd ed.). Washington, DC: Author.

Attard, J. (1984). *You can hire the perfect employee.* Westbury, NY: Caddylak Publishing.

Beach, D. S. (1975). *Personnel: The management of people at work.* New York: Macmillan.

Campbell, A. (1983). Hiring for results: Interviews that select winners. *Business Quarterly, 48*(4), 57–61.

Campion, S. E., & Arvey, R. D. (1989). Unfair discrimination in the employment interview. In R. W. Eder & G. R. Ferris (Eds.), *The employment interview—Theory, research and practice* (pp. 61–74). Newbury Park, CA: Sage.

Carlson, R. E., Thayer, P. W., Mayfield, E. C., & Peterson, D. A. (1971). Improvements in the selection interview. *Personnel Journal, 50*(4), 268–275, 317.

Eder, R. W., & Ferris, G. R. (Eds.). (1989). *The employment interview—Theory, research and practice.* Newbury Park, CA: Sage.

Equal Employment Opportunity Commission, Department of Justice, Department of Labor. (1978). Uniform guidelines on employee selection procedures. *Federal Register, 43,* 38920–39315.

Glueck, W. F. (1978). *Personnel: A diagnostic approach* (rev. ed.). Dallas: Business Publications.

Goodale, J. G. (1989). Effective employment interviewing. In R. W. Eder & G. R. Ferris (Eds.), *The employment interview—Theory, research and practice* (pp. 307–324). Newbury Park, CA: Sage.

Howell, W. C., & Dipboye, R. L. (1982). *Essentials of industrial and organizational psychology.* Homewood, IL: Dorsey Press.

Janz, T. (1989). The patterned behavior description interview: The best prophet of the future is the past. In R. W. Eder & G. R. Ferris (Eds.), *The employment interview—Theory, research and practice* (pp. 158–168). Newbury Park, CA: Sage.

Jensen, J. (1981). How to hire the right person for the job. *Grantsmanship Center News, 9*(3), 21–31.

Klingner, D. E., & Nalbandian, J. (1985). *Public personnel management: Contexts and strategies.* Englewood Cliffs, NJ: Prentice Hall.

Latham, G. P. (1989). The reliability, validity, and practicality of the situational interview. In R. W. Eder & G. R. Ferris (Eds.), *The employment interview—Theory, research and practice* (pp. 169–182). Newbury Park, CA: Sage.

Locke, E. A., & Latham, G. P. (1984). *Goal setting: A motivational technique that works.* Englewood Cliffs, NJ: Prentice Hall.

Mayfield, E. C., Brown, S. H., & Hamstra, B. W. (1980). Selection interviewing in the life insurance industry: An update of research and practice. *Personnel Psychology, 33,* 725–739.

McCormick, E. J. (1979). *Job analysis: Methods and applications.* New York: Amacom.

Meritt-Haston, R., & Weyley, K. N. (1983). Educational requirements: Legality and validity. *Personnel Psychology, 36,* 743–753.

Mufson, D. W. (1986). Selecting child care workers using the California Psychological Inventory. *Child Welfare, 65,* 83–88.

Pecora, P. J., & Austin, M. J. (1983). Declassification of social service jobs: Issues and strategies. *Social Work, 28,* 421–426.

Pecora, P. J., & Austin, M. J. (1987). *Managing human services personnel.* Newbury Park, CA: Sage.

Robertson, M. A. (1982). *Personnel administration employment interviewing guide for supervisors.* Salt Lake City: University of Utah, Office of Personnel Administration.

Ross, A. R., & Hoeltke, G. (1985). A tool for selecting residential child care workers: An initial report. *Child Welfare, 64*, 46–55.

Shafritz, J. M., Hyde, A. C., & Rosenbloom, D. H. (1986). *Personnel management in government: Politics and process* (3rd ed.). New York: Marcel Dekker.

Teare, R. J., Higgs, C., Gauthier, T. P., & Feild, H. S. (1984). *Classification validation processes for social service positions: Vol. 1, Overview.* Silver Spring, MD: National Association of Social Workers.

Zedeck, S., & Cascio, W. F. (1984). Psychological issues in personnel decisions. *Annual Review of Psychology, 35*, 461–518.

CHAPTER
9

Designing and Sustaining Effective Organizational Teams

Darlyne Bailey

The presence of teams in the workplace has a long history. However, as the type, amount, and complexity of the demands on America's human services establishment increase, organizational leaders are rediscovering the productivity of effective teams.

Teams are being used in a wide range of activities, including researching new programs and services, developing clinical treatment plans for the improved care of patients, and redesigning the organizational environment. The literature supports this posture. Almost every new book on organizational effectiveness stresses the importance of teamwork (see, for example, Clifford & Cavanagh, 1985; Pasmore, 1988; Peters & Waterman, 1982). However, despite this recognition, a study by Dyer (1987) showed that few managers actually take the time to understand when and how to develop and sustain these teams. In interviews with 300 managers from various organizations, Dyer found that less than 25 percent had instituted programs to ensure the continued success of teams. Moreover, while all these managers were on teams themselves, only 10 to 15 percent had bosses who had addressed this issue with them.

A lack of information may be the reason for this inattention. Managers may not realize that effective teams require at least these conditions: (1) an environmental context in which the organization's goals and resources support the team's needs, (2) team members with the skills necessary to accomplish the task, and (3) a manager as team leader who can keep the focus on both the task and interpersonal processes.

Thus, this chapter explores three issues: (1) the process of team development (how teams are formed and how they become functional), (2) typical behaviors of team members during the course of the team's existence, and most important, (3) the requisite behaviors and skills that effective team leaders must learn and enact (why wanting a team to be productive is just not enough).

This chapter presents these issues through an analysis of one model for the development of teams and a case vignette, and concludes with suggestions for the further development of skills in working with teams. The words *team* and *group* are used interchangeably to describe a work unit that "has a particular process of working together, one in which members identify and fully use one another's resources and facilitate their mutual interdependence toward more effective problem solving and task accomplishment" (Hanson & Lubin, 1988, p. 77).

Now more than ever, organizations need leaders who both understand the needs of human services organizations and teams and can clearly assess their abilities and reach out for help in attending to their limitations. The future of human services organizations depends on these abilities.

Organizational Teams: Past, Present, and Future

Recognition of the strength of people when they work together in organizations dates back to the 1800s. A number of scholars have made notable contributions in this area, as follows:

Late 1800s and early 1900s. The German sociologist Max Weber preached the need for (and potential dangers of) authority and rationality in working with organized groups of people (see Weber, 1930). Le Bon (1960; originally published in 1903) discovered the powerful effects of this collectivity on the individual group member. Frederick Taylor (1978; originally published in 1911), the subject of the novel and film *Cheaper by the Dozen,* studied the process of efficiency and proposed that large systems are most efficient when their organizational members are scientifically managed. At about the same time, Mayo (1933) conducted his Hawthorne Western Electric Studies and noted the relationship between group identity and cohesion in informal groups and worker productivity. Concurrently, Freud (1922) analyzed the effects of conflict in groups.

Mid-1900s. Lewin (1947), credited as the father of modern group dynamics, explored the phenomena of the formation and development of groups through laboratory and experience-based learning. Maslow (1965) and Rogers (1970) wrote about the almost limitless quality of human potential when fundamental needs are met within a culture of positive self and other regard. Almost simultaneously, Katz and Kahn (1966), McClelland (1961), McGregor (1966), and Von Bertalanfy (1968), each working separately, generated a collective description. They viewed organizations as open systems composed of subsystems of people whose level of satisfaction with the tasks, co-workers, and authorities plays a major role in determining the productivity of organizations.

Late 1900s. Ouchi (1981) and Pascale and Athos (1981) suggested that Americans have much to learn from studying alternative forms of management, such as those used in some of the highly successful Japanese organizations. One example is the quality circle, a method in which a team of employees actively participates in the resolution of the organization's problems.

Although the quality circle, as a variant of team building, continues to receive mixed reviews among American workers, an article in *Business Week* ("The Payoff from

Teamwork," 1989) helped bring the role of work groups up-to-date. In some companies, the problem-solving nature of the quality circles first evolved into what were called special-purpose teams that focused on specific tasks through the collaboration of staff and management. Then, in the mid to late 1980s, teams of employees began producing entire products instead of parts of products (such as a whole car instead of just the doors). Now called *self-managing teams*, they have also assumed responsibility for some management-level decisions. While studies continue to explore the dynamics of self-managing teams (such as their cost and benefits and the role of external leadership), the literature describes this form of organizational work group as the wave of the future (Courtright, Fairhurst, & Rogers, 1989; Manz & Sims, 1987).

As historians readily tell us, the future carries the thumbprints of the past. The first need for order within groups of people was recognized in the 1800s. The scientific management of people (often referred to as "Taylorism") was proposed in the early 1900s, only to be ameliorated by the role of social support and the need for managing conflict. The mid-1900s brought recognition of the dynamics of the evolution of groups and of how groups are most effective in raising organizational productivity when the members' individual and social needs are met. Now, in the late 1900s, American organizations in both the for-profit and nonprofit sectors are learning from overseas neighbors and experimenting with innovative designs for organizational teams.

The next section covers the general activities and requisite skills inherent in task-oriented teams. It presents many of the aforementioned values and ideologies of some of the major contributors to the current understanding of organizational teams.

Teams: Stages, Behaviors, and Skills of Leaders

Given the long-standing and robust history of organizational teams, it is not surprising that there are many models to describe their evolution. Regardless of the differences in specific responsibilities, size, and the necessary degree of internal collaboration among these teams, once formed, all these groups seem to go through similar stages.

Small-group theorists tend to see these models as developmental, with the successful movement through one stage dependent on the satisfactory completion of the stage or stages that preceded it (see, for example, Bennis & Shepard, 1956; Dunphy, 1974; Moosbruker, 1988; Neilsen, 1972). These models may have anywhere from three to seven stages, but one five-stage model (Tuckman and Jensen, 1977) is comprehensive, descriptive, and easily remembered. Tuckman and Jensen's model includes the stages of forming, storming, norming, performing, and adjourning. Using this model as a guide, one may describe the developmental challenges and skills of the leaders of managerial teams that are necessary to facilitate the team's successful movement through the stages.

Table 1 consists of four columns: the developmental stages, the general types of behaviors that team members exhibit at each of these stages, the corresponding tasks

Table 1. Team Development: Stages, Behaviors, Tasks, and Skills

STAGES	MEMBERS' BEHAVIORS	LEADER'S TASKS	LEADER'S SKILLS
1. *Forming:* People volunteer or are recruited to work together on a common task.	Questioning the leader about the group's purpose, appropriate behaviors of members, and leader's role Attributing in-team status to members on the basis of outside-of-team information Obeying the leader Discussion patterns are jerky, and there are long periods of silence	Provide structure regarding boundaries of the team (such as the frequency and place of meetings, the organization's reason for forming the team, time lines for achieving the team's task) Offer guidance in setting directions for the accomplishment of the task Solicit each member's opinions and ideas Encourage dialogue	Awareness of a personal leadership style Effective communication Thorough knowledge of the fit between the team's task and organizational goals
2. *Storming:* Individual and subgroup differences of opinions, values, skills, and interests start to surface.	Expressing opinions and disagreements Exploring the degrees of individual power and challenging the leader's role and style Attending to and avoiding the team's task Emergence of cliques and bonds	Discuss the team's decision-making process Model appropriate awareness of self and others Provide the team with the resources necessary to accomplish the task Help the team to establish procedures and norms for the resolution of conflict	Management of different values, behaviors, and skills Awareness of personal strengths and limitations Use of process and content

continued

Table 1. Continued

STAGES	MEMBERS' BEHAVIORS	LEADER'S TASKS	LEADER'S SKILLS
3. *Norming:* The team focuses on the need for order and guidelines for how to work together.	Stabilizing the team's purpose, authority relationships, individual levels. and types of participation Exhibiting in-group humor Emergence of informal leadership Establishing procedures for the resolution of conflict and the accomplishment of the task	Adhere to the team's established structure and procedures Ensure that the team's actions are in accordance with what the team *really* wants to do Infuse the team with enthusiasm and energy Reward individual and team efforts Acknowledge and reinforce the informal leadership Protect the team from outside interferences	Mentoring Management of agreement Balancing work with play Buffering the team from ongoing operations
4. *Performing:* The team delivers the completed task.	Producing results: alignment of members' energies and interests with the team's task	Vigilance: attend to the team's need for fine tuning its skills and attitudes Develop mechanisms for the continued monitoring of the team	Visioning Listening with the "third ear" Evaluation
5. *Adjourning:* The original need for the team no longer exists.	Assessing process and product Dissolving the team	Publicly acknowledge the team's accomplishments	Positive regard of self and others

SOURCE: B. W. Tuckman and M.A.C. Jensen, "Stages in Small Group Development Revisited," *Group and Organization Studies*, 2, 419–427. Copyright © 1977 by Sage Publications, Inc. Reprinted by permission of Sage Publications, Inc.

for the team leader, and the behavioral skills that are necessary for the leader to help the team accomplish its goals in ways that are efficient in terms of time and resources and satisfying to the individuals and the group as a whole.

Stages of Development

In the *forming* stage, people come together to work on a common task. Whether some of these people have previously worked together on a similar project or all have joined in the past to accomplish a different goal, the point remains that this is the first time that all these individuals are uniting to work on this task. Amid questions about the purpose of the group, the role of the leader, and attributions regarding each member's potential power in the group and real influence outside the group, the leader must provide general guidelines for the group and take steps to establish a group culture that fosters and rewards the free exchange of ideas and opinions.

"We had a wonderful group established. Harmonious. Supportive. Even established our own goals and norms. Then our boss came back from her meeting and we got task oriented very quickly."

To accomplish these tasks, at this stage the leader must have both a strong sense of self-awareness and an understanding of the interrelatedness of the team's task and the organization's goals. Moreover, the leader must be able to communicate this personal and professional information in a way that models candor and appropriate self-disclosure and acknowledges the value of the team to the effectiveness of the total organization. It is these skills that will help the group members begin to risk sharing their ideas, an activity that will move the group from forming into storming.

In the second stage, *storming,* as individual group members and small sub-groups continue to share their different perspectives, other differences become more noticeable. Differences in values, types and levels of skills, and degrees of interest in and commitment to the group's task are only a few of the many areas that may become reasons for members to be attracted to or repelled by each other. As these differences emerge, members also begin to explore their own leadership abilities, often by challenging the role and style of the designated leader. At this time, the leader must continue to model self-awareness and help the group establish guidelines, yet focus more explicitly on issues of self in the context of others and on procedures for resolving conflicts and making group-level deci-sions. While ensuring that the team has the concrete resources (such as time, space, and materials) that are required to accomplish the task, the leader must now demonstrate additional skills to equip the team members with the necessary intellectual and emotional tools. The leader's ability to recognize and appreciate the sundry differences that arise in this group will serve as a guide for how the members can utilize these differences to make the team's time together more productive. The leader's knowledge of the difference between the group's *process* (the methods and procedures the group uses to achieve its goals) and its *content* (the activities and issues that a group discusses and enacts to achieve its goals) must be used to help the group work effectively in both areas. It is only when the group as a whole agrees on how it will disagree that it is able to move into the third stage of development.

In the stage of *norming,* the team must continue its work on establishing "codes of conduct" for how the members will interact. With the abatement of the tensions surrounding the issues of individual identity and authority, the bonding of members to the subgroups, the bonding among the subgroups, and the purpose of the team, informal leaders start to emerge as the group determines exactly how it will complete the task. Amid a strong sense of group identity, the leader must continue to focus on content and process by helping the group adhere to its procedures; ensuring that the necessary resources are maintained; enthusiastically rewarding the efforts of individuals, subgroups, and the team as a whole; and supporting the members who assume leadership roles. Moreover, the leader must help the group build on its new process for disagreeing by teaching its members how to manage agreement—how to avoid the trap of agreeing just to agree that members often submit to at this stage to maintain the group's harmony. When the group learns how to balance work with play and agreement with disagreement, it is then able to accomplish the task and moves into the performing stage.

This fourth stage, *performing,* is really the payoff, when the team's energies and interests are focused on completing the task. The leader's role is offstage directing—attending to the fine tuning of the members' skills and feelings of being team players while assisting the team to develop skills to use in monitoring the execution of the task. Modeling skills of visioning (communicating a sense of what this team can be like when the task is completed); responding to the individuals' and team's felt yet often unspoken needs, desires, and fears; and joining the team in the collective evaluation of the finished product move the team to the final stage.

In this fifth stage, *adjourning,* members acknowledge and assess the total process and content of the team as they move toward dissolution. Concurrently, the leader informally and publicly recognizes the team's accomplishments as belonging to the *entire* team. The primary skill at this time is the leader's ability to have a positive regard for her or his role in this process and for the roles and responsibilities of the other members. The worth of the product is thus a symbol of a job well done by an effectively functioning team.

Although these team behaviors and the accompanying tasks and requisite skills of leaders are understandable, teams often get "stuck" in one or more of these stages. At these times, the leader's skills are best appreciated for their combined effect of facilitating the group's development. To understand these leadership skills better, consider some key moments in the development of a social service agency's planning team. This group consists of members of the board of trustees and the staff. Although this organization and its personnel are fictitious, the issues and process are true to life.

The Case of the Eastside Youth Center

Because of rapidly shrinking resources, particularly money and appropriately trained personnel, as well as the changing needs of the community and the demand for increased accountability from funding bodies, the Eastside Youth Center (EYC) has decided to develop a three-year strategic plan. This process will enable EYC to revisit the agency's mission statement, staffing patterns, and programs and to forecast the changes that are needed in the structure or operations to help the agency become a multiservice family center.

At a recent monthly meeting, the board unanimously decided to hire a local consultant to outline the strategic planning process and help the organization move through it. Because of limited funds, the consultant agreed to meet with a planning team at the beginning and six months later and, if necessary, to meet periodically with the team leader to answer questions and suggest subsequent steps.

The executive director and members of the board selected a planning team of four board members and three staff members. The president of the board was quickly appointed the team leader for the same reason she had earlier been voted president: a sound background in leadership training, some of which she had obtained on her own and the rest of which her place of employment had provided.

Forming

At a half-day workshop for the team, the consultant described the major steps and issues of a good strategic plan. The team members asked many questions, and everyone left the meeting feeling comfortable and confident about the pending process. However, two weeks later, at the first real meeting, the members focused the discussion more on themselves than on the plan. They began to refer to their community and business status and to position themselves to influence the others.

The group also began to question the expertise of the team leader. Whenever the leader would try to refocus the conversation, the group fell silent. The leader then began to make fewer statements and ask more questions, such as: "Given the fact that the team is to develop a plan to recommend to the board at the end of six months, how frequently do you want to meet?" And, "What ideas do each of you have about the process as a result of our workshop with the consultant?" The members slowly began to respond to the leader's questions, offering their ideas and deciding that the group would meet for three to four hours every other week.

In the next two meetings, the group began to explore the specifics of the task more actively, with the leader modeling skills of active listening, asking open-ended questions, and providing basic information about the mechanics of the planning process.

Storming

In the fourth meeting, the leader noticed that the members were talking to her less and arguing more among themselves. A week earlier, she had telephoned the consultant and had happily reported the team's progress. The consultant reminded her of the "calm before the storm" and urged her to remember her conflict-mediation skills. So when the members began to quarrel about the superiority of one person's ideas over another's and to imply that the board members' and staff's intentions were different, the leader pointed out what they were doing. She noted the benefits of each subgroup's perspective and asked the entire team to decide the type of process they would use for appreciating and then using the differences they had identified earlier.

At first, the leader was accused of not being direct enough. Then she was told that she was too dictatorial. The leader maintained her position and noticed that the next three meetings were attended by only two board members and two staff members. She began to urge the group to talk about the content of planning, as well as the process they were using to work as a team.

Norming

In the eighth meeting, the members began to talk about wanting more guidelines for the team. A lively discussion ensued about requirements for attendance and procedures to use for resolving disagreements. The leader told the story of the "Abilene Paradox" (see Harvey, 1974), in which an entire group of people agreed to do something that actually was bad for the group and that no one really had wanted to do—a case of mismanaging agreement. Sprinkled throughout this otherwise serious conversation were quips and jokes about the leader and the team members. There was a general feeling of camaraderie and anticipation as the group reviewed its progress to date and articulated future steps.

During the next two meetings, the leader began to notice that one board member was taking a leadership role within the group by starting the meetings, soliciting comments, and then summarizing a seemingly disparate list of ideas. She began to support this man's behavior and met with him twice outside the group to get his ideas about how the group could finish the plan. Once, during a monthly meeting of the entire board, when a motion was made to expand the team's responsibilities, the man supported the leader in refusing this additional work. At the leader's suggestion, a prepresentation party was held for the team members at this man's house—a celebration of all the work that had been done and a rehearsal of the team's recommendations to the rest of the board.

Performing

Just before the team submitted its plan, it had its final meeting with the consultant to get another perspective on the recommendations. The leader encouraged the team to be strategically creative with its suggestions and then facilitated a discussion about its work as a team. All the members were animated about their work together over the past several months and felt as though each had played a significant role in the process. The consultant also was satisfied with the results and suggested that the team volunteer to monitor the effectiveness of the plan, pending its ratification by the rest of the board. The group agreed and immediately began to formulate a mechanism for the continued evaluation of both the implementation of the plan and the process of the team.

It is not surprising that when the team presented the three-year strategic plan for the agency, the board and the executive director were pleased. The discussion was animated, creative, and productive. The board voted to continue the team for another six months to oversee the plan and assess future steps, such as installing another monitoring team and rotating members through it. The meeting ended with the team leader publicly thanking her colleagues and distributing framed certificates of appreciation to each member of the team.

Adjourning

Even though the original team was going to stay intact, the new tasks and responsibilities were different. The leader encouraged the team to celebrate the ending of the initial work. She began this closing by sharing her perceptions of the team's progress, focusing on both the process and the product. All the members expressed their views and, while praising themselves and the leader, began to talk about the first steps to take in their new roles as monitors of the plan.

This case demonstrates the five stages of Tuckman and Jensen's (1977) model of team development. It is now important to note four facts. First, while a team progresses through these stages, it may also regress owing to a change in the membership, responsibilities, or the need to work through the issues presented at an earlier stage.

Second, a team's developmental stage may have nothing to do with its age. Depending on the roles and responsibilities of a team, its relationship to the rest of the organization, and the effectiveness of its leader, a team that has been working together for two years may be stuck in an early stage, such as storming. It is likely to stay at that stage unless it is helped, whereas a much newer team may rapidly progress through the various stages.

Third, although there are clear benefits to establishing work teams, there are also some costs, or what Schindler-Rainman (1988) called "negative aspects," to using teams. Some reasons to avoid forming a team include the incompatibility of the members' commitments, the lack of a sense of purpose and direction, a member who cannot work as part of the team, or the lack of organizational support. Thus, managers must weigh the costs and benefits of forming work teams before they actually form the teams.

Fourth, the team does not usually move from one clearly differentiated stage to the next. As with all models, this one represents an ideal type. In reality, the stages tend to be less obvious and a team may even remain between stages for awhile.

The identification of the typical behaviors of members and the skills that the management needs the team leader to possess, as well as an analysis of Tuckman and Jensen's (1977) model, all help managers become aware of the dynamics of work teams. This knowledge, combined with a clear sense of their own abilities and limitations, enables managers to help their teams become more productive for the organization and rewarding for their members.

Summary

This chapter has covered the concept of organizational teams, first as part of Weber's (1930) work on authority relationships, then as Lewin (1947) clearly described them, and finally in its current usage as quality circles, special-purpose teams, or self-managing teams. A developmental model was used to study the stages of the processes of the team's formation, maintenance, and termination. A vignette provided specific examples of the relationship among these stages, the members' behavior, the tasks of the leader, and the skills that the leader needs to accomplish his or her primary task—the facilitation of the team's development toward productivity.

From this chapter, managers should realize that teams change over time. Yet recognizing the team's stage of development at any point in time is only part of the challenge. The more important message is that managers must be willing to search for and use this information while recognizing and aligning their own abilities with the needs of the group. As organizational leaders and specialists, we know that the synergy that comes from effectively operating teams is limitless. Building teams is an ongoing process, one in which organizational managers have the most critical role.

SKILLS-APPLICATION EXERCISES

Here are some suggestions for exercises that can be used for experiential learning opportunities:

▶ You are assigned to lead a work team that has been meeting for several months. After reading the organization's charge to the team, you call a meeting and discover that only a third of the members have come. They are the same third that usually comes, and they call themselves the "real workers" on the team. What do you do and say? Why?

▶ You are hired as a consultant to facilitate the merger of two small nonprofit organizations. As part of the premerger agreement, the management teams of both agencies have been asked to form the leadership of the new organization. How would you get these people to work as a team? What initial problems or issues would you expect to encounter?

▶ You are asked to write a chapter in a new book about the development of teams, highlighting the major principles and skills that managers need to learn. What do you write about and why?

References

Bennis, W. G., & Shepard, H. (1956). A theory of group development. *Human Relations, 9,* 415–437.

Courtright, J. A., Fairhurst, G. T., & Rogers, E. L. (1989). Interaction patterns in organic and mechanistic systems. *Academy of Management Journal, 32*(4), 773–802.

Clifford, D., & Cavanagh, R. T. (1985). *The winning performance.* New York: Bantam Books.

Dunphy, D. C. (1974). *The primary group: A handbook for analysis and field research.* New York: Appleton-Century-Crofts.

Dyer, W. G. (1987). *Team building: Issues and alternatives* (2nd ed.). Cambridge, MA: Addison-Wesley.

Freud, S. (1922). *Group psychology and the analysis of the ego.* London: Hogarth Press.

Hanson, P. G., & Lubin, B. (1988). Team building as group development. In W. B. Reddy & K. Jamison (Eds.), *Team building: Blueprints for productivity and satisfaction* (pp. 76–87). Washington, DC: NTL Institute–University Associates.

Harvey, J. (1974, Summer). Managing agreement in organizations: The Abilene paradox. *Organizational Dynamics,* 63–80.

Katz, D., & Kahn, R. L. (1966). *The social psychology of organizations.* New York: John Wiley & Sons.

Le Bon, G. (1960). *The crowd.* New York: Viking. (Original work published 1903).

Lewin, K. (1947). Frontiers in group dynamics: Concept method and reality in social equilibria and social change. *Human Relations, 1,* 5–41.

Manz, C. C., & Sims, H. P., Jr. (1987). Leading workers to lead themselves: The external leadership of self-managing work teams. *Administrative Science Quarterly, 32*(1), 106–129.

Maslow, A. H. (1965). *Eupsychian management: A journal.* Homewood, IL: Irwin-Dorsey.

Mayo, E. (1933). *The human problems of an industrial civilization.* New York: Macmillan.

McClelland, D. C. (1961). *The achieving society.* New York: Van Nostrand Reinhold.

McGregor, D. (1966). *Leadership and motivation.* Cambridge, MA: M.I.T. Press.

Moosbruker, J. (1988). Developing a productivity team: Making groups in work work. In W. B. Reddy & K. Jamison (Eds.), *Team building: Blueprints for productivity and satisfaction* (pp. 88–97). Washington, DC: NTL Institute–University Associates.

Neilsen, E. H. (1972). Understanding and managing intergroup conflict. In T. W. Lorsch & P. R. Lawrence (Eds.), *Managing group and intergroup relations* (pp. 329–343). Homewood, IL: Irwin-Dorsey.

Ouchi, W. G. (1981). *Theory 2: How American business can meet the Japanese challenge.* Cambridge, MA: Addison-Wesley.

Pascale, T., & Athos, A. G. (1981). *The art of Japanese management: Applications for American executives.* New York: Wagner Books.

Pasmore, W. (1988). *Designing effective organizations.* New York: John Wiley & Sons.

The payoff from teamwork. (1989, July 10). *Business Week,* 56–62.

Peters, T., & Waterman, R. (1982). *In search of excellence.* New York: Harper & Row.

Rogers, C. (1970). *Carl Rogers on encounter groups.* New York: Harper & Row.

Schindler-Rainman, E. (1988). Team building in voluntary organizations. In W. B. Reddy & K. Jamison (Eds.), *Team building: Blueprints for productivity and satisfaction* (pp. 119–123). Washington, DC: NTL Institute–University Associates.

Taylor, F. (1978). The principles of scientific management. In J. Shafritz & P. Whitbeck (Eds.), *Classics of organizational theory* (pp. 12–19). Oak Park, IL: Moore. (Original work published 1911).

Tuckman, B. W., & Jensen, M. A. C. (1977). Stages in small group development revisited. *Group and Organization Studies, 2,* 419–427.

Von Bertalanfy, L. (1968). *General systems theory.* New York: George Brazillier.

Weber, M. (1930). *The Protestant ethic and the spirit of capitalism.* (T. Parsons, trans.). New York: Charles Scribner's Sons.

Building a Pluralistic Workplace

Regina Nixon and Margaret Spearmon

The year 2000 will usher in a new millennium that will reflect dramatic changes in the demographic makeup of the American workplace. By the end of the 1990s, changes in the economy will be matched by significant new facts in both the for-profit and nonprofit sectors. Some of these new facts are as follows:

▶ The average age of the work force will be 39, and the supply of young entrants to the labor force will dwindle.

▶ Only 15 percent of the new entrants to the work force will be native white men.

▶ Women will constitute 64 percent of the new entrants to the labor force.

▶ People of color will make up 29 percent of the new entrants to the work force, double their present share of the labor market.

▶ Immigrants will represent 22 percent of the labor force.

▶ Some 600,000 legal and illegal immigrants will enter the United States annually throughout the remainder of this century (Johnston & Packer, 1987).

Taken together, these demographic changes mean that by the beginning of the 21st century, the American work force will be different from the present one. The workers will be older, and new arrivals will be largely people of color, women, and immigrants, who will make up more than five-sixths of the net additions.

Human services organizations must begin to evaluate the managerial implications of these dramatic shifts in the labor force. During the next decade, human services managers will need skill-based competencies for effectively managing and developing a work force that is becoming increasingly heterogeneous. To meet the challenge and to continue to deliver high-quality services, managers must be committed to ensuring that they create organizations in which culturally diverse groups are not merely present, but share the governance and administration. This chapter includes a definition of and rationale for pluralism as a goal for human services management, a set of principles for pluralistic management, and a set of benchmarks to assess an organization's current position with regard to issues of diversity and pluralism.

Principles of Pluralistic Management

Pluralism is different from diversity and multiculturalism, in that the latter are passive terms, often used interchangeably, that refer to an organization in which culturally diverse groups are merely present (Blell, 1990) in the workplace. Rarely do these concepts make explicit reference to the *active* notion of power. Power plays a primary role in organizational life, and it cannot be ignored by those who strive to comprehend and improve the internal functioning of organizations (Hollander & Offermann, 1990).

Unlike diversity and multiculturalism, pluralism embraces the dimension of power because it requires that leadership and administration be shared and "guarantees that power is not the exclusive domain of any single racial, ethnic, or gender group either unintentionally or intentionally" (Blell, 1990, p. 6). Pluralism also differs from integration, in which people of color, as well as white ethnics, are asked, "explicitly or implicitly, to abandon their cultural identity to merge into the majority community" (Blell, 1990, p. 6).

Pluralistic management, then, is leadership that aggressively pursues the creation of a workplace in which the values, interests, and contributions of diverse cultural groups are an integral part of the organization's mission, culture, policies, and procedures and in which these groups share power at every level. Valuing cultural differences, equity, and shared power are at the heart of pluralistic management.

The following principles of pluralistic management draw heavily on the writings of Crable (1989), Kunisawa (1988), Copeland (1988a, 1988b), Blell (1990), and Thomas (1990) and include these beliefs:

▶ Achieving a pluralistic work force is not only a moral imperative but a strategic one.

▶ Top management must make a commitment to create a pluralistic work force before fundamental structural and systemic changes can occur in the organization.

▶ A genuinely pluralistic workplace means changing the rules to accommodate cultural differences in style, perspectives, and world views.

▶ The contemporary definition of diversity embraces groupings of individuals by race; ethnicity; gender; age; physical characteristics; and similar values, experiences, and preferences.

▶ Cultural awareness and appreciation at the individual or group level are necessary but not sufficient conditions to transform an organization into a pluralistic workplace. Fundamental changes must take place in the institution's culture, policies, and administrative arrangements.

▶ Pluralistic managers value their own cultural heritage and those of others in the workplace.

▶ Pluralistic managers understand the value of diversity and seize the benefits that differences in the workplace offer.

▶ Pluralistic managers work to overcome barriers that hinder successful and authentic relationships among peers and subordinates who are culturally different from the mainstream stereotype.

▶ The empowerment of employees through career development, team building, mentoring, and participatory leadership is a cornerstone of the pluralistic workplace.

▶ Pluralistic management incorporates issues of diversity in organization-wide policies and practices and is not restricted to equal employment opportunity (EEO) policies and procedures.

▶ Skill in pluralistic management is an integral component of managerial competence.

▶ The ultimate goal of pluralistic management is to develop an organization that fully taps the human-resources potential of all its employees.

These managerial principles resonate with two central values of the social work profession: respect for the dignity and uniqueness of the individual and self-determination (Compton & Galaway, 1979). (Although these values are often revisited with respect to social work clients, it seems reasonable to apply the same values to personnel in human services organizations.) The value of respect for the individual's uniqueness and dignity welcomes diversity. The value of self-determination encourages choice and growth. Pluralistic management operationalizes these values by communicating a positive message to personnel: "Maximum opportunities for development and growth are available to all employees because each one is valued and highly prized."

A Typology of Organizational Progression

An organization's commitment to the development of a pluralistic work force begins with confronting a critical question: "Where does the leadership in the organization currently stand on issues of diversity and pluralism?" The Equity Institute (1990) constructed a typology that managers can use to assess where their organizations stand in this respect. The typology is a useful heuristic device that describes progressive levels of "diversity awareness" in organizations.

The Level 1 organization is a *token EEO organization*. It characteristically hires people of color and women at the bottom of the hierarchy, although a few tokens will be found in mid-level management. Those in management survive as long as they are perceived as "team players," which means that they "pose no challenges to the organization's mission, policies, and practices" (Equity Institute, 1990).

The Level 2 organization is the *affirmative action organization*. It aggressively recruits people of color and women, supports their growth and development, and encourages nonracist and nonsexist behaviors. Ironically, in this type of organization people of color learn that they must suppress their cultural identities and assimilate the Anglo-Western culture to climb higher up the corporate ladder.

Women learn that they must "act like men" to move ahead. Women and people of color, therefore, are still required to conform to policies, practices, and norms that were established by white men, who are dominant in senior-level management positions.

The Level 3 organization is the *self-renewing organization.* It is actively moving away from being a racist and sexist organization and becoming a pluralistic one. The self-renewing organization examines all aspects of the organization's mission, culture, values, operations, and managerial styles to assess their impact on the productivity, development, and career advancement of employees. Moreover, it explores the value of pluralism and looks for ways to redefine the organization to include a wide range of cultural perspectives.

The Level 4 organization is the *pluralistic* organization. It represents the highest form of organizational evolution in the awareness of diversity. The pluralistic organization reflects the contributions and interests of diverse cultural and social groups in its mission, operations, and delivery of services. It seeks to eliminate all forms of cultural and social oppression in the organization, and its work force is represented by different cultural and social groups at all levels. Even more significant, diversity in leadership is reflected in the organization's policymaking and governance. Equally important, the pluralistic organization exhibits a sensitivity to issues that affect the larger community and participates in socially responsible activities and programs.

An assessment of an organization's position along the diversity-pluralism continuum leads to a trilogy of questions: At what levels should interventions be targeted—the organization, the group, or the individual? What basic skills training do managers need to move the organization toward the pluralistic ideal? At what levels of management should skill-based training be focused? The following discussion considers these issues.

Interventions to Transform the Workplace

The process of changing an organization into a pluralistic workplace requires interventions at the organizational, group, and individual levels. Interventions that focus solely on changing the attitudes and behaviors of individuals or groups toward those who are culturally different will dissipate unless the organization's values, norms, and institutional arrangements are examined, restructured, or recreated (Reddy & Burke, 1988). Although the primary targets of discrimination in organizations continue to be people of color and women, these arrangements should also be carefully scrutinized to assess their disparaging impact on all employees in the organization. Empirical data support the idea that changing policies, rules, procedures, problem-solving techniques, administration, management, operating mechanisms, and enforcement contributes to changes in behavior (Alvarez, Lutterman, & Associates, 1979). Therefore, leadership in human service organizations must be committed to laying the ax to systemic roots in addition to interventions aimed at challenging and altering the attitudes and behaviors of individuals and groups.

Basic Managerial Skills

The issues of basic skills that are necessary for management in transition and the levels of management to which these skills should be targeted are interrelated and will be addressed in relation to the specific skills discussed in the following sections. Basically, management needs three types of "core" skills to facilitate the building of a pluralistic workplace: awareness skills, organizational assessment skills, and employee-empowerment skills. Although a sizable cadre of skills are required (for example, team building, communication styles, and conflict management), only three areas that are essential for management teams in the early stages of transition to a pluralistic workplace are discussed here.

Awareness Skills

Self-analysis of the "I"

Before human services managers and volunteer boards move toward a work force in which diversity is not only "celebrated" but genuine pluralism is sought, all levels of management—from frontline supervisors to executive directors and members of the board—must confront their own and others' "isms": racism, sexism, ethnism, classism, ageism, and so on. Ample research has documented the reality of conscious discrimination against people of color and women (see, for example, Fernandez, 1981; Harlan & Weiss, 1982; Mobley, 1982; Nixon, 1985a, 1985b). Effective human services managers must therefore become proficient in evaluating their own values, biases, and prejudices toward employees who are culturally or socially different from themselves.

Awareness and analysis of self (the "I") is a fundamental skill that managers can master through appropriate training. Self-analysis involves an examination of one's attitudes and behaviors related to differences. It is a necessary condition for managing cultural diversity because most people harbor some prejudice as a result of negative messages internalized during childhood from their families, significant others, or the media. Discriminatory actions against those who are different may range from blatant stereotypes to learned attitudes that are subtle or unconscious.

Management training in self-awareness should include the clarification of values; how values define attitudes and behavior; an evaluation of values, attitudes, and behaviors; positive modeling; and behavior modification. Miller (1988, p. 194) concluded that the question has changed from asking, "Do we want this person who is so obviously different on our team?" to "Am I willing to share power with the new person? How much of my white male cultural norms am I willing to modify to work with the new person?"

Cultural Literacy ("We and They")

Culture is the sum total of the values, attitudes, behaviors, and symbols that are transmitted within groups and communicated to successive generations to provide a cognitive map for actions and interpreting reality. In other words, culture is an important lens that influences the way people think, perceive, and act.

Culture, then, to a large extent influences the values and perspectives that people bring to the workplace, how they view their roles in the organization, how they can make a contribution, how they desire to be recognized for their efforts, and how they differ in work styles and problem solving. If managers do not understand or value employees' cultural heritage, how then can they begin to tap the employees' productive and creative potential fully (Copeland, 1988a)?

In addition to the rites of self-analysis, movement toward the pluralistic ideal requires that managers have knowledge of and appreciation for their own cultural heritage ("we") as well as those of others ("they"). This knowledge constitutes cultural literacy—one's proficiency in the values, behaviors, and symbols of one's own racial and ethnic background and those of others. Achieving cultural literacy means overcoming what Kunisawa (1988) called "cultural illiteracy" (see also Buonocare & Crable, 1986).

Pinderhughes (1989) underscored the significance of feeling positively about one's own cultural identity and the ability to value those who are culturally different. She concluded that individuals who are clear and positive about their own cultural identity and its meaning are less fearful and threatened by differences.

Communication between "we" and "they" can also be troublesome because such interaction brings people together who have different ways of thinking and acting and different cognitive maps for interpreting reality. Research has documented that difficulties occur when the motives and meaning of each other's behavior are misinterpreted because the attributions are based on different cultural norms and world views (Black & Mendenhall, 1990; Bochner, 1982; Triandis, 1972).

What are the implications of cultural literacy, that is, proficiency and comfort with "we" and "they," for the transition to a pluralistic workplace? A prerequisite to effective cross-cultural communication in a diverse work environment is the proficiency of managers at all levels of the organization in cultural literacy. Such proficiency will help reduce miscommunication, inappropriate behavior, and conflict and, equally significant, increase the performance and productivity of employees. Until the leaders of human services organizations appreciate the implications of culture, work, and performance, successful cross-cultural communication and the building of "authentic" relationships will be severely hindered.

Organizational Assessment Skills

Institutional racism and sexism are formidable barriers to achieving a pluralistic workplace. If the organizational culture and institutional arrangements produce exclusionary or disparaging outcomes for people of color, women, and other groups, the "I," "we," and "they" interventions will be attempted in vain. Put another way, institutional norms, values, and arrangements that impede the growth and productivity of all groups need to be examined, changed, or restructured, or the effects of cultural literacy will be short-lived.

The initial step in organizational assessment is to train mid-level managers, senior administrators, executive directors, and volunteer boards in the skills that are necessary for formally describing the organizational culture. This culture, simply defined, is the pattern of values, norms, and artifacts that frame the foundation of institutional practices, policies, and procedures. Although the description of culture may appear to be an easy task, some organizational norms and values are "overt and pervasive," whereas others are "subtle and difficult to discern" (del Bueno & Vincent, 1986, p. 15).

Crable (1989) presented four indicators that human services organizations can use to identify and describe the key elements of institutional culture: *laws, language, geography,* and *currency.* According to Crable, the most significant laws are the "informal rules" of the organization. These laws constitute the unwritten do's and don't's for organizational behavior. Language is also a critical aspect of culture because the savvy manager "knows what you can say to whom, when you can say it, how you can say it, and where you can say it" (Crable, 1989).

Geography is another significant element of culture because it locates key players in the organization and provides some indication of what they value. Knowledge of organizational geography is a prerequisite for effective communication and knowing how to achieve goals without an excessive investment in time. Finally, the knowledge of the organization's currency, that is, "things that will buy something," is as important as knowing how to "spend or invest" it.

The systematic articulation of the organizational culture is an essential leadership skill because there is a corresponding set of policies, practices, and procedures for each cultural norm, value, and artifact that will require analysis in the organizational assessment process. Analyses of the impact of these arrangements will determine the type of rewards and resources and their availability and distribution to all persons in the workplace. Policies, practices, and procedures that are found to be dysfunctional for specific groups will require strong leadership for change. System-wide failure can be solved only by system-wide change (Crable, 1989).

Employee Empowerment Skills

Gutierrez (1990, p. 149) defined *empowerment* as "a process of increasing personal, interpersonal, or political power so that individuals can take action to improve their life situations." The empowerment process, therefore, can occur at the individual, group, and organizational levels. For more than 10 years, important developments have changed the thinking about the exercise of power in the organization. Ideas about power sharing and participatory management mirror the shift from a leader-dominated organization to an expanded view of the involvement of employees in decision making. Such changes can be attributed to the greater attention that is being paid to teamwork, as exemplified in Japanese management practices (Hollander & Offermann, 1990). These organizational styles underscore the utility of active roles for both leaders and employees and empowerment at the institutional level.

"Welcome aboard, and I think I speak for all of us when I say that we expect fresh, different and innovative ideas from you. . . . Not just more of the same old thing, right guys?"

Concepts of empowerment, power sharing, and participative leadership are at the heart of pluralistic management. The inherent value of empowering the work force through power sharing and participatory leadership is increased ownership of the agency's mission, operations, and services, along with greater satisfaction with work and productivity. Human services agencies that are moving toward a pluralistic work environment will require that managers, executives, and board members are committed to and well versed in these forms of leadership.

Career development and planning represent the empowerment of employees at the individual level. When empowerment occurs at this level, it produces a sense of personal power, mastery, and regulation of one's life (Gutierrez, 1990). The management's development of a comprehensive career-development program for employees is an essential component of the pluralistic workplace. Therefore, it is critical for managers and executives to be skilled in the identification of individuals' competencies and aspirations and the agency's developmental needs.

Career-development programming requires such specific skills as career assessment, goal-setting activities, and formal career planning. Although they would be assisted by managerial staff, employees would assume responsibility for developing a plan of action, requirements for achieving goals, and time frames. This process would give them the opportunity to develop "rites of passage" through the organization and to acquire the necessary skills, experience, and track records to advance in their careers. The next section presents a brief discussion of the managerial skills that are necessary to create a pluralistic work force and their relationship to the competing values leadership framework.

Pluralistic Management and the Competing Values Framework

A major premise of the competing values framework is that leadership skills that are essential for one sector may be antagonistic to those that are needed elsewhere (Faerman, Quinn, & Thompson, 1987). Managing in a pluralistic workplace, however, calls upon each of the skill areas identified in the competing values approach: facilitating, boundary spanning, directing, and coordinating. Although pluralistic management falls naturally into the human relations leadership model, goals related to developing a pluralistic workplace require skills drawn from all four quadrants of the framework, thereby demonstrating that competencies need not be competitive or conflicting. In other words, management in a pluralistic workplace encompasses and utilizes each of the leadership models described in Quinn's (1984) competing values approach—human relations, open systems, rational goal, and internal process.

Self-analysis skills, cultural literacy, and empowerment parallel the key leadership skills of consensus, cohesion and team building, and participatory leadership in the human relations model. The competence to assess the formal and informal organizational culture is synonymous with the boundary-spanning skills found in the open-systems model. The ability to analyze institutional policies, practices, and procedures to detect patterns of discrimination is similar to the mastery of goal setting and role-clarification skills in the rational goal model. Finally, career development and planning skills to enhance employment opportunities correspond to the program planning, monitoring, and evaluation skills of the internal-process leadership model. The following case example illustrates the principles of pluralism and the management skills that are required to move toward a pluralistic workplace.

Case Example

Nancy Todd has just assumed the position of executive director of the C. W. Jones Community Service Center. Having worked 20 years in the field of social services and with extensive supervisory and managerial experience, Nancy had dreamed of assuming an administrative position at this level. Nancy's impeccable track record was attractive to the search committee, but it was her experience and success in managing diversity in the workplace that strengthened her candidacy.

The Center

The agency was facing a period of external and internal turmoil. The state Equal Employment Opportunity Office had leveled charges of discrimination and inequitable personnel practices against it. The board of directors had been mandated to develop a strategic plan to help the center become an organization whose mission, operations, and services reflect the contributions and interests of diverse cultural and social groups.

Closer to home, community leaders were complaining that the agency's staff and programs were culturally insensitive and irrelevant. Inside the center, the turnover of staff was alarmingly high. As a result, the board aggressively sought an executive who was qualified to facilitate a process of organizational change.

The C. W. Jones Community Service Center is located in an economically deprived urban community of approximately 400,000 people, 45 percent of whom are Appalachian whites, 30 percent of whom are African-American, and 25 percent of whom are Hispanic. The center is the largest community-based agency in the city. Although the number of clients has declined in the past two years, 4,500 clients were served last year. The agency provides the community with mental health services, a day care program, after-school programs, a comprehensive program for senior citizens, and a reentry program for delinquent youths.

The center employs 275 persons, 25 of whom are managerial staff. The managerial staff is nearly all white except for one African-American woman, who was recently hired as the assistant program director. Among the educational and direct service workers, 65 percent are white, 25 percent are African-American, and 10 percent are Hispanic. Employees in these categories have an exceptionally high turnover rate. It is not surprising that both professional and paraprofessional employees complain that they are unable to move into higher-level positions and that those positions are being filled with applicants from outside the agency. People of color represent 85 percent of the staff in the clerical, food services, and janitorial jobs.

Presently, the agency is under tight budgetary constraints and needs to develop resources. Although the primary funding group is the local United Way organization, federal funds and foundation grants make up one-third of the budget.

Nancy approaches her new job enthusiastically and relishes the challenge of developing, implementing, and evaluating a strategic planning process that will bring about change in this agency. She sees the opportunity to create an organizational environment in which the philosophies, policies, procedures, and services demonstrate a commitment to valuing the diversity of people of different ages, races, ethnic backgrounds, physical abilities, and life-styles. She envisions a social service agency on the cutting edge of genuine pluralism—one that would serve as a model throughout the nation.

At the onset of Nancy's tenure in her new position, she was confronted with a situation that clearly illustrated the organization's need for change. After her first week, she received a memo from two of the program directors about the lack of cooperation from the clerical pool. The memo outlined several problems: the withholding of important information, the lack of responsiveness to telephone requests from workers, and rudeness. The program directors also noted that the staff spent a great deal of time speaking Spanish among themselves, to the consternation of the other workers. As a result, the managers requested that Nancy intervene to change the situation in the clerical pool.

Need for Strategic Planning

In her initial response to the request, Nancy held a series of problem-solving sessions with the program directors and the clerical staff to identify the key issues and steps toward resolving the problems. These sessions led to a preliminary uncovering of problems that were symptomatic of the organization's inability to manage diversity. The development of a diverse and pluralistic workplace was a priority for Nancy, but the board had decided not to begin the process for six months. This incident, however, prompted Nancy to request that the board begin work immediately. The board concurred. Within six weeks, Nancy had hired a management consultant.

At the next board meeting, it was agreed that the agency would engage in strategic planning. Nancy recognized that the concepts of diversity and pluralism must first be understood and accepted by the board and the top administrative staff. Throughout the deliberations, strategies of organizational change were examined from all angles to identify who would lose and gain in the process. It was estimated that it would require from three to five years to see the strategic plan completely implemented and an additional five years to witness the full impact of the interventions. A consensus had been achieved, and it was time to begin.

The strategic planning process was divided into two phases: Phase 1 would involve the board of directors and top administrative staff in a three-day retreat, and Phase 2 would involve all the managerial staff in a similar three-day retreat. To prepare for the retreats, the consultant spent the next two months gathering diagnostic data from the volunteers, the management, and the professional and nonprofessional staffs. This process enabled the consultant to assess the organizational climate and to determine the agency's readiness for intervention. Data-gathering techniques included interviews, focus groups, questionnaires, and a review of the agency's reports.

The consultant then presented Nancy and the board of directors with a report outlining the recommended interventions, which built on a theoretical model and strategy for organizational change. The report outlined four major efforts to be implemented during an 18-month period. The goal was to heighten awareness through the development of skills and to obtain a commitment, through planning for action, to develop and improve the management of the organization.

The proposed major efforts included the following components:

Awareness-development workshops: setting the stage. These workshops are aimed at helping participants develop skills in self-assessment (the identification of personal values and of their own cultural identities) and in identifying barriers to managing and working among people who are culturally different (an exploration of various cultures that are represented in the organization and how stereotypes and assumptions affect managers' decisions).

Awareness-development workshops: organizational culture. These workshops focus on the development of skills to identify and describe the key dimensions of culture in a given organization. The design involves a process that facilitates the participants' understanding of organizational culture and their ability to identify cultural indicators in their institution.

Organizational-assessment workshop. This workshop uses a team-building approach to engage participants in problem-solving activities directed toward evaluating the organization's mission statement, policies, practices, and programs and toward identifying factors that help the agency to adopt the goals of pluralism. Teams develop goals, strategies, and action plans that outline the steps the agency will take to eliminate all practices and policies that are discriminatory and incongruent with diversity and pluralism.

Employee-empowerment workshop. The final intervention addresses the development of managerial skills that encourage the empowerment of employees. Concepts of participatory management, team building, career development, training in valuing diversity, mentoring, and evaluating the performance of employees are reviewed. Teams are guided in problem-solving and goal-setting processes to develop strategies that will help employees to eliminate barriers to fulfilling their potential.

Facilitators use a combination of lecture, discussion, case studies, simulation, audiotapes, and videotapes in the workshops. Participants are encouraged to participate in experiential activities that are designed to facilitate the analysis of personal value systems, behavior, and experiences, followed by integration and synthesis. This process, coupled with rigorous planning for action, will propel the agency toward building a pluralistic work environment.

In his closing remarks, the consultant commended Nancy and the board of directors for embarking on this endeavor. He noted, "An institution that takes on this challenge will be confronted with conflict, but conflict can be managed. An institution that embraces the concept of pluralism and is committed to developing a work force that values diversity faces a long journey. But there is a destination, and you've charted a major segment of the trip. To be successful in the future, you must begin building today." The board unanimously approved the proposed plan and adjourned with the realization that their journey had just begun.

Summary

It seems obvious that movement toward a pluralistic workplace is a long and difficult process, yet if human service organizations are to meet the 21st century's challenge of productivity and success in the delivery of services and in fulfilling clients' needs, they must begin to press toward the mark of pluralism's high calling. Certain caveats, however, appear to be in order. Diversity and multiculturalism remain valid concepts, but they should be perceived as forerunners of the ultimate goal of pluralism. Take care not to let your goal for achieving diversity and pluralism obstruct your view of the "individual." There is a thin line between valuing differences and developing yet another set of stereotypes that obscure individual differences within a culture. Cultural literacy, then, is not a guarantee but merely a guideline for understanding and communicating with workers from different cultures. The bottom line, however, is that work performance, productivity, and culture are related. A pluralistic workplace empowers cultural differences and helps the organization prosper through the contributions of all members. When people are free to be themselves, energy, creativity, and productivity will abound in human services organizations.

SKILLS - APPLICATION EXERCISE 1

Respond to the statements on this Self-assessment Checklist for Managers. On the basis of your score, develop a personal action plan that will enhance your ability to manage diversity in a pluralistic environment.

continued

Self-assessment Checklist for Managers

To assess how hard you will have to work to effectively manage diversity, rate yourself on your responses to the statements below. Use a scale of 1 to 5 to rate how strongly you agree with the statements, 1 being low agreement and 5 being high. Place your score for each item on the blank next to that item.

_____ 1. I regularly assess my strengths and weaknesses, and consciously try to improve myself.

_____ 2. I am interested in the ideas of people who do not think as I think, and I respect their opinions even when I disagree with them.

_____ 3. Some of my friends or associates are different from me in age, race, gender, physical abilities, economic status, and education.

_____ 4. If I were at a party with people outside of my own group, I would go out of my way to meet them.

_____ 5. I do not need to understand everything going on around me. I tolerate ambiguity.

_____ 6. I am able to change course quickly. I readily change my plans or expectations to adapt to a new situation.

_____ 7. I recognize that I am a product of my upbringing and my way is not the only way.

_____ 8. I am patient and flexible. I can accept different ways of getting a job done as long as the results are good.

_____ 9. I am always asking questions, reading, exploring. I am curious about new things, people, and places.

_____ 10. I am interested in human dynamics and often find myself thinking, "what's really going on here?"

_____ 11. I can see two sides on most issues.

_____ 12. I have made mistakes and I have learned from them.

_____ 13. In an unfamiliar situation, I watch and listen before acting.

_____ 14. I listen carefully.

_____ 15. When I am lost, I ask for directions.

_____ 16. When I don't understand what someone is saying, I ask for clarification.

_____ 17. I sincerely do not want to offend others.

_____ 18. I like people and accept them as they are.

_____ 19. I am sensitive to the feelings of others and observe their reactions when I am talking.

_____ 20. I am aware of my prejudices and consciously try to control my assumptions about people.

How to score: Total your answers. If your score is 80 or above, you probably value diversity and are able to manage people who are different from yourself. If your score is below 50, you probably experience much difficulty managing diversity and could benefit from further training.

SOURCE: Excerpted from the _Valuing Diversity_ copyrighted training materials developed by Copeland Griggs Productions, Inc., San Francisco, CA. These materials may not be reproduced without written permission from Copeland Griggs Productions, Inc.

SKILLS-APPLICATION EXERCISE 2

1. As a manager in your organization, you have just hired three new employees and are in the process of developing an agenda for the orientation program. One of the topics to be covered is organizational culture. To prepare for this session, assess your organization and identify the following:
   a. Laws
   b. Language/communication
   c. Geography
   d. Currency
2. You are a management consultant. On the basis of the facts presented in the case example of the C. W. Jones Community Service Center, identify where this organization would fit in the typology of organizational progression (see pp. 157–158). Why? Support your answer with specific facts from the case study. Where would your own organization be positioned? Why?

References

Alvarez, R., Lutterman, K. G., & Associates. (1979). *Discrimination in organizations.* San Francisco: Jossey-Bass.

Black, J. S., & Mendenhall, M. (1990). Cross-cultural training effectiveness: A review and a theoretical framework for future research. *Academy of Management Review, 15*(1), 113–136.

Blell, D. S. (1990). *Redefining excellence in high education: Some recommendations in response to the pluralistic imperative at CWRU.* Cleveland: Case Western Reserve University, Office of Student Affairs.

Bochner, S. (1982). *Cultures in constant: Studies in cross-cultural interaction.* Elmsford, NY: Pergamon Press.

Buonocare, A. J., & Crable, D. R. (1986). Equal opportunity: An incomplete evolution. *Personnel Journal, 55,* 32–35.

Compton, B. R., & Galoway, B. (1979). *Social work processes.* Homewood, IL: Dorsey Press.

Copeland, L. (1988a, May). Learning to manage a multicultural work force. *Training,* pp. 49–56.

Copeland, L. (1988b). Valuing workplace diversity. *Personnel Administrator, 33.*

Crable, D. R. (1989). *Workforce 2000: Managing diversity training modules I, II, and III.* South Plainfield, NJ: Dallas R. Crable Associates.

del Bueno, D. J., & Vincent, P. (1986). Organizational culture: How important is it? *JONA, 17*(5), 15–33.

Equity Institute. (1990, June). *Renewing commitment to diversity in the 90's.* Paper presented at the institute's 16th annual nonprofit management conference.

Faerman, S., Quinn, R. E., & Thompson, M. P. (1987). Bridging management practice and theory: New York state's public service training program. *Public Administration Review, 47,* 310–319.

Fernandez, J. P. (1981). *Racism and sexism in corporate life: Changing values in American business*. Lexington, MA: Lexington Books.

Gutierrez, L. M. (1990). Working with women of color: An empowerment perspective. *Social Work, 35*, 149–153.

Harlan, A., & Weiss, C. L. (1982). Sex differences in factors affecting managerial career advancement. In P. A. Wallace (Ed.), *Women in the work place* (pp. 59–100). Boston: Auburn House.

Hollander, E. P., & Offermann, L. R. (1990). Power and leadership in organizations. *American Psychologist, 45*, 179–189.

Johnston, W. B., & Packer, A. H. (1987). *Work force 2000*. Indianapolis: Hudson Institute.

Kunisawa, B. N. (1988). *A nation in crisis: The dropout dilemma*. Washington, DC: National Education Association.

Livingston, K. (1979). *Fair game: Inequity and affirmative action*. San Francisco: W. H. Freeman.

Miller, F. A. (1988). Moving a team to multiculturalism. In B. Reddy & K. Jamison (Eds.), *Team building: Blueprints for productivity and satisfaction* (pp. 192–197). Washington, DC: NTL Institute–University Associates.

Mobley, W. H. (1982). Supervisor and employee race and sex effects on performance appraisals: A field study of adverse impact and generalization. *Academy of Management Journal, 24*, 503–612.

Nixon, R. (1985a). *Black managers in corporate America: Integration or alienation?* Washington, DC: Research Department, National Urban League.

Nixon, R. (1985b). *Climbing the corporate ladder: Some perceptions among black managers*. Washington, DC: Research Department, National Urban League.

Pinderhughes, E. (1989). *Race, ethnicity and power*. New York: Free Press.

Quinn, R. E. (1984). Applying the competing values approach to leadership: Toward an integrative framework. In J. G. Hunt (Eds.), *Leaders and managers: International perspectives on managerial behavior and leadership*. Elmsford, NY: Pergamon Press.

Reddy, B., & Burke, C. (1988). What to look for when selecting a team building consultant: Multicultural and other considerations. In B. Reddy & K. Jamison (Eds.), *Team building: Blueprints for productivity and satisfaction* (pp. 179–186). Washington, DC: NTL Institute–University Associates.

Thomas, R. (1990). From affirmative action to affirmative diversity. *Harvard Business Review, 90*(2), 107–117.

Triandis, H. C. (Ed.). (1972). *The analysis of subjective culture*. New York: John Wiley & Sons.

Getting There and Staying There: Women as Managers

Dixie L. Benshoff

Let us call the question. If the job title is manager, are women as likely as men to be recruited for the position and, further, are they apt to stay in it? This chapter addresses the following questions:

▶ Are women considered for managerial positions the same way men are?

▶ What variables can a woman control to increase her probability of promotion?

▶ Once in a managerial position, how can a woman enhance her value and secure tenure?

Women at the Top

When Captain Linda L. Bray charged a Panamanian dog kennel during the U.S. invasion of Panama in December 1989, she became the first female military officer to engage in combat. Reaction was swift and vocal. Headlines queried, "Should Women Be in Combat?" Newspapers were inundated with letters to the editor both pro and con, while women across the nation in managerial positions muttered to themselves, "We already are."

The battle to get to the "top of the heap" can often be ruthless, and the competitive edge can indeed be ego-slicing sharp. Therefore, can women, who are traditionally seen as the nurturers of relationships and as being more comfortable with a cooperative problem-solving style than a competitive one (Tanenbaum, 1989), be aggressive enough to claw their way to the summit?

The answer is not immediately clear. The U.S. Department of Labor (1983) reported that by the year 2000, 60 percent of working-age women will be working, compared to 52 percent in 1980 (U.S. Department of Labor, 1988). Furthermore, it reported that there was nearly a 125-percent increase in the proportion of managers who were women from 1972 to 1981 (U.S. Department of Labor, 1983). By 2000

The author would like to acknowledge the contributions of Denise Gibson, LISW, and Claire Draucker, PhD, without whose wisdom, patience, and editing this chapter would not have been written.

to 2010, 80 percent of those entering the work force are likely to be women, minorities, and immigrants (Schwartz, 1989). Schwartz pointed out that traditionally leaders have been recruited by enticing the top 10 percent of the senior class at the country's best universities. Historically, those individuals have been white men. Currently, however, women are graduating from prestigious universities in much greater numbers and are well represented in that top 10 percent.

Schwartz also suggested (much to the chagrin of some feminists) that real barriers to the promotability of women are gender differences in the areas of parental responsibilities, tradition, and socialization. "Such interfaces," she stated, "do not exist for men and tend to be impermeable for women" (p. 68). She indicated that "half of the women who take maternity leave return to their jobs part time or not at all" (p. 65), a factor that makes the cost of employing women greater than that of men.

Schwartz asserted, however, that both genders certainly are capable of a full range of behavior necessary to be successful managers. However, she emphasized that it is useless to argue which gender is "better" at management because a disproportionate number of women will be entering the work force and assuming managerial positions. She insisted that a "policy that forces women to choose between family and career cuts hugely into profits and competitive advantage" (p. 71).

A word of caution may be in order, however, before women begin to celebrate the inevitability of their arrival because of sheer propinquity. Without leverage, women could find themselves caught in a backlash. If fewer men—especially fewer white men—are in the work force, might they not be seen as more valuable? Men could continue to constitute the elite and demand the rewards proportionate to their availability.

This phenomenon can be seen in the profession of social work—a discipline that has traditionally been predominantly female but that tends to be managed by its male members. Gibelman and Schervish (1990), in analyzing the membership of the National Association of Social Workers (NASW), revealed that 37 percent of the men were in administrative positions, compared to 22 percent of the women.

If a woman aspires to climb the executive ladder, she must be prepared to compete with men and eventually with more and more women. To be competitive, she must be aware of the factors she can influence. To advance her career, she needs better information on opportunities and help with planning and preparing for growth.

Superstar

The woman aspiring to reach the top must work hard to be the best that she can be in her field. She must have the best training possible, perform within high standards, and be consistently dependable. Hard work and exemplary performance do not guarantee victory; they only buy a ticket to the arena. When Sturdivant and Adler (1976) surveyed 444 executives, gleaned from the 1975 edition of *Who's Who in America* and Standard and Poor's *Register of Directors and Executives,* they found no female or nonwhite executives. It can be assumed that even in 1975 women were becoming accomplished in their fields, or there would not be the high proportion of female baby boomers in management today.

Swinyard and Bond (1980) pointed out that most newcomers to top management are better educated than their predecessors. Also, those who become president of their company will probably be chosen from inside the company at the level of group (not senior or executive) vice president. What are the implications of this situation for women? It particularly affects female managers who may be wondering whether they stand a better chance of promotion by staying within or leaving their present organization.

Bowman, Worthy, and Greyser's (1965) comprehensive survey of 1,000 men and 1,000 women executives produced a startling result: "In fact, both men and women executives strongly agree that a woman has to be exceptional, indeed overqualified, to succeed in management today" (p. 4).

When Sutton and Moore (1985) tried to duplicate the survey conducted 20 years earlier by Bowman et al. (1965), they asked the respondents, "What, if anything, should be done to further the opportunities in management?" A female financial consultant and investment broker stated: "Above all the woman should be competent. Then the opportunities will be there."

Once she has established herself as a star performer, the female aspirant must develop some political savvy. Acquiring power, building helpful alliances, spending time wisely, and becoming more effective in her working relationships are demonstrated ways of becoming sophisticated in the art of obtaining and keeping a desired position.

Kanter (1979) identified three sources of power:
1. Lines of supply, or the ability to acquire resources to enhance one's domain
2. Lines of information, or the ability to access formal and informal knowledge of the internal and external environment
3. Lines of support, described best by Kanter (1979, p. 104):

> In a formal framework, a manager's job parameters need to allow for non-ordinary action, for a show of discretion or exercise of judgment. Thus, managers need to know that they can assume innovative, risk-taking activities without having to go through the stifling multi-layered approval process. And, informally, managers need the backing of other important figures in the organization whose tacit approval becomes another resource they bring to their own work unit as well as a sign of the manager's being "in."

If a woman is to been seen as competent and capable, she must achieve control over her subordinates, success in reaching bottom-line results, and autonomy to maneuver within the organization to keep her constituent area of responsibility on the cutting edge of performance. Otherwise, a qualified, competent manager, male or female, will be viewed as valuable in a direct service capacity but as lacking the strength to be a leader.

Super Mom

Any discussion of the unique conditions of the female executive is incomplete without addressing the impact of the family on the manager's aspirations. Bartolome and Evans (1980) studied the private and professional lives of 2,000 managers for five years and found that their private lives were disrupted not by the act of climbing the ladder of success but by the emotional "spillover" of negative feelings that they brought home.

The manager who is preoccupied with his or her job can benefit from coming home to a world of diversion or from a much-needed respite. But the manager who returns home every night to a "second job" of cooking, cleaning, and child care often has little time for emotional replenishment. (The temptation to bring home interpersonal problems with coworkers is discussed elsewhere in this chapter.)

Although Bartolome and Evans's study focused only on male managers, the authors acknowledged that women are generally expected to be responsible for maintaining a personal relationship. Therefore, an ambitious woman may find herself spending proportionately more energy and time nurturing her relationships at home than may her male counterpart.

A 1971/72 survey of NASW members (York et al., 1985) reported that women who were never married were employed 84 percent of the time, whereas married women were employed 46 percent of the time (using months worked after graduation). York et al. identified barriers to the advancement of women in social work administration. They found that the first snag is showing interest in administration. Although the appeal of aspiring to an advanced position constituted a variable in measuring interest, the perception that the opportunity was unavailable clearly served as an obstacle. It would be interesting to learn definitively whether women consider managerial positions to be unavailable because of their family responsibilities or because the obstacles associated with the acquisition of these positions seem too overwhelming for all but the exceptional or single person.

Acquiring Power

Mentoring or "Womentoring"?

One of the most expedient (and traditional) ways of acquiring power is through mentoring. Fitt and Newton (1981) suggested that in a successful mentor-protégée relationship, the mentor protects the protégée from political pitfalls, helps the protégée get plum assignments, and guides the protégée to a position of high visibility within the company. The mentor must also guide the protégée on issues of personal traits, such as grooming and conduct, with a supportive and caring approach.

When the mentor is a man, a potential risk in providing mentoring to women is the perception by others of a romantic involvement. After all, mentors and protégées need to spend time together working after hours or perhaps traveling. Furthermore, the mentor needs to be able to express candid opinions about the protégée's appearance, conduct, and abilities. To do so, he may need to close the professional-distance gap. The mentor frequently will take a supportive, warm, and caring approach and may extend special privileges. It can be a delicate matter to do so without giving critics (who may be destructive) the idea that the protégée succeeded not because of her intellectual capabilities but by extending sexual favors.

Vertz (1985, p. 415) stressed that for mentoring to be effective, the mentor must understand the problems inherent in being a female manager:

- Women may develop attitudes and personality characteristics that are consistent with traditional female roles.
- Women's domestic responsibilities may inhibit their career advancement.
- Organizations in which women work may be structurally biased to some extent against them.
- Other institutions, such as schools and churches, may also have qualities which constrain women's career development.
- The factors listed above—personality, attitudes, domestic constraints, and structural constraints—may result in women having job credentials that are less well-developed when compared to those of men.

Vertz addressed these issues by saying that if a woman wants to advance, she needs to have high self-esteem and be aggressive. Furthermore, women in managerial positions tend to have a nontraditional attitude toward the role of women in employment, but consider themselves feminine. As Vertz (1985, p. 417) pointed out:

A mentor's job, therefore, is to encourage and facilitate development of these personality and attitudinal attributes in those women who desire to advance. Unless the mentor is a woman, the most difficult characteristic to transmit from mentor to protégée, in this specific organization, is non-traditional gender role attitudes.

Obviously, if only superstars can be managers, there will be fewer female managers, so how many will be skilled or inclined to be mentors? And with few mentors, how can women hope to gain the information they need to get promoted? There are ways other than mentoring by which women can gain power in the organization.

Mother Earth versus Father Time

Other differences that have been found between male and female managers may suggest methods that women can use to gain more power within an organization. For instance, Josefowitz (1980) found that women managers were twice as accessible (available) to employees as were male managers. She speculated that while men use their time to achieve priorities, such as promotion, women feel a duty to be helpful to subordinates. She questioned whether a willingness to be available implies that women have a greater need to be liked. Certainly, the psychological literature on locus of control (Rotter, 1966) indicates that women are more likely than men to be external validators. In other words, women depend more on approval from others, whereas men are reinforced for being "their own man."

The cost to women, however, is obvious: lost time for future planning and more time devoted to present crises. Men who seem too busy to grant an audience without an appointment, because of their importance or increased areas of responsibilities, may be sending the subliminal message that they are more promotable than are women who selflessly assist others in their duties.

Although these views are not exhaustive, they do address the more readily apparent dynamics that women encounter. In essence, women must be competent, credible, confident, and visible. They must be cooperative enough to be accessible, but competitive enough to keep an appropriate distance, while maintaining their femininity and being careful not to evoke damaging perceptions of impropriety.

King of the Mountain versus Queen for a Day

Once a female manager receives the promotion she's been working for, she needs to establish her position quickly and confidently. Rosen and Jerdee (1980, p. 32) surveyed 1,500 readers of *Harvard Business Review* and discovered—

> ▶ Managers expect male employees to give top priority to their jobs when career demands and family obligations conflict. They expect female employees to sacrifice their careers to family responsibilities.
> ▶ If personal conduct threatens an employee's job, managers make greater efforts to retain a valuable male employee than an equally qualified female.
> ▶ In selection, promotion, and career-development decisions, managers are biased in favor of males.

The authors also pointed out that "Women must become more assertive and independent before they can succeed" (p. 43). Just how women can do so without alienating others bears further exploration. Yorks (1976), who identified issues associated with achieving and retaining managerial responsibilities, commented on the reactions of female managers when confronted with stereotypical and oppressive attitudes, such as "Women get too emotional, or they personalize things too much" (p. 15). He cautioned against women confronting others too aggressively for fear that women will unintentionally reinforce what they are attempting to counter.

Yorks also noted that a contributing factor to the longevity of managers is the realization that there is a "limited supply of political capital" (p. 15). One could speculate that men are comfortable trading (Tanenbaum, 1989), whereas women are less at ease swapping favors. Women tend to believe that people should do something simply because it is right. Successful managers do not assume that others are supportive until the evidence is apparent. Yorks specifically pointed out that women can be too trusting of other women.

Visibility is crucial, according to Yorks. The successful manager knows not only how to be in the right place at the right time, but how to talk about moments of success to others who were not there. Women who have been raised not to boast and to show interest in others' achievement, and who thus refrain from mentioning their own accomplishments, could be at a distinct disadvantage.

What Is a Woman to Do?

It seems apparent, then, that the newly arrived woman who plans on staying long enough in management to experience the benefits of her sojourn needs to increase her awareness of her position and how others perceive her. She needs to expand her repertoire of behavior in dealing with others and to be comfortable with her own authority.

Although talking about assertiveness in 1991 seems to be a cliché, it is worth repeating that assertiveness does not mean being aggressive or learning gimmicks or techniques to get one's way. It does mean using personal skills to increase one's effectiveness in getting one's own needs met without interfering with the rights of others.

Women managers must avoid the appearance of emotionalism, excitability, or irrational behavior. A man can slam his fist on the boss's desk and be seen as strong and independent, but a woman will be seen as out of control. Conversely, a man had better not cry at work, but a woman will also fare far better if she refrains from doing so. Therefore, the female manager must become objective and control the tendency to personalize. She must lower her expectations that others will cheer her or even recognize her efforts—at least outwardly.

In a recent performance evaluation, for example, a newly promoted female manager asked her boss to identify the things she did that he liked and did not like. Because he viewed her request as insecurity, she had to develop other ways to receive these cues. She observed carefully and noticed that her boss tended to smoke his pipe when he was relaxed and content, so she carefully made records of who was doing or saying what when she saw him smoking.

Informal support can encourage women to pursue achievement (York et al., 1985). In fact, women who depend on validation and recognition may become paralyzed without it. This paralysis, of course, adversely affects their performance and reinforces the idea that they are not doing well. Eventually, it becomes a self-fulfilling prophecy. Rather than deny the need for validation, women can substitute positive messages for negative perceptions. Finding someone other than family members or coworkers to vent to about the job can increase feelings of self-worth and lower the risk of being seen as dependent or insecure. Women can benefit from the consciousness-raising-group model of the 1970s and form support groups composed of other female managers.

Heed the suggestion to avoid complaining to coworkers and family members at all costs. Managers can unintentionally undermine their own authority when they appear needy to coworkers, and anyone can quickly become frustrating to family members when she or he allows the stress of a job to "spill over" at home.

Tanenbaum (1989) described a situation in which a protective, helpful husband announces what he considers to be the obvious solution to a problem about which his wife is complaining. His wife perceives his announcement as a message that she is not adequate to solve the problem herself, which only makes her feel worse. She becomes frustrated and angry, and the two quarrel. He then avoids further discussion or tells her to quit the job if it is making her crazy. She may simply have wanted to vent—not to solve the problem—which is difficult for him to comprehend because, according to Tanenbaum, men tend to communicate to solve problems, not to express feelings. Stress at work then turns into stress at home.

"No, I wouldn't call it sexist if you told me I looked pretty today. I'd call it good old-fashioned brown-nosing."

The female manager should guard against "taking care" of everyone else. Perhaps one reason women usually carry a purse is that they will have the safety pin, aspirin, extra pen, or Kleenex needed by non-purse carriers (children and men). Women have made such an issue of not making coffee that they have forgotten the point. Make coffee or provide a pen as long as this behavior is seen as being supportive and is shared by peers. In other words, you may need to protect others as you would have them protect you. A word of caution is in order, however, before you protect a dominant man in public: Make sure he wants the protection, or he may turn on you to demonstrate that he does not need it.

Set yourself up for success. Fitt and Newton (1981, p. 98) quoted a mentor discussing his female protégée: "Women frequently have less self-confidence than men about their ability to do a job well. She's better than she thinks she is. I am working to give her confidence, to let her know there's a backup here. I'm her cheerleader." Find your cheerleaders and give them something to cheer about. In what do you excel? How can you turn those skills into something visible for your organization? One woman was recently promoted to an important position in the financial department of a nonprofit organization. She was especially adept at graphic art, and on her own initiative she drew a flyer about the services that coworkers could expect from her department. The flyer increased communication and clarified expectations, much to the delight of her superior.

Do not be surprised, however, if your stroke of creative genius is not always met with unabashed appreciation. Before you invest a lot of time and energy in a pet project, seek assurance that it is needed and will be useful to whomever you wish to impress. If you meet with a negative response, abandon the idea before you become too psychologically invested in it.

We Have Met the Enemy and She Is Us

Do not be surprised if men tend to support you more often than do women. When Sutton and Moore (1985, p. 66) replicated a 1965 survey of business executives 20 years later, they found that, "unlike the male respondents in 1965, the majority of men no longer consider women temperamentally unfit for management positions and disagree with the notion that women rarely want positions of responsibility and authority." Unfortunately, however, of the women surveyed in 1985, only 51 percent indicated they would personally feel comfortable working for a woman, compared to 65 percent in 1965.

The fact that fewer women feel comfortable working for a female supervisor may reflect the fact that "pink-collar" workers, who are employed in traditionally female skilled jobs, such as secretarial work, and who do not aspire to management, often tend to be family centered. It has already been noted that the successful woman manager needs to devote more time and energy to her career than does her male counterpart. For instance, Vertz (1985, p. 417) found that "men in lower level positions are more likely to be single and responsible for chores than men in upper level positions" and that "men in upper level positions have fewer domestic chores than women in similar positions." Society may reinforce other attributes in women that are congruent with a traditional female role, thus alienating women who have adapted life-styles that are inconsistent with those traditions. For example, in her summary of the Milwaukee District Office of the Internal Revenue Service, Vertz found that women in lower-level positions were more likely to prefer male supervisors, whereas women in upper-level positions had no preference. Men, in general, were more likely to prefer male supervisors.

Kagan (1985) surveyed the readership of *Working Woman* magazine and discovered what she called career traps, one of which is particularly relevant to this discussion. Seventy-one percent of the respondents, given a choice, decided to miss a deadline so an assignment could be completed "perfectly," rather than hand in an imperfect product and be ready for more assignments. It is interesting that the minority of women who reported they would hand the assignment in as soon as it "was done as well as anyone else could do or better," reported greater satisfaction with their careers and tended to earn higher salaries (the assumption being that higher salaries indicate advanced positions). Women with lower salaries readily admitted that they rigidly performed an assignment in keeping with their own standards of perfection, and they thought that doing so was more important than completing an assignment on time. It would be interesting to learn how male managers would respond to the same question. One could speculate that women who endorse the traditional female role of being "good girls" and who work hard to please others have not learned that overachievement does not guarantee success. In fact, knowing when to stop a project to be responsive to the greater organizational climate, or at least learning how to be less intense when involved in a pet project, may actually serve women better than investing 100 percent.

Serbin, Sprafkin, Elman, and Doyle (1982) demonstrated that when children are learning social skills, girls tend to influence others with courtesy and suggestions while boys use more direct demands. For example, boys refused to stop an activity that girls protested, but did so if other boys told them to stop. Girls, on the other hand, stopped an activity when either boys or other girls asked them to.

Implications for the female manager are obvious. The female manager must quickly learn to be comfortable with her own authority. She must learn how to set limits without sounding angry; she must learn to express anger without sounding aggressive; and she must learn how to delegate, hold others accountable, and take charge without alienating.

Take My Wife—Please!

A female manager must have a sense of humor and know how and when to use it. Men use sarcasm and putdowns with each other to increase their sense of camaraderie. The woman who witnesses this behavior and protests it may be asked in a subtle way to relinquish her privilege of being part of the team.

Women should resist the temptation to use self-deprecating (typically female) humor. In an experiment at the University of Wisconsin, Canton and Zillman (cited in Friedman, 1990) found that people tend to find jokes funnier when females are disparaged. Men who are occasionally self-deprecating may be seen as magnanimous enough to admit their mistakes and reveal their fallibility, whereas women who make self-disparaging remarks tend to be accepted at face value. Furthermore, men rate self-deprecators as being less confident, less intelligent, and less witty (Friedman, 1990). So once again, women have a difficult assignment: to be assertive enough to fend off putdowns, but careful not to alienate the joker. Although this task may seem impossible, remember that women have been balancing unwieldy loads of cultural messages for countless years. Be sexy, but do not be inappropriately seductive. Be friends, but do not be flirtatious. Be available, but do not be annoying. Be decisive, but do it my way.

Honest, Honey, Your Check Is in the Mail

A final note. Women who strive hard to discover the formula for becoming and remaining successful may be disappointed to learn that their compensation will more than likely be less than what a man would earn in the same position. In their thoughtful discussion of compensation and gender issues, Rosen, Rynes, and Mahoney (1983) noted, for example, that the average annual salary for a female college graduate is $20,000, compared to $19,000 for a male high school dropout. Overall, women still earn only 68 cents to every dollar earned by men (Earlenbaugh, 1989).

Nonetheless, women who make it to the top seem to get there by intellectual achievement, political savvy, poise, sophistication, and perhaps an uncanny way of decoding the mixed messages sent their way. They may be staying at the top partly because they have support from their families, as well as from others outside their families and workplaces, to supplement their female ego needs that are not met in the predominantly male work environment. Once at the top, they are adept at taking charge without alienating others and can communicate their achievements with confidence and by putting others at ease. Women managers have a firm foothold on the pinnacle of success, and if predictions are accurate, more and more women will soon be at the top.

Summary

More and more women are entering the work force. It remains to be seen whether, given their acculturation to be cooperative and nurturing, they will be considered for managerial positions the same way men are. Society still expects women to take major responsibility for what Hochschild (1990) called "the second shift"—caring for their families as well as their careers. It would seem that this dual role expectation would impede women's ability to rise to management because of their own reluctance and the system's assumption that divided attention is the same thing as distractibility.

The literature suggests that female executives tend to be exceptional in their fields. Having demonstrated consistent stellar performance, successful female managerial candidates will need to acquire and maintain power, build helpful alliances, and manage time wisely. Traditional methods of achieving these results, such as mentoring, contain special problems for women that must be addressed. Female managers need to develop a keen awareness of interpersonal dynamics that contribute to credibility and visibility. They cannot afford to become complacent and just tend to their jobs. It is crucial that they learn how to substitute negative messages that they sometimes send themselves with positive ones. Doing so will help them "personalize" less and gain more confidence. With greater confidence, they will have more success and will tend to see themselves in a more positive light.

Women need to develop support groups that will help them to increase their self-esteem and raise their consciousness about effective strategies of coping and excelling. The successful female manager should avoid the tendency always to depend on her family and her coworkers to provide the support that she needs and values. She will do well to guard against taking care of everyone else and learn to deal in trade—not in a ruthless, narcissistic way, but in a way that ensures there will be some return on her investment of energy.

Women in demanding jobs need to work on their need for recognition and attention. If women truly have a tendency to be less comfortable with internal validation and require more external support and recognition, the female executive may need to learn to get such support and recognition somewhere other than at work.

Women in managerial positions need to learn to let go of ideas that are not well received. When women do not perceive they are heard, they tend to continue to repeat themselves until the desired response is forthcoming. This pattern of communication can cause them to be perceived as "nagging" or as being so rigid that they are seen as self-righteous and, therefore, not team players. The female executive needs to discover ways to promote her ideas when they are truly important to her but to let go of those that may not be as high on her list of priorities.

Women who aspire to be managers or who are ensuring their tenure need to discover who truly supports them. It is a mistake to assume that the willingness to support an individual in becoming successful is based on gender, for the issue is more complex than that. In addition, it is in the best interest of successful managerial candidates to avoid the tendency to do assignments "perfectly," at the expense of deadlines. "Good girl" rules do not always apply in the workplace, and the successful female manager will benefit from a less-intense approach to pet projects.

Finally, female executives need to develop and use generously a sense of humor. Even here, however, they cannot afford the luxury of pure spontaneity. If a female manager tends to engage in self-deprecation, she should drop these jokes from her repertoire and share only anecdotes and stories that enhance her credibility. With increased awareness of pertinent dynamics and the determination that got her to the top in the first place, today's female manager can possess the special constellation of skills that will ensure the stellar performance of herself and her agency in the year 2000 and beyond.

SKILLS-APPLICATION EXERCISE

Julia has been recently promoted. Before her promotion, she was friends with Gwendolyn, who is now one of her support staff. Lately, Gwendolyn has been boasting to other coworkers about her influence with Julia, and Julia has been having difficulty getting Gwendolyn to complete assignments that are consistent with Julia's directions. Julia should

____ A. Tell Gwendolyn she no longer wants to be her friend and that she should shape up or expect to be fired.

____ B. Work behind the scenes to get Gwendolyn transferred to another department.

____ C. Confront Gwendolyn by pointing out how uncomfortable she is with the situation and, if necessary, spelling out the consequences of Gwendolyn's behavior.

____ D. Say nothing and assume that the situation will eventually get better.

____ E. Be broad-minded enough to know that maybe Gwendolyn's way of completing assignments could actually be helpful.

____ F. Attempt to get close to Gwendolyn. Go out some night with her and confide in her about personal problems so that she understands that Julia needs her support.

Discussion: Alternative A makes Julia look emotional, and therefore she could be vulnerable to Gwendolyn's criticism. Gwendolyn could complain to her peers or sabotage Julia's work. Alternative B may work, but it could also backfire. Any leak to Gwendolyn could result in Gwendolyn getting support from others for Julia's disloyalty and deviousness. Alternative C makes it clear to Gwendolyn that Julia will not allow Gwendolyn to use their relationship for her own personal gain. Julia can let Gwendolyn know that if Gwendolyn continues to put her in an awkward position, she will have to use her authority. An appropriate confrontation with a gentle but firm tone communicates to Gwendolyn that Julia is comfortable with her authority and will continue to enjoy an appropriate relationship with Gwendolyn, but will set limits if Gwendolyn's behavior exceeds the limits of the boundaries of that relationship. Alternative D is tempting and is presumably practiced frequently. It is dangerous,

continued

however. Passivity can erode authority. There is no reason to believe that the situation will get any better through inaction. Alternative E is another form of passivity. Women who tend to doubt themselves to avoid conflict simply do so in an effort to gain control over their own anxiety. Regardless of whether Gwendolyn's way is better or not, it is not the way that Julia directed the assignment to be done. Julia could invite Gwendolyn to make suggestions, but she should not allow her to disregard Julia's intentions. Alternative F diminishes professional boundaries. It is appropriate for Julia to share with Gwendolyn that she needs Gwendolyn's support at work, but this must be done in the context of the professional relationship. By confiding in Gwendolyn about personal problems, Julia is sending her a confusing message. New professional boundaries now exist; and just as there are ground rules for social relationships outside of work, there are ground rules for behavior at work that must not be violated.

References

Bartolome, F., & Evans, P. (1980). Must success cost so much? *Harvard Business Review, 58*, 137–148.

Bowman, G., Worthy, N., & Greyser, S. (1965). Are women executives people? *Harvard Business Review, 43*, 14–29.

Earlenbaugh, D., (1989, January 26). Average annual earnings. *Beacon Journal,* C1.

Fitt, L., & Newton, D. (1981). When the mentor is a man and the protégée a woman. *Harvard Business Review, 59*, 56–58.

Friedman, P. (Ed.). (1990, April). *Women and humor—Don't let the joke be on you.* (Available from the Pryor Report, 400-3 College Avenue, P.O. Box 1766, Clemson, SC 29631.)

Gibelman, M., & Schervish, P. (1990). *Social worker professional activities survey: Report and analysis of findings.* Unpublished report, National Institute of Mental Health–National Association of Social Workers.

Hochschild, A. (1990). *The second shift.* New York: Avon Books.

Josefowitz, N. (1980). Management men and women: Closed vs. open doors. *Harvard Business Review, 58*, 65–75.

Kagan, J. (1985, October). Who succeeds, who doesn't. *Working Woman, 113*, 154.

Kanter, R. (1979). Power failure in management circuits. *Harvard Business Review, 57*, 103–113.

Rosen, B., Rynes, S., & Mahoney, T. (1983). Compensation, jobs, and gender. *Harvard Business Review, 61*, 170–190.

Rosen, G., & Jerdee, T. (1980). Sex stereotyping in the executive suite. *Harvard Business Review, 58*, 30–43.

Rotter, J. B. (1966). Generalized expectancies for internal versus external control of reinforcement. *Psychological Monographs, 80*, 1–28.

Schwartz, F. N. (1989). Management women and the facts of life. *Harvard Business Review, 67*, 65–77.

Serbin, L., Sprafkin, C., Elman, M., & Doyle, A. (1982). *Canadian Journal of Behavioural Science, 14*, 350–363.

Sturdivant, F., & Adler, R. (1976). Executive origins: Still a gray flannel world? *Harvard University Review, 54*, 125–131.

Sutton, C., & Moore, K. (1985). Executive women—20 years later. *Harvard Business Review, 63*, 42–66.

Swinyard, A., & Bond, F. (1980). Who gets promoted? *Harvard Business Review, 58*, 6–18.

Tanenbaum, J. (1989). *Male and female realities: Understanding the opposite sex.* Sugarland, TX: Candle Publishing Co.

U.S. Department of Labor, Women's Bureau. (1983). *Time of change: 1983 handbook of women workers.* (Bulletin 298). Washington, DC: U.S. Government Printing Office.

U.S. Department of Labor, Women's Bureau. (1988, July). *The Women's Bureau: A voice for working women.* Washington, DC: Author.

Vertz, L. L. (1985). Women, occupational advancement, and mentoring: An analysis of one public organization. *Public Administration Review, 45*, 415–423.

York, R., Henley, C., & Gamble, D. (1985). Barriers to the advancement of women in social work administration. *Journal of Social Service Research, 9*(1), 1–15.

Yorks, L. (1976). What mother never told you about life in the corporation. *Management Review, 65*(4), 13–19.

Suggested Reading

Austin, C. D., Kravetz, D., & Pollock, K. L. (1985). Experiences of women as social welfare administrators. *Social Work, 30*(2), 173–179.

Chernesky, R. (1983, Fall/Winter). The sex dimension of organizational processes: Its impact on women managers. *Administration in Social Work, 7*(3/4), 133–143.

Chernesky, R. (1987, Spring). Six new books on women managers. (Book Review Essay). *Affilia: Journal of Women and Social Work, 2*, 61–64.

Chernesky, R., & Bombyk, M. (1988, Spring). Women's ways are effective management. *Affilia: Journal of Women and Social Work, 3*, 48–61.

Hooyman, N. R., & Cunningham, R. (1986). An alternative administrative style. In N. Van Den Bergh & L. Cooper (Eds.), *Feminist visions for social work.* Silver Spring, MD: National Association of Social Workers.

Martin, P. Y. et al. (1983). Advancement for women in hierarchical organizations. *Journal of Applied Behavioral Science, 19*(1), 19–33.

Weil, M. (1987). Women in administration. In O. S. Burden & N. Gottlieb (Eds.), *The woman client.* New York: Tavistock.

Dismissing Problem Employees

Robert F. Rivas

Dismissing employees may be seen as a final and negative part of the overall employment process. Even though managers and supervisors sometimes find it necessary to dismiss employees, little attention has been paid to the issue of dismissal in social work. The human services literature has few references to dismissal, despite social workers' need to understand the process and use it appropriately (Rivas, 1984).

Several texts on social work management do not include information about dismissal, although there have been interesting treatments of the functions of human resources management in human services administration (for example, see Bertcher, 1988; Hasenfeld, 1983; Patti, 1983; Slavin, 1978; Weiner, 1982). The literature on social work supervision offers little information on dismissal as well. Kadushin (1976), however, introduced the concept of administrative supervision, which involves supervisors exacting performance from employees. Administrative supervision is also concerned with issues of compliance, noncompliance, and sanctions in social service employment. Munson's work (1979) also contains articles that help explain these processes.

It appears that the literature does not consider the dismissal of employees a viable prerogative for the human services. Instead, it stresses the tasks of developing and educating staff (see, for example, Bertcher, 1988). When discussing control and the use of authority, the literature tends to deal with larger structural issues, such as organizational controls and leadership styles (Patti, 1983).

This chapter discusses the dismissal of employees as part of an overall supervisory process that requires specific procedures to be followed and skills to be utilized. The discussion of the manager's personnel function emphasizes the categories of job separation and the types of employee problems that result in dismissal. The supervisory process is explored, and a paradigm is offered for understanding how the supervision and dismissal of employees are connected within the organizational context. Finally, the specific skills and procedures that are needed to dismiss problem employees are described.

This chapter originally was published as R. F. Rivas, "Perspectives on Dismissal as a Management Prerogative in Social Service Organizations," Administration in Social Work, 8(4) (1984), 77–92. *Revised and reprinted with permission of The Haworth Press, Inc.*

Dismissal and Human Resource Management

Human services managers are concerned with the work of their organizations and the employees who carry it out. Because human services organizations are labor intensive, they are highly dependent on the quantity and quality of workers who deliver social benefits and services. Thus, a particular importance accrues to the human-resources management aspects of the delivery of human services.

Human resource management may be conceptualized as a continuum of these activities: recruiting, selecting, inducting, training, supervising, and evaluating employees. Each activity is connected with the dismissal process in two ways: An employee can be dismissed during each of these "stages" of employment, and the dismissal process often depends on how well each function has been carried out during the employment process.

Recruitment and selection usually require a number of steps. As Patti (1983, p. 138) noted, "some would argue that there are no managerial decisions that so vitally influence the ultimate success of a program than the choice of its personnel. [Recruitment and selection involve] maximizing the fit between the jobs that must be done and the people who will do them." Managers develop job descriptions, advertise, form a pool of applicants, match the qualifications of the applicants with the job descriptions, and select the most appropriate candidates. Agency policies usually formalize the process, which may also be heavily regulated or influenced by civil service law, labor and employment laws, union contracts, affirmative action plans, and professional personnel standards. In this chapter, these issues are discussed more fully in relation to dismissal than to recruitment.

Induction, training, supervision, and evaluation are also ongoing concerns for managers, although the responsibility for these activities is often delegated to line supervisors. In larger organizations, these functions may be carried out as a staff function of the personnel department or the department of human resources management. During induction, managers or supervisors set beginning parameters for workers' functions. Workers seek the structure of the agency's rules and policies for direction in their work (Lewis & Lewis, 1982). Training closely follows induction and may take the form of training in a field of practice (such as geriatrics or corrections) or in a method of practice (general practice or specialized practice). More specialized training may be offered under the staff development function.

Supervision in human services organizations is considered to be within the scope of human resource management, although in social work it tends to be a distinct method of practice. Supervision can provide employees with education, support, feedback on performance, and professional development. Kadushin (1976) suggested that supervision can be conceptualized as either administrative, educational, or supportive. However, it is particularly within the structure of administrative supervision that the adequacy of employees' work is evaluated. In this regard, Kadushin (1976, p. 51) noted that supervisors are responsible "for seeing that the work is done . . . that it is done in accordance with agency policy and procedures and . . . [that] it is being accomplished at a minimally acceptable level." Hence, the process of dismissal can be linked directly to the function of supervision of employees.

Considering the extent to which the literature emphasizes educational or supportive supervision, it is not surprising that supervision is seen as inimical to the control aspect of management or to the ultimate managerial sanction of dismissal. In fact, the two concepts represent one of the paradoxes of "competing values" in the social work managerial process. The terms *education* and *support* are usually not used in the same context with the term *dismissal* in relation to the overall supervisory function, perhaps because "social work supervision has been primarily sensitive to, and aware of, the human being rather than the organization" (Kadushin, 1976, p. 115). Although Kadushin noted that social work has attempted to accommodate the use of power and authority and the supportive or educational models of supervision, the literature appears to underemphasize those control structures that permit the dismissal of employees.

Although dismissal is rarely conceived of as part of the continuum of human resource activities, it is a valid part of the larger activity of the separation or termination of employees. *Separation* has a neutral connotation and thus may be considered part of the normal cycle of personnel activities for an organization.

The Phenomenon of Separation

All organizations lose employees for various reasons. Resignation and retirement may be basically healthy actions for both the employee and the organization. Layoff, while usually not desirable from any standpoint, does not necessarily carry a negative connotation about the performance of the worker or the organization. Leaves of various types (vacation, military, educational, sick, parenting and family, jury, and holiday) are another form of employee separation, albeit temporary and without a negative connotation. The separation of employees, especially resignations and retirement, may be considered the last or final activity in the continuum of personnel functions. Layoffs and leaves can legitimately be placed on the end of the continuum, but dismissal does not fit as easily, since it is not seen as a normal or desirable outcome of the personnel function. It is, perhaps, treated as taboo. As Strauss and Sayles (1980) noted, dismissal is often viewed by employers and employees as "industrial capital punishment," and thus the strong negative connotation may have obscured the dismissal prerogative in the social work literature.

Dismissal

Dismissal is the discharge of an employee from an organization because of his or her unsatisfactory job performance, violation of a contract, or the commission of acts that violate the policies or personnel standards of the organization, or the *Code of Ethics* (NASW, 1990) and *Standards for the Classification of Social Work Practice* (NASW, 1981). These other violations appear to be somewhat different from unsatisfactory performance. Essentially, dismissal resulting from violation of a contract, organizational policy, personnel standards, or ethics constitutes what may be considered dismissal for cause. Dismissal for cause is more easily applied by managers, particularly when the act of the employee is in clear violation of some prescribed standard of conduct or in gross violation of an agency's rules. Dismissal for unsatisfactory job performance may not be as easily applied, particularly because of difficulties associated with the employee-evaluation process in the human services.

Evaluation

To dismiss an employee on the basis of unsatisfactory performance, it is first necessary to document and evaluate his or her performance. Kadushin (1976, p. 277) described evaluations as troublesome processes for social workers, noting that they "tend to be avoided if not actively resisted." Some reasons for this phenomenon are that evaluations explicitly call attention to the difference in status between the supervisor and the supervised, reflect on the supervisor, evoke strong negative feelings, and are discouraging to workers (Kadushin, 1976, pp. 277–278).

The evaluation of a worker's performance may pose other problems. Social work managers must exercise judgments about their employees, a process that may run counter to the tenet of being nonjudgmental. When the performance of employees is inadequate, managers may believe that with additional educational or supportive supervision, the employees can change and improve and that organizations have the responsibility for providing these tools to help employees change.

A host of other difficulties can accompany the evaluations of employees. Many managers and supervisors do not observe their employees' performance because of the nature of the service that is rendered and the confidentiality of employee-client relationships (Hoshino, 1978). In these circumstances, they must rely on case recordings, supervisory discussions with employees, and other indirect means. Because the service technologies of social work cannot be specified as clearly as the technologies of other professions (medicine or nursing, for example) or the technologies of production (business and factory work, for instance), an aura of mystery still hovers over what constitutes an effective or efficient service (Newman & Turem, 1978). Hence, it may be difficult to evaluate an employee's performance in relation to the service technology.

If evaluation is fraught with problems, dismissal based on an evaluation is also difficult. Supervisors' reluctance to evaluate employees and their tendency to view employees as resources to be developed through educational and supportive supervision influence human services managers to develop, rehabilitate, or remotivate inadequate employees before considering dismissal or an alternative. Once the line is crossed from this developmental approach to the dismissal approach, however, a return to development is generally impossible.

Issues Involved in Dismissal

There has been little research on the extent or circumstances of the dismissal of employees in human services organizations (Dworaczek, 1983). Yet there is evidence that human services managers have spent a "majority of their time and energy in relations with subordinates where obtaining compliance and cooperation was, at least implicitly, their principle concern" (Patti, 1977, p. 16). Although the extent of this phenomenon is unclear, some of the factors that influence the use of dismissal can be identified and discussed.

Job Ownership

A range of issues relate to job ownership or tenure in human services employment. The employee in a bureaucracy, for example, tends to see employment as tenured. Civil service regulations, grievance procedures, the influence of unions, and the influence of law tend to support the employee's view that once he or she is past the probationary period, the organization cannot remove him or her. The stereotypical view of the employee in a bureaucracy suggests that the employee, rather than the organization, controls the circumstances of employment.

There may be some basis for this position. Given the supportive and educational nature of supervision during the probationary period, the employer may be reluctant to exercise the dismissal option, even though dismissal during probation is far less complicated than it is afterward. Once probation is over, additional information is required to document an employee's inadequate performance. As time passes, managers can feel a progressive loss of job ownership to their employees, which makes the evaluation of performance for the purposes of dismissal a progressively time-consuming and problematic activity.

The concept of "lifetime employment" is increasingly being seen as beneficial for both the organization and the employee. Borrowed from the Japanese, "lifetime employment" has been instituted in a number of U.S. companies with a view toward treating employees as both investments and assets (Luxenberg, 1983). Although yet a young movement, this concept could influence the general climate of employment in many organizations and lead employees to believe further in their rights to job ownership.

Dismissal as a Management Prerogative

Long experience with legislation and executive orders concerning affirmative action, equal opportunity employment, and antidiscrimination may have eroded the view that dismissal is the first prerogative of management. The influence of labor law has sparked debates about the rights of management and workers. Fisher (1973, p. 40) noted that "supporters of management rights have urged basically that all rights in the employment relationship not won by contract or forbidden by law belonged to employers. Supporters of worker rights argued that labor possessed some 'inherent' rights quite apart from contracts or laws." Laws regulating employment have tended to act as "a public curb on management rights."

The place of management rights in the employment situation is difficult to understand because of the many influences and restrictions applied to the circumstances of employment. Ewing (1983) suggested, for instance, that the right of management to fire employees is the basis of its authority. However, the court decisions reviewed by Ewing were often inconsistent in their findings; some supported management's prerogative to fire, whereas others warned management to exercise its rights carefully and within the limits of legal precedents. The resulting conflict, court decisions, and inconsistencies confuse the issue of "wrongful discharge."

The Influence of Unions

The strong influence of unions in organizations also has tended to constrain management's use of the dismissal prerogative. Fisher (1973) noted that the National Labor Relations Act of 1935 was passed largely as a supportive statement of workers' rights, particularly the right to organize in their own behalf. The organization of the work force and the presence of union contracts tend to require managers to exercise due process in disciplinary actions, particularly in cases of dismissal. Dismissal may have been effectively rendered "a last resort" in dealing with union employees because of the formality of procedures governing any disciplinary action against them.

Antidiscrimination Laws and Dismissal

The federal government restrains organizations from dismissing employees on the basis of discrimination with regard to race, color, religion, sex, and national origin. Federal legislation, including Title VII of the Civil Rights Act of 1964 and the Equal Employment Opportunity Act of 1972, provides for a number of guarantees against discriminatory dismissal by employers. Other laws have enlarged the definition of discrimination to include the categories of age (1967), pregnancy (1978), and disability (1973). These laws cover both public and private employees and are enforced through the Equal Employment Opportunity Commission (EEOC) (Lewis & Lewis, 1983). Since 1972, the EEOC can take employers to court to enforce the antidiscrimination laws in these categories. In addition to federal legislation, many states have passed similar antidiscrimination laws. Federal employees and employees of organizations under governmental contract are also protected by executive orders that parallel this federal legislation.

The rights of employees under antidiscrimination laws have been expanded in a sense. An employee is free to file a complaint with the EEOC if he or she feels that the dismissal was based on discrimination. In considering whether to dismiss employees, managers must give careful attention to due process and must document the employees' performance before dismissing them.

Dismissal and Supervision

Having considered some of the larger issues involved in the prerogative to dismiss employees, this chapter now considers dismissal as an organizational process. To do so, it examines dismissal in relation to the supervisory function of management.

A Typology of Supervision

Kadushin (1976) suggested that supervision can be administrative, educational, or supportive. This chapter offers an alternative typology that more clearly specifies the types of supervision provided to an employee in relation to the employee's position with the organization over time. In addition, the typology accounts for the relationship between the type (and extent) of supervision and the professional employee's need for increased autonomy over time.

Figure 1 illustrates the relationship of supervision to autonomy over time. The upper portion of the figure represents the extent of the organization's use of supervision. The lower portion suggests the level of autonomy exercised by the employee in relation to the organization's use of supervision. As an employee progresses through the probationary period, the extent of supervision decreases and the employee's level of autonomy increases. Although the figure is only a model, it graphically represents how the supervision and autonomy of employees are related. In the early stages of employment, an employee is subject to a far greater level of supervision than during the later stages.

Figure 1 also suggests that differential supervision occurs over time. At the point of hiring, the employee is provided with probationary supervision, which is usually intense and involves a great deal of cost and effort for the supervisor and the organization. During probation, the employee is carefully oriented, inducted, and monitored for minimally acceptable performance. As the employee moves from probationary to permanent status, supervision continues to be intense. The nature of the supervisory relationship appears to take on an educational flavor, with both the organization and the supervisor assuming considerable responsibility for schooling the employee.

At some point, the organization and the supervisor gradually reduce their educational commitment to the employee. The employee is then expected to

Figure 1. Typology of Supervision

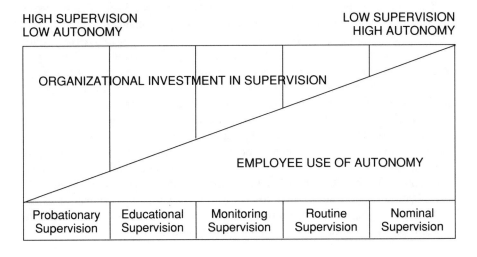

HIGH SUPERVISION
LOW AUTONOMY

LOW SUPERVISION
HIGH AUTONOMY

ORGANIZATIONAL INVESTMENT IN SUPERVISION

EMPLOYEE USE OF AUTONOMY

| Probationary Supervision | Educational Supervision | Monitoring Supervision | Routine Supervision | Nominal Supervision |

perform adequately, and the supervisor monitors the performance. Monitoring supervision requires less organizational and supervisory investment than does educational or probationary supervision. As the employee begins to function more effectively, supervision becomes somewhat routine. The organization and the supervisor can expect that as the worker's autonomy increases, the investment in supervision decreases. Finally, supervision becomes nominal, in that little is required for the highly autonomous employee.

Although it is not represented in Figure 1, another type of supervision requires a great deal of organizational and supervisory investment. Adversarial supervision occurs when the organization and supervisor determine that an employee cannot maintain his or her performance at an acceptable level or that the organization cannot raise the level in a cost-effective fashion. At this point, the organization prepares for the dismissal of an employee by carefully documenting his or her poor performance. During this time, the relationship between the supervisor and employee may take on an adversarial quality.

Although this typology represents a theoretical version of supervision, it helps to clarify the ideal in terms of the autonomy of employees. It suggests what the organization may expect to invest in supervision and how, over time, the costs of the investment should decrease while the return on the investment (the employee's autonomy) should increase. It also suggests that dismissal can be related to performance over time and investment in supervision.

The Relationship of Supervision to Performance

The concept of the organization's investment in the supervision of employees is important. It is clearly impossible for an organization to maintain a high level of supervision and an ongoing, intense investment of supervisory resources in employees. The employees' autonomy and performance should increase over time. Figure 2 illustrates the ideal relationship of supervision to employees' performance.

Theoretically, supervision progresses over time from high to low, while performance progresses over time from low to high. In practice, the investment in supervision and the employee's level of performance progress on the basis of the employee's need for supervision and the organizational resources that are available. There is, however, a point at which the organization cannot continue to invest a great amount of resources in supervising an employee. During probation, the organization expects to do so, but when the employee attains permanent status, the organization expects not to have to return to the level of its earlier investment. Similarly, it expects that once probation is over, the employee will not return to the lower level of performance allowed during that period.

Figure 2. The Ideal Relationship of Supervision to Performance

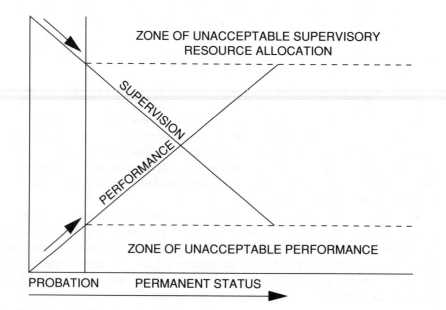

The unacceptable levels of supervision and performance are indicated in Figure 2 as the zones of "unacceptable supervisory resource allocation" and "unacceptable performance." These zones signal the organization that the cost of supervision, relative to the employee's level of performance, may be too high to maintain. It is, theoretically, when an employee falls into the zone of unacceptable performance that dismissal may be in the best interests of the organization on the basis of cost-benefit considerations.

Supervision, Performance, and Dismissal

Figure 3 illustrates how the process of dismissal is represented in relation to cost-benefit considerations. As an employee's performance declines, the investment in supervision increases. Eventually, the employee enters the zone of unacceptable performance, and the organization responds by increasing its supervisory invest-ment. In the absence of an improvement in performance, the organization may no longer be able to invest resources at that level and may choose to dismiss the employee. Figure 4 depicts a similar decision that is made on the basis of an employee's failure to reach the zone of acceptable performance by the end of the probationary period.

Figure 3. The Dismissal Decision

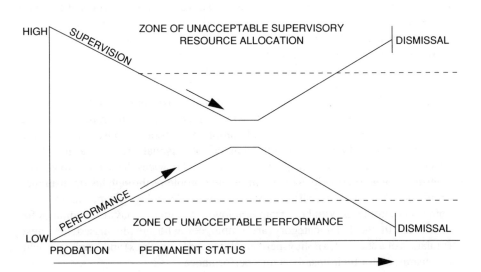

Figure 4. Dismissal During Probation

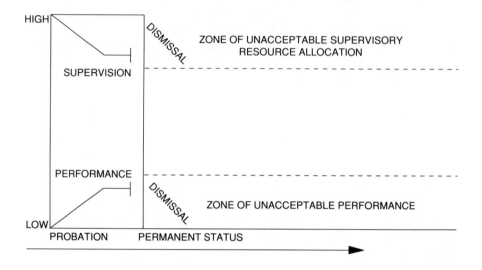

Dismissal: Practice Perspectives

Dismissal remains the ultimate penalty (Strauss & Sayles, 1980, p. 220). Many practical considerations are involved in using dismissal. The cost of replacing and retraining new workers is high. Dismissal may have a negative effect on the morale of the other employees in the organization, and it may create other staff problems. (In some instances, however, employees welcome the dismissal of an employee who does not perform to expectations or who violates a policy or ethics.) The organization should consider many factors that are external to the employee's performance when contemplating dismissal.

In considering dismissal, managers should distinguish between "employees with problems" and "problem employees." In the former category are employees whose performance may be impaired by family problems, substance abuse, mental health problems, financial concerns, or other sources of personal stress. It has long been accepted that organizations (especially in the social services) have much to gain by offering such workers help in overcoming their problems through health insurance provisions or employee assistance plans. However, employees who cannot overcome such problems with help from employers eventually may be candidates for dismissal. In the latter category are employees who are dismissed for cause (violation of a contract, a policy, personnel standards, or ethics) and employees who are dismissed for their unsatisfactory performance.

Managers should consider several fundamental principles of practice when they exercise the dismissal prerogative, some of which vary with the reason for dismissal. In extreme cases of dismissal for cause, an employee should be suspended (with pay, if necessary) until a full investigation of the infraction or violation is carried out. If the violation involves the safety of clients (as in the abuse of clients or the violation of ethics), care should be taken to prevent the employee from having official contact with the clients until the investigation is completed. In other "for cause" situations, decisions about suspension depend on the seriousness of the situation, the circumstances under which the violation took place, and the motivations of the employee.

"Apparently, they've just eliminated your box from the department's organizational chart."

Cases of dismissal for unsatisfactory job performance (including the performance of employees with problems who have failed to respond to "rehabilitative" efforts) have several practice considerations. Before the dismissal, an employee should receive adequate warning, in writing, about the intention to dismiss (Halloran, 1981). Huberman (1975) described a four-step sequence of fact-finding that should precede dismissal for unsatisfactory performance, including a casual, private warning; a repeat of the reminder; a discussion with the employee with other managers present; and a final discussion with a warning that further problems will result in dismissal. Strauss and Sayles (1980) suggested that disciplinary action before dismissal should be immediate, that an employee should be given advance warning, and that an employee should be treated with consistency and without regard for his or her personality.

The Dismissal Interview

The dismissal interview is certainly one of the more difficult tasks of organizational life. Anxiety levels are high, negative feelings are present, and relationships may well be adversarial. The following are suggestions for overcoming or at least ameliorating some of the difficult feelings and processes in which an employer and a dismissed employee often engage.

▶ *Pay attention to the evaluation process.* Several questions need to be considered before the dismissal interview. Does any documentation lead to conclusions other than imminent termination? Who, if anyone, will be surprised by the dismissal? Has the alleged misconduct been adequately investigated? Does the employee's salary record reflect his or her unsatisfactory performance? Have other employees been treated differently under similar circumstances? (Jensen, 1981). In general, the issue of due process should be considered as well. Has the employee received the benefit of due process in the evaluation and disciplinary process?

▶ *Choose the right time and place.* Although it has been suggested that Friday afternoon is an ideal time to dismiss an employee, timing is really a function of the circumstances of the dismissal and the good judgment of the employer. In the human services, other concerns affect the time and place for dismissal. For example, issues of termination from clients, including clients' records and record keeping, need to be worked out with the employee in a responsible manner. In addition, care should be taken to assure privacy and confidentiality for the employee during the dismissal interview. These human concerns and ethical issues should be part of the planning phase of dismissal.

▶ *Prepare for the interview.* Planning for a dismissal interview is important, but plan for it without trying to "write" the script. The employee's record should be reviewed and past disciplinary actions noted. It also may help to use the skill of "tuning in" to an employee's situation. Shulman (1979, p. 18) noted that tuning in is an effective skill that prepares the interviewer to understand the client's situation, a form of preliminary empathy. At this time, "finding the right words" can be considered. Even the most skilled interviewers have some difficulty choosing words to inform an employee that he or she is being dismissed.

▶ *Begin with a clear statement of purpose.* This generic skill is useful for all interviews, but its use in the dismissal interview signals to the employee the seriousness of the interview. The clarity of the statement is most important. It should be short, to the point, and framed in clear language. For example, "We are here to discuss your performance on the job" or "I have made some decisions about your job performance."

▶ *Clearly and factually state the action being taken.* It is difficult to find just the right words to tell an employee, "You're fired," without making the action seem harsh. An effective statement is, "I have decided to dismiss you as an employee of the agency" or "As of today, you are being dismissed from employment with us." It is best to avoid euphemisms, such as "letting you go," or other general statements.

▶ *Clearly state the reasons for your action.* If the dismissal is for cause, clearly indicate this—for example, "The reason for your dismissal is because you violated agency policy, and despite warnings, continued to violate policy." If the dismissal is for performance, indicate the employee's shortcomings and the processes used to evaluate them. For example, "On the basis of our recent performance evaluations, you have not been able to form helping relationships with your clients, nor have you kept adequate records on the clients." Avoid euphemistic expressions such as, "You don't seem to be working out" or "You don't seem to be the right person for the job." Be factual and stick to observable, behavioral criteria. It is also important to use clear, nonverbal cues to accompany the statement of dismissal and the reasons for it. Nonverbal messages, such as body language, posture, gestures, and paralanguage (the vocal quality of the message) should bespeak the assertion of authority that is being exercised. Do not send mixed messages.

▶ *Do not negotiate.* At this point in the dismissal process, the decision has been made. Further evidence, arguments, or considerations should not be entertained. It may be necessary to explain this fact to the employee and to repeat that the decision is final and not open to further consideration.

▶ *Inform the employee fully about appeal or grievance procedures.* An employee can often make use of the appeal or grievance machinery in the organization if the organization has such a policy. An employee should be informed of all such rights.

▶ *Offer support when possible.* Although a dismissed employee may find it difficult to accept support from an employer, some effort should be made to acknowledge the difficulty of the situation for the employee and to offer to help in other areas. An employer can make suggestions for new employment, further education, behavioral change, or counseling. Although support can be offered, "another chance" should not be implied.

▶ *Take personal responsibility for the dismissal.* The employee is being dismissed from the organization. The person dismissing him or her is the agent of the organization and should act accordingly. Avoid placing the blame on the organization. Do not contradict the facts or try to ameliorate the situation by speaking for yourself or disagreeing with the dismissal.

Summary

The dismissal of employees is a troublesome process. The extent to which employers use their prerogative to dismiss is unknown. Dismissal is sometimes shrouded in secrecy and constrained by law, agency policy, union contract, and a host of other factors. Before an employer dismisses an employee, he or she must have clear evidence of misconduct or evidence of inadequate performance that is based on the processes of supervision and evaluation. Substantial documentation is necessary. The dismissal interview requires advance preparation, the use of assertive behavior, clear messages, and empathy and fairness in dealing with the dismissed employee. Although dismissal is generally an unpleasant process, it is sometimes necessary to maintain the effectiveness of the agency or organization as a service delivery vehicle. A primary concern of managers must be the quality of the service being provided; sometimes the dismissal of an employee is the only recourse available after other developmental and remedial approaches have failed.

SKILLS-APPLICATION EXERCISE

The Case of John B

John B is a new employee of the Cosmos Child Care Center, a residential treatment center for emotionally disturbed children. He has been employed for the past four months as a member of the direct care staff. His duties include caring for the physical and emotional needs of a group of eight children and seeing to the needs of their daily life in a small-group-home setting.

John's supervisor, Alice G, has been carefully monitoring John's work as he has progressed through his employment at the center. She has given John two written performance appraisals, one after the first month of employment and another after the third month. John's probationary period is scheduled to last for six months.

John's performance appraisals have been based on Alice's observations of John's behavior with the children in his care. Alice pointed out to John that while he was on the job, he seemed distant and discourteous to several of the children. Often, when the children would ask him for help with some activity, he would become silent and not respond. She noted that this behavior was

continued

difficult for the children to understand. Alice observed this behavior on four occasions, and on the last two, she raised her concerns directly with John when they had a private moment together.

John's reaction to these two encounters was strange. He did not respond to Alice and simply stared at her while apparently trying to control his nonverbal behaviors, particularly his facial expressions. In their last encounter, Alice became personally uncomfortable with John's lack of reaction and blank stares.

Alice received reports from other staff members who worked with John that confirmed that John's behavior was strange. Several staff members thought that John might be mentally ill.

Alice decided to have another conference with John to bring up the negative reports by the staff and to ask John's perception of his situation. Upon learning of the negative comments made by his colleagues, John confided to Alice that he had grown up in a residential treatment center for children and felt that he knew what was best for the children in his care. He also asserted that the children did not need a social worker getting involved in their lives. John continued to assert that he knew what was best and that other staff members did not have the same insights he had because of his personal history.

After this conference, Alice reflected on the facts of John's employment as she knew them. John was in the fourth month of his six-month probationary period. He had had two performance appraisals and several supervisory conferences. John's behavior, as observed by Alice and by the staff, was strange and disturbing. The messages his behavior sent were unclear and upsetting to the children in his care. John did not display insight into his behavior when questioned about it. John grew up in a residential treatment center and has some strong opinions about caring for children.

Discussion Questions

1. On the basis of the facts of this case, does Alice G have sufficient cause to terminate John's employment?
2. If John's employment is terminated, what reasons will Alice give John for her action?
3. What effect will John's probationary status have on the firing process?
4. How might Alice phrase a final verbal warning to John about his problem behavior with the children?
5. If Alice decides to terminate John's employment, what would constitute a clear, concise statement informing him that he is being fired?

Answer Key

1. Alice G probably has sufficient reason to terminate John's employment because of his behavior with the children, his lack of insight into his behavior, and his inability to change his position to conform to the

continued

demands of the agency. In addition, the retention of John would require an inordinate allocation of supervisory time, which the agency could not afford.

2. Alice should cite John's behavior with the children and point out that it is confusing to them. She should note that John has shown a pattern of failing to meet the children's needs for assistance. She should cite his past performance appraisals and bring up incidents that she directly observed, rather than the staff's reports.

3. The fact that John is on probation probably makes it easier to dismiss him. Probation is usually considered a time during which an employer can dismiss an employee without a great deal of process. However, ethical, professional social work practice should include due process for all personnel on the employment continuum.

4. A clear statement of the desired outcome should be used, worded in the form of a reachable, behavioral goal. One example might be, "John, by the time of our next conference, you will need to be more attentive to the requests of the children. I will observe you during your shift and will observe your expressions and actions toward the children's requests. If you are unable to be more attentive, I will have to dismiss you from the agency."

5. If she dismisses John, Alice should begin with a clear statement describing the action she is taking. She might begin by saying, "John, based on your job performance, I have decided that effective immediately, I am dismissing you from employment with the agency."

References

Bertcher, H. (1988). *Staff development in human service organization*. Englewood Cliffs, NJ: Prentice Hall.

Dworaczek, M. (1983). *Dismissal of employees: A selected bibliography*. Monticello, IL: Vance Bibliographies.

Ewing, D. (1983). Your right to fire. *Harvard Business Review, 61,* 32–38.

Fisher, R. (1973). When workers are discharged: An overview. *Monthly Labor Review, 96,* 4–17.

Halloran, J. (1981). *Supervision: The Art of Management*. Englewood Cliffs, NJ: Prentice Hall.

Hasenfeld, Y. (1983). *Human service organizations*. Englewood Cliffs, NJ: Prentice Hall.

Hoshino, G. (1978). Social services: The problem of accountability. In S. Slavin (Ed.), *Social administration: The management of the social services*. New York: Haworth Press.

Huberman, J. (1975). Discipline without punishment lives. *Harvard Business Review, 53,* 6–8.

Jensen, J. (1981, September–October). Letting go. *Grantsmanship Center News,* 37–43.

Kadushin, A. (1976). *Supervision in social work*. New York: Columbia University Press.

Lewis, H., & Lewis, M. (1982). *The intellectual base of social work practice*. New York: Haworth Press.

Lewis, J., & Lewis, M. (1983). *Management of human service programs*. Monterey, CA: Brooks/Cole.

Luxenberg, S. (1983, April 17). Lifetime employment: U.S. style. *New York Times*.

Munson, C. (Ed.). (1979). *Social work supervision*. New York: Free Press.

National Association of Social Workers. (1981). *Standards for the classification of social work practice*. Silver Spring, MD: Author.

National Association of Social Workers. (1990). *Code of ethics*. Silver Spring, MD: Author.

Newman, E., & Turem, J. (1978). The crisis of accountability. In S. Slavin (Ed.), *Social administration*. New York: Haworth Press.

Patti, R. (1977). Patterns of management activity in social welfare agencies. *Administration in Social Work, 1*, 5–18.

Patti, R. (1983). *Social welfare administration*. Englewood Cliffs, NJ: Prentice Hall.

Rivas, R. F. (1984). Perspectives on dismissal as a management prerogative in social service organizations. *Administration in Social Work, 8*(4), 77–92.

Shulman, L. (1979). *The skills of helping: Individuals and groups*. Itasca, IL: F. E. Peacock.

Slavin, S. (Ed.). (1978). *Social administration: The management of the human services*. New York: Haworth Press.

Strauss, G., & Sayles, L. R. (1980). *Personnel: The human problem of management* (4th ed.). Englewood Cliffs, NJ: Prentice Hall.

Weiner, M. (1982). *Human services management: Analysis and applications*. Homewood, IL: Dorsey Press.

CHAPTER

13

Managing Organizational Decline

Richard L. Edwards and John A. Yankey

Reductions in funding frequently have a strong negative effect on the delivery of services and, therefore, on the clients who are served. What is less obvious is the impact of budget cuts on the lives of those people who strive to serve clients. This chapter addresses the impact of budgetary reductions on managers and staff in human services organizations. It draws on the literature on retrenchment and cutback management, as well as on the authors' personal experiences as upper-level managers in organizations that experienced major cuts in funding that necessitated significant reductions in programs and staff.

A New Era of Fiscal Austerity

During the 1980s, human services organizations entered a new era characterized by declining economic conditions. It represented a dramatic change after nearly 50 years of almost uninterrupted growth.

When Ronald Reagan assumed the presidency in 1980, he quickly followed through on his campaign pledge to make significant realignments in the priorities of the federal budget. As a result, the nation entered a round of reductions in federal spending for social programs. During fiscal years 1981 and 1982, most programs that were aimed at serving the poor, as well as a range of other federal social programs, suffered from severe budgetary cuts.

The initial impact of the reductions in the federal budget on state and local governments was felt differentially. Some states and localities were able to use their resources to buffer the impact of the federal cuts, whereas others immediately had to reduce staffing and services.

During the early years of the Reagan administration, the issue of managing under conditions of decline, or what has been labeled "cutback management," was frequently addressed both in the professional social work literature and at a variety of professional conferences (Austin, 1984; Bombyk & Chernesky, 1985; Hirschhorn, 1983; Knighton & Heidelman, 1984; Pawlak, Jeter, & Fink, 1983; Turem & Born, 1983). However, interest in the subject soon waned when the initial impact of the federal budgetary cuts passed. The subsequent impact was lessened, partly because although federal funding for some social programs was further reduced in the following years, the reductions were of a much smaller magnitude than the earlier ones and funding for some other social programs even increased slightly. In addition, many states, as well as the voluntary sector, absorbed part of the burden.

Now, however, we are entering a new era, a second round, in which funding for social programs will continue to be threatened for years to come. This era was initially heralded by the enactment of the Gramm-Rudman-Hollings Balanced Budget and Deficit Reduction Act of 1985. Named after its original cosponsors, it was an important piece of federal legislation because it mandated major reductions in the federal budgetary deficit each year and a balanced federal budget by fiscal year 1991. Commenting on the effect of the act, Greenstein (1986, p. 1) was prophetic when he stated:

> In the years ahead, our nation will have to make hard choices on what should be reduced or eliminated, what should be maintained, and what, if anything, should be increased. Decisions must also be faced on whether to raise revenues. The choices made will shape our society for years to come.

Between 1985 and 1990, given the enormity of the federal deficit, the deficit-reduction targets of the act generated vigorous debates on national priorities. However, by the end of the decade, it was apparent that the deficit-reduction target for fiscal year 1991 would not be met.

In 1990, Congress engaged in a bitter fight over the budget, finally passing the Omnibus Budget Reconciliation Act (OBRA) of 1990. The OBRA includes cuts in spending and increases in revenues that are aimed at reducing the federal deficit by $42.5 billion in 1991 and $496.2 billion over five years. It extends the Gramm-Rudman-Hollings law through 1995, establishing new deficit-reduction targets for each year.

One of the most significant features of the OBRA is the setting of caps on discretionary spending for the next five years; entitlement programs are not included in the caps. Unlike previous legislation, however, the OBRA established separate caps for domestic, defense, and international accounts, and no funds may be transferred among those accounts.

The establishment of separate caps, along with the inability to transfer funds, marks a shift from the battles over funding for defense versus domestic programs toward a focus on which programs will be funded within each category. Initially, domestic programs were provided with inflation-level funding, but all new initiatives must be funded by reductions in other domestic programs. The overall impact of the OBRA is that federal funding for domestic programs can be expected to become much tighter—and, with the war in the Middle East in winter 1991, it is clear that there will be no "peace dividend."

Unlike the earlier round of cuts in the federal budget, it is improbable that states, localities, or the voluntary sector can buffer the impact in the current round of cuts.

In 1991, 40 states faced budgetary deficits (Tolchin, 1991, p. A10). Corporations and other voluntary organizations are unlikely to be able to provide significant amounts of additional funding for human services programs. Thus, all signs point to a new era of fiscal austerity for human services programs that will likely persist for many years.

As federal funding for many human services programs decreases, an increasing number of human services managers will be confronted with the issue of retrenchment. The next round of cutbacks will undoubtedly result in layoffs and will call for different kinds of skills than most human services managers have heretofore been required to have. However, some important lessons can be learned from the experiences with the round of cutbacks that occurred in the early 1980s.

The Management of Decline

It is important for human services managers to recognize and understand the organizational and individual responses that tend to accompany declining resources if they are to be expected to develop adequate organizational and personal coping mechanisms. Regrettably, however, human services managers, like their counterparts in other fields, tend to be inadequately prepared to manage effectively under conditions of decline. This tendency is not surprising, since most managers have more training for and experience in responding to conditions of growth. As Boulding (1975, pp. 8–9) pointed out:

> We are very ill-equipped for the management of decline. For several generations, a considerable portion of the human race, and the United States in particular, has enjoyed growth in almost all aspects of social life. . . . All of our institutions and ways of thinking have survived because they were well-adapted to an age of rapid growth. If this age is now coming to an end, large adjustments will have to be made in our ways of thinking, in our habits and standards of decision making, and perhaps even in our institutions.

Growth has been viewed as consistent with the ideology and values of our culture, which considers growth and expansion to be primary indicators of effectiveness. Growth is also consistent with social work values that stress that adequate services should be available to all in need. The idea that "bigger" or "more" is better has been internalized by human services managers and their staffs, as well as by many others in this society.

Whetten (1980) noted that our culture views bigness as a highly desirable characteristic. The enhancement of economies of scale, the ability to absorb shocks that accompany environmental changes, and increased productive capacity are among the presumed benefits of largeness. Managers tend to be regarded as successful if they produce more, obtain larger budgets, and expand their organizations, but ineffective if they do the reverse.

Consequently, management training programs have not generally focused on the development of skills related to managing under conditions of decline. That they have not is not surprising, since most current organizational theory is based on assumptions of growth. Decline tends to be either ignored or treated as an aberration.

Responses to Decline

The traditional emphasis on organizational growth is being assaulted by the realities of decline, and nowhere is this situation truer than in the human services. Managers are finding that their knowledge and skills are inadequate for the challenges presented by decline. As a result, the following conditions can be observed in organizations and agencies that are experiencing decline or cutbacks in funding:

▶ high levels of manager and staff stress
▶ low trust, secretiveness, and centralization
▶ increased conflict and decreased morale
▶ conservatism and aversion to risk
▶ staff turnover and a self-protection orientation (see Cameron, 1983).

Under conditions of growth, the availability of slack resources makes it possible to overcome most of these problems. That is, when there are sufficient resources, people are more likely to be able to get what they want from the organization. The staff feel more secure; slack resources create conditions in which experimentation and innovation are possible. In addition, slack resources create buffers for the staff and for the organization. When there are no slack resources, the personal skills of the manager become more critical for the effective management of the organization.

In organizations that are experiencing cutbacks, there is often a "mean mood" because the staff feel insecure. Scapegoating is common, since managers are often blamed for the decreased resources, and the staff believe that the manager should have foreseen the problems and taken earlier actions to lessen their impact.

Because managers in organizations that are experiencing cutbacks do not have slack resources, they are less able to neutralize conflicting interest groups and buy internal consensus. "Adaptation by addition" is no longer possible, and managers have to contend with high levels of stress in themselves, as well as in their staff members. This stress often results in a restriction of the flow of communication in the organization, both from the top down and from the bottom up.

Concern for human relationships tends to be substantially reduced in such organizations, and relationships among managers and their staffs tend to become more formalized. Decision making tends to be more centralized, as managers begin to feel a need to maintain control and "play things close to the vest."

A feeling of impending crisis often pervades the organization as individual staff members fear they may lose their jobs, and the turnover of staff rises because those who can leave often do. Those who are unable to leave, for whatever reasons, often become embittered, feeling as though they are "trapped." For the organization, this atmosphere creates a major personnel problem, since those staff members who are best able to leave are often those who are the most capable. Consequently, the organization runs the risk of losing its best staff. Managers are aware of this possibility and often tend to guard against it by keeping bad news to themselves, thus intensifying their own stress and the mistrust of their subordinates.

Impact on Staff

The literature on cutback management tends to focus more on the impact of cutbacks on managers and managerial strategies for dealing with declining resources than on other staff members. However, all staff are clearly affected by cuts in funding, even when their particular jobs are not lost. Despite staff members' best professional efforts to avoid letting their concerns interfere with their relationships with clients, it is not reasonable to assume that clients are not adversely affected. Consequently, it is essential that managers in organizations that are experiencing declining resources concern themselves with the range of reactions of their staff members.

Austin (1984, p. 428) suggested that staff members in organizations that are experiencing declining resources often go through the following five-step process that is similar to Kübler-Ross's stages of death and dying: (1) denial and isolation, (2) anger, (3) bargaining, (4) depression, and (5) acceptance.

The first reaction of staff members to the possibility or reality of cuts in funding is often denial and isolation or withdrawal. The staff members initially express the belief that rumors of such cuts are exaggerated or that their particular agency, unit, or program will not be affected and often justify this by pointing to the quality of services they provide. Many staff members also react by attempting to withdraw from any discussions of cuts, taking what may be labeled an "ostrich" approach.

As staff members become more aware of the reality of cuts in funding, they often react with anger, which is frequently focused on the agency's administrators, who are blamed for the situation. The anger stems from the staff's fear that they may lose their jobs, and local targets are much more accessible than are far-off policymakers.

As their initial anger subsides, the staff members may begin to acknowledge the reality of the situation and begin to bargain for the survival of their particular unit, program, or job. When such bargaining fails, they tend to become depressed. At this point, they may feel helpless and hopeless, believing that the situation is beyond their control. If they are able to work through their depression, they will settle into a state of acceptance.

Unfortunately, not all staff members who are affected by cutbacks are able to work through these stages to the point of acceptance. Many leave the organization while they are still angry or depressed. Thus, managers who are involved in organizations that are facing a decline in resources need to recognize that these stages are normal concomitants of the situation and to find ways to help their staff members negotiate through them.

Managerial Strategies

The literature on cutback management suggests that managers tend to deal with conditions of decline by focusing increasingly on internal organizational concerns to the relative exclusion of external concerns. This focus on internal concerns is a common theme identified in the literature, and a number of authors have suggested that the tendency to do so is dysfunctional. Austin (1984, p. 428), for example, noted that the management of cutbacks requires administrators to play two major roles: the cheerleader and the strategic planner.

> The cheerleader role involves the administrator's capacity to engage in problem finding as well as problem solving, to model the learning process so that staff can participate in organizational and personal renewal, to increase staff involvement in all levels of decision making, and to take care of the "managerial self" to maximize effectiveness. The role of strategic planner includes the ability to develop viable policy and program options for both the agency's governing boards and its staff to consider and debate, to develop and maintain interagency networks for support and collaboration, to acquire skills and resources to market new and existing agency services, to manage computerized information systems, and to plan for staff involvement in seeking organizational excellence.

Weatherley (1984) considered two types of executive leaders that may emerge in organizations faced with cutbacks: the technician and the statesman. The technician views the organization and its staff as a means to an end and when confronted with decline is likely to attempt to maximize organizational efficiency, going to great lengths to avoid having the organization perceived as one that is declining. Furthermore, the technician generally assumes an authoritarian, top-down managerial style and exhibits a short-term perspective. The statesman, on the other hand, views the organization and its staff "as a social entity meeting certain needs of its participants and embodying certain values that emphasize service, however that may be defined" (p. 41). The statesman generally assumes a democratic managerial style, while exhibiting a long-term perspective. Finally, the statesman is attentive to the informal organizational structure, showing real concern about clients, as well as staff at all levels in the hierarchy. Weatherley concluded that "an organization led by the pragmatic technician concerned primarily with short-term survival may inadvertently and incrementally adopt policies that undermine its long-term viability and subvert its mission" (p. 44). The statesman, Weatherley suggested, must also deal with current crises, but views them in the context of a broader vision that seeks to protect and promote organizational values. Thus, in weighing different policies, the statesman will consider their long-range implications for the organization and its staff, as well as their immediate impact.

In their discussion of cutback management, Bombyk and Chernesky (1985) identified two leadership models, the Alpha style and the Beta style, which are similar to the two leadership styles identified by Weatherley. The Alpha style, they suggest, is a "leadership style that focuses on hierarchical structure, clear definitions of power and authority, and on rewards to promote individual achievement and compliance with the rules [and] . . . is based upon a belief that problems are essentially technical matters and that solutions can be engineered" (p. 49). The Beta style is characterized more by a concern for people and processes and less by a task orientation. It emphasizes collective problem solving, sharing information, and attention to the needs and feelings of staff members. Bombyk and Chernesky argued that "the strengths of the Beta style for cutback management lie in its fluid conception of power, its empowerment of staff and clients to be co-participants in the decision making process, and its ability to tolerate the chaos and uncertainty of the organization's retrenchment phase" (p. 56).

Certainly, managers and staff members in organizations that are experiencing declining resources often are confronted with competing values. Environmental conditions may dictate that certain aspects of organizational life should be empha-sized and this emphasis can, and often does, have an adverse effect on other aspects. For instance, one of the first actions managers might take when confronted with declining resources is to institute a freeze on hiring and to order that positions that become vacant through attrition be left unfilled. The managers would then develop revised budgetary projections that take into account "savings" they would expect as a result of not filling positions that became vacant through retirements or resigna-tions. As Turem and Born (1983, p. 207) noted:

> Superficially, attrition seems a reasonable, conflict-avoiding response to newly imposed fiscal constraints. By combining attrition with hiring freezes, administrators may avoid the bureaucratic, union, and interpersonal hassles related to layoffs and quell the disruption of staff morale (and thus staff performance) that "RIF" (reduction in force) rumors may have stirred up.

However, they pointed out that attrition is not a good way to deal with budget cuts because

> at best, attrition represents personnel decision by default; at worst it is a tactic to avoid confronting issues that should be addressed squarely regardless of their unpleasant-ness or difficulty. Attrition, like across-the-board reduction, does not require human service professionals to undertake the arduous task of defining and setting priorities on specific goals of each service program. Both approaches ignore the possibility that the value of maintaining established staffing patterns in certain areas may more than justify making disproportionate cuts in other areas.

When attrition and hiring freezes are instituted, the staff may have to assume a greater work load, such as carrying increased caseloads. This change may be regarded as a move to make the staff more productive and the agency more efficient.

However, over time, such a strategy may have an adverse affect on the cohesion and morale of the staff. It is possible that staff will experience higher levels of stress, which may lead to greater absenteeism and perhaps to increased turnover.

Another common response of managers to declining resources is to attempt to trim the "frills" from the budget by reducing or eliminating various support services, including janitorial, equipment and building maintenance, secretarial, and other services. In addition, such benefits as reimbursement for continuing education or professional development activities are also frequently sharply curtailed or eliminated. Managers do so to protect or shield their professional staff members as long as possible, out of a desire to maintain direct services to clients.

Over time, however, these actions also lead to increased stress in staff and may contribute to a turnover in staff, with the result that the agency may ultimately find itself with a predominantly younger, less experienced staff that is not able to provide the same quality of services that more experienced staff who were with the agency longer might have been able to provide. The net result is that the agency may experience communication problems, the flow of information may be impeded by not having sufficient support staff, and the agency will be increasingly less stable. All these conditions may curtail productivity (the delivery of services), which, in turn, may have a further adverse affect on funding.

Yet another common strategy that managers use to deal with declining resources is to institute "across-the-board" cuts. The idea behind this strategy is that the organization will continue to do all it has been doing, albeit on a reduced level. This approach is intuitively appealing, since it seems to be an equitable way to share the pain involved in cutting back and "no program, provider, or client constituency can claim to have been singled out to bear the brunt of retrenchment" (Turem & Born, 1983, p. 206).

For the manager, an across-the-board approach to dealing with declining resources may be the least painful. And it may be effective when the reductions in resources are relatively small and it is deemed that such reductions are likely to be short term. However, when reductions in resources are major and are likely to persist for a long time, the across-the-board strategy may lessen the effectiveness of all aspects of the organization's programming. In the long run, it may be far better for the organization to do fewer things well than to do many things poorly.

Dealing with Staff

Managers who confront the specter of declining resources can take a number of specific actions to help their staff members deal more effectively with the situation. First, however, they must recognize that their own levels of stress are likely to increase. Therefore, they must take steps to identify the sources of this stress and handle it. Identifying and dealing with stress are likely to involve grappling with a paradox, since managers tend to react to their own increasing stress by withdrawing, keeping information to themselves, and becoming more autocratic in making decisions. These tendencies must be fought, however, and efforts must be made to be more open about sharing information and decision making. In addition, managers need to attend to their own stress through a variety of stress-reduction techniques, from doing more physical exercise to creating and participating in support groups with other managers who are in a similar situation.

Particular attention must also be paid to those in the organization who will have the responsibility and burden of telling others that they are being laid off or that their

"After the layoffs, no one was left who knew how to fill out purchase requisitions, expense vouchers or make coffee."

jobs are eliminated. This is an extremely stressful task that often falls on middle managers, and its impact should not be overlooked.

Managers need to be aware that an important component of their activity in dealing with declining resources is the management of rumors (Hirschhorn, 1983). They must decide what to tell the staff and when to tell it. Rumors not only structure and reduce anxiety, they give the staff a way to make sense of the situation. In other words, rumors often enable staff to gain a sense of control. Managers can counteract rumors, to a large extent, by recognizing the purposes that rumors serve and by providing alternative mechanisms for the staff to meet their needs for greater control. These mechanisms include helping staff members at all levels in the organization to structure their anxiety by engaging them in planning activities, as well as by providing them with opportunities to express the negative feelings they are bound to have. Planning groups can be established and charged with developing a range of best case–worst case scenarios with a set of alternative decisions for each scenario.

Managers may also engage staff planning groups in an examination of the agency's mission and goals to identify the "core program." Such identification can be helpful in the subsequent development and structuring of a plan for handling decisions about retrenchment or layoffs. As Hirschhorn (1983) noted, managers must often confront the need to make trade-offs between the issues of fairness and strategy. When layoffs are contemplated, managers generally desire a fair process, yet they often would also like to be able to keep those staff members who are most likely to prove valuable to the agency in the future. A consideration of the agency's core program helps to identify those individuals within the organization who have the knowledge and skills that make them best able to further the core programming.

Of course, union contracts and civil service regulations may set limits on a manager's ability to make staffing decisions under conditions of decline. When such contracts or regulations exist, it is incumbent upon the manager to be well informed about their requirements and restrictions. When no such contracts or regulations exist, the manager may have more latitude in making decisions about retrenchment. In either case, to the extent possible, decisions about who to keep and who to let go should be based on judgments about which staff members can contribute most to the organization's core programming and which will best enable the organization to be positioned to take advantage of environmental opportunities that may arise in the future.

When decisions are made to lay off particular staff members, these individuals should be informed as early as possible to afford them the maximum chance to find other jobs. Staff whose positions are being eliminated should be provided with a range of supports or outplacement services. These supports may include providing them with assistance in preparing résumés, assuring them that they will be able to get reference letters that indicate the circumstances under which their employment was terminated, and giving them opportunities to ventilate their feelings about the situation. In addition, it may be helpful to arrange for a representative of the local unemployment compensation office to meet with the staff to explain how they may apply for unemployment compensation, how long it will take for them to receive their first check, how much money they can expect to receive, and for how long they may be eligible to collect benefits. This kind of information is essential to staff members who have to plan how they will manage their lives in the period immediately after being laid off. Furthermore, every effort should be made to help staff find out about other employment opportunities.

Managers should engage in planning activities that are aimed at defining the primary functions of their organizations and developing strategies for the future. They need to be aware that cutbacks "may alter an organization's strategic position in a network, reduce its relative power, and increase its dependency on other organizations" (Friesen & Frey, 1983, pp. 36–37). Thus, it is important for managers to consider how their organizations will relate to other organizations: whether they will enter coalitions, attempt to keep a monopoly over their services, or look for new markets or opportunities for services.

Managers also need to become actively involved in the development of resources. These activities may range from grant writing, obtaining contracts, and instituting fee-for-service programs to devising strategies for making use of volunteers and paraprofessionals and building relationships with policymakers. In short, managers who are confronting declining resources "need to develop both technical skills (i.e., how to raise new funds) and interactional skills (i.e., how to build a constituency)" (Friesen & Frey, 1983, p. 37).

Summary

Managers of human services agencies are confronting a new era of fiscal austerity. In the 1990s, they will continue to experience the financial consequences of Ronald Reagan's "New Federalism," the Gramm Rudman Hollings legislation, and the OBRA of 1990.

The significant decline in financial resources is likely to result in the following conditions: (1) increased levels of stress for both staff members and managers; (2) mistrust, secretiveness, and centralization; (3) increased conflict and decreased morale; (4) conservatism and an aversion to taking risks; and (5) the turnover of staff and a self-protection orientation. The absence of slack resources compounds the managers' capacity to deal most effectively with these conditions. However, the flip side is that downsizing has the potential for revitalizing organizations.

To be effective, human services managers must recognize their own stress and learn to deal with it. Having done so, they should involve staff in identifying the organization's core program and delineating the agency's mission, primary functions, and goals. At the same time, they should pursue resource-development strategies to increase revenues. If layoffs are necessitated by dwindling resources, they should be handled in a straightforward, honest manner, and outplacement assistance should be provided to staff who are losing their jobs. It is evident that these varied responses to organizational decline will require both technical and interactional skills.

SKILLS-APPLICATION EXERCISE

You are the manager of a county child welfare department. Your programs include adoption services, in-home family-unification services, foster care services, and services (counseling and public education) to prevent physical and sexual abuse. Your funding sources include governmental grants (65 percent), fees (30 percent), and some small grants from foundations and corporations (5 percent). You have been advised that your governmental funding will be reduced by 20 percent over the next two years.

You have been requested by the board of county commissioners to submit your plan for dealing with these budgetary cuts. What managerial actions or approaches would you take? Include in your design how you would respond to the following:

1. What activities can the agency stop performing?
2. What activities can you get other agencies to do?
3. What activities can be performed more effectively?
4. How can you reduce the cost of labor?
5. How can you increase the agency's revenues?

References

Austin, M. J. (1984). Managing cutbacks in the 1980s. *Social Work, 29,* 428–434.

Bombyk, M. J., & Chernesky, R. H. (1985). Conventional cutback leadership and the quality of the workplace: Is beta better? *Administration in Social Work, 9*(3), 47–56.

Boulding, K. (1975). The management of decline. *Change, 7*(5), 8–9, 64.

Cameron, K. S. (1983). Strategic responses to conditions of decline: Higher education and the private sector. *Journal of Higher Education, 54,* 359–380.

Friesen, B. J., & Frey, G. (1983). Managing organizational decline: Emerging issues for administration. *Administration in Social Work, 7*(3/4), 33–41.

Greenstein, R. (1986). *Hard choices: Federal budget priorities in the Gramm-Rudman-Hollings era.* Washington, DC: Interfaith Action for Economic Justice.

Hirschhorn, L. (Ed.). (1983). *Cutting back: Retrenchment and redevelopment in human and community services.* San Francisco: Jossey-Bass.

Knighton, A., & Heidelman, N. (1984). Managing human services organizations with limited resources. *Social Work, 29,* 531–535.

Pawlak, E. J., Jeter, C. S., & Fink, R. L. (1983). The politics of cutback management. *Administration in Social Work, 7*(2), 1–10.

Tolchin, M. (1991, February 4). Cuts after decade of cuts: Governors grim at meeting. *New York Times,* p. A10.

Turem, J. S., & Born, C. E. (1983). Doing more with less. *Social Work, 28,* 206–210.

Weatherley, R. (1984). Approaches to cutback management. In F. D. Perlmutter (Ed.), *Human services at risk* (pp. 39–56). Lexington, MA: Lexington Books.

Whetten, D. A. (1980). Sources, responses, and effects of organizational decline. In J. Kimberly & R. Miles (Eds.), *The organizational life cycle* (pp. 342–374). San Francisco: Jossey-Bass.

COORDINATING SKILLS

M anagerial coordinating skills encompass the roles of monitor and coordinator. Competencies for the role of monitor include receiving and organizing information, evaluating routine information, and responding to routine information. Competencies for the role of coordinator include planning, organizing, and controlling. The chapters in this section focus on these internal, control-oriented roles and competencies as human services managers seek organizational stability and continuity.

Mary Kay Kantz and Kathryn Mercer discuss how to write effectively. They argue that human services managers must "gain control" over their writing so that it works for them, and they focus on the difficulties of getting started and overcoming these start-up barriers. Special attention is paid to the purpose of the written communication and to the audience to whom the communication is to be directed. Generating information and organizing ideas are suggested as the next essential steps in effective writing. Kantz and Mercer believe that writing skills are important in both the monitoring and coordinating roles and that documentation, record keeping, and technical writing, as well as other internal and external written communication, contribute to the efficient flow of work. Thus, to the extent human services managers can efficiently collect, organize, and disseminate information, they are likely to be more successful, especially in hierarchically oriented organizations.

Perry P. Heath focuses on the impact of an information-based society. He suggests that the increased sophistication of technology may create a new realm of "entrepreneurial adventure" to try the unprecedented and that authority, in the future, may be less a function of organizational hierarchy than of knowledge and how to gain access to and use information. He offers a series of action steps to facilitate the introduction or enhancement of technology in human services organizations: developing a means of building technological awareness, providing training that answers questions, creating an organizational attitude that supports risk taking, and including technology-related agenda items at conferences and seminars. Heath views managerial leadership to be essential for the implementation of computer systems in human services organizations. He presents numerous examples of computer applications to undergird his view that such systems can influence planning, organizing, and controlling, as well as receiving, evaluating, and responding to information. To the extent that routinization can lead to stability and an increasingly efficient work flow, Heath concludes that information technology will provide new opportunities for human services managers and organizations.

Claudia J. Coulton presents a compelling and persuasive argument for the role of quality assurance in carrying out the monitoring and coordinating roles. Describing the purpose of quality assurance as the continuous promotion and enhancement of the quality of services provided by human services organizations, she recognizes the difficulty of defining this ever-elusive concept. Coulton suggests that quality assurance comprises three interrelated aspects: structure, process, and outcome. She notes key definitional parameters as currently being important: the given time and place in an organization's functioning, the expectations of receivers and providers of services, and the values of those involved in designing and implementing quality assurance approaches. In addition, she provides a detailed description of the elements of such a program, including the establishment of the appropriate structure for quality assurance and the components of and steps in designing the monitoring and evaluation system. Coulton, like other authors in this section, demonstrates the interrelatedness of skills in carrying out the managerial roles of monitoring and coordinating. Quality assurance programming, to be maximally useful, requires some development of all the competencies associated with these roles.

Paul A. Kurzman emphasizes the risks and liabilities that human services organizations encounter and the monitoring and coordinating roles of human services managers in establishing and managing risk-management activities. He identifies the most frequently noted risks—the duty to warn if clients disclose an intent to harm themselves or others, to maintain confidentiality, to ensure the continuity of services, to properly diagnose and treat clients, and to avoid sexual impropriety—and discusses the recommended responses, including insurance protection, legal counsel, staff training, and internal audits. Kurzman provides useful insights into the rationale and practices for each of these potential responses. The implicit themes of stability, continuity, reliability, and technical competence permeate his views of the necessity for human services managers to deal proactively with the risks their organizations face.

14

Writing Effectively: A Key Task for Managers

Mary Kay Kantz and Kathryn Mercer

There are several problems with paper. One is that there is so much of it around that most of us are stumbling over it, drowning in it, and wasting lots of time dealing with it, both at home and in the office. Another problem with paper is that from time to time you have to write on it. And whenever you do, you put a little bit of yourself down on the paper to be examined and judged by someone else. Solely on the basis of what you set down on paper, someone may decide whether you are managing your organization efficiently or whether you have exercised your professional judgment wisely.

There is something fleeting about a judgment or opinion that is expressed orally; it is less available for scrutiny than is the written word and it will probably be less far reaching in its impact. But ideas can be transformed by writing. Once put down on paper, mere suggestions or daily routines become rules and policies. And one person's (perhaps ill-informed) opinion becomes the last word on the subject.

So as a human services manager you cannot afford to be a poor writer. If the words you put down on paper are not clear to your reader, they can take on a life of their own that is contrary to your intent. Or they can die on the spot, when you want them to come alive and make the reader take action. For example, you may need to be able to convey your thoughts effectively in writing to obtain funding for a new project, to get approval for additional staffing, or to get the go-ahead for new programs and services. If you cannot convey the necessary information clearly, concisely, and persuasively, you lose. If you cannot do it efficiently—meaning it takes you or a staff member a long time to complete a report or a request for funding—you lose.

Then how do you win? How do you get control over your writing so you can improve it and make it work for you? Is it even possible to improve your writing if all those years in the classroom doing grammar exercises did not help? It is indeed possible, and it is worth the effort.

Getting Started

The best way to start is to identify your strengths and weaknesses as a writer, so you can plan your program of improvement. You can use the same framework both to evaluate your writing and to work on improving it—that is, look at your writing as including three distinct components: content, organization, and style.

Unfortunately, most of us have had our hands slapped often enough, literally or figuratively, over errors in grammar and punctuation that we tend to think only of checking for those kinds of mechanical problems ("style") in dealing with our writing. In fact, content is the most important consideration. Writing is communication, the exchange of messages. So the message, the meaning you wish to convey in your writing, is of prime importance. The organization of content and attention to details of style are separate matters, to be dealt with after you have decided on your message. Learning to recognize and deal separately and explicitly with these various components of the writing process will enable you to build on your writing strengths and systematically overcome your weaknesses.

Evaluating and Improving Content

In reviewing your writing to determine whether your message is clear and complete, check for (1) its focus on purpose and (2) its focus on the audience.

Purpose

Focusing on the purpose of your writing should be your first consideration. This means being aware of the general purpose of the writing—to inform, to persuade, and to motivate—as well as the objectives of the specific task at hand.

It is surprising how often writers fail to convey the message they have in mind simply because they have not taken the time to think about why they are setting something down on paper. Instead, they sit down and start to write whatever comes to mind. It may well be that what they write has more to do with their emotional state at the moment or the distractions of the day than with the essence of their message.

For instance, a supervisor may write a simple memo announcing the agenda for an upcoming staff meeting. Her purpose is to see if anyone has anything else to add to the agenda. The memo evolves into an explanation of why the meeting was postponed from last Thursday's original meeting date, how the current severe weather conditions have affected the ability of staff members to make early morning meetings, why the staff meetings have been so long and drawn out lately, and so on. The supervisor is angry about some of these matters and apologetic about others. Some of them may be worth adding to the agenda so that solutions can be found. But in the meantime, these extraneous items have distracted the reader of the memo, who is now less likely to respond to what the supervisor wanted in the first place.

You can avoid this problem by taking a few minutes before drafting a document to list the points you want to make. For purposes of evaluation, try backtracking through several pieces of your writing and list the separate points you made in each. Check to see how many of the points really support your purpose in writing the document. How often did you include irrelevant ideas or comments that may distract the reader or be counterproductive to your purpose?

It is easier to weed out irrelevant points when they stand alone in a list than when they are embedded in a completed text. More important, when you simply list your ideas—without being concerned with constructing well-formed sentences and coherent paragraphs—you allow your thoughts to flow more freely and creatively. Stopping frequently in your writing to check the spelling of a word or to decide just how you want to start a paragraph is likely to cause you to lose your train of thought, or worse, to neglect to pick up on spur-of-the-moment ideas that just may lead to the solution for which you are looking.

In more complex writing tasks, you will need more than a quick listing of ideas to keep you on track (some other approaches are discussed later). But the same principle applies. Deal first with the message: your purpose for writing. If you let yourself fall into the grammar-picker syndrome—proofreading continuously as you write, afraid that a mistake in punctuation will get past you—you may have trouble producing as creative or as thorough a piece of writing as you would like. Work on developing your thoughts and speaking directly to your audience, knowing that you can correct grammatical problems later.

Audience

An awareness of your audience must also be at the heart of the writing process. Sometimes the audience seems to be of less immediate concern because you are writing for the same audience all the time (your staff, for instance) and you have developed a sense of how to talk to this group. Other times, the sense of the audience is closely tied in with the purpose of the writing and must be carefully considered if you are to get your message across. For example, your goal may be to obtain funding from a particular source, and that source has a tendency to fund only specifically defined activities because of the predilections of the original benefactor. Your goal, then, is not just to ask for a grant, but to appeal to the interests of the benefactor as seen through the eyes of the fund's administrator.

Before you write, find out as much as you can about your audience. If you lack the time or resources to find out as much as you need to know, then conjure up an audience for your own benefit. Make it as close as possible to the audience you believe you are addressing. Then *speak* to that audience. How would you convey your message to that audience in person, one to one? Try to speak as directly to that audience on paper as you would in person. Sometimes, especially if your writing project calls for creativity, it may be helpful to forget about the audience until you have had time to explore fully your own ideas on the subject you will be addressing. Too much focus on your audience too early in the process may stifle creative thought. You may subconsciously supply answers to a problem on the basis of what you believe your audience would like you to be thinking. However, you must deal with the demands of your audience before the writing task is finished.

Another point to consider in terms of audience is the use of jargon. It is obvious that the use of professional jargon may create problems for a nonprofessional audience. But problems also may arise from the overuse or indiscriminate use of such language in writing for members of the "in" group. The standard argument, of course, is that jargon allows for the precise expression of concepts that are central to the work of the profession. But often such language actually is used to mask imprecise and unclear thinking. The solution is to think through the ideas you wish to express and make sure you have resolved the problem or fully developed your idea or proposal before you try to convey your thoughts to the reader. Then, having developed and understood the idea yourself and having decided to address an audience that is conversant with the jargon, you can safely revert to that special form of language for the benefit of precise expression.

"Quite frankly Kevin, I'd be hesitant to accept an annual report submitted in green and yellow crayon."

Organization

Your audience will not respond to your message unless the message is clear, and the message will not be clear unless it is well organized. Your thoughts do not have to be well organized as they tumble from your brain onto the page; usually they are not. The problem is that many people expect that they will be and consequently do not make an effort to organize their thoughts.

The process of organization, however, is separate from the idea-generating process. And most people are better at one than the other. In either case, writing tends to go faster and to bring forth more original thought, regarding both solutions to problems and methods of expression, when the process of generating the message precedes the process of organizing it for presentation to a reader.

The traditional approach, the sit-down-and-just-start-writing approach, may still be all you need for brief, routine writing tasks. But for more complex or more critical pieces, you may find free writing to be of value. This method is based on the concept of dealing separately with the separate components of the writing process. Many writers today use the free-writing approach to overcome writer's block and to get more ideas per minute down on paper. The idea is simply to start writing in whatever form feels comfortable to you. The easiest way is just to list your thoughts and perhaps (for later organizational purposes) to number each separate thought. You should feel free to let your mind wander where it will as you write, jotting down even half-thoughts, tangential ideas, and distractions. Start your pencil moving and keep it moving no matter what, taking no time out to check spelling or to correct punctuation or to decide how to phrase an opening sentence. You can even interrupt yourself in the middle of a thought.

Free writing can be done as an exercise to loosen up before beginning a writing project—in which case it does not matter what you write about. Or it can be done as the initial phase of your real task. At any point in the free-writing process, you can stop jotting down ideas and begin to organize your material. Although you treat idea generating and organizing as two separate processes in free writing, you use them in tandem, moving one or the other to the forefront as you choose.

There are many different organizational patterns you can follow for different writing tasks (some will be discussed later in this chapter). But in this initial phase—your free-writing session—simply group like ideas with like ideas. Nothing fancy or complicated.

Free-Writing Model

For example, suppose you decide to draft a memo proposing that your staff be given some kind of training in writing. You want to come up with some practical suggestions for doing so and you want to be persuasive, but you are not quite sure where to start. A free-writing exercise might produce the following list of ideas:

1. In an office setting it is important to be able to communicate clearly.
2. Many people have trouble finding the time to write.
3. Maybe it's because they put it off because they don't want to do it.
4. Maybe they don't want to do it because they are embarrassed by their writing skills.
5. A lot of people have negative feelings about writing because teachers in the past have criticized whatever they have written.
6. But now we're not in school.
7. On the other hand, some people have never had any significant help with their writing.
8. Professionally, it is important to appear well on paper. It indicates you have a solid educational background and looks good to others.
9. It helps you get ahead professionally if you can communicate effectively, spoken and written.
10. What about social work profess'ls in particular? Who do they have to communicate with?
11. There are many audiences for a s.w. profess'ls writing—clients, lawyers, judges, foundations and other sources of support, the general public, co-workers, and supervisors.
12. How can—Maybe the approach should be a *series* of workshops or seminars by *different* people, might make it more interesting—how to meet all the different needs?
13. I would like to improve the speed of my writing—getting something into a finished form—different projects have different requirements as far as what "finished" means—getting into a finished form without wasting a lot of time that I need for other things. Same for others?
14. Maybe I should do more writing than I have been doing—just on my own—to get up to speed.
15. But are there helpful techniques for doing this?

At this point you may decide to start organizing these thoughts to see where you are. Let us assume that you look over the list and see four groups of ideas (A, B, C, and D). You run down your list, jotting the appropriate letter in front of each numbered idea:

> A for ideas 1, 8, and 9
> B for ideas 2–7
> C for ideas 10, 11, and 13
> D for ideas 12, 14, and 15.

Now you are ready to do a quick outline of your material, not worrying about the form, such as the following (the numbers in parentheses are the numbers of your original ideas):

> A. Importance of writing in an office setting (1)
>   —Credibility (8)
>   —Professional development (9)

B. Why social work professionals would need help with writing
    —Many procrastinate (3)
      —Why?
        —No time (2)
        —Embarrassed by lack of skills (4)
          —Why? Baggage from the past (5)
          —But time to let that go (6)
      —Others really do lack basic skills (10)
C. What kind of help is needed (10)?
    —Audience (10/11)
    —Efficiency (13)
    —Purpose (13)
D. Kinds of help available?
    —Self-help (14/15)
    —Workshops (12)

From the rough outline that emerges, you can begin to see which topics are worth developing and which points may be omitted. You can begin to firm up your ideas of audience and purpose if those points have not yet been clarified. By expanding the entries in the outline into complete sentences, you can sharpen the focus of your thoughts. And without the pressure of producing a finished product on the first try, you have more room for creative problem solving.

Free-Writing Exercise

To experience the free-writing process and to compare it with the more traditional approach to writing, try these exercises.

Choose one of the following assignments (A–C). Spend about 20 minutes responding to it, following Instruction 1. Then choose a second assignment and spend the same amount of time responding to it according to Instruction 2. Complete just as much of the assignment as you can reasonably do in the allotted time. Then compare the results by answering the questions that follow the assignments.

Instruction 1: Draft the memo, newsletter article, or whatever, in the format in which such a document would actually appear. Remember to start each paragraph with a topic sentence that tells clearly what the paragraph will be about and end each paragraph with a conclusion. Make transitions between paragraphs clear. Do your best to avoid errors of grammar, punctuation, spelling, sentence structure, and choice of words.

Instruction 2: List your thoughts and suggestions as they come to you. Number them if you wish. Do not worry about organization, paragraph or sentence structure, grammar, spelling, or punctuation. Write down your thoughts just as they come to you.

Assignments

A. Write a letter aimed at persuading a legislator to endorse proposed public funding of a particular human services project.

B. Write an opinion-page article for your local newspaper, encouraging the general public to support a particular human services program.

C. Write a memo to the director of the undergraduate social services training program at your local university, who has asked your advice in designing a program to train and place student interns in social service agencies in your community.

Evaluate Your Work

Compare the writing you did according to Instruction 1 with what you did according to Instruction 2.

1. How many paragraphs did you write in 1?

2. How many different ideas did you express in 1? 2?

3. Did you write anything that surprised you in 1? 2? What was it?

4. How did you feel about each of these writing assignments?

5. Who was your audience, what was your purpose in 1? in 2?

Some writers find that they are skilled enough to write a final draft at the first attempt, and some writers find that for routine tasks they need or want to take the time for only one draft. But many experienced writers find that some form of free writing helps them develop their writing skills and produce more thoughtful and well-organized written work. Although it is a multistep process, free writing can actually help you become a much more efficient writer—to get more good writing on paper faster—compared with the writer who tries to do a final draft all at once.

Style

Although it is better *not* to worry about punctuation, grammar, sentence structure, and so on while you are busy defining and organizing your message, you *must* deal with this aspect of your writing before you are finished. Your credibility will suffer if you do not.

But it is relatively easy to clean up your prose after you have made the big decisions about the content and arrangement of your message. And there is no law that says you have to do it yourself. Sometimes another pair of eyes can be a great help and timesaver when it comes to proofreading. Do not be embarrassed or hesitant about asking a colleague to proofread your writing. Your willingness to take this step simply demonstrates your commitment to improving your writing— for your own sake and the benefit of your organization.

In dealing with problems of style, identify (perhaps with the help of your proofreader) several specific problems that seem to recur in your writing. Browse through some of the many excellent books on writing that you will find at your library or bookstore (many are listed at the end of this chapter) and set a little time aside each week to work on one problem at a time. It is not a difficult task, just one that requires some dedication. You can truly accomplish on your own what all the knuckle rapping of your elementary school teachers could not achieve. Your computer can also provide some help at this point. Get in the habit of using its spell-checking feature and investigate the possibility of acquiring grammar-checking software (such as RightWriter). Just remember to use these features thoughtfully. They will help you, but they will not do all the work; they respond mechanically to their tasks and need some input from you.

Using This Information

Human services managers often function as problem solvers. Their clients present dilemmas that have personal, social, and legal implications. The managers are asked to assess the situation, to form an opinion, and to communicate that opinion to an audience. The audience might be a funding source, the government, a board of directors, the agency's staff, or clients. Usually there is no single correct view of a given situation. Thus, the reader needs sufficient information to be persuaded or to reach an independent decision. The professional's written opinion will serve its purpose if it is based on logically connected arguments that lead to a clearly formulated conclusion. To communicate the logical problem-solving process to another person, a clear organizational plan is needed.

Identify the Purpose of Your Writing

The first task is to identify your mission in preparing a document. Take a few minutes to think about what you need to say, why you need to say it, and to whom. A clear summary will help you maintain your focus throughout the writing process.

For example, assume that you are a manager of a child protective services agency (CPS). You have been requested by the state funding agency to justify your request for additional personnel. Here is the statement of purpose you have drafted:

> As an administrator of a child protective services agency (CPS) operating in a major metropolitan center, my goal is to educate and persuade the state funding agency (the audience) that CPS is understaffed.

Generate Information

To begin preparing this report, you make a list of ideas that have led you to believe that the deficiency in staffing poses an immediate problem. You jot down examples, statistics, background material, major factors, and minor factors. In making this list, you do not worry about the order of the information or how the information will be structured in the report.

Some of the ideas you generate in this information "dump" include the following:

▶ The number of child abuse reports increased 20 percent in the last year.

▶ New state and federal legislation requires extensive investigation and documentation.

▶ Numerous CPS workers have complained about their inability to do the job.

▶ Worker's caseloads are up 12 percent.

▶ During the past month, CPS was sued by a parents' group for its failure to use reasonable efforts to reunify families.

▶ CPS lost 10 workers in the past two months who discussed "burnout" in their termination meeting.

Clustering and Organizing Ideas

Several organizational schemes can be used to convert a rambling list of ideas into a coherent persuasive report. All schemes have the goals of (1) putting similar thoughts together in groups, (2) arranging the items within each group in a logical order, and (3) connecting those groups in a coherent fashion.

You separate the six ideas you just listed into three categories:

▶ External pressures—legislation and increased reporting

▶ Internal pressures—increased caseloads, complaints, and burnout

▶ Danger signals—lawsuits and the attrition of workers.

Grouping and labeling separate ideas will give a basic structure to the writing and help the reader absorb the information.

You next look for a unifying theme and message that will connect one group to the next.

Here the theme that emerges is that the problem—understaffing—is a result of the worker's response to increased external demands on the agency. The persuasive message of the report could be that corrective action is needed before there is further disintegration of the agency's ability to function as indicated by the lawsuit and an increased turnover of staff.

The writing's theme or message should match the statement of purpose written at the beginning of the process. A theme helps generate an order for the groups and a sequence of information within each group. Some ways to arrange information include chronology, geography, analytical deduction, steps in a process, and comparison or contrast. In the CPS example, you decide to combine two sequencing methods.

First, you decide to trace chronologically the sequence of external events that led to the problem of understaffing. Then, you plan to present and interpret data to show the current impact on the agency and to forecast the future inability of the agency

to render needed services. Ideally, this analytical process will persuade the reader that your proposed solution—increased funding—is imperative.

Organizing the Persuasive Document

Once ideas have been generated, clustered, and organized, you are ready to draft the document.

1. *Identify the problem or issue to be addressed.* The reader needs to know the subject of the document at the outset.

2. *Introduce your position in a lead paragraph and give a road map.* The position statement controls the organization of the memo. It states "up front" the solution to the problem and summarizes the reasons for your conclusion. The lead paragraph tells the reader where you are going and how to get there.

3. *Control the discussion through assertive paragraphs that focus on a single idea.* One method of writing persuasively is to divide the document into ARAC arguments. ARAC stands for assertion, rule, analysis, conclusion.

Assertion: For each topic or idea, begin by stating your position on that topic. Write one sentence that directly states your major point.

Rule: Identify the relevant authority that supports your position—a statute, statistics, literature you have consulted, and so forth.

Analysis: Use the rest of the paragraph to support and explain your position. Use the facts of the situation you are analyzing to demonstrate how you arrived at your position.

Conclusion: Restate your position on the topic of the assertive paragraph, indicating where you have been.

The first sentence of the next paragraph should be linked to the last paragraph and direct the reader to the next subtopic or topic. Thus, the four-step process begins again.

4. *Use organizational signals.* The reader needs signals so the direction and flow of the writing are always apparent. The way the prose appears on the formatted page focuses the reader's attention on your important points and leads the reader to the appropriate conclusions.

First, use the paragraph to indicate your separate topic organization. Each paragraph should address only a single topic. The break between paragraphs will allow the reader to see the topic organization of your writing.

Second, begin new paragraphs with topic and transitional sentences to give continuity and cohesion to your writing. These sentences provide the reader with a point of view for looking at a paragraph. Transitional sentences explain to the reader how one point leads to the next.

Third, use signposts. Signposts are periodic indicators of where your argument has been and where it is going. They help redirect the reader back to the larger pattern, placing all the pieces in the larger context. Consider using headings as signposts. These breaks in the writing allow the reader to catch a breath and rejuvenate. They also visually demonstrate the structure of your argument and give the reader a sense of your major points.

5. *Conclude your argument.* Confidently restate your position, putting everything into perspective. This conclusion sums up the entire analysis—all the issues and subissues. It may also recommend future action.

Demonstration of ARAC

The following exercise demonstrates the ARAC method for organizing a persuasive memorandum.

You are a supervisor of child protective services. The court has asked the agency to assess and draft recommendations as to whether a child is neglected or dependent. You are familiar with the state statutes that define dependency and neglect.

Section 51 defines a neglected child as any child

(A) Who lacks proper parental care because of the faults or habits of his or her parents. . . .

(B) Whose parents neglect or refuse to provide him or her with proper or necessary subsistence, education, medical or surgical care, or other care necessary for his or her health, morals, or well-being.

To show neglect, you must show that the parent was at fault. However, the court can find a dependent child when there is no parental fault.

Section 52 defines a dependent child as any child

(B) Who lacks proper care or support by reason of the mental or physical condition of his or her parents. . . .

(C) Whose condition or environment is such as to warrant the state, in the interests of the child, in assuming his or her guardianship.

A child protective service investigation revealed the following facts concerning the Dorwins. Is state intervention appropriate in this case? You may classify the child as a dependent child or a neglected child in your recommendation.

The Dorwins[1]

Mr. and Mrs. Dorwin . . . were reported to a child protective agency in a large metropolitan city. They had moved to the city from a farming community. Mrs. Dorwin, who was twenty-eight years old, had been reared in a poverty-stricken rural area. She had completed six years of formal education. Her family had lived in a shack

---

[1]*Reprinted by permission of Beacon Press from* When Parents Fail, *by Sanford Katz, copyright © 1971 by Sanford Katz.*

without electricity or plumbing. Both her father and sister had been hospitalized several times because of mental illness.

Mr. Dorwin was thirty-one years old; he was raised in an urban area of a predominantly rural state. Because of his mother's mental illness and his father's alcoholism and abusive treatment of his children, Mr. Dorwin and his brothers and sisters lived with and were raised by a relative. Mr. Dorwin completed eight years of formal education. An auto mechanic, he had a criminal record for drunkenness and assault and battery on his wife and children. He seldom worked steadily. The Dorwins were married when Mrs. Dorwin was six months pregnant.

Mr. and Mrs. Dorwin had moved into an attractive, well-kept apartment, later to be evicted for nonpayment of rent and causing damage to the residence. The walls of their present apartment were dirty, with large holes where plaster had been removed. The floors were uncared for; garbage and feces were spread throughout the rooms. The house had a strong urine odor. The five Dorwin children (ages ten, nine, seven, five, and four) were dirty, poorly clothed, and malnourished. Frequently they were seen begging in the streets for scraps of food. Neighbors reported that the children were often left alone at night or with an alcoholic uncle as a baby sitter. Often the children slept on sodden mattresses without sheets. Sometimes they all slept in the same bed with their mother. Neighbors said that the parents frequently swore at their children. The children themselves said they were afraid of their father, who often struck them in the head with his fist. The children were also witness to physical battles between their parents.

The children were absent from school between fifty and sixty days during the year. When they did attend, they were dirty. Their peers rejected them. They had few playmates. Frequently they were without money for lunch or for recreational activities. Teachers reported they fell asleep in class. Although they exhibited average intelligence on standard psychological tests, they consistently failed in school. David (age seven) was sent home from school after seven days because he, like his sisters Donna (age five) and Sonia (age four), was not toilet trained and could not control himself in the classroom. The three older children had severe visual problems, but the Dorwins never followed through with an ophthalmologist's recommendation for treatment. Nor did the Dorwins cooperate with a physician who was treating Donna for a painful bowel disease that could have been cured by their supervising a simple program of diet and medication for the girl.

1. *Identify the issue*

Is state intervention appropriate on the basis that the Dorwin children are neglected or dependent?

2. *State your position*

The Dorwins' five children are neglected under section 51 because (1) they lack proper parental care owing to the faults of their parents and (2) their parents have refused or neglected to provide them with necessary subsistence, education, and medical care necessary for their health and well-being. State intervention is imperative for the safety, health, and welfare of the children.

Here the statute itself suggests an organization for the persuasive memorandum. Section 51 identifies two ways that children could be neglected—the lack of proper parental care owing to parental fault and parental neglect or refusal to provide necessary care. From the facts, arguments could be made supporting each alternative. Thus, the memo can be separated into two major topics.

3. *Outline topics and subtopics to be discussed and create a roadmap for the reader.*

> The Dorwins have failed to provide for their children in three ways: First, the Dorwins have provided substandard housing and living conditions. Second, the Dorwins have a violent and unloving relationship with their children. Third, the Dorwins have refused to cooperate with a physician's recommendations for treating the visual impairments and physical diseases of their children.

The factual information is clustered around three topics, each of which demonstrates that the children are neglected.

4. *Draft assertive ARAC paragraphs. Begin by explaining to the reader the authority on which you rely (in this case the statute's requirements.) Then, break the argument down into subarguments. Under each argument, demonstrate the application of the statutory requirement by using the facts. Use signposts when they are helpful. When you have finished your arguments, conclude. Here is an example of the remainder of the persuasive memorandum.*

Topic paragraph: sets up the analysis and presents the author's position

The Dorwins are responsible for the neglect of their children. Section 51 indicates that a child is neglected if his "parents neglect or refuse to provide him or her with proper or necessary subsistence, education, medical or surgical care, or other care necessary for his or her health, morals, or well-being." Thus, the statute requires a demonstration that (1) the child lacks proper parental care and that (2) this lack of care is the fault of the parents. Under this definition, the Dorwin children are physically, educationally, and medically neglected.

Topic: inability to provide necessary subsistence

The Dorwins have neglected their children. *[This is the assertion.]* A parent's failure to provide a suitable living environment, restful sleeping conditions, or warm clothing and sufficient food evidences neglect. *[This is the rule. It is a good idea to use some authority for these statements if there is any. For example, a well-respected author could be quoted.]* The Dorwin apartment where the five children and their parents live is dirty. The walls of their present apartment have large holes where plaster has been removed. The floors are uncared for. On the day of my visit, garbage and feces were spread throughout the rooms. The house had a strong odor of urine. The children sleep on sodden mattresses without sheets. Sometimes they all sleep in the same bed with their mother. The five Dorwin children (ages 10, nine, seven, five, and four) were dirty, poorly clothed, and malnourished. Neighbors reported

Topic: lack of proper parental care owing to the parents' fault

that frequently they were seen begging in the streets for scraps of food. *[In the application section, facts are mustered in support of the paragraph's position. The rule is applied to the current situation.]* Thus, the Dorwins have failed to provide their children with adequate subsistence for their well-being. *[Conclusion: The original assertion is restated.]*

The parents have shown an uncaring attitude toward their children. *[This is the assertion.]* Parental alcoholism that has a detrimental impact on the child and domestic violence are indicators of neglect. *[This is the rule.]* Mr. Dorwin has a criminal record for drunkenness and assault and battery on his wife and children. Neighbors said that the parents frequently swore at their children. The children themselves said their father often struck them in the head with his fist. The children were also witness to physical battles between their parents. Neighbors reported that the children were often left alone at night or with an alcoholic uncle as a baby-sitter. *[This is the application]*. Because of Mr. Dorwin's drinking and his violent conduct toward his children and his wife, the children are fearful. State intervention is necessary to protect them from this unloving environment. *[This is the conclusion.]*

Topic: unattended medical problems

The children are also medically neglected, since the Dorwins have failed to provide medical treatment that would alleviate their children's visual and physical impairments. *[This is the assertion.]* Parents have an obligation to give their children basic medical care for diseases, even those that are not life threatening. *[This is the rule.]* The three older children had severe visual problems, but the Dorwins never followed through with an ophthalmologist's recommendation for treatment. Nor did the Dorwins cooperate with a physician who was treating Donna for a painful bowel disease that could have been cured by their supervising a simple program of diet and medication for the girl. *[This is the application.]* In the latter situation in particular, the Dorwins have no excuse for failing to provide simple medical care that would greatly improve their daughter's health and comfort. *[This is the conclusion.]*

Concluding paragraph: shows impact of parental neglect on the children

In sum, the Dorwin children have been physically and emotionally neglected by their parents. The children's totally inadequate school performance evidences the detrimental impact that their environment has had. The children were absent from school between 50 and 60 days during the year. When they did attend, they were dirty. Their peers rejected them. They had few playmates. Frequently, they were without money for lunch or for recreational activities. Teachers reported they fell asleep in class. Although the children exhibited average intelligence on standard psychological tests, they consistently failed in school. David (age seven) was sent home from school after seven days because he, like his sisters Donna (age five) and Sonia (age four), was not toilet trained and could not control himself in the classroom.

The state has authority to adjudicate the Dorwin children neglected because Mr. and Mrs. Dorwin are responsible for their children's condition. Section 51 requires a showing of parental fault. Although the

Recommendation: file neglect charges, not dependency charges, because evidence shows parental fault parents have had limited formal schooling and a familial background that may have inadequately prepared them for parenthood (which would support a finding of dependency, not neglect), the Dorwin's elaborate refusal to provide the children with basic medical care, their violent behavior, and the presence of feces and urine in the household show neglect.

Summary

Focusing on the purpose of written communication is the first step in effective writing. An awareness of the specific audience for whom you are writing is a second essential ingredient. Organizing the message—which is separate from the idea-generating process—constitutes yet another critical task in communicating effectively in the written mode. Finally, proofreading your writing for punctuation, grammar, sentence structure, and other style problems shows your commitment to improving your writing.

The free-writing approach may be used to overcome writer's block and to generate ideas. It is an approach that can be used as an exercise to loosen up before actually beginning a writing task or it can be the initial phase of your task.

There are different approaches to clustering and organizing ideas you have generated. All of these approaches have the goals of (1) putting similar thoughts together in groups, (2) arranging the items within each group in a logical order, and (3) connecting those groups in a coherent fashion.

Once ideas have been generated, clustered, and organized, you are ready to draft the written document. This draft should (1) identify the problems or issues to be addressed, (2) introduce your position and give a "roadmap," (3) use assertive paragraphs that focus on a single idea, (4) use organizational signals, and (5) conclude your argument.

Suggested Reading

Dumaine, D. (1989). *Write to the top: Writing for corporate success.* New York: Random House.

Elbow, P. (1972). *Writing with power: Techniques for mastering the writing process.* New York: Oxford University Press.

Fowler, H., & Aaron, J. (1989). *The Little, Brown handbook* (4th ed.). Glenview, IL: Scott, Foresman.

Hill-Miller, K. (1983). *The most common errors in English usage and how to avoid them.* New York: Arco.

Kaye, S. (1989). *Writing under pressure: The quick writing process.* New York: Oxford University Press.

Kilpatrick, J. (1985). *The writer's art.* Kansas City, MO: Andrews & McMeel.

Mack, K., & Skjei, E. (1979). *Overcoming writing blocks*. Los Angeles: J. P. Tarcher.

Schertzer, M. (1986). *The elements of grammar*. New York: Macmillan.

Shaw, H. (1986). *Spell it right* (3rd ed.). New York: Harper & Row.

Stott, B. (1984). *Write to the point, and feel better about your writing*. Garden City, NY: Doubleday Anchor Press.

Strunk, W. Jr., & White, E. B. (1979). *The elements of style* (3rd ed.). New York: Macmillan.

Venolia, J. (1987). *Rewrite right*. Berkeley, CA: Ten Speed Press.

Zinsser, W. (1985). *On writing well*. New York: Harper & Row.

Zinsser, W. (1989). *Writing to learn: How to write—and think clearly—about any subject at all*. New York: Harper & Row.

15

Managing Information Technology

Perry P. Heath

Information technologies are changing the way people communicate with each other, where they work, how they earn a living, and how they entertain themselves. These changes in daily activities, driven by advances in computers and microelectronics, are creating new economic and societal patterns. The changes are epochal, predated only by the agricultural and industrial eras.

The totally information-based society will not come to be for many years, but the magnitude of its impact must be kept in mind when one examines trends in information technology that are only now beginning to influence human services managers. Although information technology is already providing new ways to do things that have already been done, its most profound effect is creating—and will continue to create—a new realm of entrepreneurial adventure in which the unprecedented is tried because the usual is no longer satisfactory. Although this axiom is most visible in the for-profit business world, human services organizations are also businesses and must respond to environmental changes. The technology is structuring that new context and forming the basis for strategic planning in all sectors of business, including nonprofit (United Way of America, 1989a).

Shoshana Zuboff, of the Harvard Business School, is representative of experts in workplace technology. She noted that the "informating" capabilities of computer technologies are not yet well understood, although the information produced is an important organizational resource (United Way of America, 1989b). Recognizing the value of the information and using it effectively and creatively are key issues for organizations that are seeking to be more accountable and competitive.

Managerial authority has been built on an exclusive control of an organization's knowledge base. This control is diminishing, which supports the notion of a competing values framework of leadership behavior. Because the computer integrates information across space and time, many people have virtually instantaneous access to information. Authority is becoming less a function of an organizational hierarchy and more related to a knowledge base to assume responsibility. Administrative collaboration is increasing. The manipulation of data and information is seen as a method of problem solving and social exchange, particularly given the advances in information-communication technology. Zuboff claimed that these new relationships are producing a deeper sense of collective responsibility for and joint ownership of organizations.

Heretofore, it was thought that to be a successful computer user, a knowledge of programming was necessary. A user had to have a solid background in mathematics to work with the computer's "logic." That situation simply is no longer true. Instead, a commitment to learn how computers can enhance productivity is essential. The more a user can learn about how the machine can be used to accomplish more work faster, better, and cheaper, the more valuable the user will be to an organization. This knowledge is particularly relevant in the human services sector, where resources are scarce, technology is limited, and tradition is fixed. Learn what the computer can do and use your imagination, and productivity will skyrocket.

Software Is Key

The most important thing to remember about any computer is that, by itself, it is worthless. The "chips," drives, monitor, and keyboard provide power, but without software they are as useless as a car with no engine. In other words, the key to using a computer effectively lies in the software. By mastering the concept behind the "Big Four" software applications, a manager can begin to take advantage of information technology. Then, with some imagination and creativity, the increases in productivity will become readily apparent (Glossbrenner, 1985). The major— Big Four—software applications that are now on the market for general use by managers are as follows:

Word processing. The essence of a word-processing package is the production of text. Almost without exception, anything now done on a typewriter can be done more quickly and with greater ease using a computer and word processor. Text can be recorded once for use, manipulation, and reproduction, saving hours of retyping. If changes need to be made later, the document can be recalled, changed, and printed. The style of print is limited only by the printer's capabilities. The benefits of word processing truly become evident when multiple revisions and larger quantities of text are needed. For example, the personalization of numerous form letters is a simple task with a word processor.

Database management. This software puts a great deal of power at the disposal of a manager. A database is a collection of related information. For example, clients' files, employees' records, and phone directories are databases. The essence of a database management program is the retrieval of information—facts, figures, and relationships—that may be needed at any given time. The power and flexibility offered by database management are important in virtually all aspects of an organization's business.

Electronic spreadsheets. Paper-and-pencil spreadsheets have been staple management tools for years, used to organize and present the facts and relationships that are relevant to a project. Similar to figures on an income tax form, the figures in one block of a spreadsheet are typically the result of calculations involving numbers from other blocks, some of which may be scattered in various places. Virtually everything in a spreadsheet that is calculated is based on something else in the spreadsheet. With paper and pencil, changing one figure would necessitate making multiple changes throughout the document. In the past, two spreadsheets were usually prepared—the best case and the worst case. An electronic spreadsheet eliminates those limitations. By asking the computer to do multiple calculations, you can get answers to a multitude of "what-if?" questions almost instantaneously. The new assumptions are the only figures to be entered after the base sheet. Press a button, and the computer will perform all the necessary recalculations. Therefore, a manager can test a vast array of assumptions and use the results to make better-informed decisions.

Data communications. The last of the Big Four applications to be mastered, data communications is one of the most prolific in terms of tangible information. Fax machines and modems are part of the explosion in data communications. Of the four applications, data communications is the most computer-oriented because there is no antecedent. Data-communications programs do not process text or data, as do the others; they provide "enabling" features that allow computers to converse with each other, typically through the telephone lines or via cables that connect computers. A wealth of information is now available through on-line services for retrieving information. The process begins when the user dials into a typically larger computer that stores huge amounts of information. The repositories of information are called, oddly enough, databases. The great advantage to the manager is instantaneous access to information. These on-line services are costly, but considering the expense of paying someone to do the research, it is easy to justify their cost.

Thousands of computer software packages are available. There are computer-aided-design programs, graphic packages, and integrated software facilities that allow communication between packages. There are applications for virtually every need, and the number is growing at an incredible rate. Consequently, one does not need to know a programming language unless one chooses a career in software development. A manager will probably never have to master more than a few programs, but knowledge of the many things a computer can do and creativity and imagination in using them will maximize his or her performance and productivity.

Managers' knowledge of the technology, which is changing rapidly, is critical if automation is to be used to achieve any degree of production capacity. It is equally important to the growth of office and business technology for those who use the technology to accept it widely. This acceptance has several implications that will be addressed later.

Organizations, including human services agencies, are rapidly approaching a time when most of their employees will have been introduced to and accepted the computer era. These workers will not attach the mystique to the technology that previous generations of workers did. Workers who learned the technology in school will tend to embrace it rather than fear it. They will become agents of change by convincing their older associates to be more receptive to the advances. A manager can undertake several steps to facilitate the introduction or enhancement of technology.

Develop a means of increasing the staff's awareness of technology. Establish an organizational policy on information technology. The critical element in this policy will be the recognition that information is as much a resource as is the work force, plant, and equipment. Managers look to policy for guidance; such a policy will place technological considerations in the management decision-making process.

Provide training that answers questions. Most managers, particularly in human services organizations, lack the skills and knowledge that are necessary to operate the technology effectively. They must first become aware of the potential of the technology and then must convey that knowledge to employees who can effectively use the information. Managerial training should focus on helping managers understand the types of processes and outputs they can ask the technology to produce for them. This training, however, threatens managers' sense of security and self-esteem while incorporating increased responsibility. Training for managers should be built into the existing managerial roles of planning, organizing, controlling, producing, and evaluating. Training must be continuous, not a one-shot process. The management of information resources implies the constant upgrading of personnel, along with the level of informational literacy within the organization.

Create an organizational climate that supports risk taking. As with any technology or change, it takes time to master its use. Managers must have an entrepreneurial spirit about the use of computers.

Include technological items on the agendas of conferences and seminars. When possible, managers should encourage their staff to attend professional conferences at which technological issues are discussed. Successful user applications should be nontechnical, presented by manager-users, and accompanied by displays and demonstrations of the applications. Successful users can be a gold mine of support and information.

Implementation of the System

Managerial leadership is paramount in the implementation of an automation system. The appropriate approach can have a considerable impact on the successful development and implementation of the system. Some important factors include these:

▶ Support of the top management: the direction, support, and control provided by those at the agency's highest administrative levels

▶ Phases of development: adherence to the fundamental processes of planning and implementing any organizational system

▶ Cost-benefit analysis: management's understanding of the major costs and assessment of whether the projected outcomes justify the expenses

▶ Resources: the availability and provision of resources, including staff, hardware, and software for proper implementation

▶ Project management: the programmatic and technical leadership provided for the project, combined with realistic planning, control over the timely completion of activities and high-quality products, and the avoidance of cost overruns

▶ Team approach: the effective collaboration of technical and user staff in building and installing the system.

By understanding these factors, managers can play a critical role by being committed to the development of the system, overseeing the proper administration of the project, and approving the continuation of the work at key points. The development of the system is thus a managerial issue, not just a technical matter (Cotter, 1981). When executives fail to cope with or control the development of automated systems, the objectives are either not defined or are poorly defined; development is piecemeal with no overall plan; implementation is hurried and therefore ineffective, inefficient, and fraught with problems; the morale of staff is low; management's informational needs are disregarded; and the system may even be abandoned. Top management's abdication of responsibility for and lack of involvement in decision making regarding the management information system (MIS) may be the major cause of the failure or faulty implementation of automated data-processing efforts. To paraphrase an old motto of IBM: Think before deciding on any action regarding the planning and implementation of an automated MIS. Remember, never change the way business is conducted to conform to a computer system; change the computer system to conform to the business.

Case Example

The literature overflows with admonitions that increased productivity and greater accountability are the norms for today's human services manager and cannot be overstated. The availability of resources, coupled with the demand, has placed the human services system in a mode of constant change. The following case example illustrates the process of introducing a computerized system into an agency and the benefits that can result.

Cuvo, Hall, and Midler (1988) investigated the computerization of a central intake unit of a large social service agency in response to the recent emphasis on accountability. The agency's goal is to deliver efficient and high-quality services to clients. The ability to control the point at which some 13,000 clients enter the system determines how well the agency is fulfilling its obligations to funders and implementing its existing intake policies. The agency has seven locations. The project's goal was to provide clients with confirmed appointments at the time of their initial call and to shift the time-consuming scheduling process away from direct service providers. As predicted, cost-effectiveness and productivity increased, as did the number of service hours provided.

The agency's creation of a central computerized intake unit resulted from two interrelated decisions: to transform intake from a predominantly clinical to a predominantly administrative function requiring certain clinical skills and to standardize and limit the agency's first contact with clients. This computerization allowed the agency to include former secretaries on the intake staff, which invoked resistance from the practitioners who thought that the support staff was assuming therapeutic roles. The assumption was challenged and diffused. Redefining intake as an administrative function transformed the nature of the initial contact with the clients. The goal was not to reinvent the intake system, but to apply computer technology to the process.

In the early stages of implementation, inevitable problems arose, and unanticipated benefits accrued. Central intake had a dramatic and immediate effect on the agency. Other changes were more subtle but far-reaching. The most obvious change to clients was an end to the delays in service. One of the most significant long-range

"He's perfect. I'll take him."

effects was the redefinition of roles within the organization. Job responsibilities were broadened and increased at various levels of the agency. Although the tasks involved did not include complex new skills, the computer demanded concentrated attention and reduced the amount of paperwork. The new system modified the role of administrators. New tasks of coordination and supervision emerged. For example, enlistment of staff support and the negotiation of new concerns became a high priority. Automation made the administrators more managers and coordinators of personnel and less interpreters of policy.

The process required the hiring of new staff members, such as the coordinator of intake services, to tighten the administrative control of this consolidated intake function. For the agency's chief administrators, the benefits of the central intake system included an increased capacity for analysis and creative problem solving. The database yielded several new pieces of information: a more reliable waiting list, the therapists' actual schedules, and more complete information about prospective clients. This additional information allows the administrators to make better-informed judgments; they can examine staffing patterns, determine peak hours of service, and evaluate new programs and the need for new services. Cuvo, Hall, and Midler (1988) concluded that standardized intake is a crucial means of achieving the primary goal of service to clients. The computerized intake system has had a major effect on the agency's organizational structure; managerial capabilities; and, to a lesser extent, social work practice.

Applications for Social Workers

Parker, Chynoweth, Blankenship, Zaldo, and Matthews (1987) discussed the availability of computer software for the social work practitioner and manager. They concluded that the costs of numerous software applications vary dramatically with advances in technology. For a relatively nominal fee, clinicians can utilize software to record data and to help them understand, manage, and treat clients. Managers can use software for planning, reporting, and evaluation. Researchers can access powerful data-analysis tools and procedures at a minimal cost. Clinical supervisors can monitor the progress of student interns, and instructors who develop courses, evaluate students, and generate publishable material can be more productive. Computer technology can be applied in screening of clients, writing, billing, office management, and reporting to regulatory agencies and funders. In short, the computer can be used to deal creatively with the multiplicity of problems that confront social work practitioners and managers.

The computer is incapable of doing anything without a precise, clear, step-by-step set of instructions on how to proceed with its task. The effectiveness and creativity of a variety of software applications have been reviewed in the literature. Ethical issues and the "depersonalization of social work" will not be addressed here.

Instead, a brief recap of the categorical opportunities for automation support, presented by Parker et al. (1987), will be presented.

Therapeutic Applications

Therapeutic applications have only recently been tested and are not universally accepted. Parker et al. (1987) refer to a variety of effective software applications, from the completion of rote tasks to the treatment of people with learning disabilities or hearing, vision, or memory impairments. Among the many tools for evaluation is the Clinical Measurement Package, developed by Hudson (Nurius & Hudson, 1989). Hudson's software utilizes a single-subject design and measures the severity of problems in 13 areas. The system provides interpretive reports and scores that facilitate client-therapist communications and the therapy process. Hudson's approach manages to avoid some of the pitfalls of mere data collection and collapse.

Computers have had an impact in such areas as family and marital therapy, geriatrics, and institutional care, where coordination of care is important. Some of the least controversial clinical applications are in self-help therapies: relaxation, hypnosis, nutrition, weight loss, smoking cessation, and so on. Managers must be attentive to the applications in all facets of social work practice and management.

Goodman, Gingerich, and de Shazer (1989) evaluated the use of an "expert system" on clinical practice. Such systems, sometimes called artificial intelligence, are computer programs that embody the expertise of a human expert that can be consulted on a specific problem. These researchers developed BRIEFER, a prototype expert system that is designed to advise family therapists on what intervention to give clients at the conclusion of the initial session.

During the early development of MIS, computer applications were limited to quantifiable problems. Consequently, there were few innovations for the human services field because most applications were being developed for standard financial and mathematical routines. Recent advances, however, have made it possible for computer technology to be applied to an array of human services problems. Expert systems use "rules of thumb" to solve problems.

BRIEFER was developed around a specific therapy approach—the brief approach—that focuses on solutions, rather than on problems. The therapist helps the client identify suitable solutions. If the solutions have already been identified, they are used as the foundation for establishing therapeutic goals. The system is not quite so simple as "enter data, get results," but the basis for therapy is formed in the approach and uniqueness of therapy. The application asks questions via input during breaks in the interview session. The software then compares the responses and formulates recommendations. The purpose of Goodman, Gingerich, and de Shazer's research was to assess the feasibility of expert systems technology for brief family therapy. The study found that the advice given by BRIEFER closely paralleled the intervention that was originally provided in the studied cases, which lends credence to the usage of expert technology. In addition, the response to the software by therapists and trainees generally has been positive.

Goodman, Gingerich, and de Shazer expressed a guarded optimism that a complete expert system can be developed that will be able to offer valid and useful advice to practitioners who are conducting brief therapy. With expert systems technology, computing capacity can be applied to the complex problems with which clinicians must deal. Expert systems also have important implications for training, research, and the development of theories. However, the ethical ramifications and acceptance of their use have not yet been investigated.

Games have been a part of human services practice for many years. Computers increase the power, sophistication, and possibilities of using games in the human services. Computer games are viewed as useful tools that will make an increasing contribution to the human services as practitioners and scholars become more familiar with computers. Games enhance motor skills, as well as comprehension and concentration (Resnick & Sherer, 1989).

Computers are also excellent tools for taking histories. In many instances, the client can use the computer to answer standardized questions. The software's ability to alter subsequent questions on the basis of a client's response allows for the more detailed and efficient study of the client.

A client's ability to directly input information in a computer, instead of going through an interviewer, has been shown to be advantageous. Resnick and Sherer (1989) cited several studies to support this conclusion, including those of adolescents who revealed their history of substance abuse more readily in computer interviews and sexually dysfunctional individuals who were more willing to provide data related to their problem to a computer than to a clinician. A computer-based questionnaire can be developed to meet almost any organizational, project, or clinical purpose.

Other Applications

Human services researchers or authors can easily capitalize on the current technology. With all the word-processing features now available, they can paginate and footnote their documents and link them to graphics and other software packages. This kind of power, once available only on large mainframe computers, is now accessible with personal computers as well.

The most straightforward application of computer technology to the purposes of professional social work practice is in the management of social agencies. Miller (1986, p. 54) offered a word of caution, however: "A well-administered agency may become better as a result of computerization; a badly run organization cannot be salvaged by any purchase of hardware or software. Computers can maintain a marvelously precise ledger sheet, but they cannot spend money wisely."

Administrative applications have been created to meet the most acute demands. Reporting requirements, whether by funders, boards of directors, or governmental agencies, represent a tremendous challenge for the integration and accuracy of data. Quality-assurance packages can link specific forms of documentation and hence can result in increased productivity and improved accountability. Some packages can be programmed to create reminders of deviations from the norm, to monitor screening protocols, and to perform a variety of "watchdog" functions. Other automated business functions that were previously discussed include processing of forms, accounting, and word processing.

The substitution of a computer program for the clinical insight of a trained diagnostician is a dream (or nightmare) of the distant future. The problem lies in reducing an enormously complex and ambiguous process to a precise and well-defined algorithm (Miller, 1986). Nonetheless, software designed to perform psychological testing and assessment is becoming more commonplace. This development is in concert with Hudson's assessment tools (see Nurius and Hudson, 1989). The proliferation of software to administer, score, and interpret a variety of diagnostic instruments is largely a response to the distinct advantages that automation provides.

The costs of computer software and hardware will continue to decrease with the advent of new and improved technology. The increased use of the computer will improve the care, diagnosis, treatment, and assessment of clients and decision making by practitioners. Social work managers must be open to accepting the advances and be willing to learn sophisticated methods of information management, adopt new and unfamiliar technologies, and creatively apply computers in their respective settings.

Case Study

The United Way of the Greater Cheerlessly Area in Cheerlessly, Pennsylvania, is a relatively small federated fund-raising, fund-distribution, and community problem-solving organization. In 1982, the agency's annual fund-raising appeal raised approximately $450,000, which was distributed to 22 human services organizations. The first full-time executive director had recently been hired, and the volunteer leaders became committed to stimulating the growth and development of the organization in an effort to increase needed funding for health and human services in the area. Up to that time, all systems were manual and were maintained by a full-time executive secretary, with help from the volunteers. If growth and service to the community were to be increased, automation would have to be considered.

The director managed a minimal operating budget and had limited computer knowledge, but was determined to achieve the levels of community problem solving that the volunteers had set as goals. The process of implementing an automated MIS was begun. The advantage at the outset was the commitment and support demonstrated by the leadership. The perils were recognized, too. Costs, training, data input, information gathering, and continuing support were among the issues to be considered.

The director gathered appropriate information from other, mostly larger, United Way agencies that had undergone automation. An analysis was conducted of cost projections and the requirements for staffing, information, and future development. First, an oversight committee was established to monitor the process and to perform most of the tasks involved. Volunteers with the necessary expertise were recruited to serve. They included the board treasurer, who could speak to the agency's financial capacity and the availability of resources; data-processing professionals from two local companies, who could help assess organizational needs; and others who were aware of the available hardware and software applications. Advice and guidance were also sought from United Way of America, the national service organization.

The director and key volunteers developed a list of functions that were performed by the agency and grouped them into several areas: financial, text processing, and information management. The financial needs were related to the accounts payable and general ledger systems. Text was primarily generated to support the planning and allocations functions, as well as general correspondence. The need for marketing and communications materials (graphics support) was identified, but tabled for future implementation. There was a conscious effort not to go overboard. After all, the initial purpose was merely to make information more readily available. The information management needs, including databases that were necessary for the effective operation of the annual campaign, were the most important. Information on accounts, the development and tracking of volunteers, pledge transactions, and accounts receivable were deemed to be the highest priorities for automation.

Having determined the organization's needs, the committee decided that an assessment of available software and hardware or other acceptable solutions was the next task. It called on United Way of America to provide information on current field applications and costs. Several alternatives were presented. The volunteers were familiar with applications to meet the financial and text needs, but accepted suggestions from United Way of America. Costs were assembled and bids were sought. Other alternatives, including the purchase of services through a service bureau, the leasing of equipment, and the hiring of a consultant, were also considered during the cost-analysis phase. The committee decided to purchase existing software because the software was reliable.

Nontangible implications of the system were evaluated. Training, policies, and procedures regarding data input and integrity and ongoing upkeep and migration would be needed. The committee decided to purchase hardware from a local vendor and to purchase the campaign and supporting software from vendors that were affiliated with United Way of America. With the bids in hand, cost considerations were important. Funding was sought and obtained from the community foundation. The system was ordered. By today's standards, it was an albatross. It included a Radio Shack model 12 with two eight-inch floppy disk drives and 64K RAM and a DMP21000 dot matrix printer.

That was the beginning of automation for the United Way of the Greater Cheerlessly Area. Automation immediately proved to be beneficial. Three successive campaigns achieved double-digit increases, the ability to personalize a variety of form letters was a great advantage, and monitoring and tracking reduced the loss of pledges. The system was cost-justified in about a year.

There were negative consequences that followed the implementation of the system, however. The part-time support staff member left because of an inability to adjust to automation. The demand for information by the volunteers and agencies was too great for the staff to handle. Training became an ongoing concern as new software packages were introduced. The incidental costs of an automation system had not been fully explored and considered in the budgeting process: ribbons, paper, and diskettes are costly.

Today, the United Way of the Greater Cheerlessly Area is an exemplary community problem-solving model among organizations of its size in the United Way system. With the capacity to maintain and manipulate information related to human services issues in the community, it is truly viewed as a resource, change agent, fundraiser, and problem solver.

Summary

Human services organizations have been reluctant to use or even investigate information technology because of a lack of information and resources and the fear that it will "depersonalize" the profession. However, managers and clinicians now face challenges to their accountability, efficiency, and effectiveness that can be eased by an appropriate MIS.

Software and hardware developments that are meaningful and cost-effective are making automation appealing. Managers must be entrepreneurial in their approach to developing and implementing computer systems. They must be informed about the advantages and capacities of such systems, which can enhance decision making, productivity, and accountability. The human services sector has been laggard in adopting new technologies. It is now time to take advantage of the state-of-the-art proved systems.

SKILLS - APPLICATION EXERCISE

Conduct an analysis of the systems needs for your organization. Determine the types of work that should be automated, the various alternatives available, cost considerations, and recommendations. Several steps need to be taken. Develop a problem statement, a broad acknowledgment of the situations that warrant

continued

further study. Gather information from staff, clients, and others who will be affected by any changes. This information must be taken into account when you search for solutions, including hardware and software. Then develop a statement of exactly what is to be accomplished and how its completion will be measured and to what level or degree.

References

Cotter, B. (1981). *Planning and implementing social service information systems: A guide for management and users* (Vol. 25). Washington, DC: Project Share.

Cuvo, D., Hall, F., & Midler, G. (1988). Computerizing central intake: A means toward accountability. *Social Casework, 69*, 214–223.

Glossbrenner, A. (1985, Fall). The only computer skills you need for success. *National Business Employment Weekly*, 5–12.

Goodman, H., Gingerich, W. A., & de Shazer, S. (1989). BRIEFER: An expert system for clinical practice. *Computers in Human Services, 5*(1/2), 53–67.

Miller, H. (1986). The use of computers in social work practice: An assessment. *Journal of Social Work Education, 3*, 52–60.

Nurius, P., & Hudson, W. (1989). Computers and social diagnosis: The client's perspective. *Computers in Human Services, 5*(1/2), 21–35.

Parker, M. W., Chynoweth, G. H., Blankenship, D., Zaldo, E. R., & Matthews, M. J. (1987). A case for computer applications in social work. *Journal of Social Work Education, 2*, 57–68.

Resnick, H., & Sherer, M. (1989). Computer games and the human services. *Computers in Human Services, 5*(1/2), 89–109.

United Way of America. (1989a). Communication and information technology. In *What lies ahead: Countdown to the 21st century* (pp. 90–96). Alexandria, VA: Author.

United Way of America. (1989b). Trend 7: Automation. In *The future world of work* (pp. 37–42). Alexandria, VA: Author.

Developing and Implementing Quality Assurance Programs

Claudia J. Coulton

Quality, both real and perceived, is fundamental to the success of any service organization. Consumers, clients, and patients consider quality in deciding whether to use services and in choosing providers. When service organizations are nonprofit, quality is one of the chief determinants of whether an organization has fulfilled its purpose and is worthy of continued or increased support from the community.

Human services managers may be unique in the degree to which quality, rather than profit or compliance with public policy, is the measure of their performance (Patti, 1987). Yet the uncertain and individualized technology and the predominance of professionals and paraprofessionals in human services organizations make guaranteeing quality a complex and difficult managerial task. The manager must combine the technical skills of data gathering and analysis with the ability to facilitate consensus, learning, and changes in behavior and in the system.

Quality assurance is an approach to managing the quality of the products of human services organizations. Quality assurance programs systematically and continuously examine the quality of services, identify any deficiencies, determine the sources or causes of the problems, and engage in correcting the problems. Quality assurance has borrowed many of the statistical quality-control techniques from industry, added the problem-solving tools from industries' experience with quality circles and teamwork, overlaid an understanding of group process, and adapted them to the context of the professional culture. It is a continuously evolving set of principles, procedures, and techniques that are widely used in health, mental health, residential treatment, and family and children's service organizations of various sizes and auspices. Quality assurance programs and activities are mandated by many accrediting bodies and are required for participation in many state and federal programs.

This chapter begins with an overview of quality assurance, including its purpose, history, definitions, and basic principles. It then describes the steps in developing a complete quality assurance program and presents an example of a quality assurance activity.

Overview

Purpose

The purpose of quality assurance is to continually promote and enhance the quality of the services that an organization provides. Quality assurance is essential to achieving the objectives of any human services organization. Quality assurance activities typically focus on those functions of the organization that involve the provision of services to consumers, clients, or patients. Human services organizations may have objectives other than serving clients, such as education, research, and advocacy, but these objectives are not typically the focus of the types of quality assurance programs discussed in this chapter.

History and Mandates

Human services organizations have attempted to enhance the quality of their services since their inception, but until recently, their efforts were not mandated or systematized. Supervision, in-service training, certification, and case conferences are all examples of activities that were intended to promote high-quality services. Yet they were based on assumptions about the quality of care and how it could be improved, whereas today's approaches to quality assurance are based on an actual analysis of the services that are being provided.

Systematic quality assurance programs came into being in the 1970s under the impetus of several federal programs (Coulton, 1982). Two of the most important programs for human services were the requirements for evaluation and monitoring built into Title XX (social services provisions) of the Social Security Act and the Professional Standards Review Organizations, created through amendments to Title XI of the Social Security Act. These regulations set in place the expectation that providers and purchasers of a service had the responsibility to examine that service and to judge its quality.

The early methods used to study quality were rudimentary and cumbersome by today's standards and were based primarily on case-by-case reviews (Coulton, 1978; Rehr, 1979). They often used implicit criteria, rather than explicit standards, and involved considerable subjectivity. The reviews typically covered only small samples of the total population of consumers and seldom measured actual outcomes.

The present approaches have been shaped by practitioners, researchers, and professional and accreditation organizations that are concerned with making quality assurance more efficient and increasing its ability to bring about a better quality of care for all clients (Coulton, 1989). A fundamental shift has been to move from case-based to statistical models for examining quality. This shift has been made possible by the rapidly growing technology of clinical information systems that integrate data on clients' characteristics, services, providers, and outcomes.

A key actor in the development of current methods of quality assurance has been the Joint Commission on the Accreditation of Health Care Organizations (Lehmann, 1987, 1989). This commission accredits many organizations for the provision of health, mental health, rehabilitation, and substance abuse services and has developed quality assurance requirements that have common elements for all these settings. Many state agencies have adapted their quality assurance requirements to fit the commission's approaches, and professional organizations are collaborating with the commission to develop specific methods for their specialties (Vourlekis, 1990). The steps for developing a quality assurance program presented later in this chapter are consistent with the approach required by the commission.

Defining Quality

Quality is an elusive concept that implies value. A service that is of high quality has features that are valued by relevant individuals or groups. Quality assurance programs seek ways to objectify what are essentially subjective phenomena so they can be examined.

A definition of quality depends upon the state of the art at a given time and place, the expectations of the receivers and providers of services, and the values of those involved. Defining quality for any particular service is, therefore, a complex process. The reality is that quality assurance is seldom successful in taking all these perspectives into account. For example, home-based services to a frail elderly population may be judged to be of good quality if people are maintained in independent living for as long as possible. However, what is actually possible to achieve may depend on the availability of such technologies as meal deliveries, nutritional supplements, and telecommunications. While the elder may value his or her prolonged independence, the family members may experience this period as prolonged anxiety and a burden. Providers may differ with clients in how they weigh the risk of injury and when they judge that remaining in the home is too dangerous.

Quality is thought to be made up of three interrelated aspects: structure, process, and outcome (Donabedian, 1982). *Outcome* refers to the quality of the results. Care of adequate quality leaves the client or patient in a state or condition that is considered desirable. Outcomes of adequate quality are those that can reasonably be expected, given current knowledge and capability. For example, one aspect of the quality of services for drug dependence is the degree to which clients become drug free. A reduction in the frequency of drug use would not be considered an outcome of adequate quality because current theory and research generally suggest that abstinence is necessary to control addiction. Similarly, in the field of mental health, a desired outcome is that former long-term patients of mental hospitals are able to function in a community setting. It would not be reasonable to require that patients become symptom free because complete remission is not expected in most cases, given the current state of treatment.

A second way of evaluating quality is to examine the process of services or care. Were services delivered according to currently available standards of practice? Did the provider carry out the proper actions in the way they should be performed? For example, providers may agree that all adolescents who are admitted to a treatment center should be evaluated for the risk of suicide according to a protocol. The process would be considered of adequate quality if all steps of the protocol were completed at the time of admission. A second illustration of the quality of the process is taken from hospice services. Suppose that providers agree that all patients should have the opportunity to express their preferences about where they will die. Evidence that such discussions took place would be indicative of adequate-quality service from a process perspective.

Structure refers to a third aspect of quality and asks whether the "inputs" to the services are adequate. Were the staff properly trained, and were their qualifications adequate for the practices they performed? Were the facilities, support services, and

"Since that last interview only took nine minutes, your client-per-hour ratio increased to seven, which moves you up a notch to fourth fastest intake worker. However I've noticed your effectiveness-per-client index has fallen."

administrative arrangements proper? Were the incentives in the system those that promote good quality? For example, providers believe that some abused children can be maintained in their homes if the situation is judged to be safe, but realize that this is a difficult and risky judgment. Suppose there is agreement that only a senior social worker can make this assessment. Using a structural definition of quality, one would ask whether all senior social workers who perform such assessments had adequate training and experience to do so. Another illustration of structure relates to incentives for providing high-quality services. Imagine that a program to prevent children from dropping out of school paid contract workers only for the time they spent in therapy sessions with the children, but the general standard in the field was that school and home contacts were essential to the success of the program. The structure would include a disincentive to make these needed contacts and would be considered to have a negative impact on the quality of the program.

These three aspects of quality are interrelated. If the techniques and methods of delivering services have been fully tested and are well known, there is considerable certainty that following the proper process will lead to desirable outcomes. However, the state of the art for many types of clients and services is such that although there is agreement on the objectives of services, practitioners provide the services in their own unique ways. Under these circumstances, outcomes may be a more valid indicator of quality. Also, when outcomes are not what they should be, processes usually need to be examined. The structural aspects of quality may be responsible for poor processes or outcomes, such as when providers are allowed to perform tasks for which they are not adequately trained or there are incentives to deliver a service to clients or patients who are not good candidates for the particular intervention. The analysis of outcomes often leads to the identification of problems in the structure of services.

Assumptions and Issues

Underlying quality assurance programs are some fundamental assumptions that provide a necessary context for these programs to be effective. First, the responsibility for quality rests at all levels of the organization, from the chief executive to the provider of service. There must be mechanisms at all these levels to facilitate involvement in the quality assurance effort. The quality assurance function must be directly accountable to the chief executive, so that problems that are affecting quality at all levels and parts of the organization can be corrected.

Second, the provider of service is viewed as the cornerstone of quality. Providers are to be involved in all aspects of the quality assurance process, from defining quality, to examining the actual provision of services, to finding and remedying problems.

Third, although quality has many subjective elements, quality assurance strives for objectivity. Thus, providers should not judge the quality of their own work, but should participate with peers in objective definition and review. Groups of individuals who are involved in providing like types of services should work together in the quality assurance process.

Fourth, most deficiencies in quality are assumed to be a function of problems in systems, protocols, procedures, training, or information, rather than in the motivation or capability of individual practitioners. Quality assurance should be structured not only to uncover such common problems but to identify the rare instance of the ignorance, incompetence, or impairment of providers.

Two issues that commonly arise in examining quality are cost and risk. The relationship between the cost of services and quality is not well understood, but there is tremendous pressure today to control the costs of all types of programs. Ideally, before a service program is established, studies of cost-effectiveness would have uncovered the optimal level of resources that are needed to provide an acceptable quality of service. But that is seldom the case. In the absence of information about cost-effective services, proposed standards for quality are typically based on what can be achieved for currently prevailing expenditures. However, the findings of a quality-assurance analysis may reveal that resources can be shifted from one activity to another and that doing so will lead to an overall improvement in the quality of services throughout the organization.

Human services organizations are increasingly facing the possibility of risk, in the form of litigation, so risk management has become an important activity. Quality assurance relates to that part of risk that is due to the injury or dissatisfaction of clients. An effective quality assurance program should result in the reduction of risk to clients. Areas of high risk should be targeted for an intensive quality review.

Elements of a Quality Assurance Program

Quality assurance programs systematically and objectively examine services, determine whether services are appropriate and adequate, and correct any identified deficiencies. *Monitoring, evaluating,* and *problem solving* are the terms often applied to these three elements of the process. Steps for establishing these processes are described next.

Establish a Structure

The complexity of the structure for quality assurance depends on the size and components of the organization. In an organization in which services are delivered by several departments or program areas, persons who are responsible for quality assurance are appointed in each area. In addition, at the executive level, persons are assigned responsibility for organization-wide quality assurance. Lines of communication are established between and among these quality assurance committees or groups. The quality assurance structure, plan, activities, findings, and actions are documented in writing, and minutes are kept of the meetings of these quality assurance groups.

Develop a Monitoring and Evaluation System

Designated providers work together to develop a method for measuring the quality and appropriateness of services in their area. The method is viewed as constantly evolving as knowledge, the need for services, and techniques develop. Several basic steps must be taken to create a useful method (the Joint Commission on the Accreditation of Health Care Organizations has put forward terminology for these steps that will be used here, so the reader whose organization is undergoing accreditation can relate this material to those standards).

Delineate the Scope of Services

Monitoring and evaluation activities need to cover the range of services that are provided and the range of clients who are served. To begin this delineation, providers can ask themselves what they do and for whom they do it. These questions should lead to their listing the major client-related tasks and functions of their department or program area that come under the purview of the quality assurance program. For example, the scope of service of a hospital social work department may include discharge planning, psychosocial evaluation, counseling, health education, information and referral, and case management.

Identify the Important Aspects of Service

Not all aspects of the provision of service and their results can be examined. It is most crucial to focus on those aspects of a service that are important to its overall quality. Service or program activities that are received by a large number of patients are important to quality because of their high volume. Other aspects of service pose a considerable risk to clients. Also important for quality assurance are those aspects of service that are known to be difficult or problematic. Again, with regard to a hospital social work department, important aspects of care may include assessment, the timeliness of service, case finding, interdisciplinary collaboration, the involvement of family members, and the resolution of problems.

Designate Measurable Indicators

An indicator is not a direct measure of quality, but a sign that can be observed. It should be correlated with quality, but indicators are seldom relevant to quality in all cases. To the extent possible, the indicators that are chosen should tap the important aspects of service that have been identified. Some indicators may tap more than one aspect.

Indicators may reflect either appropriateness, process, or outcome. Indicators of appropriateness reflect whether the service should have been given (or whether a needed service was omitted) or was given in the proper amount. For example, an indicator of inappropriate entry into a program may be clients who terminate before completing 20 percent of the planned sessions. Indicators of process examine how the service was delivered, whereas indicators of outcome reveal results for the client.

In selecting indicators, practitioners should take validity, reliability, sensitivity, specificity, and feasibility into account. A valid indicator of quality is one that tends to reflect the actual quality of service and not some other factor, such as the characteristics of clients. For example, the ability to tie one's shoes would not be a valid indicator of the outcome of rehabilitation in children, because this ability is confounded with age. It could be made valid by applying it only to clients over age six.

Reliability refers to the stability of measurement of an indicator. For example, injuries among home-care patients may be an indicator of the quality of home-based services, but will not be useful if providers differ in their practices of reporting them.

An indicator with acceptable sensitivity will capture most cases of poor quality. An indicator with acceptable specificity will correctly classify most cases of acceptable quality. For example, an indicator of the quality of discharge planning might be readmissions within 30 days. If most patients who received poor-quality planning ended up being readmitted within that time frame, the indicator would have high sensitivity. If most readmitted patients were recipients of poor-quality planning, the indicator would also have high specificity.

Finally, the feasibility of an indicator must be considered. Can the indicator be measured using available data, or does it require special data-gathering activities? What is the cost of obtaining the necessary data?

Establish Standards for Evaluating Indicators

An indicator is a sign that quality may not be adequate and that further investigation is needed. A rule must be specified for determining when such investigations should take place. For each indicator, some standard of performance (called the threshold for action by the commission) is specified.

Thresholds for action may be tied to a specified rate or level of an occurrence over a designated period or to each instance of an event. An example of a rate as a threshold can be seen in a rehabilitation program using the rate of dropping out as an indicator of the quality of the admissions process. The staff specifies that an acceptable dropout rate is below 15 percent of those enrolled in a 90-day program. Thus, the dropout rate is examined every 90 days and further evaluations are undertaken if it exceeds the 15 percent threshold.

An illustration of a sentinel event as a threshold for action comes from a residential treatment program for adolescents. The staff has selected children who are absent without leave as an indicator of the quality of the assessment process, an important aspect of care. Since absence without leave is a rare but dangerous event, every instance of it is immediately investigated by those who are responsible for quality assurance. The threshold for action is defined as one incident. In other words, 0 percent is considered acceptable.

Standards or thresholds for action are debated among practitioners. For some types of indicators that are extremely risky and dangerous, the threshold is obvious; every instance calls for action, the standard is zero. More often, however, some occurrences of the indicator are expected even when service is of the highest quality. Then a threshold for action is often based on past experience, professional judgment, or the professional and scientific literature. For these types of indicators, it is preferable that there be widespread discussions of reasonable standards that go beyond a single agency or organization. In many instances, professional organizations are beginning to define reasonable standards for their members on the basis of either empirical studies or carefully gathered professional judgments.

Develop a Method for Data Collection

A measurement plan is specified for each indicator. Providers determine the sources of data, whether a sample or total population will be used, how often the data will be gathered, and the persons who are responsible for gathering and reporting the data. Common sources of data include the records of clients or patients, computerized information systems, billing records, reports of incidents, log books, minutes of staff meetings, and questionnaires. Random samples, rather than the entire population of clients, are typically used when data gathering is laborious. When reviews of records or surveys of clients are the sources of data, data may be gathered on a probability sample of the size that will yield acceptable accuracy.

The rehabilitation program that has chosen the dropout rate as an indicator will be used to illustrate the data-collection method. The plan calls for attendance records to be the source of data, and a dropout is defined as an unplanned absence of more than one week. The entire population of clients will be used and the secretary of the program will examine and record the status of dropouts at the end of every month. The rate will be examined by the head of the quality assurance committee to determine whether it exceeds the 15 percent threshold. Further evaluation and problem solving will be undertaken by the committee if the rate is excessive.

Analyze the Problem and Improve the Quality

Once the quality-assurance monitoring system is in place, the persons who are responsible for quality assurance will regularly examine data on the key indicators and draw conclusions about whether standards have been met. They will keep careful records of the results of these reviews and communicate the findings to the departmental or program staff and to the persons who are responsible for quality assurance at the executive level. When problems are identified, action will be taken to solve them. The results of this action will also be documented and communicated. The steps in this quality-improvement process are as follows:

Examine Services and Analyze Problems

Periodically, thresholds on particular indicators will be exceeded. When they are, the persons who are involved in the aspects of service related to the indicator must conduct an in-depth evaluation. The purpose of this analysis is, first, to determine whether there is indeed a problem of quality. Because indicators are merely signs, not definitive determinations of quality, staff may discover reasonable explanations for the indicator exceeding the threshold other than problems with quality.

More commonly, however, some real deficiencies will be revealed, and the task of the investigators is then to discover the reasons for the problems. The investigators may have to collect additional data and examine patterns and trends in greater detail. Discussions with providers may shed light on the sources of the difficulties. An in-depth peer review of specific providers may be deemed necessary. For example, an in-depth analysis of the excessive dropout rate described earlier may find that the increase occurred at the time the size of the program was expanded. Discussions with staff and a review of records reveal that in many cases the clients' motivation and the family's support for rehabilitation were not explored before the clients were admitted. Thus, the improper assessment of motivation and support is identified as a possible explanation for the high dropout rate.

An in-depth examination of patterns and trends in services most commonly reveals problems that are occurring throughout the program and that involve most or all providers. Occasionally, the deficiencies in practice may be provider specific. Such deficiencies may be discovered when individual patterns of practice are compared across providers. In any such comparisons, it is necessary to adjust for differences among providers in the types of clients they serve and the severity of the problems with which they deal.

Solve Identified Problems

Upon discovering particular sources of the deficiencies, the staff members who are involved specify a method for improving the quality of service or care. One or more persons are designated as responsible for carrying out these activities. Corrective action often includes training and education; changes in protocols, policy, or procedures; and administrative or personnel actions. Closer monitoring may also be a problem-solving tool.

Assess the Effectiveness of Actions

The success of corrective action should be revealed by continued monitoring of the indicators of quality. The indicators that previously exceeded the threshold should now fall into the desirable range. This evidence of improved quality should be documented and reported to the executive levels of the organization.

In the event that the indicators of quality do not improve, further analysis is needed. Three possibilities should be considered. First, the validity, reliability, or specificity of the indicator may have changed. If so, a change in the measurement technique may be needed. Second, the original analysis of the problem may have been erroneous. In this case, additional sources of the problem may be uncovered. Third, the corrective action may have been implemented incorrectly or may have been an insufficient response to the problem, so the activities to improve quality may need to be continued.

The Quality Assurance Cycle

The monitoring, evaluation, and problem-solving cycle is repeated continuously throughout the organization. This cycle is represented graphically in Figure 1. Monitoring continues as planned while problems of quality are being assessed and solved.

The documentation and communication of findings within the organization are fundamental to the effectiveness of the effort. Management's commitment to the process is essential for maintaining the staff's enthusiasm and support for the process. The mark of an effective quality assurance program is that numerous problems are uncovered and that efforts to improve quality are continuously under way. Staff will become committed to the process when they see that their ability to deliver high-quality services has increased.

A Case Example

This section presents selected aspects of a quality assurance program that illustrate the principles and steps discussed in this chapter. The scenario is a medium-size community mental health center with several clinical departments and programs. The executive is redesigning the quality assurance program to include the continuous monitoring, evaluation, and problem-solving cycle just presented. The executive begins by providing an in-service training program for the staff on the philosophy and principles of quality assurance and the important role that providers play in the process. The training program also emphasizes the interconnection among the assessment of quality, the improvement of quality, and professional accountability.

Figure 1. Quality Assurance Cycle

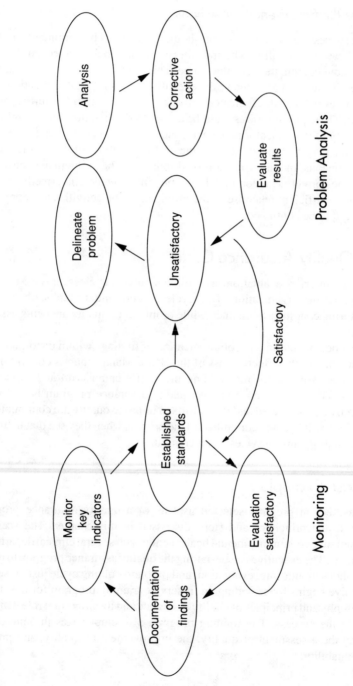

The executive asks the directors of departments and programs for advice on the composition of the organization-wide quality assurance program. Six individuals who represent the major functions of the organization that affect quality or have a role to play in its assessment are invited to join. The executive decides to chair the committee and to assign an administrative assistant 25 percent of the time to perform staff functions for the committee, such as preparing minutes and reports, circulating reports from various departments and programs, and ensuring that all necessary actions are taken.

The agency-wide quality assurance committee prepares a written quality assurance plan for the agency. As part of this plan, each department and designated program area will carry out quality assurance monitoring and evaluation. The executive and the assistant work with all the directors to begin these activities with their staffs. The experience of one program is described in detail.

The day treatment program is a six-month, five-day-a-week rehabilitation program for chronically mentally ill people who are living in the community. Its director assigns three service providers to develop a method of monitoring and evaluating the quality of care. The three begin by discussing the scope of services that the program offers. They conclude that individual, group, and family treatment; social skills training; housing placement; readiness for employment training; and case management constitute the bulk of their services.

The next step they undertake is to identify the important aspects of care—those that are problem prone or high risk or that affect a large number of clients. The admissions process, involvement with clients' families, completing referrals, and success in placing clients in housing and jobs are identified as areas that are important to the quality of the program and where problems may arise. These aspects of care are shared with the remainder of the program staff, who support these choices.

The group members begin the difficult task of identifying measurable indicators for these aspects of care. After weeks of deliberation, they suggest a set of indicators, along with thresholds for action and sources of data. For each indicator, they provide a rationale, so that the link to quality is clear. The indicators are presented in Table 1.

A system for gathering the data on these four indicators is set in place. The committee reviews findings at specified intervals. During the first six months of monitoring, two indicators reach the threshold for action.

The first indicator requiring in-depth evaluation is job training and housing placements. Two incidents of failed placements occurred. Each is examined in depth by the committee. Clients' records and interviews with pertinent staff members and the clients' families are used to determine any deficiencies in quality that were involved. It is discovered that in both incidents the clients' families were not fully supportive of the plan. The staff decide to add a family meeting as a required element of the placement protocols and designate the program director to implement the plan. A report documenting the findings and action is submitted to the agency-wide quality assurance committee. Monitoring of this indicator over the next six months reveals no cases of failed placement.

Table 1. Example of a Monitoring and Evaluation Plan for Day Treatment

Aspect of Care: Admissions screening and assessment.
Indicator: Patients admitted to the program who are asked to leave or drop out after the two-week test period.
Rationale: If the admissions assessment is thorough and accurate, most clients who start the program will be functioning at an acceptable level for participation in the program. They and their families will also have received sufficient information about the program to judge their own readiness. Admitting people to the program who leave prematurely is disruptive to other members of the group and leads to feelings of failure for the clients involved.
Measure: The number who left after two weeks this month/the number who were admitted this month.
Source of data: Computerized client information system—monthly.
Threshold for action: Exceed 5 percent.

Aspect of care: Involvement of clients' families.
Indicator: Families can correctly identify treatment goals and elements of the day treatment program for clients.
Rationale: For clients who live with their families, family members can support the clients' progress more effectively if they are aware of the components of the program and of the goals established with the clients.
Measure: Families who accurately identify four out of five program components and treatment goals/ clients who are living with their families.
Source of data: A family survey form sent quarterly to a random sample of 30 families.
Threshold for action: Below 85 percent.

Aspect of care: Housing and job-training placements.
Indicator: Clients who stay fewer than two months in housing or job placement.
Rationale: Preparing a client for housing and job placement involves assessing both the client and the environment, preparation of the client and environment for the move, and support and assistance during the transition. If a client actually reaches the point where he or she moves, the failure to remain is an undesirable outcome and may be related to deficiencies in the placement process.
Measure: Every incident of short-term removal from placement.
Source of data: Housing and job-incident reports.
Threshold for action: 0 percent.

Aspect of care: Completion of referrals.
Indicator: Clients who successfully complete the transition to outpatient treatment.
Rationale: One aspect of readiness for discharge from day treatment is the client's ability to use less-intensive outpatient services. Failure to follow through with this referral could lead to a return of symptoms, hospitalization, or both.

The second indicator that reaches the threshold for action is the successful completion of referrals. A more refined analysis of the six-month trends reveals that the lowest level of success in referrals was to agency X. This finding is reported to the agency-wide quality assurance committee. The committee notices that two other program areas had identified problems in referrals to agency X. The agency executive takes responsibility for corrective action and is able to enter into a collaborative agreement with agency X that includes several methods of facilitating referrals. Subsequent monitoring of this indicator reveals improvement.

At the end of the year, the day-treatment quality assurance committee prepares a report summarizing its findings on all indicators, the results of the in-depth evaluations that were undertaken when thresholds were reached, the actions that were taken, and the evidence that quality improved. The group also decides that in the coming year it will identify several additional aspects of care and indicators to expand its monitoring system.

Summary

Quality assurance is directly tied to the mission of most human services organizations: to provide high-quality services. A collaborative process between managers and providers, quality assurance combines skills in data collection and analysis, consensus building, and problem solving.

Quality assurance programs must be accountable to the highest levels of the organization while involving those who directly produce the services. Today there is wide agreement that the steps in quality assurance involve the ongoing monitoring of important aspects of service, the analysis of identified problems, and corrective action. The process is continuously evaluated and improved.

One of the greatest benefits of quality assurance is that it has the capacity to change behavior. Furthermore, because the measures and analyses of problems are created by providers, it can continually adapt to changes in scientific knowledge or the state of the art. Thus, it can move practice forward to the highest levels of quality possible at any given time.

SKILLS-APPLICATION EXERCISE

One of the most difficult parts of developing a quality assurance program is the identification of key indicators that can be monitored. Select a type of service or program with which you are familiar. Respond to the following items:

- ▸ Briefly describe the program or service. Who receives it? Who provides it? What is its purpose?
- ▸ Identify three important aspects of the service. Consider aspects that are high volume, problem prone, or high risk.
- ▸ For each aspect, identify a measurable indicator of performance and provide a rationale for using this measure.
- ▸ For each indicator, state the data you will use and a threshold for action.

References

Coulton, C. J. (1978). *Social work quality assurance programs: A comparative analysis.* New York: National Association of Social Workers.

Coulton, C. J. (1982). Quality assurance for social services programs: Lessons from health care. *Social Work, 27,* 397–403.

Coulton, C. J. (1989). Quality care assurance. *Mt. Sinai Journal of Medicine, 56,* 435–439.

Donabedian, A. (1982). *Explorations in quality assessment and monitoring (Vol. 2).* Ann Arbor, MI: Health Administration Press.

Lehmann, R. (1987). Joint Commission sets agenda for change. *Quality Review Bulletin, 12,* 72–75.

Lehmann, R. (1989). Forum on clinical indicator development: A discussion of the use and development of indicators. *Quality Review Bulletin, 15,* 223–227.

Patti, R. J. (1987). Managing for service effectiveness in social welfare: Toward a performance model. *Administration in Social Work, 11,* 7–22.

Rehr, H. (1979). *Professional accountability for social work practice.* New York: Prodist.

Vourlekis, B. (1990). The field's evaluation of proposed clinical indicators for social work service in the acute care hospital. *Health and Social Work, 15,* 197–206.

Managing Risk in the Workplace

Paul A. Kurzman

> The life of the law has not been logic: it has been experience; the felt necessities
> of the time, the prevalent moral and political theories, intuitions of public policy,
> avowed or unconscious, even the prejudices which judges share with others, have
> a good deal more to do than syllogism in determining the rules by which we should
> be governed.
>
> —Justice Oliver Wendell Holmes, Jr.

In the direction of human services agencies today, few topics cause more concern to managers than the issue of risk management. This concern is with good reason because of the increase in litigation against human services agencies and social work practitioners.

Much of the current vulnerability results from changes in the practices and funding of agencies. Human services agencies are seen no longer merely as compassionate caretakers, but as professional service providers. Youth-recreation programs, senior citizens' outings, crafts projects, and remedial reading programs have been supplemented (if not supplanted) by sophisticated employment, child development, group home, employee assistance, and family treatment programs. Similarly, voluntary charitable giving to fund programs (through theater benefits, bequests, thrift shops, community foundations, and United Way contributions) has given way to major contracts and fee-for-service arrangements with governmental agencies, which now provide the bulk of the agencies' income. Human services agencies are no longer playing "sandlot ball"; they are playing in the "big leagues" and have correspondingly big risks to manage (Antler, 1987; Bernstein, 1981).

The Legal Environment

In tandem with these organizational changes has come recognition of social work as a full-fledged mental health profession. Social workers are, by far, the largest professional group in the human services arena. Merely 15 years ago, in 1976, only 19 states provided for the legal regulation of social work practice; in 1991, 49 states do. Similarly, professional social workers enjoy vendorship status in 24 states today, whereas vendorship for social work did not exist in a *single* state 15 years ago (Whiting, 1990). With licensure and vendorship have come the authority to be direct and independent providers of clinical treatment services, generally without referral from or supervision by psychologists or physicians. Increasingly, clinical social workers make the diagnoses, provide the treatment, authenticate clients' claim forms, and authorize third-party reimbursements, not only with private insurance carriers, but with CHAMPUS and Medicare. Today, social workers serve as expert witnesses in courts of law, as mental health managed-care experts for major health insurance carriers, and as framers of clinical service regulations in the departments of both state and federal governments.

As lawyers and colleagues have noted, "professionals are held to a higher standard of behavior in their professional capacities than that of the general population" (Watkins & Watkins, 1989, p. 36). Hence, the recent recognition of social work's autonomous professional stature by the government, insurance companies, courts of law, and the public has helped to create new forms of exposure and greater risk in practice. Some service settings, of course, involve inherently higher levels of potential peril than do others. Voluntary agencies with foster care, adoption, day care, debt management, family planning, protective service, group home, camping, residential treatment, and sexual dysfunction programs, for example, place practitioners and managers at particularly high levels of risk. Even the public sector of social work practice is no longer protected. As Besharov (1985, p. 13) noted:

> Courts and state legislatures have all but abolished the doctrines of sovereign, governmental and public official's immunity, so suing public social service agencies and their employees has become progressively easier. Similarly, the abolition of the doctrine of charitable immunity has exposed private agencies and their employees to greater liability.

Agency executives also must "look within" to managing their risks as employers in a competitive and heterogeneous world. For example, do women have access to senior positions in the same way men traditionally have? Are minorities of color well represented on staff, not just at the clerical or custodial level, but in professional, supervisory, and executive positions? Are appropriate accommodations made for the handicapped, both as staff and as clients, in a barrier-free environment? Are ageist and homophobic biases toward colleagues and clients dealt with promptly, honestly, and openly? Many of these issues are dealt with, in part, when a union represents staff or when strong organizations are present in the broader community to ensure nondiscrimination and the ongoing accountability of agencies to their consumers of service.

The foregoing realities would be cause enough for concern if social workers were well prepared for risk-management issues in their graduate social work education. However, many have suggested they are not (Albert, 1986; Barker, 1984; Besharov,

1985; Brieland & Lemmon, 1985; Schroeder, 1982). The NASW *Code of Ethics* and the State Licensing Board *Code of Professional Conduct* are rarely mentioned in the curriculum; moreover, the *legal* dimension of ethical issues in practice receives scant attention, despite the suggested guidelines of the Commission on Accreditation of the Council on Social Work Education. Hence, social work managers may have little preparation for this critical dimension of their professional responsibility. This situation is certainly no better with respect to members of other disciplines who are involved in the human services. Indeed, agency executives may be talented clinicians, skilled supervisors, wise administrators, and even creative fundraisers, but managing the agency's legal obligations, on the one hand, and its legal vulnerability, on the other hand, are areas for which they are apt to be unprepared and unqualified. Moreover, because staff are likely to perceive themselves as "good-doers" and "do-gooders," risk management may seem an oxymoron (Barton & Sanborn, 1978; Everstine & Everstine, 1986).

Competing Values

As Quinn and Rohrbaugh (1981) suggested, there are competing values that underpin any assessment of the effectiveness of an organization. Organizations that follow an "open systems" model, for example, may value behaviors and outcomes that would be perceived as less important to leaders who pursue a "rational goal" model. Simply put, "the Competing Values Approach suggests that the selection of various criteria of effectiveness reflects competing value choices" (Edwards, 1987, p. 5). As a manager, should one emphasize chance taking, creativity, and innovation or rules and regulations that may reduce risk, exposure, and potential organizational jeopardy, from without and within? Does promoting innovation and decision making at the level closest to the client enhance the agency's posture or place its stability (in an unstable world) at too great a risk (Kurzman, 1977)?

To many observers, the term *risk management* connotes caution, collaboration, and consultation. Professionals, who are trained to have expertise in autonomous practice, may perceive such an agenda as a series of illegitimate boundaries circumscribing their judgment, discretion, and freedom to maintain client-centered interventions. Too much management of risk indeed may inhibit the freedom one wishes to promote to keep the agency at "the cutting edge"—competitive and therefore stable in an ever-changing external world.

As Lewin and Cartwright (1964) noted, a dynamic field of forces conditions and constrains managers' decisions. It is *normal* that conflicting interests compete for a manager's attention. In fact, recognition of, and a healthy respect for, the inevitable competing values just noted can lead managers to a different use of self that may strike a proper balance among the several forces over time. A competing values approach gives recognition to this reality and provides a useful framework for analysis and conceptualization. The approach both highlights elements and values that are often overlooked (such as risk-management activity) and encourages the manager to place the need for action in this arena in a broader perspective that may condition implementation. Quinn and Rohrbaugh's (1981) perspective can prod the human services manager to initiate instrumental activities toward the legitimate protection of the agency, its staff, and the clients it serves without placing an inappropriate or exclusionary value on this activity over others. In Simon's (1961) terms, an acknowledgment of competing values can lead to the development of a "satisfying" model of management that recognizes legitimate contending interests among the field of forces, without and within.

The Risks

As the references to this chapter indicate, many books have addressed the vulnerability of social workers and the liabilities inherent in practice. However, less emphasis has been placed on the human services agency per se and on the role of the agency executive or manager in establishing and managing risk-management activities. This section examines the major risks that need to be managed and the complexity of the competing values that must be squarely addressed.

Six risks that are present in prototypical social work agency-based practice are most frequently noted. If these risks are not understood and approached from a preventive posture, they most likely will result in litigation or claims of unethical practice. (Note: Although the following is addressed primarily to social workers, it is also applicable to other professionals in human services agencies.)

Best known perhaps may be the worker's and agency's *duty to warn* if the client discloses an intent to harm himself or herself or others. Codified in what has become known as the Tarasoff Decision, a ruling by the California Supreme Court in 1976 imposed upon the therapist the duty to "exercise reasonable care" in the protection of a potential victim from the violent acts of a client (Weil & Sanchez, 1983). The court concluded that therapists have "an affirmative duty to warn and protect" when they determine, through appropriate standards of their profession, that their clients present a serious danger of violence to a particular person or persons (*Tarasoff v. Regents of the University of California*, 1976). Although the Tarasoff case was decided by a state court and thus technically may be of limited jurisdictional value, few cases have had as far-reaching an effect (Hull & Holmes, 1989, p. 34). Several landmark decisions in subsequent years affirmed the Tarasoff principle and extended its intent to cover nonlicensed "mental health counselors," as well as licensed mental health providers (*Hedlund v. Superior Court of Orange County, CA*, 1983; *Jablonski v. U.S.*, 1983; *Peck v. Counseling Service of Addison County, VT*, 1985).

In the Tarasoff Decision, the court said, in part,

> When a therapist determines, or pursuant to the standards of his profession should determine, that his patient presents a serious danger of violence to another, he incurs an obligation to use reasonable care to protect the intended victim against such danger.

The discharge of this duty may require the therapist to take one or more of various steps, depending on the nature of the case. Thus it may call for him to warn the intended victim or others likely to appraise the victim of the danger, to notify the police, or to take whatever other steps are reasonably necessary under the circumstances.

A second area of risk to agencies comes ironically from the *duty to keep confidential* material that is shared with the agency and its practitioners in the course of the professional relationship. Section II-H of the NASW *Code of Ethics* (National Association of Social Workers, 1990), for example, states that "the social worker should respect the privacy of clients and hold in confidence all information obtained in the course of professional service." However, confidentiality is not absolute, which is why section II-H-1 of the code provides that the worker should share confidential material "only for compelling professional reasons" (see also Promislo, 1979; Wilson, 1978).

What the Tarasoff Decision did was to delineate one such "compelling professional reason" and to clarify that the code's "should" may imply an *obligation* to act and disclose. In the words of the Tarasoff Decision: "The protective privilege ends where the public peril begins."

Indeed, the concept of client confidentiality is governed for social workers (in 44 of the 49 states in which the profession is regulated) as "privileged communication." The state statutes provide protection for clients similar to the protection they enjoy in the context of their relationships with attorneys, the clergy, and physicians (Knapp & Vande Creek, 1987; Vande Creek, Knapp, & Herzog, 1988). However, almost all such statutes make exceptions to privilege for such disclosures as the intent to commit a crime or a harmful act to self or others and disclosure of the abuse or neglect of children. In fact, most states today have a specific law that mandates all licensed professionals to report known or suspected cases of child abuse and would define the failure to report as a *prima facie* case of unprofessional conduct.

A third professional obligation involves the *duty to ensure continuity of service* to clients under care. The expectation is that the agency will not abandon or neglect a client who needs immediate care or currently is under its care without making reasonable arrangements for the continuity of service. Such a duty obligates the agency to uncooperative and "undesirable" clients, whose hostility and initial unresponsiveness may indeed be a symptom of their need and their disorder. Being able to demonstrate outreach, empathy, flexibility, and appropriate referral to an alternate provider may be essential (Meyer, Landis, & Hays, 1988; Saltman & Proch, 1990). Similarly, the *duty adequately to record* services provided is incumbent on all agencies and practitioners (Schrier, 1980). As social workers achieve the status and recognition of vendors, accurate and timely recording becomes essential to ensure that both agencies and clients are properly protected for the receipt of third-party payments. The failure to support a diagnosis from the American Psychiatric Association's (1986) *Diagnostic and Statistical Manual of Mental Disorders (Third Edition—Revised)*, commonly known as DSM-III-R, in an agency recording that has been provided to an insurance carrier to justify a fee payment may be defined as an act of fraud within state statutes. In addition, many states that license social workers define the failure to provide adequate recordings of services to clients and to retain such records for a specified number of years as grounds for charges of professional misconduct.

Social workers also have a *duty to diagnose and treat their clients properly*. This is a major issue for agencies that have weak procedures for supervisory review and few standards to support interprofessional consultation and referral (Reamer, 1989). The failure to refer a client to a physician to rule out biological, organic, or

"According to the Tarasoff Decision, I'm obligated to warn the people below of your intention to jump on them."

genetic conditions that may trigger psychological symptoms is perhaps the largest arena of risk. Alexander (1983, p. 5) noted that half the claims for erroneous diagnoses made under the NASW Insurance Trust's professional liability insurance program were based on a charge that the clients' problems were actually medical, not psychological. In addition, agencies need to provide for consultation in psychosocial areas for which social workers may still be poorly trained, such as learning disabilities and substance abuse.

The expectation that agency practitioners will reach an appropriate DSM-III-R diagnosis also implies that this correct diagnosis will be recorded on insurance forms to Medicaid, Medicare, and such private insurance carriers as Blue Shield. Because social workers now have greater recognition as eligible vendors of psychotherapeutic treatment, care must be taken that errors in diagnosis, whether intentional or inadvertent, are not recorded. Research (Kutchins & Kirk, 1987) has shown that clients may place pressure on providers to report *less* severe diagnoses than are indicated because of their fear of the potential adverse effects of labeling. Staff may conversely feel pressure to *increase* the severity of the diagnosis falsely or to exaggerate symptoms so the client or agency can qualify for third-party payments.

Finally, there is a risk to practice inherent in the *duty to avoid sexual impropriety.* Sexual acts performed under the guise of therapy are not permitted between clients and workers (Schultz, 1982). Virtually all the codes governing the professional conduct of social workers in the 49 states (and three jurisdictions) that regulate social work practice make this prohibition explicit. Moreover, section II-F-5 of the NASW *Code of Ethics* (NASW, 1990) makes no exceptions to its unequivocal statement: "The social worker should under no circumstances engage in sexual activities with clients." Such activity cannot be defended in the guise of "supporting the transference" or helping to "overcome sexual inhibition or dysfunction." Given the position of trust that the agency *shares* with its practitioners, courts may view employers as having culpability as well. The potential perils here are even greater than with the risks previously described because most insurance policies *exclude* intentional wrongdoing, such as sexual involvement with clients. For the 455 agencies and 47,800 individual social workers it covers, the NASW Insurance Trust's professional liability insurance covered claims of sexual involvement until 1985. However, the staggering increase of such claims in the 1980s led the insurance company to exclude them from coverage thereafter (Besharov, 1985, p. 179). Agencies and supervisors, moreover, generally will be viewed in the role of *respondeat superior* and share civil liability for such wrongful acts committed by those under their supervision or in their employ (Watkins & Watkins, 1989, p. 48).

By highlighting these most serious risks and duties, one can see that great caution and sound judgment are needed at the helm of the human services agency today. (For a more extensive list of categories of risk and liability, see Besharov, 1985, pp. 2–9.) The litigious environment in which professionals currently practice makes it imperative that managers plan to reduce the agency's exposure while preserving a spirit of flexibility and innovation. Procedures have to be put in place because good intentions are an insufficient protection. In addition to the possibility of government-sponsored criminal actions against agencies and their practitioners, civil actions by clients are becoming more common and more successful. The defense against torts, such as the negligence of agencies and malpractice by individuals, requires as careful thought as do preparation of the budget and staffing the board of trustees.

Recommended Responses

A series of four major recommendations flow from this discussion. They reflect a focus on the competing values that are intrinsic to the issues at hand and therefore deal with process and goals, the maintenance of and competition among systems, planning and training, and both internal and external loci of organizational concern.

Insurance Protection

No agency can afford to be without adequate forms of insurance. Such coverage should include (1) premises liability, covering all sites at which services may be delivered; (2) agency professional liability, including the activities of all staff, paid or volunteer, consultant or employee; (3) coverage of officers and directors, to shield members of the board of trustees from individual and collective personal liability in the performance of their fiduciary duties; (4) vehicular insurance, generally at a level higher than the mandated state minimum; and (5) bonding for all officers and staff who have the authority to sign contracts or manage the agency's income and assets. Such casualty policies should cover the agency and key participants for most losses and damages, including negligence, provided that one cannot prove nonfeasance or malfeasance. In addition, insurance generally provides for the funding of the potentially expensive legal defense against charges that may be brought, regardless of the outcome. Without adequate insurance, winning a case in court may actually be a Pyrrhic victory (Jones & Alcabes, 1989). Out-of-pocket legal fees and court costs for the individual and the agency may be so high that, in effect, one "loses" even when one wins. In sum, it is essential for the agency to obtain insurance coverage that is commensurate with the organizational scope and clinical complexity of its practice (Tremper, 1989, pp. 144–165).

Legal Counsel

Every agency should establish legal counsel in the same way it sets up an ongoing relationship with an accountant or psychiatric consultant. One should not wait until a crisis occurs and try to select an attorney under pressure. Most agency administrators try to ensure that one or more attorneys serve on their board of directors, so they can get the frequent informal advice they may need on such issues as reviewing a lease, framing an amendment to the bylaws, and signing a new governmental contract, usually on a *pro bono* basis. However, there are good reasons why an independent counsel is warranted. First, some legal opinions may involve a potential conflict of interest for a board member because the questions involve actions by the board itself or one of its members. Second, the legal issues may be outside the board member's legal specialization and expertise. Third, the individual (or organization) that is taking legal action against the agency may be a client of the board member's firm.

Whether done by a board member or an external counsel, new legal agreements and contracts should be fully reviewed before they are signed. Given the principle of *respondeat superior* noted earlier, it also is important for an attorney to ensure that the agency's insurance covers persons, for example, who will be agents of the agency's service (under the supervision of the agency's employees), such as student interns, VISTA workers, community volunteers, and psychotherapy trainees (Cohen & Marino, 1982, p. 315). On a proactive basis, as well, an attorney should regularly explore the major federal, state, and local statutes (and case law) that govern the agency, its funding, and its professional practice.

Staff Training

The best way to avoid trouble is to prevent it from occurring. Social workers know the value of education and prevention, often deploying these skills on behalf of clients with remarkable creativity and success. As managers, however, social workers often forget to apply what works in direct practice to the *organizations* for which they now are responsible ("Social Work and the Law," 1984).

In addition to ongoing clinical training activities that may accompany monthly administrative meetings or periodic case conferences, it may be wise to institute quarterly half-day sessions for formal administrative training. Such sessions not only provide the line staff with the information they need for advancement into administrative positions, they send the message that organizational issues are everyone's concern (Besharov & Besharov, 1987; Sharwell, 1982). Experts can be invited to speak, or staff with special expertise can lead the sessions. From a risk-management perspective, among the important items to cover are (1) state laws governing the requirements and procedures for reporting known or suspected cases of child abuse or neglect; (2) principles that are embodied in the Tarasoff Decision with regard to the "duty to warn" when there is serious potential danger by a client to self or to others; (3) current federal and state regulations on the recording and maintenance of records; (4) statutes on privileged communication governing the several mental health professions and the specific principles of confidentiality embodied in the professions' ethical codes; (5) the proper completion of insurance forms for third-party reimbursement, including the appropriate use of the several axes of the DSM-III-R; (6) additional training for proper differential diagnoses in areas in which mental health professionals are likely to be poorly trained, such as learning disabilities, organic pathology, psychopharmacology, and chemical dependence; and (7) relevant state rules and standards of professional conduct for the licensed health professions (Hardcastle, 1990; Wodarski, 1980).

Special emphasis must be given to the need to train staff to avoid even the *appearance* of sexual impropriety. Occasionally, it may be appropriate, for example, for a therapist to hug clients momentarily to console them; to stroke their wrists briefly during a moment of stress; or to compliment clients on their dress or appearance if this is a new sign of strength and self-esteem. It would be naive, however, not to understand that there is a thin line that would be easy for the therapist to cross. Moreover, one must remember the clinical dictum, especially in working in the context of a transferential relationship with troubled clients, that "perception is reality." The alarming rise in charges of professional misconduct that have been brought before disciplinary committees of licensing boards and committees of inquiry of professional associations in the past few years charging psychotherapists with both heterosexual and homosexual sexual misconduct must be understood and underscored. As was noted, such charges against social workers have become so prevalent in recent years that a cap has been placed on professional liability insurance coverage when a sexual impropriety by a worker has been documented (Besharov, 1985, p. 179).

Furthermore, agency managers should note that this issue is not profession specific. The American Psychological Association's (APA's) recent study showed that "in the past 10 years, 45% of all malpractice awards through APA's professional liability coverage have dealt with therapist-patient intimacy" ("Therapist-Patient Sexual Intimacy," 1988, p. 13). Bringing in a member of an NASW or APA chapter's Committee on Inquiry to discuss the respective provisions of the *Code of Ethics* in this area is warranted. In addition, it may be wise to invite a member of the disciplinary panel of the relevant state licensing board to speak about standards for licensure and case law experience regarding sexual impropriety. The need to train staff members to avoid even the possible *perception* of improper behavior in their speech, conduct, and presentation of self is crucial to limiting an agency's exposure. If such a transgression occurs, the staff person should be quickly identified as "an impaired professional" and referred for appropriate help, while the client's needs and rights are served and protected.

Internal Audit

All agencies conduct a *fiscal* audit each year, if only because it is required by funding bodies and by the Internal Revenue Service as a condition for maintaining their tax-exempt—501[c][3]—status. What most managers fail to do, however, is to retain outside experts to conduct a periodic *program-and-management* audit to ensure that risks are being properly managed. The items that an external and board auditor might jointly review with a senior member of the managerial staff should include the following:

▶ Are the agency's governmental licenses (such as those with the department of mental health, division of substance abuse services, and board of social welfare) in order?

▶ Are all professional staff currently licensed and registered for practice?

▶ Are provisions for emergency actions (fire drills, the involuntary hospitalization of clients, the safety of staff, and the reporting of accidents) well known and regularly updated?

▶ Are premiums for all forms of casualty insurance coverage paid and current?

▶ Are procedures for the management of clients' records being properly followed?

▶ Are governmental vouchers and records of Medicaid insurance reimbursements being maintained, in keeping with contractual requirements?

▶ Are supervisory evaluations being conducted and reviewed in a timely fashion? A biennial internal management audit of the appropriateness of such standard operating procedures and the staff's adherence to their provisions is a preventive risk-management activity that may pay big dividends for the agency, the staff, and the clients served.

Summary

New opportunities have brought new risks. As licensed professionals who are managing regulated agencies in the context of a litigious society, managers of human services agencies can no longer consider risk management to be a luxury. The demands of clients, funding sources, and the standards of the profession suggest that managing risks is part of the prudent manager's responsibility for a logical strategy of primary and secondary prevention. That is, risk management is better conceptualized as a proactive strategy of affirmation than as a reactive response to a crisis. Managers who organically build in this function as a normal component to their administrative role and function should not find this activity any more burdensome than hiring staff and balancing the budget. Although human services managers have to respond to many competing values as they manage their internal and external environments, the growth and stability of agencies are dependent on the managers' competent performance of risk-management functions. Human services agencies have legitimate "survival needs" because they must coexist with internal and external forces that constantly impinge on them. In a sense, they are social organisms that reflect the legitimate competing values to which they must respond. In this context, agencies must manage risks to thrive and survive, often in turbulent times, because clients—often with few options in life—are depending on them.

SKILLS-APPLICATION EXERCISES

▶ You are the manager of a hospital-based employee assistance program (EAP) that provides free and confidential professional mental health and substance abuse services to all hospital employees and their families. An emergency room nurse voluntarily comes to the EAP to see a social worker on your staff about her cocaine and alcohol addiction, which she says, "seems to be getting worse." Because she is exceedingly good at what she does, and generally careful about when she "snorts" and drinks, her addiction has not been detected by supervisors or peers. She wants help for her problem, but only if she can stay on her job and only if the EAP worker promises her confidentiality. Provided that the EAP staff make these two promises, she indicates she will do whatever they recommend, including coming in for daily EAP sessions, gradually eliminating her use of alcohol and cocaine, and joining Alcoholics Anonymous and Cocaine Anonymous in the community. She reminds your staff person that she is a voluntary self-referral and of the EAP's long-standing and well-known promise of confidentiality (Kurzman, 1988). Without revealing the client's identity, your EAP social worker wants to know if you will permit him to honor the client's requests. What do you do, and why?

▶ Your agency has received a letter from a prominent negligence attorney in the community alleging that a male social work psychotherapist at your agency made explicit verbal and physical advances to a female client during several treatment sessions. It is said that the client, in the context of a transferential treatment relationship, was sufficiently encouraged and enticed by these alleged advances that she became more seriously ill. In addition, she lost her well-paid job as a certified public accountant because she could no longer concentrate at work. She further claims, through her attorney, that the social worker's advances alienated the affection of her husband, who wants a divorce. The client's attorney wants to meet with you to explore a $1 million settlement, in lieu of a protracted, public, and potentially more costly outcome of litigation against you, the worker, and the agency. As the executive director of the agency, would you meet with the client's attorney? What would be your short- and long-range plans of action?

▶ You are the new executive director of a moderate-size, multiservice voluntary agency with many governmental contracts, local purchase-of-service arrangements, foundation grants, and a small freestanding licensed mental health clinic. You have a diverse professional and paraprofessional staff and the immediate support of three experienced assistant executive directors—for program, development, and administration. What would be your plan of action, during your first year, to assess the adequacy and sufficiency of your agency's risk-management policies and procedures?

References

Albert, R. (1986). *Law and social work practice*. New York: Springer.

Alexander, C. A. (1983, November 21). Professional liability insurance: Jeopardy and ethics. Paper presented at the 1983 Professional Symposium, National Association of Social Workers. National Association of Social Workers, Washington, DC.

American Psychiatric Association. (1986). *Diagnostic and statistical manual of mental disorders. Third edition—revised*. Washington, DC: Author.

Antler, S. (1987). Professional liability and malpractice. *Encyclopedia of Social Work* (18th ed., pp. 346–351). Silver Spring, MD: National Association of Social Workers.

Barker, R. L. (1984). The Tarasoff paradox: Confidentiality and the duty to warn. *Social Thought, 10*(4), 3–12.

Barton, W. E., & Sanborn, C. J. (Eds.). (1978). *Law and the mental health professions*. New York: International Universities Press.

Bernstein, B. E. (1981). Malpractice: Future shock of the 1980s. *Social Casework, 62*(3), 175–181.

Besharov, D. J. (1985). *The vulnerable social worker*. Silver Spring, MD: National Association of Social Workers.

Besharov, D. J., & Besharov, S. H. (1987). Teaching about liability. *Social Work, 32*, 517–522.

Brieland, D., & Lemmon, J. (1985). *Social work and the law*. St. Paul, MN: West Publications.

Cohen, R. J., & Marino, W. E. (1982). *Legal guidebook in mental health*. New York: Free Press.

Edwards, R. L. (1987). The competing values approach as an integrating framework for the management curriculum. *Administration in Social Work, 11*, 1–13.

Everstine, L., & Everstine, D. S. (1986). *Psychotherapy and the law*. Orlando, FL: Grune & Stratton.

Hardcastle, D. A. (1990). Legal regulation of social work. *Encyclopedia of Social Work 1990 supplement to the 18th edition* (pp. 203–217). Silver Spring, MD: NASW Press.

Hedlund v. Superior Ct. of Orange County, 34 Cal 3d 695 (1983).

Hull, L., & Holmes, G. (1989). Legal analysis and public agencies: The therapist's duty to warn. *New England Journal of Human Services, 9*(2), 31–34.

Jablonski v. U.S., 712F. 2d 391 (1983).

Jones, J. A., & Alcabes, A. (1989). Clients don't sue: The invulnerable social worker. *Social Casework, 70*, 414–420.

Knapp, S., & Vande Creek, L. (1987). *Privileged communication for mental health professionals*. New York: Van Nostrand Reinhold.

Kurzman, P. A. (1988). The ethical base for social work in the workplace. In G. M. Gould & M. L. Smith (Eds.), *Social work in the workplace* (pp. 16–27). New York: Springer.

Kurzman, P. A. (1977). Rules and regulations in large-scale organizations: A theoretical approach to the problem. *Administration in Social Work, 1*, 421–431.

Kutchins, H., & Kirk, S. A. (1987). DSM-III and Social Work Malpractice. *Social Work, 32*, 205–211.

Lewin, K., & Cartwright, D. (1964). *Field theory in social science*. New York: Harper & Row.

Meyer, R. G., Landis, E. R., & Hays, J. R. (1988). *Law for the psychotherapist*. New York: W. W. Norton.

National Association of Social Workers. (1990). *Code of ethics*. Silver Spring, MD: Author.

Peck v. Counseling Service of Addison County, 499 A-422, VT (1985).

Promislo, E. (1979). Confidentiality and privileged communication. *Social Work, 24*, 10–13.

Quinn, R. E., & Rohrbaugh, J. (1981). A competing values approach to organizational effectiveness. *Public Productivity Review, 5*, 122–140.

Reamer, F. G. (1989). Liability issues in social work supervision. *Social Work, 34*, 445–448.

Saltman, A., & Proch, K. (1990). *Law in social work practice*. Chicago: Nelson-Hall.

Schrier, C. (1980). Guidelines for record-keeping under privacy and open-access laws. *Social Work, 25*, 452–457.

Schroeder, L. O. (1982). *The legal environment of social work*. Englewood Cliffs, NJ: Prentice Hall.

Schultz, B. (1982). *Legal liability in psychotherapy: A practitioner's guide to risk management*. San Francisco: Jossey-Bass.

Sharwell, G. R. (1982). Avoiding legal liability in the practice of school social work. *Social Work in Education, 5*, 17–25.

Simon, H. A. (1961). *Administrative behavior* (2nd ed.). New York: Macmillan.

Social work and the law. (1984). *Practice Digest* (whole issue).

Tarasoff v. Regents of the U. of California, 17C. 3d 425, 551, p 2d 344 (1976).

Therapist-patient sexual intimacy. (1988, September–October). *EAP Digest, 13*.

Tremper, C. R. (1989). *Reconsidering legal liability and insurance for nonprofit organizations*. Lincoln, NB: Law College Education Services.

Vande Creek, L., Knapp, S., & Herzog, C. (1988). Privileged communications for social workers. *Social Casework, 69*, 28–34.

Watkins, S. A., & Watkins, J. C. (1989). Negligent endangerment: Malpractice in the clinical context. *Journal of Independent Social Work, 3*(3), 35–50.

Weil, M., & Sanchez, E. (1983). The impact of the Tarasoff Decision on clinical social work practice. *Social Service Review, 57*, 112–124.

Whiting, L. (1990). *State comparison of laws regulating social work*. Silver Spring, MD: National Association of Social Workers.

Wilson, S. J. (1978). *Confidentiality in social work*. New York: Free Press.

Wodarski, J. S. (1980). Legal requisites for social work practice. *Clinical Social Work Journal, 8*, 90–98.

PART

5

DIRECTING SKILLS

Managerial directing skills encompass the roles of producer and director. Competencies for the producer role include personal productivity, motivating others, time management, and stress management. Competencies for the director role include taking the initiative, goal setting, and effective delegating. The chapters in this section offer wide-ranging perspectives on these roles and competencies.

Douglas C. Eadie describes the field of strategic planning and management, emphasizing that the central issue for human services organizations is to keep a dynamic balance between themselves and their external environments. According to Eadie, "strategic issue management" describes the entire process, from global strategies to detailed planning for action. He describes the steps in the process— identifying values and clarifying the organization's vision, scanning the external environment, scanning the internal environment, identifying and selecting the strategic issues, formulating strategies, and implementing strategies—and presents examples of how the process may be applied to nonprofit organizations, including human services organizations. Implicit in this chapter are emphases on rationality, analytic approaches, economic considerations, the clarification of goals, productivity, interpersonal benefits accruing from the skillful carrying out of the planning process, and taking action. Value is placed on increasing both efficiency and effectiveness. Eadie believes that the enhancement of the relative position of an organization in its environment is a key function of human services managers.

Myron E. Weiner looks at the complex and challenging subject of how to motivate employees. Paying attention to the nature and process of motivation, the necessity for human services managers to individualize their motivational approaches, and the blending and linking of the performance of individuals and the organization, Weiner provides a specific framework for thinking about motivation. He offers an overview of theories of motivation, pinpoints the employee's job as the link between the individual and the organization, and highlights the Job Characteristics Model of the motivation to work. Emphasizing the importance of individual and collective approaches to evaluating the performance of employees, Weiner suggests a variety of skills that managers need to carry out the roles of director and producer, including the clarification of goals, the blending of goals, "performance linkage," providing feedback to employees about their performance, the design of jobs, job-role linkage, job training, and career development.

Laurie Newman DiPadova and Sue R. Faerman discuss the management of time, stressing the competencies of personal productivity, goal setting, taking the initiative, delegating, and managing stress. They argue that the effective management of time is a personal responsibility and can be a "learned skill"—that human services managers can increase their ability to accomplish more in less time by working smarter, not harder. To support their view, they explore some of the myths of time and time management and present detailed techniques for improving the use of time: organizing one's self, organizing at work, and helping others to be organized. These techniques cut across a number of skills, including goal setting, clarifying roles, establishing clear expectations, determining priorities, motivating oneself and others, delegating tasks or functions appropriately, planning, and managing stress.

Kenneth R. Wedel, in writing about designing and implementing effective performance contracts, presents a typology of purchase-of-service approaches, including cost-oriented, performance-based, and performance-incentives contracting. He presents a set of criteria and guidelines for human services managers to design and implement their purchase of services. He suggests that managing for performance requires skills in planning, negotiating, and monitoring, as well as in goal setting, establishing clear expectations, planning, rational analysis, and taking the initiative. Wedel believes that performance contracting can stimulate entrepreneurship, involve human services managers and organizations in profit-making ventures, and stimulate appropriate behavior in the marketplace if human services managers use the approach to create certain outcomes.

John A. Yankey and Mark I. Singer deal with a relatively new topic in human services management: managing mergers and consolidations. They draw conceptual distinctions between these two strategies of organizational restructuring and suggest that there are four phases to a merger or consolidation, including deciding whether to explore it, deciding on a potential partner, planning for its implementation, and implementing the new structural arrangement. Yankey and Singer present three approaches to deciding on a potential partner for a merger or consolidation and offer a number of suggestions regarding the information that needs to be generated to make such a decision. Similar suggestions are presented for planning and for implementing the merger or consolidation. They emphasize that both process and substance are critical to the successful conclusion of mergers and consolidations. The roles of both producer and director are emphasized, especially competencies in planning, clarifying and setting goals, rational analysis, motivating others, using authority, and delegating responsibilities.

CHAPTER 18

Planning and Managing Strategically

Douglas C. Eadie

Strategic planning and management processes have been widely used in the for-profit sector for the past quarter century, and their application is now spreading rapidly in the human services. Sound reasons exist for the growing use of these processes in human services organizations:

▶ Social workers work in an evermore complex and rapidly changing environment that places a premium on flexibility, adaptability, and the conscious management of change—in missions, strategic directions, plans, and programs. Strategic planning and management processes focus on the management of change, whereas traditional long-range planning approaches have basically projected current activities into the future—on the assumption of continuing environmental stability.

▶ There is also increasing competition among nonprofit, public, and for-profit organizations in many fields, from education and training to health and human services, and organizations that are able to plan and manage strategically are far better equipped to survive and flourish.

So strategic planning and management techniques are quickly becoming a staple in the human services manager's cupboard. However, talking about them is far easier than putting them to practical use in the near term, with concrete results and at an affordable cost. The popular adage, "No pain, no gain," is all too true in applying strategic techniques. Not only are these techniques technically demanding, their application inevitably involves significant costs, most notably the time of board members and managers. And no simple cookbook can be followed to plan and manage strategically. Rather, a broad logic and methodology must be adapted to the specific needs, circumstances, capabilities, and personnel of particular organizations.

The history of planning in nonprofit and public human services organizations is replete with tales of woe, as elaborate, ambitious planning processes have failed to achieve the expected results or have even broken down midstream. This chapter prepares the reader to venture confidently onto the complex, shifting, and occasionally even treacherous terrain of strategic management, to recognize certain guideposts, to spot and avoid certain pitfalls, and ultimately to find a path that will lead to successful application.

The chapter first describes the rapidly changing field of strategic planning and management, with special attention to a variation on the theme that is proving especially useful in the nonprofit and public sectors: strategic issue management. The process of designing applications to fit particular organizations is then described, after which two special issues are briefly addressed: the role of the nonprofit board in strategic planning and management and the tie between strategic management and the annual operational planning and budget preparation process. Finally, a practical exercise provides the reader with an opportunity to try some of the techniques.

Logic and Methodology: An Overview

Strategic management is a balancing act; its primary purpose is to maintain a dynamic balance between an organization (its mission, goals, plans, and resources) and its external environment. The balance is maintained by ensuring that the organization's scarce resources are invested to take maximum feasible advantage of opportunities (for new or additional revenues, new customers or clients, or new products or services) and to deal effectively with challenges (the decline or disappearance of a major source of revenue or the appearance of a significant competitor).

Strategic planning and management is a relatively new and rapidly developing field, especially in the human services sector where its presence is just now being felt (Bryson, 1989; Bryson & Roering, 1987; Eadie, 1989; Olsen & Eadie, 1982). One of the most important innovations in the field in recent years has been the rejection of the notion that the primary product of this process is a weighty, comprehensive plan that encompasses all an organization's activities. It is now widely accepted that the real product is organizational change in response to environmental change, not the elaborate codification and projection into the future of current programs and functions. Indeed, experience has shown that, in a time of often dizzying environmental change, the production of massive documents may be a harmful waste of time.

The term *strategic management,* which is now used far more widely than the term *strategic planning,* developed in response to the early overemphasis on the production of documents at the expense of attention to actual change. *Strategic management* encompasses not only the formulation of strategies, but their implementation, and is best seen as an ongoing process (Bryson, 1989; Eadie, 1989; Tichy, 1983).

Another major current in the field is the attention paid to the collective involvement of people in fashioning and implementing strategies (Robinson & Eadie, 1986). The fact is that people do it, not computers, forms, procedures, or six-pound documents. Now that people are recognized as being important for the formulation of successful strategies, developing the human resource and building strong teams are rightly seen as critical to the success of strategic management (Gluck, 1985; Nutt & Backoff, 1987).

There are strategies and there are strategies. A community may stage a series of participatory meetings that result in a vision and a set of broad directions for development—a kind of global strategy far removed from detailed action planning. A human services organization may develop such a global strategy as well. But the community or the human services organization may also formulate detailed action strategies (specific change targets, or initiatives, along with implementation plans) to address particular issues that have been identified. These are also strategies. And to narrow the focus even further, a particular division or department in a nonprofit organization may produce its own strategies, including both a global strategy and detailed action strategies.

The point is that saying that an organization is engaging in strategic management means nothing until the kind of strategy being produced is known. As will be explored later, until an organization knows the kind of strategy it wants to produce, it cannot determine the specifics of the process required to produce it.

"The strategic plan says we facilitate the timely flow of inter-departmental and external communications. . . . So try not to think of yourself as 'just a mailroom clerk.' "

Strategic Issue Management

Strategic issue management is increasingly used to describe the entire process, from the development of a global strategy through the generation of detailed action strategies. As will be seen, the focus on strategic issues safeguards against using the process merely to describe and codify what an organization is already doing. Therefore, strategic issue management has sometimes been called "management by selection" (Eadie, 1986, 1987a, 1987b; Eadie & Steinbacher, 1985).

The principal elements in the process are the clarification of values and vision, external environmental scanning, internal environmental scanning, the identification and selection of strategic issues, the formulation of strategies, and implementation of strategies. The following discussion addresses both the content involved in each element and the process used to generate it, drawing on real-life examples.

Clarification of Values and Vision

The clarification of values and vision provides the strategic issue management process with a kind of "natural law": a strategic backdrop for scanning the environment, selecting the issues, and gaining information about the strategies. Without this backdrop, the strategic management process would be like an automobile engine without a driver or a steering wheel: undirected motion and energy.

Values are the most cherished principles—the "golden rules"—that guide an organization's planning and management activities. A vision is a word picture of an organization's desired impact on or contribution to its community or service area and of the organization's role in the community.

The Lorain City (Ohio) School District board (Eadie, 1990d, pp. 12–13), meeting with the district's top administrators and faculty leaders, fashioned a statement of values that includes the following points:

- We believe that a complete education includes both academic and life skills.
- We believe that education should be a lifelong endeavor.
- We believe that all students can learn.
- We believe that student pride in accomplishment and sense of self-worth are critical to success in learning and in life.
- We believe that our schools should be a safe, attractive, nurturing environment for our students.
- We believe in strong parent involvement in our schools.

At a two-day session, the board of the Southeastern Minnesota Private Industry Council, in Rochester, mapped out a vision of the council's role in the community that consisted of the following principal elements (Eadie, 1990e, p. 5):

- A council providing strong leadership in the design—and the management—of the local employment and training system

▶ A council whose leadership results in a more effective employment and training system that includes strategic planning, a rational division of labor among providers, and the coordination of resources

▶ A council that is the single most important employment and training resource to local elected officials, in planning and program development and in support of economic development

▶ A council that mobilizes diverse, growing resources to address employment and training needs, but that grows in a disciplined fashion

▶ A council that aggressively leads in identifying and addressing community-wide employment and training needs.

Statements of values and vision are often fashioned in intensive, facilitated work sessions involving board members and top managers. Certainly, something this important to the long-term success of an organization should not merely be delegated to staff and then passively reviewed by a board. The board and staff of the Bexar County Local Development Corporation, in San Antonio, Texas, for example, developed detailed impact and role statements as part of a vision exercise in a day-long work session, after which the vision statement was refined by the staff working with a consultant and confirmed in a follow-up session of the board (Eadie, 1990b, 1990c).

External Environmental Scan

In light of its vision and mission, what information must an organization have about the world in which it works to spot issues and formulate effective strategies? The environmental scan answers this question. The vision and mission provide the boundaries that keep the scan from being an overwhelming task.

Developing the Content

Whether the scan is prepared by a staff task force and then reviewed in an intensive board-staff work session or is developed in a work session, the point is to identify the national, state, regional, and local trends and conditions that need to be understood to fashion a strategy. The Southeastern Minnesota Private Industry Council, for example, was interested in (1) federal legislation and program guidelines related to economic development and training, changing standards and practices in the employment and training field, developing service delivery technologies, and national and global economic change; (2) state gubernatorial directions, legislation, and programs in employment, training, and related social service areas; and (3) the local economy (the mix of businesses and employment in different industrial classifications) and demography (population by age, sex, race, income, and education), and various social "pathologies" that would affect its plans and delivery of services, such as the rate of high school dropouts, teenage pregnancies, and single-parent families living below the poverty line.

Analysis of Stakeholders

In the quest for statistics, it is all too easy to forget that an organization's environment also consists of other entities that significantly influence or have the potential to influence an organization's vision, mission, and strategies. These influential organizations are often loosely known as "stakeholders," and understanding them is a critical part of the external environmental scan.

Stakeholders may be understood in terms both of organizational characteristics and actual and potential relationships with the organization. Organizational characteristics include vision, mission, priorities, plans, resources, style of operating, track record, and, what is most important, perceptions of the organization. Vis-à-vis the organization, a stakeholder may be a cooperator, a partner in a joint venture, a provider of resources, a provider of legitimacy (blessing the organization's endeavors), a wielder of authority, a competitor, a paying customer, or a client.

The Lorain City School District's board and staff, for example, devoted considerable attention to the district's relationships with the county and city governments, with local civic organizations, and with neighborhood associations (Conley & Eadie, 1990). The board of the National Association of County Training and Employment Professionals (Washington, DC), in the course of a day-long work session with senior staff, identified among its key stakeholders the National Job Training Partnership, with which it had a partly competitive, partly cooperative relationship. It was noted that the "current uncertainty in its mission and goals as it goes through a difficult transition" made it highly difficult to assess the potential working relationship with the partnership (Eadie, 1987a, p. 5).

Customers and Clients

When analyzing stakeholders, human services organizations must distinguish between paying customers and clients because the two groups involve different relationships that require special management. Clients of a county welfare agency, for example, do not directly buy the services they receive (although, indirectly, they may pay through taxes), but the state department of welfare and the county commissioners are direct customers with considerable power over the mission, plans, and programs of the welfare agency. The point is that the service delivered to the client is only one kind of product; other kinds may be delivered to the paying customers (for example, county commissioners may view the movement of welfare clients into training programs and, ultimately, to paying jobs as the preeminent product of the agency).

Organizations within Organizations

Keep in mind that the external environment of an organization may include the wider organization to which it belongs. So, for example, the environment of the

Oswego County (New York) Department of Employment and Training includes the remainder of the Oswego County government. Therefore, when the executive staff of the department met for a day to scan its environment, it identified as two of its primary stakeholders the county legislature and the county administrator, who was described as "familiar with—and supportive of—the department's mission, strategies, and programs," easily accessible to the department, closely tied to the local Republican party structure, and a "hard-nosed" decision maker. It was believed that the county legislature perceived the department positively, seeing it as an "effective performer and a modest consumer of county resources" (Eadie, Rose, & Bellow, 1988, p. 22).

Internal Environmental Scan

Organizational Resources

The foundation for identifying strategic issues is fully in place when an organization leaves its external environment and looks inward, assessing its resources, its strategies, and its organizational strengths and weaknesses. Resources are human, financial, and technological. When an organization looks inward, it must understand how well it is staffed (the number of staff and their experience, education, and training), its sources of revenue and what is happening to them (are certain federal grants in decline?), and the extent to which it is using state-of-the-art technologies.

Strategies in Place

The assessment of existing strategies has two components: (1) evidence of the organization's performance toward achieving stated program goals and (2) the experience of the organization in managing major initiatives for change. Analyzing the organization's performance related to stated goals can be a straightforward process, but only if reliable data on performance are systematically collected and analyzed; otherwise, the assessment may involve considerably more work. The analysis of initiatives for change, in terms not only of the outcomes achieved but of how efficiently the change process was managed, provides important insights into an organization's ability to handle change in the future. Two examples from recent strategic issue management processes are the Southeastern Minnesota Private Industry Council's analysis of its Campus Connection program, which provides at-risk high school students with an intensive summer residential experience on a college campus, and the Lorain City School District's large-scale implementation of a magnet school program as a response to court-ordered desegregation.

Organization's Strengths and Weaknesses

The analysis of the organization's strengths and weaknesses is the culmination of the internal environmental scan. The analysis will inevitably overlap with the analysis of resources and the assessment of strategies in place, but the point is to understand the competitive position of the organization in its wider environment. For example, the board and staff of the Bexar County Local Development Corporation identified several strengths, such as the presence of two county commissioners on its board, the absence of any directly competitive organization in its market and service area, and its close ties to local school districts. The list of competitive weaknesses includes the corporation's narrowly representative board, "which limits the corporation's clout and networking capability," and its lack of local credibility (Eadie, 1990b, p. 4).

Preparing the External and Internal Scans

Although it is possible to develop the external and internal environmental scans in an intensive, facilitated work session with no formal staff preparation, environmental analysis is such a complex and critical activity that, if possible, staff preparation for a work session is advisable. A frequently used approach is to impanel task forces to develop briefings for an upcoming work session (Wyckoff, 1988).

In carrying out their task, the task forces go through five major steps: (1) identifying the types of data to be gathered and the specific elements of the data, (2) determining the sources of data and how to tap them, (3) collecting the data, (4) determining how to convey the data (presentation and format), and (5) analyzing the significance of the data for the organization that is doing the scanning.

The Southeastern Minnesota Private Industry Council, the Lorain City School District, and the National Association of County Training and Employment Professionals, among others, specified that their environmental-scan task forces present their scans in the form of attractive, easy-to-understand visuals, using bulleted points, charts, and graphs. Although the board and staff members who participated in the work sessions at which the scans were reviewed received hard copies of the visuals, no weighty documents were prepared and disseminated. The task forces spent as much time deciding creative ways to convey the information (pie charts, line graphs, and bar charts) and assessing its significance as they did collecting it.

Identifying and Selecting Strategic Issues

What Are Strategic Issues?

Strategic issues may be thought of as major *change challenges*—opportunities and problems that appear to demand an organizational response, so a successful balance can be maintained between the organization's internal and external environments. Opportunities are principally avenues to organizational growth—through the delivery of new services or products, through tapping new sources of revenue, and through addressing new needs (these avenues of growth or levers are obviously intertwined and are never mutually exclusive). Problems are conditions, events, or trends that threaten to reduce an organization's resources, its programs, or its competitive position (including its reputation and political clout).

No scientific test can determine whether an issue is truly "strategic" or merely "operational." Certainly, in the course of an organization's annual operational planning and budget preparation process, many issues arise that relate to refining and adjusting operating programs, and they can involve major expenditures (such as instituting a new computer registration system in a recreational department). However, some issues always rise above others in terms of the stakes involved (both benefits and costs) and their complexity.

It is worth noting that because strategic issues often cut across organizational functions and departments, they require organization-wide attention; similarly because they sometimes transcend organizations, they require that different organizations cooperate in addressing them. Also, issues may relate to administrative or managerial concerns, as well as to the content of programs and services.

Some Examples

The Southeastern Minnesota Private Industry Council identified not only a number of needs in the community to which it might respond in expanding the scope of its program, including women reentering the work force, illiteracy in the workplace, and pregnant teenagers, but such critical managerial issues as the need for stronger board leadership and for a conscious, systematic strategy of public information and education. The strategic issues identified by the Oswego County Department of Employment and Training included three stakeholder relationships that deserved special attention: with the Department of Social Services (in relation to implementing welfare-reform legislation), with the state employment service (in relation to colocating programs), and with Operation Oswego County (in relation to integrating strategies for economic development and training).

Generating Strategic Issues

One effective way to generate strategic issues is through brainstorming work groups within the context of a one- or two-day work session at which an organization's vision and mission are clarified and its external and internal environmental scans are reviewed. The purpose of the work groups is to generate major change challenges that can then be discussed by all participants of the work session in a plenary session—not to rank order or select issues.

The Lorain City School District employed four brainstorming work groups to generate change challenges: the content and delivery of the educational program, pupil services, governance and administration, and community affairs and relations (Eadie, 1990d). The Western Michigan Regional Planning Commission in Grand Rapids used four: transportation, economic development, land-use planning, and a catch-all category—emerging opportunities (Eadie, 1988). The Alamo Area Council of Governments (San Antonio metropolitan area) utilized six: aging, health, and human services; economic development, employment, and training; physical development; public safety; services to local government; and emerging opportunities (Eadie, 1990a).

Selection of Issues

As a preface to the selection of strategic issues, keep in mind that any organization's resources in time, energy, dollars, political capital, and so forth are not only finite, they are usually stretched to the limit in the public and nonprofit human services sectors. Therefore, it is highly unlikely that many strategic issues can be effectively addressed at any one time. Selectivity is thus more than a virtue; it is a necessity.

There is no simple or scientific way that one can choose which issues to address in the near term through the formulation of strategies. Some believe that a highly effective approach is to analyze issues in these two ways:

▶ Evaluate the potential cost that the organization might bear if it does not move forward now in addressing a particular issue, considering both direct costs (dollars, lost credibility, human pain and suffering, and so on) and lost benefits (lost revenue from a grant not obtained).

▶ Assess the organization's ability to have a positive impact on an issue within the resource constraints. A school district may, for example, think more than twice about taking the lead in addressing the drug dependence of students because of the complexity of the issue and the substantial costs involved in addressing it comprehensively.

The ultimate decision on which issues to tackle in the near term will depend, then, on a rough cost-benefit analysis. The objective is a set of issues that promises the most potential benefit (and avoided costs) for the price in time, dollars, and political capital.

Formulation and Implementation of Strategies

Formulation of Strategies

Once the strategic issues to be addressed have been selected, task forces often are appointed to fashion action strategies to address them. A staff steering committee, comprising senior managers, may be used to review the work of the strategy-formulation task forces, and the board will, of course, ultimately review and approve the task force's recommendations. The steps involved in formulating strategies are these:

▶ Get a firm grasp on an issue by breaking it down into its various subissues. This step inevitably involves the task force doing a more detailed, second-stage scan of an issue than was possible when it identified and selected the issues.

▶ Determine which subissue to tackle.

▶ Brainstorm action initiatives to address each of the subissues and to select the initiatives that appear to yield the most benefit for the cost, within acceptable resource limits.

▶ Fashion detailed implementation plans that set forth a schedule of events, specify who is accountable for what action, and detail the costs involved.

Implementation of Strategies

Implementation involves three key issues: (1) the organization's commitment, (2) the allocation of resources, and (3) the implementation structure and process. Commitment means that the policy body, the chief executive officer, and senior managers, at least, are committed to the results anticipated from implementing proposed strategies, to the roles that must be played to implement these strategies, and to the costs that must be incurred. The wider the ownership that is felt for an organization's strategy, the more likely the strategy is to be fully implemented. This fact argues for widespread participation in strategy-formulation task forces as a vehicle for building ownership; another vehicle is effective internal communication.

Financial resources can be explicitly allocated to implement strategies through the annual operational planning and budget preparation process by ensuring that the work of the task forces feeds into the budgetary decision-making process in a timely fashion. Another approach is to allocate dollars from a contingency fund established to finance innovation and change.

Finally, a structure and managerial process will be required to ensure the full and timely implementation of the strategy. This process may include a steering committee of senior administrators that meets once a month, a technical coordinating committee that provides detailed guidance, implementation task forces that provide hands-on management of the implementation process, a high-level staff person to coordinate the whole effort, and a system for regularly reporting progress and resolving problems.

The Design Applications

Experience with failed planning processes has at best made many managers of public and nonprofit human services organizations skeptical of planning initiatives; at worst, it has bred cynicism. Processes have collapsed midstream because organizations have lacked either the capability or the commitment required to implement them. Other organizations have faithfully gone through all the steps in their planning processes, only to find that the results were not worth the effort (witness the many shelves groaning under the weight of never-consulted tomes on planning that are covered with dust).

The purpose of design is to ensure that an organization achieves precisely what it wants through its planning process, at a cost that it can afford. Through design, the outcomes or products to be generated are identified, the process and structure required to produce the outcomes are developed, and the resources required to implement the process are specified. Armed with a sound design, an organization can move forward with confidence to implement the techniques of strategic issue management, knowing that it has the capability to implement a process that will produce the outcomes it wants.

Developing the Design

The design process is a prelude to applying strategic issue management that is typically initiated by the chief executive officer and preferably involves both board members and senior staff. In one or more intensive work sessions, process outcomes are identified and the process and structure of strategic issue management are worked out. The resources (time, consulting fees, and so on) that are required to implement the process should also be spelled out. The design should be described in a document that is formally reviewed and accepted by the board, the chief executive, and senior managers.

A Word on Outcomes

There are two primary categories of outcomes in the strategic management process: those that relate directly to the kinds of strategies that will be generated and those that are process-related "spin-offs." For example, an organization that is facing a fiscal crisis may determine in the design process that it will deal during the first cycle of strategic issue management with only one issue—the enhancement of revenue—and that the primary outcome of the first-year planning effort will be a detailed action strategy to deal with that overriding issue. Another organization may determine that during its first cycle, its whole focus will be on the generation—in a concentrated work session of the board and executive staff—of a vision for the organization and a set of broad strategic directions. A third organization may decide to engage in the full-blown process, from environmental scanning through the identification of issues to the selection of issues to the formulation of strategies for action.

The foregoing are direct, content-related outcomes. In addition, organizations can identify some less direct—but not necessarily less important—outcomes. For example, building a team of executives may be an important outcome of the process, as may strengthening the leadership role of the board. Another outcome may be to increase the staff's morale or to strengthen the public's understanding of the organization's mission and goals. All these outcomes—direct and indirect—will drive the development of the process and structure of strategic issue management.

Also driving this development are what may be called "rules of the game." For example, an organization may specify in its design that any strategies that its task forces recommend during the first cycle must be achievable within current resource limits or specify precisely how the additional required resources will be obtained. An organization may specify in its design that a highly controversial matter should not be raised during the process (for example, the distribution of syringes to drug addicts as a tactic to prevent AIDS). The point is to ensure through these rules that the strategic ship does not hit an iceberg that could have been avoided through forethought.

A Word on Process and Structure

Designing the process and structure to achieve the identified outcomes basically involves determining what should be done, when it should be done, and by whom it should be done. This determination will, of course, be driven by the identified outcomes, the rules of the game, and the organization's capability. It is important that the reader not underestimate the potential for any process to collapse midstream if it is not carefully designed. The strategic management effort, no matter how modest or elaborate, will not be an established organizational routine during the first one or two cycles; it will always be threatened by the press of day-to-day events and loyalties to established organizational units (in contrast to ad hoc task forces). Like a crustacean, if it is not protected by a hard shell of formal process and structure, the effort can quickly ooze away.

Examples of structure are a board task force to formulate a statement of vision; a staff task force on environmental scanning; a two-day work session of the board and staff to review and confirm the statement of vision, discuss the environmental scan, and identify strategic issues; and the use of task forces to formulate strategies.

The Organization's Capability

Whether an organization is able to carry out a design successfully depends on its capability. Although organizational capability is a nebulous concept, practical experience suggests that the following factors should be explicitly considered.

First is the commitment of the board and chief executive officer to the process, in terms both of the outcomes to be generated and the costs that will be incurred in going through it. The board's and chief executive's participation in developing the design and reviewing and approving it will help ensure this commitment. The commitment of the organization's senior managers will also be critical to the success of the design.

Second, people make or break strategic management processes, so understanding the human-resource dimension is critical to developing a sound design. Obviously, skills and experience deserve consideration. A staff that has never participated in strategic planning and management activities will be less capable than one that has. Also important is the organization's internal climate. Skepticism of planning based on negative experiences or a general malaise related to working conditions will definitely lessen the staff's capability to engage in strategic management activities.

Third, time and attention are also important aspects of organizational capability. An organization that is severely understaffed will be hard-pressed to devote time to strategic management. Similarly, one that is grappling with one or more crises, such as a looming budget deficit, an audit uncovering irregularities, or a political battle with the county commissioners, will be less able to devote attention to strategic issue management.

Finally, money is always an important aspect of capability. Doing strategic issue management costs money—for work-session space, the production of materials, and external technical assistance.

Following the inexorable rule that the strategic management process and the organization's capability must match, an organization can always reduce its expectations of outcomes and the demands of the process or spread a process out over a longer period. But keep in mind that systematically strengthening capability may be part of the strategic management design. For example, funding from foundations may supplement the organization's budget. Orientation and training sessions may enhance skills while reducing skepticism. And participation in shaping the design may counter low morale.

Boards and Budgets
Board Leadership

Without question, the boards, commissions, councils, and other policy bodies of many human services organizations are highly frustrated these days at what they rightly consider to be their vaguely defined, often obviously unimportant roles (Carver, 1990). It is common to see the "illusion of control" that comes from two equally unimportant and unproductive kinds of board work: paying inordinate attention to the review of trivial details, such as detailed reports of payments to vendors, and thumbing through finished documents, such as a completed, bound budget, and asking random questions.

The process of strategic issue management provides ample opportunity for a board to be fully engaged in carrying out important leadership responsibilities: in defining outcomes of the process and confirming the design, in formulating statements of vision and mission, in reviewing the environmental scans and identifying strategic issues, in selecting the issues to be addressed, and in reviewing the strategic actions that are recommended to address the selected issues.

A particularly effective device is to stage an intensive one- or two-day work session or series of sessions for the board and staff, at which much of the foregoing work is done. The Bexar County Local Development Corporation, for example, held two intensive strategic work sessions, two months apart. At the first meeting, a one-day session, a statement of vision and set of organizational values were formulated in brainstorming groups, a broad scan of the environment was done, competitive strengths and weaknesses were examined, and objectives for the board's leadership were developed. At the second meeting, a two-day session, the statements of vision and values were refined and confirmed; a detailed environmental scan, developed by a consulting firm, was reviewed; strategic issues were identified; and possible actions were brainstormed.

Such board-staff work sessions are likely to be successful if the outcomes and agenda are agreed to in advance, a comfortable off-site location is used, preparation is meticulous, and adequate time is allowed. Professional facilitation can also help, particularly when highly complex and possibly emotional or controversial issues are being addressed.

The Budget Connection

An explicit connection is needed between any strategic issue management effort and that "Mississippi River" of planning, the annual operational planning and budget preparation process. Two obvious connections are these:

▶ Scheduling the formulation of statements of vision and mission, the environmental scan, and identification of issues so they can be factored into the budgets of operating units (the strategic input will help guide preparations of the budget at the operating-unit level, where trends, conditions, and issues are, indeed, pertinent in shaping budgets)

▶ Ensuring that the recommendations of strategy-formulation task forces include detailed cost estimates and that the cost estimates are considered part of the decision-making process on the budget.

Summary

This chapter has traced the rapid development of strategic management in the public and nonprofit human services sectors, from the original notion of heavily documented comprehensive planning to the more action-oriented process of strategic issue management. Strategic management enables an organization to respond effectively to challenges in its environment, both significant opportunities and major constraints or problems. The key elements of the process are the clarification of values and vision, external and internal scanning, the identification and selection of issues, and the formulation and implementation of strategies.

The chapter examined the design process, through which an organization ensures that it achieves what it wants from the application of strategic management at a cost that it can afford. The design spells out the outcomes or products that the strategic-management application will generate and details the structure and process required to achieve the outcomes. As part of the design process, an organization explicitly determines that it has the capability to implement the process or will build the requisite capability.

SKILLS-APPLICATION EXERCISES

- If the organization you work in has a vision and a mission, describe them. If not, create a statement of vision and mission for your organization.
- What is your personal vision, in terms of career aspirations and personal life-style? Scan your environment—externally and internally—and identify any strategic issues you are facing in light of your vision. Formulate broad strategies to address those issues.
- Make a list of stakeholders of the immediate organizational unit in which you work and of the organization in which your unit fits. Analyze each stakeholder's characteristics and the relationships—actual and potential—that your unit and organization may have or build with each stakeholder.
- You also have stakeholders with whom you must deal in your career and personally. Name a few of the most important and analyze their characteristics and the nature of your relationships with each. Fashion stakeholder-management strategies to ensure that the working relationships are effective.
- Scan the external and internal environments of the organization you work in to (1) identify major trends and conditions and (2) assess the organization's resources and strengths and weaknesses.
- On the basis of this scan, identify some strategic issues that your organization may need to address and evaluate the potential costs (direct or in lost benefits) of *not* addressing each issue.
- Select one or two of what appear to be the most critical issues and brainstorm possible initiatives to address them. Identify for each initiative the anticipated impact on the issue and the costs (time, money, political capital) that may be anticipated in implementing it.
- Your organization is considering undergoing a process of strategic issue management. Assess your organization's capability to undertake such an ambitious project, paying special attention to the barriers that may be faced.

References

Bryson, J. M. (1989). *Strategic planning for public and nonprofit organizations*. San Francisco: Jossey-Bass.

Bryson, J. M., & Roering, W. D. (1987). Applying private-sector strategic planning in the public sector. *Journal of the American Planning Association, 53*, 9–22.

Carver, J. (1990). *Boards that make a difference*. San Francisco: Jossey-Bass.

Conley, G. N., & Eadie, D. C. (1990). Strengthening board strategic leadership. *Economic Development Commentary, 13*, 4–11.

Eadie, D. C. (1986). *Strategic issue management: Improving the council-manager relationship*. Washington, DC: International City Management Association.

Eadie, D. C. (1987a, November 6). *Report to the National Association of County Training and Employment Professionals: Report on the NACTEP Board Strategic Work Session—October 22–23 in Orlando*. Shaker Heights, OH: Strategic Development Consulting.

Eadie, D. C. (1987b). Strategic issue management: Building an organization's strategic capability. *Economic Development Commentary, 11*, 18–21.

Eadie, D. C. (1988, February 6). *Report to the Western Michigan Regional Planning Commission: Report on the Commission's January 21–22 Strategic Work Session*. Shaker Heights, OH: Strategic Development Consulting.

Eadie, D. C. (1989). Building the capacity for strategic management. In J. L. Perry (Ed.), *Handbook of public administration* (pp. 162–175). San Francisco: Jossey-Bass.

Eadie, D. C. (1990a, August 3). *Report to the Alamo Area Council of Governments: Work Session Report*. Shaker Heights, OH: Strategic Development Consulting.

Eadie, D. C. (1990b, June 18). *Report to the Bexar County Local Development Corporation: Report on the June 2 Strategic Work Session*. Shaker Heights, OH: Strategic Development Consulting.

Eadie, D. C. (1990c, July 31). *Report to the Bexar County Local Development Corporation: Work Session Report*. Shaker Heights, OH: Strategic Development Consulting.

Eadie, D. C. (1990d, August 17). *Report to the Lorain City School District: Report on the August 10–11 Strategic Work Session*. Shaker Heights, OH: Strategic Development Consulting.

Eadie, D. C. (1990e, June 15). *Report to the Southeastern Minnesota Private Industry Council: Work Session Report*. Shaker Heights, OH: Strategic Development Consulting.

Eadie, D. C., Rose, S. D., & Bellow, N. J. (1988, July 11). One job training program's plan for the future. *County News*.

Eadie, D. C., & Steinbacher, R. (1985). Strategic agenda management: A marriage of organizational development and strategic planning. *Public Administration Review, 45*, 424–430.

Gluck, F. W. (1985). A fresh look at strategic management. *Journal of Business Strategy, 6*, 4–21.

Nutt, P. C., & Backoff, R. W. (1987). A strategic management process for public and third-sector organizations. *Journal of the American Planning Association, 53*, 44–57.

Olsen, J. B., & Eadie, D. C. (1982). *The game plan: Governance with foresight*. Washington, DC: Council of State Planning and Policy Agencies.

Robinson, R. V., & Eadie, D. C. (1986). *Building the senior management team through team issue management*. Washington, DC: International City Management Association.

Tichy, N. M. (1983). *Managing strategic change*. New York: John Wiley & Sons.

Wyckoff, M. A. (1988). Strategic management planning in Region 8: A case study. *Planning & Zoning News, 6*, 14–18.

Motivating Employees to Achieve

Myron E. Weiner

In general, the supervisory and managerial task of motivating employees of human services organizations to achieve is simple. It becomes a complex, often difficult, challenge when one takes into consideration the uniqueness of each employee and the wide variety of organizational settings in which they work. This chapter deals with this challenge. It first identifies the skills necessary for motivating employees and then provides an opportunity to further analyze the skills and to practice using them. Although the motivation of employees is a familiar subject, this chapter provides a specific framework for the task, which is common to all human services organizations.

Human behavior is bedded in motives—the needs, desires, aspirations, drives, and impulses of an individual that are directed toward achieving some conscious or subconscious goal. Motivation, therefore, is something internal to a human being. In organizational settings, supervisors or managers cannot affect a worker's internal state; they can only create an environmental condition so that an employee can expect that his or her motives will be satisfied through the achievement of the organization's work.

As Kolb, Rubin, and McIntyre (1984, p. 67) noted,

> The prime task for managing motivation, therefore, is channeling and directing human energy toward the activities, tasks, and objectives that further the organization's mission. . . . Managers cannot motivate a worker to achieve, for example, but they can create expectations in the work place that achievement will be rewarded.

What, then, are the skills required for creating expectations in the organizational environment that will motivate people to achieve? At present, most experts tend to agree on three sets of fundamental skills for this task:
- ▶ *Understanding* the nature and process of motivation
- ▶ *Individualizing* one's approach to the task of motivating employees
- ▶ *Blending and linking* the performance of individuals and the organization

Understanding Motivation

The first skill required for motivating people to achieve is *understanding*. The management must understand what motivates human beings; the relationship among human beings, organizations, and individuals or groups; and individual and organizational achievement.

Theories of Motivation

There are two categories of theories of motivation: content theories and process theories. The former focus on what motivates people, the latter on how people are motivated.

Content theories identify the basic needs of human beings. They all share a common premise: an unsatisfied need becomes the driving force for behavior directed toward satisfying that need. For several years, the dominant content theories of motivation were taken from the works of Maslow (1943); Herzberg, Mausner, and Snyderman (1959); McClelland (1976); and Alderfer (1972). Figure 1 illustrates these popular content theories and indicates the types of needs that motivate people.

Maslow's hierarchy of needs is the oldest and most familiar content theory of motivation. It proposes that although people's physiological and safety needs are linked to work situations, the potential of work environments to satisfy the needs for belonging, self-esteem, and self-actualization is the strongest source for motivating workers to achieve. Herzberg's theory has also been popular for several decades. It divides needs into two categories: *hygiene* factors (pay, working conditions, policies, supervision, and interpersonal relations) related to the needs for physical safety and belonging and *motivator* factors (responsibility, advancement, recognition, and achievement) related to the needs for self-actualization and self-esteem.

McClelland's and Alderfer's content theories are simpler; both propose that people have essentially three needs that are the foundation of their motivation. For McClelland, the three needs are the need for achievement (the desire to perform with excellence or to excel), the need for power (the desire to influence and control others), and the need for affiliation (the desire for close interpersonal relationships). For Alderfer, the three needs are the need for existence (the need to satisfy hunger, thirst, and shelter), the need for relatedness (friendship and affection from others), and the need for growth (the desire for creativity, status, and advancement).

Process theories define motivation as a process of choices that people exercise in given situations. The four most popular process theories of motivation include expectancy theory, operant theory, equity theory, and goal-setting theory.

In *expectancy theory,* the particular behavior an individual chooses depends on what he or she believes will result in some desired reward. This process involves three steps: (1) expectancy, the individual's estimate of the probability that a given level of effort

Figure 1. Content Theories of Motivation

Maslow's Hierarchy of Needs	Herzberg's Two-Factor Model	McClelland's Motive Model	Alderfer's ERG Theory
Self-actualization needs (opportunity, growth)	Motivators: achievement, recognition	Need for achievement	Growth desires
Self-esteem needs (recognition, status)	Work itself Responsibility Advancement	Need for power	
Belonging needs (friendship, affection)		Need for affiliation	Relatedness desires
Safety needs (security, safety)	Hygiene: company policies Supervision Pay Interpersonal relations Working conditions		
Physiological needs (hunger, thirst, sex)			Existence desires

SOURCE: W. A. Randolph and R. S. Blackburn, *Managing Organizational Behavior.* Copyright © 1989 by Richard D. Irwin, Inc. Reprinted by permission of Richard D. Irwin, Inc.

will result in a desired level of performance; (2) instrumentality, the person's estimate of the probability that the level of performance will be rewarded as anticipated; and (3) valence, the value placed by the individual on each of the possible rewards. With *operant (reinforcement) theory,* desired behavior is rewarded and undesirable behavior is punished. In *equity theory,* an employee is motivated by comparing his or her efforts and production with some internal standard of performance or with the performance of others. According to *goal-setting theory,* employees and organizations both set goals that influence individual and organizational behavior. The degree to which these two sets of goals are congruent determines the level of effort by employees to achieve organizational goals.

As was just noted, people are self-motivated. All a manager can do is to create organizational conditions by which motivational energy can be released to achieve goals and outcomes that benefit both the individual and the organization. To structure environmental and organizational conditions, a supervisor or manager needs to have a good understanding of *motivators* (content theories) and *motivational processes* (process theories). The two sets of theories work hand in hand. For example, all the content theories of motivation indicate that recognition is a strong motivator. The several process theories of motivation provide optional approaches to structuring organizational environments differently so that the need for recognition can be tailored to the specific employee and the particular situation.

Employees, Organizations, and Performance

In addition to understanding what motivates employees in human services agencies, supervisors or managers must understand the relationship between the performance of employees and the performance of the organization. What links individuals (employees) to organizations? The answer is simple: the *job*. The job is the vehicle by which an individual makes a living, seeks a career, and becomes part of the job market in a country's economy. The job is also the means by which an organization can get its tasks and functions completed and its mission achieved. Therefore, in every economy there is an implicit formal or informal "inducements/contributions" contract that links workers, organizations, and performance, as shown in Figure 2.

Figure 2. Inducements/Contributions Contract

THE INDIVIDUAL	THE ORGANIZATION
1. The job links the individual to a career and status/role in a social system and thus helps meet personal needs and aspirations.	1. The job provides qualified human resources (energy and skills) necessary for the achievement of organizational missions.
2. Limits are placed by the organization on the individual's behavior.	2. Receives a limited array of the individual's total possible behaviors.
3. Quid pro quo: Defines tasks the individual is expected to do and rewards to be received.	3. Quid pro quo: Defines tasks the individual is expected to do and the rewards to be received.
4. Provides opportunities, constraints, and "sphere of action" for career building.	4. Exchanges inducements for efforts today, opportunity for career development.

The inducements/contributions contract flows from the fact that the job is the linchpin between the individual and the organization. The job is the foundation for the process by which individuals are motivated to invest their energy and efforts to achieve individually and collectively.

Because the job is so critical to motivating people to achieve, it is natural that a great deal of attention has been focused on designing the organizational work environment. In recent years, one of the more popular models for work design has been the job characteristics model of the motivation to work (see Figure 3).

Understanding this model sufficiently to shape the work environment is a critical skill for linking the performance of individual employees to the organization's

Figure 3. Job Characteristics Model

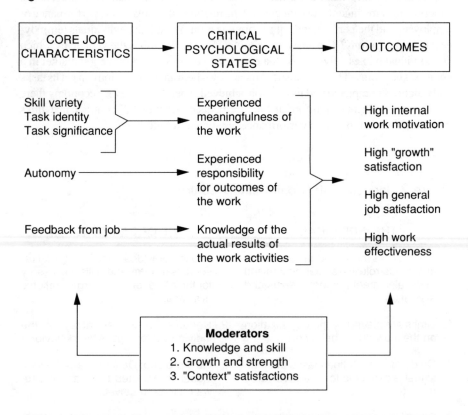

Source: J. R. Hackman and G. R. Oldham, *Work Redesign*. Copyright © 1980 by Addison-Wesley. Reprinted by permission of Addison-Wesley Publishing Co., Inc., Reading, MA.

performance. Although most of the terminology in this model is self-explanatory, the following three terms deserve special attention: (1) *skill variety:* the extent to which a job involves different types of tasks that require a variety of skills; (2) *task identity:* the extent to which the job requires the performance of a task from beginning to end; and (3) *task significance:* the importance of the job in relation to the total work effort of the organization. Whereas an employee was once expected to adapt to a specific job, current thinking suggests that both the employee and the job should mutually adapt or be adapted.

Performance and Outcome Measures

The performance of employees—individually and collectively—can be quantified. The most common measures of performance are work units, unit costs, or some relationship between the two. Performance can also be measured according to qualitative-effectiveness criteria. Though more difficult to quantify, the impact and outcomes of services on clients can be measured to identify the quality of the services that are delivered.

Are there other outcomes that represent individual achievement? On the positive side, achievement can be measured in terms of job satisfaction and commitment. *Job satisfaction* is a positive orientation or feeling toward the job. An employee can be satisfied with his or her pay, opportunities for promotion and career advancement, bosses (supervisors), coworkers, the work itself, and working conditions. *Commitment* is the strong belief and attachment to an organization and its goals and values. It is generally measured by the desire to remain part of the organization and a willingness to expend great effort for the organization, its mission, and its functions.

Some negative outcomes also relate to performance and achievement, for the individual and for the organization. In addition to low productivity that can be quantified, negative outcomes can be measured in terms of tardiness, turnover, lack of creativity, stagnant personal and professional growth, absenteeism, stress, and resignation or dismissal.

Individual achievement, performance, and outcomes need continuous measurement. If they are negative, they have an obvious impact on an organization and on workers, individually and collectively. But even when they are positive, it takes effort by supervisors and managers to sustain and augment the productivity and effectiveness of services, for the individual as well as for the organization.

Individualizing One's Approach

Henry Rogers was the head of one of the largest public relations firms in the United States. In writing his strategy for creative management (Rogers, 1986), he noted the following:

> You cannot motivate people through mass appeal. You cannot motivate people by
> staff meetings. You cannot motivate people by sending out memos "to our staff." It
> doesn't work . . . you have to do it one to one. It takes a lot of time and a lot of effort,
> but it pays off. You must understand that everyone is not motivated in the same way.
> Each of your employees is probably motivated by something different. (p. 55)

The message is clear: To be effective in motivating people to achieve in human services organizations, you will need an individualized approach.

There are no magic techniques for getting to know someone. It takes an investment of time and energy and calls on all the interpersonal communications skills that you have. To improve this process, many organizations help their managers, supervisors, and workers gain better insight into themselves and appreciate differences among the employees with whom they work by using such instruments as LIFO (Atkins & Katcher, 1976), the Myers-Briggs Type Indicator (Briggs-Myers, 1980), and the Keirsey Temperament Sorter (Keirsey & Bates, 1984). All these instruments are directed toward helping people get to know themselves and their coworkers better, to individualize coworkers, and to appreciate their individual differences.

Employees know, however, when managers have a genuine interest in their well-being and professional and personal growth. They know if they are being treated uniquely, as a human being, or if they are being dealt with as a number, a thing, or only a cog in the machine.

At the very least, it is necessary to meet frequently with all employees and to keep good records on them. A single piece of paper or a file folder that summarizes each employee's career growth and plan, professionally and in the organization, is a powerful technique for helping motivate employees to achieve their maximum.

This skill is as simple as taking a few minutes to send each employee a birthday card or, better still, to celebrate the birthday during a coffee break. Commonsense skills for an individualized approach to employees are far better than is any high-level management technology.

Blending and Linking the Individual's and Organization's Performance

The final skill required to motivate human services employees to achieve is that of blending and linking the personal-professional goals of employees with the organization's goals (see Figure 4). In brief, these skills include communicating clearly organizational performance goals to employees, continuously ascertaining each employee's personal and professional goals, and blending and linking these two sets of goals.

Although it is true that organizational environments are primarily created and structured by others, a supervisor or manager still has the primary role of shaping

Figure 4. Blending: The Critical People-Management Skill

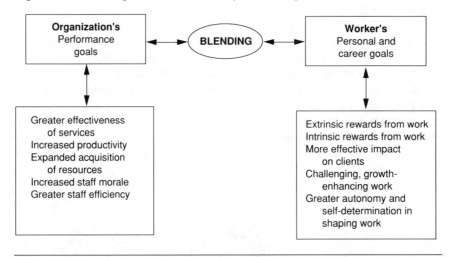

SOURCE: M. E. Weiner, *Human Services Management: Analysis and Applications,* 2nd ed. Copyright © 1990 by Wadsworth, Inc. Reprinted with permission.

the environment for groups of employees. As Weiner (1988, p. 158) noted, this can be done with the following set of blending and linking skills:

Goal clarification: clarifying the goals for each employee, as well as for the organization, primarily in terms of outcomes for clients and secondarily in terms of the growth and development of employees and of the organization

Goal blending: blending organizational goals with workers' personal goals and aspirations

Performance linkage: linking the worker's expectations with organization's achievement of goals

Performance feedback: continuously letting workers know how their performance as individuals and in groups contributes to the achievement of outcomes and goals

Job design: blending the content of work (tasks, functions, and relationships) with intrinsic-extrinsic job rewards and job qualifications (skills, knowledge, and abilities)

Job-role linkage: shaping challenging and growth-enhancing roles for workers that generate self-responsibility and self-managing work groups (Peters, 1987) toward achieving more effectively linked client-organizational outcomes

Job training and career development: providing opportunities for employees' careers to grow through orientation, professional development, and training

Work participation: involving workers in processes that will mutually enhance their job satisfaction and outcomes for clients.

Understanding and using these skills, individually and in combination, are critical for motivating employees to achieve.

Blending and linking skills need to be integrated. For example, even in human services organizations, in which the ability to reward employees is limited, the following suggested mechanisms for rewarding achievements illustrate the way in which a number of blending skills can be interrelated to link the goals of workers and the organization: time off, over and above the normal vacation; more of what they like to do, less of what they do not like to do; interesting assignments and challenging tasks; a favorable interpretation of the rules; exceptions from annoying regulations; more freedom—more authority and more autonomy; praise and recognition (an announcement in the presence of their peers that a job was particularly

"Terry is our so-called motivation expert."

well done); awards and other symbols of accomplishment; access to top managers or outsiders; prizes, even if inexpensive and fun; educational opportunities; the chance to have lunch with someone special.

Summary

The primary resource of any social work organization is its employees. If employees are properly motivated, the energy and effort that they will invest in the achievement of the agency's tasks, goals, and mission is bounded only by the limits of time, physical energy, and skills. The key to motivating employees is to create the conditions that open the floodgates of physical, emotional, and intellectual effort that can be harnessed and directed toward the achievement of organizational goals.

This chapter has concentrated on three sets of skills that are necessary to unlock those floodgates of motivational energy that employees represent, individually and collectively: (1) understanding the nature and process of motivation, (2) individualizing one's approach to the task of motivating employees, and (3) blending and linking the individual's and organization's performance. For supervisors and managers of human services organizations, mastering these skills is a critical and rewarding challenge.

SKILLS-APPLICATION EXERCISES

This chapter identifies the three sets of skills required to help motivate people to achieve in organizational settings. To better recognize and identify these skills, it may be helpful to examine and analyze a number of cases and vignettes that illustrate them.

Exercise 1

Trapped

The first exercise deals with *what* motivates people to achieve. As you read the following vignette, try to identify the different needs of employees in the workplace. Also, try to classify these needs in terms of the theories of Maslow, Herzberg, McClelland, and Alderfer.

Jack Thomas feels trapped—trapped by the 23 years he has invested in the state government's pension system. Initially as a supervisor and now as district office manager for the department of human services, he feels

continued

underpaid, overworked, overstressed, and unappreciated. Even though he is a key executive in a billion-dollar operation that is essential to the U.S. economy, he is always the subject of disparaging remarks by his friends and family members who work for the corporate world. He is, after all, nothing more than "a state employee." He knows that his friends and relatives believe he could not compete in the business world, and through the mediocrity of the government civil service, his longevity has promoted him to his level of incompetence. Although Jack is thankful that a dedicated cadre of talented supervisors have devoted their careers to the department, he also recognizes the high turnover rate in the office, particularly among the best and brightest social workers who move on to nonprofit agencies or start their own private practices.

The fact that as a devoted member of the social work profession he is committed to the less privileged in our country cannot even be discussed in today's greed-oriented society, where "bottom-line" values permeate everyone's personal and community lives. Not only does Jack feel that his career has stagnated, he knows that the workers in the district office feel the same way. The social and economic problems of the disadvantaged and minorities in the state are increasing, despite all the efforts of Jack and his colleagues. Morale is so low that managers, supervisors, and workers do not even pull together as a team. They are separated by different programs in the department and by different civil service classifications: workers against supervisors, supervisors against managers, social workers against eligibility technicians and child support enforcement clerks, clerical union members against managers, and so on. There are no incentives beyond annual performance evaluations that result in the awarding of increments and that are generally pro forma.

Workers take the maximum number of days of sick leave each year. In his 23 years, Jack has heard every excuse imaginable for being late to work. Tension and stress in the office have always been high, and many employees have filed for worker's compensation because of it. A few of his best friends have turned to substance abuse. Even though Jack's life is consumed with completing productivity reports, he receives little, if any, feedback from the upper management, for himself or for his workers, that would indicate that their hard work is being recognized. When he first became a supervisor, Jack dealt with all his coworkers as individuals, treating each of them uniquely. As he rose in the management ranks, pressures of the work gave him little time; he felt too overwhelmed. In time, he became like all the others in top management, detaching himself from his subordinates and keeping them at arm's length. The majority of communications with staff are through memos, even though Jack knows this is the worst way to try to deal with each coworker uniquely.

As he looks around the overcrowded, unattractive office, all Jack can see is gray—gray office furnishings, gray workers, gray clients, and gray

continued

prospects for improvement. He walks over to his wall calendar and, as he has been doing daily this past year, crosses off today's date. Only 1 year, 11 months, and 14 days left before he is eligible for retirement.

Does this vignette sound familiar? The organizational environment of human services agencies is challenging, to say the least. Although the vignette was written purposely in extreme terms to illustrate the different *content* theories of motivation, understanding the level of satisfaction of needs is the first skill required to help motivate people to achieve more, both for themselves and for the organization.

Reread the vignette and complete the Checklist of Content Theories of Motivation for Jack, referring to the content theories of motivation found in Figure 1.

Checklist of Content Theories of Motivation

	Probable Level of Needs Satisfaction		
Theories	Low	Moderate	High
Maslow's Hierarchy			
Physiological needs	[ ]	[ ]	[ ]
Safety needs	[ ]	[ ]	[ ]
Belonging needs	[ ]	[ ]	[ ]
Self-esteem needs	[ ]	[ ]	[ ]
Self-actualization needs	[ ]	[ ]	[ ]
Herzberg's Model			
Hygiene (maintenance)	[ ]	[ ]	[ ]
Policies	[ ]	[ ]	[ ]
Supervision	[ ]	[ ]	[ ]
Pay	[ ]	[ ]	[ ]
Interpersonal	[ ]	[ ]	[ ]
Working conditions	[ ]	[ ]	[ ]
Motivators			
Achievement	[ ]	[ ]	[ ]
Recognition	[ ]	[ ]	[ ]
Work itself	[ ]	[ ]	[ ]
Responsibility	[ ]	[ ]	[ ]
Advancement	[ ]	[ ]	[ ]

continued

Checklist of Content Theories of Motivation (continued)

Theories	Probable Level of Needs Satisfaction		
	Low	Moderate	High
McClelland's Model			
Affiliation	[ ]	[ ]	[ ]
Power	[ ]	[ ]	[ ]
Achievement	[ ]	[ ]	[ ]
Alderfer's Model			
Existence desires	[ ]	[ ]	[ ]
Relatedness desires	[ ]	[ ]	[ ]
Growth desires	[ ]	[ ]	[ ]

Your rating should probably indicate primarily a *low* level of satisfaction of needs for all the motivational needs of Jack (and most likely those of his colleagues). Perhaps a few needs could be rated "moderate"; they would be related to his retirement pension, which tends to provide security (safety). They may also be related to his feelings toward the work itself; despite his pessimism, he has devoted 23 years to being a social worker for the disadvantaged.

Exercise 2

Terry's Team

The following case vignette is more upbeat. Try to identify the four *process* theories of motivation: expectancy, operant conditioning, goal setting, and equity.

They had a great reputation in the department, and they were all proud of it. It had taken Terry many years to build her team and, even more important, much effort to keep the members glued together as a team. It did not just happen.

1. Long ago she adopted Michael LeBoeuf's principles of management: reward people for right behavior and you get the right results; fail to reward the right behavior, and you are likely to get the wrong results. You do not manage people, you lead them. Once you set up a positive reward system for achieving the right goals, people quickly become their own best managers. And that means more time and freedom for you—a pretty good reward in itself (Rogers, 1986, p. 35).

2. Their collective reward was a week away. Terry had convinced a friend of hers to give her "team" the use of the family's beach cottage for the long Columbus Day weekend. The weather was holding up, and they would enjoy

continued

a few days of fun—eating and interacting, along with holding their annual informal goal-setting sessions. Together they would set the team's goals for the coming year. Then each member would indicate his or her contribution to the group's goal, along with his or her targets for professional growth in their separate individualized development plans (IDPs). Together with Terry, the team had initiated the IDP program two years ago.

3. In preparation for the Columbus Day retreat, Terry had finalized the latest monthly productivity report for the team showing the 12-month results for each member of the team and for the total group. The data made monthly and year-to-date comparisons with targets that the team had set at last year's retreat, both for the group and for each member separately. Despite drops in productivity in other units of the department and the tightening financial situation, Terry knew the team would feel good that each of them and the team as a whole had exceeded not only the performance milestone targets, but the past years' productivity records.

4. Terry was pleased. As she was getting ready to leave for the day, Joe Baker (one of her veteran team members) popped his head into her office and said, "I worked it out, Terry. As you requested this noon, I can stay late tonight and finish the client impact survey report. If all goes well, the draft will be on your desk when you come to work tomorrow morning." Terry responded, "Great, Joe. I don't have to tell you how important it is for all of us to get that report to the Central Office on time." Terry knew that Joe wanted to receive the top team bonus this year and possibly a promotion. For sure, he wanted a superior annual performance review. The chances for the bonus were 75 percent, a good review was practically assured, and even the promotion had a 50 percent chance.

Each paragraph in this vignette illustrates one of the process theories of motivation. Identify them by placing the number of the paragraph next to the following theories.

___ Expectancy theory
___ Operant conditioning (reinforcement theory)
___ Equity theory
___ Goal-setting theory

The answers are 4, 1, 3, and 2. Now, consider how you would rate Terry in terms of utilizing the blending and linking skills to motivate employees to achieve.

Rating Terry's Blending-Linking Skills

Skills	Poor	Good	Excellent
Goal clarification	[ ]	[ ]	[ ]
Goal blending	[ ]	[ ]	[ ]
Performance linkage	[ ]	[ ]	[ ]

continued

Rating Terry's Blending-Linking Skills (continued)

Skills	Poor	Good	Excellent
Performance feedback	[ ]	[ ]	[ ]
Job training/career development	[ ]	[ ]	[ ]
Worker participation	[ ]	[ ]	[ ]

From the minimal evidence in this vignette, one would have to rate Terry good or excellent on each of these blending and linking skills required for motivating employees to achieve.

References

Alderfer, C. P. (1972). *Existence, relatedness and growth.* New York: Free Press.

Atkins, S., & Katcher, A. (1976). *LIFO: Life orientations.* Beverly Hills, CA: Human Resources Technology Co.

Briggs-Myers, I. (1980). *Introduction to type.* Palo Alto, CA: Consulting Psychologists Press.

Hackman, J. R., & Oldham, G. R. (1980). *Work redesign.* Reading, MA: Addison-Wesley.

Herzberg, F., Mausner, B., & Snyderman, B. (1959). *The motivation to work.* New York: John Wiley & Sons.

Keirsey, D., & Bates, M. (1984). *Please understand me: Character and temperament types.* Del Mar, CA: Prometheus Nemesis.

Kolb, D. A., Rubin, I., & McIntyre, J. (1984). *Organizational psychology: An experiential approach to organizational behavior* (4th ed.). Englewood Cliffs, NJ: Prentice Hall.

Maslow, A. (1943). A theory of human motivation. *Psychological Review, 80,* 370–396.

McClelland, D. C. (1976). Power is the great motivator. *Harvard Business Review, 54,* 100–110.

Peters, T. (1987). *Thriving on chaos: Handbook for a management revolution.* New York: Harper & Row.

Randolph, W., & Blackburn, R. (1989). *Managing organizational behavior.* Homewood, IL: Richard D. Irwin.

Rogers, H. (1986). *The one-hat solution: Roger's strategy for creative middle management.* New York: St. Martin's Press.

Weiner, M. (1988). Managing people for enhanced performance. In R. Patti et al. (Eds.), *Managing for service effectiveness in social welfare organizations* (pp. 147–160). New York: Haworth Press.

Managing Time in the Organizational Setting

Laurie Newman DiPadova and Sue R. Faerman

From time to time, you probably feel that you cannot do all the things you want to accomplish. Everybody is making demands. Each task seems more important than the others. You have endless things pressing on you, but you do not know where to start. What do you do next? Which is more important? Why can't you begin and get these things out of the way? How can you handle everything? Every new task simply adds to your already stress-filled situation.

If you ever feel this way, you are not alone. Research indicates that managers identify time-management problems as their greatest source of stress (Mintzberg, 1973; Whetten & Cameron, 1984). The challenges of managing time, however, are not unique to managers. Many individuals in all walks of life experience the feeling of not having enough time. Moreover, because people see managing time as a life-management skill, the frustration of not having enough time sometimes translates into guilt or anxiety. People often interpret their difficulties in handling the hours of the day as an indication that they are unable to manage other areas of their lives.

It is not surprising that there are abundant sources of sound advice for managing time. Courses for improving time practices abound for virtually everyone—employees, college students, homemakers, children, and volunteers. Informative books on the subject can be found in virtually any bookstore (see, for example, Knaus, 1979; Lakein, 1973; Mackenzie, 1972; Winston, 1983).

Given the universally acknowledged problem of time management and the extensive resources suggesting remedies, it is ironic that many individuals still experience considerable stress because of too little time. The question is: Why do so many people still feel stressed and discouraged regarding their use of time? One reason stems from the fact that since everyone has the same 24 hours to manage, there may be a tendency to compare oneself unfavorably with other people who appear well organized and accomplished. In doing so, individuals neglect to give themselves credit for what they are doing well. The unfortunate inclination to focus on shortcomings without acknowledging strengths simply fosters discouragement, which may, in turn, inhibit the energy needed to make changes.

Second, feverishly managing one's time—suddenly embarking on strict schedules, carefully monitoring each conversation, and accounting for minutes wasted—
may increase stress dramatically. Paradoxically, the result is often a reduction of
productive time.

Finally, time-management problems may sometimes be a manifestation of
unresolved deeper concerns in a person's life. Individuals may budget their time, as
they would their money, but never understand why their time-management problems are so persistent. Rather than approaching time as a resource to be budgeted
and accounted for, this chapter focuses on managing *oneself* in relation to time
(Mackenzie, 1972). *Self-management* includes managing schedules, calendars, and
everything from paper to attitudes to relationships.

The purpose of this chapter is to help you decide how to improve your use of time.
It is not the intention to posit the perfect time-management formula; rather, a variety
of techniques are suggested.

The following assumptions underlie this chapter. First, time management is a
personal responsibility. People make decisions in life for which they must bear the
direct consequences. Other people cannot be blamed for one's frustration. Hence,
each person must examine his or her own situation and explore the actions that can
be taken to change it.

Second, improving time-management skills means increasing the ability to
accomplish more in less time by working smarter, not harder. Planning does not
waste time; it focuses efforts. The time spent planning ultimately yields greater
productivity.

Third, time management is a learned skill. People are not born good time
managers. Their current practices are a result of learning. Sometimes these behaviors result from faulty beliefs and attitudes. When individuals correct misconceptions, they are better able to unlearn what they no longer need and learn new
techniques.

Fourth, time management for managers differs from time management for
nonmanagers. Although everyone can benefit from basic time-management methods, the supervisory role of managers suggests unique opportunities, challenges,
and techniques in this regard. For example, managers can delegate to their
employees; they are also expected to assist employees with their time-management
efforts.

Finally, time management is individualized. Individuals cannot look at what
others do as an accurate gauge of their personal progress. Everyone approaches his
or her work and personal responsibilities in a different manner. As a result, this
chapter offers some suggestions to consider, not rules by which to abide.

The remainder of this chapter discusses both the organizational context of time
management for managers and individual behavior in organizations. In addition, it
presents time-management techniques that have proved helpful to managers.

The Organizational Context of Time-Management Issues

Managers and their employees operate in formal organizations. Within these organizations, many structures and processes affect how individuals manage their time. Some enhance how people use their time, whereas others create time-management problems.

Several organizational structures and processes create paradoxes for managers. For example, many forces in organizations operate to control and standardize people, yet the organizations—as well as the people—often need individuals to contribute their unique skills, perspectives, and creativity. Trying to balance these two forces can lead managers to communicate with mixed messages and conflicting expectations. A second example arises when managers need to accomplish their tasks, yet be available to respond to interruptions from others. Handling interruptions, while sometimes seen as a time waster, is actually part of the manager's job. A final example occurs when managers are promoted from the professional ranks without appropriate opportunities for managerial education and development. Generally, when social workers are promoted to managerial levels, it is because of their ability to excel in social work. When the social worker-turned-manager still wants to be a social worker, conflict will likely arise as the manager continues to spend time engaged in social work.

In addition to the paradoxes created by organizational structures and processes, individuals bring into the organization false beliefs or myths about how to manage their time. The combination of myths and paradoxes can create additional problems for managers. Myths are particularly important to recognize, not only for the manager's own time-management efforts, but to enhance attempts to assist employees. The following are five myths of time management. You can probably think of others. As you examine this list, consider the extent to which you subscribe to each myth.

Myth 1: Being busy means being productive. The truth is, the active person may be disorganized, inefficient, and ineffective. This myth is especially harmful because it encourages us to look at activity, rather than at the quality of work being produced.

Myth 2: Only upper management can make the most important decisions. In reality, decisions should be made at the lowest possible level in the organization because persons lower in the hierarchy are more familiar with the circumstances. This myth often causes time to be wasted because decisions at the lower levels generally require less time than do decisions at the upper levels.

Myth 3: The best decisions are the delayed decisions. Although it may be wise to defer decisions until information is available, it is not possible to have all the information or to know with certainty each consequence of various courses of action. This myth is destructive because many managers use it to procrastinate.

Myth 4: The quicker things are done, the better. Hastening a decision without the critical facts or initiating an action prematurely without taking the time to elicit input from key people can spell disaster. This myth is often used by people who "do not have the time to plan."

Myth 5: It takes too much time to delegate. Although the skills of effective delegation may require time to learn and apply, delegation saves time and empowers employees. This myth is deceptive because the refusal to delegate locks managers into the mentality of always having too much to do.

As is readily apparent, accepting these myths hinders the pursuit of positive courses of thinking and action. In camouflaging the truth, myths make it more difficult to take corrective action. The first step in time management is to recognize and reject these myths as a basis for action.

Furthermore, managers and employees need to recognize that they control the bulk of their time. The extent of control is related to the level of initiative taken (Oncken, 1984). For example, if your style is low initiative, so that you wait to be directed in each step of a given assignment, your boss will need to require frequent reporting to check your progress. In this situation, your time is being controlled by your boss. Conversely, if you take the initiative and act on your own, you will maintain more control over your time. Also, as a manager, you can train and encourage your staff to control their time by providing opportunities for them to act independently, rather than requiring that they take continual direction from you. Again, doing so frees you to control your time. Having examined the organizational context, the chapter now turns to the topic of procrastination and how it affects individuals as they work.

Procrastination

Are you among the many who consider themselves to be procrastinators? Do you find yourself putting off necessary tasks and consequently elevating your levels of guilt, frustration, and stress? Do you engage in this behavior on a regular basis? If so, this section may help you understand why you procrastinate. Even if you do not procrastinate, you may find this section useful in dealing with others who do.

From time to time, everyone puts things off. Sometimes it is helpful to postpone things; other times it is self-defeating. The key is being able to determine when delaying things is beneficial and when it is indicative of a harmful habit. It may be functional at times to put off a task until more information is available or to defer making assignments on a project until your employees draw their current activities to a conclusion. Delaying things may be as functional as not turning the car off the road before one reaches the driveway.

Procrastination develops when tasks are habitually postponed until the last minute, causing considerable suffering and anxiety in the interim. As Knaus (1979) put it, many who procrastinate "place themselves on psychological trial daily."

It is important to note that procrastination is not the result of laziness, irresponsibility, or the lack of discipline. Such beliefs merely add to procrastinators' tendencies to denigrate themselves, feeding their self-defeating behaviors. Consequently, traditional admonitions to "just do it" are consistently ineffectual in dealing with procrastinating behaviors. Rather, it is important to understand the underlying reasons that lead you to procrastinate.

Psychological Functions of Procrastination

Even when procrastination appears to be harmful and a problem, it often meets a person's psychological needs. Individuals procrastinate to avoid inner conflicts and to protect self-esteem (Burka & Yuen, 1983). For example, procrastinating important tasks may reflect a basic fear of failing to perform perfectly. Individuals also tend to procrastinate when they wish to avoid a task they consider unpleasant or distasteful. Keep in mind that if some need was not being met by procrastinating, the behavior would not be so consistently used.

Understanding the needs that are met by procrastination is the first step in changing this behavior. If you procrastinate, ask yourself, What do you get out of it? Why do you put off things that should not be delayed?

Researchers have identified a number of beliefs and attitudes that are associated with procrastination. Although an exhaustive presentation of these views is beyond the scope of this chapter, the most common ones are included in the "Procrastinator's Code":

The Procrastinator's Code[1]

I must be perfect.
Everything I do should go easily and without effort.
It's safer to do nothing than to take a risk and fail.
I should have no limitations.
If it's not done right, it's not worth doing at all.
I must avoid being challenged.
If I succeed, someone will get hurt.
If I do well this time, I must always do well.
Following someone else's rules means I'm giving in and I'm not in control.
I can't afford to let go of anything or anyone.
If I expose my real self, people won't like me.
There is a right answer, and I'll wait until I find it.

Do any of these statements reflect your view of yourself? Can you identify ways in which you have received any of these messages in your life? Do any of the people with whom you work seem to operate under these premises? If so, recognize that these beliefs are self-defeating and that procrastination is a way of dealing with them.

---

[1]*From Jane B. Burka and Lenora M. Yuen,* Procrastination, *© 1983 by Jane B. Burka and Lenora M. Yuen. Reprinted with permission of Addison-Wesley Publishing Company.*

The fact that procrastination is a learned behavior is an important point. A learned behavior can be unlearned and replaced. Breaking the procrastination habit involves identifying those inner conflicts and relearning more positive and less self-defeating ways of dealing with them. The next section explores more specifically the dynamics of procrastination in an organization.

Procrastination in the Organizational Setting

Tendencies to procrastinate may accelerate in the organizational setting. It is ironic that although procrastinators often experience their lives as being out of control, individuals tend to use procrastination to assert a measure of control over their life. Organizations are controlling entities with rules, procedures, and a hierarchy of people telling you what to do. Putting off the completion of assigned tasks is one attempt to exert control over your destiny. Similarly, when individuals find it difficult to be open with their bosses about what they can do or feel comfortable doing, they may put off a task rather than say no. If you find that you procrastinate more at work than in other areas of your life, you may wish to explore your response to control.

Paradoxically, procrastination is a prescription for the loss of control, rather than for the gain of control. First, you lose freedom when the task is "hanging over your head," taking up energy and providing cause for worry. Waiting until the last minute also means that the deadline—not you—determines your schedule. Furthermore, if procrastination is carried to extreme and poor work performance results in disciplinary action, demotion, or dismissal, the freedom-giving benefits that organizations offer, such as income and the opportunity for worthwhile work, are denied.

Breaking the habit of procrastination is difficult because it meets psychological needs. Although it is hard to do, progress can be made. Consider the following steps:

1. Analyze your situation to see if you accept any beliefs listed in the Procrastinator's Code. If so, understand that these beliefs are false and that correcting them is a first step in changing your procrastinating behaviors.
2. Take a sheet of paper and write out each statement from the Procrastinator's Code that you tend to accept.
3. Examine each faulty belief. For example, if you wrote "I must be perfect," examine that statement critically. Ask yourself questions such as these: Why must I be perfect? Was I taught that I had to be perfect to be loved? What is the worst thing that can happen if I am not perfect?
4. Contradict the belief. Do it in writing. For example, write why perfection is an unreasonable expectation for any human being to hold. Write why self-improvement is reasonable.
5. Instead of trying to achieve perfection (or any other faulty belief), direct your energies toward accepting yourself as a person of worth.
6. Refuse to see yourself as lazy or undisciplined and insist on viewing procrastination as a signal to investigate your assumptions about yourself.

Many find that exploring these assumptions is the beginning of a meaningful self-improvement journey.

7. Pursue the subject by exploring published works by therapists and researchers who offer meaningful suggestions. These works will assist you in rethinking these potent misconceptions.

Not all procrastination can be assumed to be a function of subconscious psychological dynamics. Many times those who procrastinate simply have not learned some basic time-management techniques. The following section reviews a variety of proved techniques.

Time-Management Techniques

Like most of us, you have probably decided that your management of time may need some adjustment and fine-tuning. This section offers several time-management techniques to assist you in deciding what changes to make in your life. Before you go further, however, you need to understand how *not* to approach these techniques. Do not assume that these techniques are what perfect time managers do. Probably, efforts to implement all these suggestions will not be appropriate for you. It is unlikely that all of them are applicable to your situation now, although you may find other suggestions more helpful later in your career. In addition, this section is not intended to exhaust the possibilities of techniques that may be useful to you.

The following collection of proved techniques is divided into two groups: (1) organizing yourself and (2) helping others to be organized. As you review this section, you may think of additional techniques that you need to implement. You are also encouraged to use the references at the end of this chapter to pursue these topics further. The important thing is to assess your situation, decide what to do next, and begin to do it.

Organize Yourself
Organizing the Day

Keep a calendar. Combine all your appointments on one calendar: office appointments, social engagements, volunteer obligations, personal and medical appointments, trips, and so on. Keeping a separate calendar for work is less practical and often results in your making several appointments for the same time. Although your life takes place in multiple settings, it is only one life and it needs one comprehensive calendar. Keep this calendar with you at all times and refer to it. Writing down appointments not only diminishes the chances of forgotten obligations, it frees your mind of details. Rather than remember the dozen different appointments you have, all you have to do is remember two things: check your calendar and keep it current.

Write everything down. In a notebook or a part of your calendar, keep a master list of things to do as they occur to you. *Jot down everything*: work-related assignments, letters to write, appointments to schedule, arrangements to make, items to pick up at a store, and so forth. Do not worry about organizing at this point. Just focus on having one place to write down everything. The value of putting things in writing cannot be overstated; you are not plagued mentally keeping track of things that you are afraid of forgetting.

Do not fall into the trap of thinking you do not have enough time to plan. Imagine taking an extended travel vacation without bothering to plan it. You would return frustrated because the weeks had gone by and you had not seen everything that you had expected to see. Imagine the same trip with planned airline flights, hotel accommodations, and lists of sights to visit. In which situation would you get the most out of your time?

Planning is simpler than it may appear when you use the master list as the raw material of your planning. Take a few minutes every day to review your master list and decide when you need to do what. Write any appropriate items on your calendar. Mark off things you did the day before.

Keep a daily to-do list. From the master list, compile a list of things to be done that day. Decide which items you can delegate to someone else. It is all right for the master list to be messy and marked up; it is for your use only. Remember that it is simply a tool for putting on paper everything you have in your mind that you have to do.

Set priorities among the items on your to-do list. Do not expect to accomplish everything on your list. Distinguish the importance of the items using the ABC method: A items are the most important, B items are moderately important, and C items are the least important. Although the C items may be the easiest to do, resolve to tackle the A items first. If you focus on getting the Cs out of the way first, then most of your life may be spent on lower-priority items, rather than on what you regard as important (Lakein, 1973).

Schedule appropriate things to do on your calendar. Transfer items from your to-do list onto your calendar. You do not have to place everything on your calendar, but some things need to be scheduled. For instance, if you need to make an airline reservation by a certain date in order to qualify for a discounted fare, schedule that in. The financial savings may be substantial.

Analyze your master list. If you find that some items on your list just are not getting done, ask yourself: Why am I putting this off? Do I really have to do it? Do I resent having to do it? Did I overextend myself and try to do too much? If I do not act on this at all, what will happen? What are my options? Make your master list a learning tool, as well as a planning tool.

Make your calendar and master list an integral part of your day. Like using your toothbrush every morning, eventually you will not need to make a conscious decision to use your calendar and master list.

Organizing at Work

Reduce the information overload. Have on hand two file folders labeled "Action" and "To File," respectively. Divide all incoming papers into two groups: those that take more than five minutes to read, and those that take less time. Sort the papers using the TRAF system (Winston, 1983), as follows:

1. Most of the paper and mail you receive takes fewer than five minutes to read. Resolve to handle these pieces of paper only once.

T = *Toss* ads, seminar notices, for-your-information weekly reports, and other disposable papers. Freely use the "quick toss" method of paper management.

R = *Refer* papers to other people (colleagues, staff, and others) for action, review, or response.

A = *Act* on papers that require your personal attention. Place them in the Action folder for completion.

F = *File* papers. Write on the document the name of the file into which it should go and a discard date. Place it in the To File folder for filing later.

2. Place papers that take five minutes or more to read in the Action folder.

3. Schedule time for acting on the papers that are in the Action folder.

Set up a tickler file system. Winston (1983) also recommended the following system: Number file folders from 1 to 31, indicating the day of the month. Also, take 13 folders and label ones for each month of the year plus one for "Next Month." Simply put the papers that need action this month into the numbered file according to the date on which you have to respond. Place papers for next month in the Next Month file. Use the rest of the months' files in like manner. On the first day of the following month, file the contents of the Next Month file into the current month's numbered file and place the contents of the following month into the Next Month file. You can use these files as reminders of action you have to take, as well as for knowing where to find some of the current papers you need.

Handle telephone calls efficiently. Treat telephone calls as meetings. Plan for the calls ahead of time. When possible, have a prearranged written agenda in hand. At the same time, when you hold a scheduled meeting with someone in your office, treat unexpected telephone calls as interruptions. Respect the time of the person in your office by telling the caller that you will call back.

Design your work space. Have your work area laid out in such a way as to minimize unnecessary movement. Keep supplies and materials that you use frequently in a designated place on or near your desk. When you need uninterrupted time, keep your door shut. Have the file folders and a wastebasket in easy reach for TRAFing your papers.

Schedule interruptions. Restrict your "open-door" policy to certain periods unless something critical happens. Restrict telephone conversations. Answer and make telephone calls during certain periods only. If possible, have messages taken that you can answer later.

Answer mail quickly. When possible, write responses on letters or memos, photocopy them for your files, and return the originals.

Delegate papers and assignments when possible and appropriate. Delegation is not only an important managerial competence (Quinn, Faerman, Thompson, & McGrath, 1990), it is also a proved time-management technique. Delegation saves time and indicates respect for the person one delegates to. Consider the nature of the task and the needs and abilities of the individual before you delegate. Be certain to communicate your expectations clearly and offer to assist the person in the delegated task, if necessary.

Do not accept upward delegation from employees. Be aware of who owns the problem. If you are not careful, you can find yourself working for employees by taking on assignments they give. This situation can be remedied in part by insisting that when they bring you a problem, they offer a solution.

Tackle your Overwhelming A. The focus of this group of strategies is coping with tasks you find overwhelming and difficult. Usually, these tasks are important (labeled "A" on your to-do list), large, complex, of long duration, and appear to be difficult. Many times they are tasks that have not been tackled previously. Lakein (1973) termed these tasks "Overwhelming As." The following suggestions draw on Lakein's work:

1. Identify your Overwhelming A. That is, choose a task that you have difficulty with because of its size, complexity, expected duration, or all three.

2. Assess the appropriateness of the Overwhelming A. Be sure that you should embark on this task. If you have designated it as something you should do, but you find yourself continually resisting it, perhaps it is not right for you. It may be *too* overwhelming. Ask yourself: Is it realistic? After decades away from school, deciding to work for an advanced degree when you have just taken on a new job may be impractical. Listen to your intuition. Once you decide on an Overwhelming A, proceed with the following steps, keeping in mind that if you find you are being unrealistic, you can always reassess your choice.

3. Divide and conquer. Take a few minutes to write out the components of the task. Break the task down to the smallest possible parts.

4. Use the Swiss cheese method. Take 5 to 10 minutes to work on the first part of the task. This part may be as simple as making a telephone call to request needed information. Use 5- to 10-minute breaks to punch holes in your Overwhelming A. Notice the sense of personal energy you receive after using the first 5 to 10 minutes.

5. Refuse to underestimate the usefulness of small (5- to 10-minute) spans of time. Recognize that a lot can be accomplished in these periods. You can use them to work on your Overwhelming A.

6. Create block time. Schedule 30 minutes or more as protected block time to work on your high-priority items. Know your most productive times of the day and create block time during those periods. Consider this time as important as a scheduled meeting.

A final Lakein principle: When you have 5 to 10 minutes, ask yourself: "What is the *best* use of my time right now?"

Helping Others to Be Organized

As a manager, you are responsible for helping staff members organize their time. First, you are instrumental in organizing their time for them, as in scheduling meetings, setting expectations, and giving assignments. In addition, the staff members may look to you for indications of how they should manage their time. The following are suggestions especially for managers in the organizational setting.

Manage your meetings carefully. Meetings take up a large percentage of a manager's work. Managers report that almost 60 percent of their time is spent in scheduled meetings and 10 percent is spent in unscheduled meetings (Mintzberg, 1973). The management of meetings, then, is a crucial aspect of managing your time

"Pencil me in at 7:00 p.m. for fifteen minutes of coloring and story-telling."

and your employees' time. Proved meeting-management techniques include the following (Quinn, Faerman, Thompson, & McGrath, 1990):

1. Set a time limit for your scheduled meetings. Setting a time limit creates the expectation of having to finish the business at hand within designated time limits.

2. Hold meetings only when needed. Feel free to cancel meetings once in a while. Doing so may improve the quality of the meetings that are held.

3. Prepare an agenda for the meeting. Using clear objectives of the meeting and inviting only those who need to attend, prepare an accurate agenda for the meeting. Distribute the agenda beforehand and follow it during the meeting. An agenda helps participants to be prepared; it also clarifies what needs to be accomplished during that time. Consulting with participants beforehand, in developing the agenda, further enhances their participation.

4. Start meetings on time. Starting meetings on time not only models an expectation that schedules will be kept, but shows respect for the time of the individuals who made the effort to arrive at the appointed time.

5. Prepare minutes promptly and follow up on the issues of the meeting. Distribute the minutes in a timely manner and check on any assignments that have been made. Doing so trains people to understand that most of the work takes place outside meetings, not in meetings.

6. Hold routine meetings at the end of the day. Energy and creativity are usually low toward the end of the work day, and quitting time will help enforce the meeting's timely finish.

7. Stand up during short unscheduled meetings. Standing helps ensure the brevity of the meeting. Be aware that sitting down may signal a longer meeting than is necessary.

Model sound time-management practices for your staff. Make no secret of your calendar, your master list, or your to-do list. Find ways to let the staff know that your time—and their time—is important.

Communicate carefully. Practice reflective listening skills. Make sure that your messages are clear to your staff. Remember that clear communication is your responsibility.

Assist employees to establish priorities for their work. This type of help is actually a way of clarifying your expectations of the staff. If you have given an employee three assignments, be sure to indicate which aspects of those assignments have priority.

Allow your employees to say no to you. Good time managers are aware if they have too much to do. Recognize that "saying no to the boss" is awkward at times. As a manager, encourage your employees to evaluate their time critically and to let you know if they feel overloaded. Such encouragement will promote discussion and save you time and difficulty later.

Take advantage of opportunities for staff development and training. Enhance your time-management skills and those of your staff. Good training is a sound investment in performance and productivity.

Summary

This chapter has explored the organizational setting of time-management challenges for managers, as well as some of the dynamics of procrastination. It considered suggestions for improving your use of time, several of which bear repeating. First, you constantly make decisions as to the best way to use your time. Important techniques to consider now may not be significant later. Be aware that time management is a dynamic process. It requires reassessment as situations change. Such changes are not cause for discouragement. Be realistic and recognize that the demands of changing situations require you (and your plans) to be flexible.

Second, remember that implementing new techniques is not easy. It may be more difficult at first, but eventually the techniques you choose will become a matter of habit. Finally, be assured that you are probably a better time manager than you give yourself credit for. Be generous with yourself—give yourself credit for your time-management strengths. In so doing, you empower yourself to make the changes you desire.

Analysis Exercise: The Case of Frank Franklin

Monday morning Frank Franklin,[2] a unit manager at Lincoln County Department of Social Services, reported to the office promptly at 8:30 A.M. After washing out his cup, Frank poured some coffee and walked over to Bonnie Winston's desk. As one of his new employees, Bonnie had attended a training course the previous week, and Frank wanted to know how the course had gone. He also needed to catch Bonnie up on a few issues that had arisen while she had been out and to give her information she had asked him to obtain for a report that she is writing for him.

Leaving Bonnie, Frank stopped by the washroom before heading back to his desk. There he found a memo detailing new policies concerning the personal use of county vehicles by employees while on county business. Basically, the policy stated that employees were not allowed to use the vehicles to pick up or drop off relatives or friends while en route to or from official business. Frank was surprised by the news and went to ask Ralph Larowe, another unit manager, if he had read the memo. Although Ralph was a good colleague, who would always help you out if you were in a tough spot, he did have a reputation for talking; once he started, it was hard to get him to stop. Around 9:30, Frank finally indicated that he had some important work and would have to return to his desk. In fact, Frank needed to get started on the new budget. The branch chief had said that she wanted the first draft by the end of the week.

---

[2]*Adapted from Training Materials for* Getting Work Done Through Others: The Supervisor's Main Job *(Albany, NY: Advanced Human Resources Development Program, New York State Governor's Office of Employee Relations & the Civil Service Employees Association, Inc., 1987). Adapted with permission of the New York State Governor's Office of Employee Relations.*

When Frank got back to his office, Bonnie was waiting to talk to him. Some pages were missing from the information he had obtained for her. She wanted him to track them down.

At 10:00 the branch chief telephoned and asked Frank to find a report detailing program expenditures over the last three years. The branch chief also expressed her concerns over the new vehicle policy and discussed (at length) the absurdity of the policy, given its low potential for saving money or improving image and its likely negative impact on the employees' morale. Clint Thompson, the administrative assistant, would usually be the one to locate the report, but he was upstairs attending a meeting of the Employee Assistance Program's peer counselors. Frank decided to locate the report himself. But trying to understand Clint's filing system confused him, and after 20 minutes he decided to wait until Clint returned to the office. It was now almost 11:00, and there was not enough time to begin working on the budget before Frank's 11:30 lunch meeting. Frank cleaned up his desk instead, preparing himself for an efficient afternoon.

Returning to work at 1:00 P.M., Frank quickly glanced over the departmental newsletter and noticed that the Monthly Activities Reporting Form (LC-1013) had arrived. He decided to start filling it out. He had considered working on the new budget, but decided to give himself an hour to work on the monthly report, assuming that he would have from 2:00 to 4:30 to work on the budget. It was 1:30 before Frank remembered to ask Clint to find the report that the branch chief had requested.

About 15 minutes later, Clint returned with two reports. One report listed program expenditures over the past two years, and the other listed program expenditures over the past five years. There was no three-year report, and Clint said that he was pretty sure that there never had been one. Frank asked him to look one more time.

At 2:00 Clint returned and this time insisted that there was no three-year report. Frank called the branch chief to ask which report she wanted, but her secretary said that the branch chief was upstairs at a meeting and it was not clear when she would return. Frank left a message and told Clint to return to his other work.

Frank went back to his desk, returned two telephone calls, and decided to work a little longer on the monthly report. It was only the 20th of the month, but Frank had not gotten as far as he had expected in the hour he had promised himself.

When he next looked at his watch, he noticed that it was almost 3:00. Now there surely was not enough time to work on the budget before the end of the day. A project like the budget is best accomplished when a large block of time is available. Frank knew that by the time he had gathered up all the materials he needed to work on the budget, it would be just about time to put them away. Frank decided that he would see what other tasks he had on his "to-do" list and plan to work on the budget the next day.

Discussion Questions

1. What are some of the problems Frank Franklin has in managing his time? Which myths of time management has he accepted? What other difficulties does Frank have in getting his work done? If his productivity today is typical, what will happen to his levels of stress and frustration in the coming months?

2. What behaviors would Frank need to change to improve his use of time? What techniques would he find particularly useful to implement?

3. What specific time-management issues does Frank have in dealing with his employees? His peers? His boss? What can he do to gain more control of his time?

4. How often have you found yourself in Frank's situation? What has your analysis of Frank told you about yourself?

Analysis Exercise: When Do You Procrastinate?

Listed next are 12 commonplace behaviors and feelings.[3] Review this list and, in each case, identify examples in your own life that *reflect* or *refute* this type of behavior or thinking. After reviewing the items, respond to the questions that follow.

Example

Problem	Evidence
1. I delay until the eleventh hour before beginning important projects.	Reports often started near the deadline; pay taxes late; usually make travel arrangements just before the deadline.

Please complete the inventory with a view toward presenting a fair picture of yourself.

Problem	Evidence
1. I delay until the eleventh hour before beginning important projects.	
2. I remain angry for long periods, contemplating how I will take revenge on an adversary.	
3. I feel overwhelmed.	
4. I fail to return phone calls.	
5. I show up late for appointments.	

continued

---

[3]*Adapted from William J. Knaus,* Do It Now *(Englewood Cliffs, NJ: Prentice Hall, 1979), pp. 10–13. Adapted with permission of the publisher, Prentice Hall Press/A Division of Simon & Schuster, Inc., New York, NY 10023.*

Problem	Evidence

6. I collect materials to use on a project and then delay doing the project.
7. I avoid situations in which I believe I won't be successful.
8. I delay sending out correspondence.
9. I feel as though there is just one crisis after another in my life.
10. I tell myself that tomorrow I'll begin.
11. I feel that I lack drive or energy.
12. I often agree to do things I don't really want to do because I have a hard time saying no.

Discussion Questions

1. What are the ways in which you procrastinate most frequently? Do you see patterns in your procrastinating?

2. When you find yourself procrastinating, what excuses do you give yourself (and others) for this behavior? How can you become more aware of when you are procrastinating, as opposed to having a legitimate reason for delaying doing something?

3. In what areas do you not have a problem with procrastination? What can you learn about yourself from these areas that can help you with areas in which procrastination is a problem?

SKILLS-APPLICATION EXERCISES

The following are two skills-application exercises. The first exercise gives you the opportunity to look at some of your general problems in time management; the second helps you to plan to improve your time-management skills on a specific project on which you are currently (or will soon be) working.

Exercise 1: How Well Am I Using My Time?

In responding to the following questions, you should identify some of your own time-management problems and find ways to improve your use of time.

Discussion Questions

1. Think about how you managed your time last week. Remember, be generous with yourself and give yourself credit for positive accomplishments.

continued

Identify specific problems that you had in accomplishing a task or tasks. The rest of this exercise will focus on the problems.

2. What are some of the problems you have in managing your time? Which myths of time management have you accepted? What other difficulties did you have getting your work done?

3. What time-management techniques could improve your use of time? What steps do you need to take to adopt them?

4. What specific time-management problems do you have in dealing with your employees? Your peers? Your boss? What can you do to change the situation?

5. Choose one or two specific situations in which you find yourself procrastinating. Identify several ways in which you can change your behavior in these situations. Now identify what you can do the next time you find yourself in the situation. For each situation, try to think about what might happen to prevent you from changing your behavior. What can you do now to decrease the chances of that happening?

Exercise 2: Overcoming Your Overwhelming A

Identify a project on which you are currently (or will soon be) working that you find overwhelming or difficult to think about. Respond to the following questions and statements in terms of this project.

1. Begin by thinking about the ways that this project seems overwhelming to you. How have you reacted to these feelings? How have these feelings affected your ability to make progress on this project? How can you use Lakein's (1973) approach to help you finish this project?

2. Is this project appropriate for you? Do you have the correct skills to carry out this project? Is this the correct time for you to be embarking on this project? Are there other reasons why this may not be the right project for you? If you decide it is inappropriate, decide what steps you need to take to discontinue working on the project. If you decide it is appropriate, continue responding to the questions and statements that follow.

3. What are the components or tasks of this project? Try to break the project into the smallest tasks possible.

4. Think about how long it will take to complete the various tasks. Divide your list among tasks that will take only 5 to 10 minutes to complete, tasks that may take up to one hour to complete, and tasks that will take more than one hour.

5. Identify several tasks that will take only 5 to 10 minutes to complete and schedule time to complete a few of them.

6. Identify which tasks need a block of time to complete and schedule time to complete the first one or two of them. In scheduling blocks of time, remember to consider what time of day you work best.

7. Identify what you need to do to remind yourself to return to the list of 5- to 10-minute tasks, when this time is available.

8. Finally, schedule some time, one or two weeks from now, when you can review your progress. Be proud of what you have accomplished. Review what still needs to be done and plan for the next period.

References

Burka, J. B., & Yuen, L. M. (1983). *Procrastination: Why you do it, what you can do about it*. Reading, MA: Addison-Wesley.

Knaus, W. J. (1979). *Do it now*. Englewood Cliffs, NJ: Prentice Hall.

Lakein, A. (1973). *How to get control of your time and your life*. New York: New American Library.

Mackenzie, R. A. (1972). *The time trap: How to get more done in less time*. New York: McGraw-Hill.

McCay, J. T. (1959). *The management of time*. Englewood Cliffs, NJ: Prentice Hall.

Mintzberg, H. (1973). *The nature of managerial work*. Englewood Cliffs, NJ: Prentice Hall.

Oncken, W. (1984). *Managing management time*. Englewood Cliffs, NJ: Prentice Hall.

Quinn, R. E., Faerman, S. R., Thompson, M. P., & McGrath, M. R. (1990). *Becoming a master manager: A competency framework*. New York: John Wiley & Sons.

Whetten, D. A., & Cameron, K. S. (1984). *Developing management skills*. Glenview, IL: Scott, Foresman.

Winston, S. (1983). *The organized executive: New ways to manage time, paper, and people*. New York: W. W. Norton.

21

Designing and Implementing Performance Contracting

Kenneth R. Wedel

Purchase-of-service contracting (POSC) for the delivery of government-sponsored services is firmly established in the human services. The reasons for contracting out services vary as widely as the expectations for services. Nevertheless, it may be generalized that policymakers and human services managers share an underlying hope that clients of contracted services will receive appropriate and high-quality services. This chapter is concerned with the knowledge and skills that managers of both public- and private-sector human services organizations need to maximize performance contracting and the controversies involved in the practice.

Performance contracting is one of a number of arrangements used by governmental sponsors who interact with nongovernmental sectors to obtain goods and services, deliver statutory care or services, demonstrate innovative approaches in implementing policies, evaluate programs, and sponsor basic research. Figure 1 shows the various arrangements that governmental sponsors commonly use for these purposes.

It is probably safe to say that in all governmental funding arrangements to nongovernmental entities, a desired level of "performance" is implicitly expected. Even the gift relationship identified in Figure 1 usually includes at least a call to "carry on the good work." Nevertheless, the ways and means of making explicit the desired standards of performance vary greatly among the funding arrangements. The examples in Figure 1 are seen as a continuum of the attention given to performance, from the least (gifts or subsidies) to the most (POSC–incentive contracting).

An *incentive contract,* by definition, is intended to motivate the contractor (Riemer, 1968). Although the incentive is often economic, this chapter explores the possibilities for other types of incentives in performance contracting for human services. Consistent with the literature on governmental contracting, the terms *incentive contracting* and *performance contracting* will be used interchangeably.

The author is indebted to Georgia Berry for the case example presented in this chapter.

Figure 1. Governmental Funding Arrangements

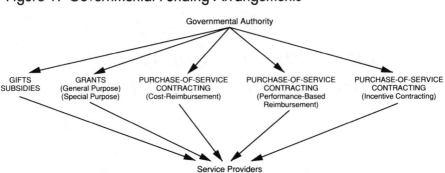

Governmental grants that are general purpose tend to have broad guidelines for performance. An audit trail typically documents whether funds were channeled to meet appropriate objectives, such as serving eligible clients. More specific guidelines for performance usually accompany special-purpose grants, such as a grant to support the planning of the Ninth National Conference on Child Abuse and Neglect.

Of particular interest are the variations in POSC. When the cost-reimbursement modality is used, POSC may differ little from grant arrangements. Contracted services are reimbursed on the basis of the costs incurred, such as when a contract calls for case management services to an unspecified number of clients at an agreed-on cost for the contract period. Performance-based POSC involves the specification of service units at an agreed-on cost, with reimbursement by the government at an agreed-on rate. One example is when there is an agreed-on cost for each hot meal actually delivered to a specified group of clients.

Finally, in performance contracting, levels of performance are predetermined and an incentive is offered for achieving the highest levels of performance specified in the contract. Performance contracting results, for instance, when a contractor is offered a financial incentive in the form of added reimbursements for each successful placement of a client in an alternative care situation within a standard time.

Any of the funding arrangements identified in Figure 1 may be accompanied by different expectations of interorganizational relationships with government-sponsored and nongovernmental entities that receive funds. Instead of engaging in an extended discussion of these relationships, this article examines what is likely to be expected when POSC, especially a performance-contracting arrangement, is deemed appropriate and utilized.

Typology of POSC Contracts

Three general modalities of POSC approaches can be identified from the broad categories of governmental funding arrangements in Figure 1. The approaches are classified according to how services are reimbursed. The modalities are *cost-oriented contracting*, which emphasizes the effort and resources that are expended in the delivery of services; *performance-based contracting*, which concentrates on outputs, usually in units of service and cost per unit of service; and *incentive (performance) contracting*, which focuses on outcomes in terms of qualitative or quantitative factors. Within each general modality, there are a number of more specific types of contracts. Table 1 presents the various types of contracts, along with their identifying features.

Criteria for Applying POSC

The government's decisions about contracting out services may be influenced by many sources. Sometimes the decision-making process is influenced by potential service providers' advocacy efforts or other political influences (Malka, 1990; Massachusetts Taxpayers Foundation, 1980). Nevertheless, models and guidelines exist to help policymakers determine how POSC is to be applied. One set of guidelines, developed by Kettner and Martin (1986), lists six empirically derived categories (with subcategories) for decision making in POSC: (1) productivity, fiscal, and cost considerations; (2) planning, designing, and funding considerations; (3) improvement of services to clients; (4) governmental organization and policy considerations; (5) legal requirements; and (6) politics and loyalties.

Once a governmental sponsor decides to contract out a service, further considerations are necessary to determine the type of contract that should be issued. Suggested guidelines at this level are more tentative because many factors may be involved. As a general rule, however, the information in Table 1 under each type of contract offers a conceptual starting point for explaining the intended purpose and determining when each type of contract is applicable.

Cost-oriented and performance-based contracts are commonly used in the human services. The trend, however, is toward a greater reliance on performance-based contracts. For example, reports of contracts for services for the aging have emphasized the purported benefits of reimbursing contractors on the basis of units of service at specified unit prices (Hasler, 1985; U.S. Department of Health and Human Services, 1982).

Performance contracting has seen limited application in the human services, at least if judged by the dearth of literature on the subject (Wedel & Colston, 1988). In some other governmental arenas, notably defense and aerospace, it has been used extensively. It is in the literature of these latter fields that a substantial amount of research and theoretical issues have been presented (DeMong, 1978; DeMong & Strayer, 1981; Fisher, 1969; Fox, 1974; Hunt, 1971, 1984; Nolan, 1980; Pace, 1970; Scherer, 1964). Although there are some obvious differences between the "typical" contractor for national defense or aerospace projects and for the provision of human services, the conceptual underpinnings and practical applications can be identified for the use of performance contracts.

Table 1. Typology of Contracts

Cost-Oriented or Performance-Based Contracts	Performance/Incentive Contracts
1. Firm Fixed Price Fixed-price, lump sum, or unit cost is specified. Price remains firm for life of contract. Contractor assumes complete responsibility for profits (excess program resources) or losses. Applicable when contractor is able to assume risks that may occur. Applicable when sponsor's resources are firm and fixed. Applicable when costs can be estimated with reasonable accuracy. One of the easiest and least costly contracts to administer. **2. Fixed Price Redeterminable** Fixed-price contract with special clauses for increasing or decreasing the price. Applicable when cost factors are subject to variation during the term of the contract. Applicable when the sponsoring agency has flexibility in funding arrangements.	**3. Cost Sharing** Contractor receives a predetermined portion of the total costs for delivering the service. Applicable when both the sponsor and the contractor are willing to share the costs of the services. Applicable as a method for allocating scarce social services resources. **4. Reimbursement of Costs** Provides for payment to the contractor of allowable costs incurred in the delivery of services. Applicable when the sponsor is able to assume risk in covering all the actual costs incurred. **5. Cost Plus Fixed Price** In addition to the actual costs of delivering the service, the contractor receives a negotiated percentage of the costs as profit (excess program resources). Appropriate when resources in excess of actual costs can be justified by both the sponsor and the contractor.	**1. Cost Plus Incentive Price** Target costs and performance objectives are established. The contractor receives funds for the cost of services at a predetermined minimum level of service. If services are judged to be of greater quality than minimum, the contractor receives additional funds—usually to a maximum amount. Applicable when it is appropriate to encourage the contractor to improve performance. Applicable when the sponsoring agency has flexibility in funding arrangements. **2. Negotiated Performance Contract** Negotiated on the basis that a certain level of performance will be achieved. If the level of performance is reached, the contractor receives a predetermined price (usually a high rate of profit or excess program resources). If the level of performance is not reached, the contractor receives no funding or a token payment. Applicable when measurable indicators of quality are available. Applicable when high risks and liberal funding arrangements are possible.

The underlying theory of performance contracting is basic. A contractor can be encouraged, through the use of incentives written into the contract, to perform in ways that maximize certain desired results. Usually, the incentives offered are economic rewards for high-level performance, but, as discussed in the next section, a number of other considerations enter the picture.

With the conceptual overview of types of contracts in mind, attention can turn to the basic elements of POSC contracts and the steps required to write a performance contract.

Preparing a Contract for Performance

It is important to remember that the programmatic aspects, not the legalistic aspects, of contracts are being considered. The latter are appropriately the domain of the legal profession, and it is strongly advised that managers rely on legal experts to ensure that the terms of the contract reflect precisely the understanding and expectations of all parties. Therefore, it is essential that program staff work closely with legal counsel to develop or review a contract before the organization enters a contractual agreement. The concern here is to structure the contract in such a way that it will result in the best possible services to clients, and legal counsel can be of assistance in this regard. However, the knowledgeable manager must first make clear what is desired in the contract from a programmatic point of view.

Ideally, a service contract would include the basic components of a contract that are presented in Table 2. In addition to the criteria specified in Table 1 and the common basic components of contracts set out in Table 2, an additional set of assumptions will need to be considered in the preparation of a performance contract:

▶ Authority through statutory and administrative policy is required to allow a governmental organization the flexibility to price services according to levels of performance.

▶ It is feasible to delineate the levels of performance of a service through empirical measures.

▶ There are incentives that will encourage a service contractor to enter a performance contract and be willing to continue as a contractor.

Under a performance contract, the governmental sponsor and the contractor agree on the services to be provided and on a specific set of performance targets or requirements, the achievement of which is linked to payment or another type of reward or penalty.

Several steps are required in a performance contract to establish what is meant by performance and to determine what has taken place upon completion of the service. Figure 2 presents a dynamic framework to help guide the preparation of a performance contract.

A critical ingredient in a performance contract is the explication of incentives to encourage contractors to meet or exceed selected levels of performance. The

Table 2. Components of a Contract

- ▶ A detailed description of the service, including a statement of goals and objectives
- ▶ Criteria and procedures for monitoring the service
- ▶ Criteria and procedures for evaluating the service
- ▶ Procedures for resolving disputes
- ▶ Procedures for changing the orientation-direction of the service
- ▶ Formulas and circumstances under which funding would continue
- ▶ Procedures for winding up the service
- ▶ Obligations of both parties to end the service

---

premise is that organizations have incentive systems that induce their members to cooperate or contribute toward the achievement of goals and that it is possible to specify incentives that will represent members' interests. There are many possible incentives, but there may also be potential constraints and limitations on just what kind of incentives can be offered to the contractor. As a general rule, for instance, strictly financial "profits" or extra cash funds may be the most difficult to offer. Fortunately, other types of incentives may stimulate high-level performance.

On the basis of their review of the literature, Knoke and Prensky (1984) classified incentives for the organizational system as utilitarian, normative, and affective (see Table 3).

Utilitarian incentives come to mind most readily when the subject of performance contracting is introduced. Additional fees or reimbursements can be offered on the basis of performance, as can in-kind goods or services, specialized training, and other staff-development activities. Additional examples include offers of flexible options for the delivery of services, the waiver of specific bureaucratic requirements, and the awarding of credit points for the next round of competitive bidding on a contract.

Normative and affective incentives tend to be less tangible than do utilitarian incentives. In some cases, however, they may be important motivators of performance. Normative incentives include possible special recognition by the media of the contractor's performance, such as best in the state; recognition of the contractor's commitment to a population that has special needs; and the achievement of a level of performance as an important indicator for a marketing strategy.

Affective incentives are particularly elusive when they are applied to performance contracting. Nevertheless, they can be strong, as in the case of a provider agency's involvement in collaborative planning and decision making for services on the basis of its exemplary performance as a contractor.

The categories of these various incentives are not mutually exclusive. For instance, a financial reward that is given to a contractor for superior performance

Figure 2. Performance-Reimbursement Cycle

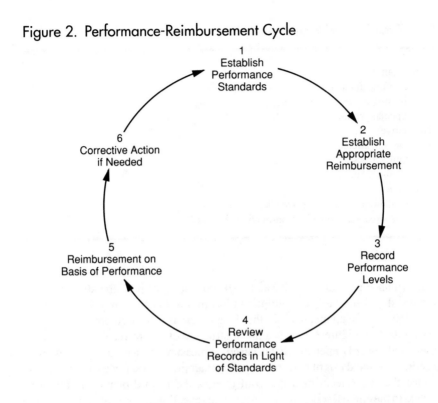

may also be a strong normative incentive. Furthermore, staff in the contractor's organization may be motivated by working with colleagues who are recognized as highly competent.

The classification of incentives presented here may also help the human services manager to examine whether members of the organization realize that performance incentives are being offered. A persuasive case can be made that performance contracting will work effectively only when the individuals who are performing the services relate positively to the incentives. Once the desired incentives are chosen, they must be programmed into the contract document. Finally, and equally important, each category or type of incentive can be used to examine the presence of disincentives to high levels of performance at both the organizational and individual-member levels.

The approaches that can be used to link rewards for meeting or exceeding standards of performance are discussed next. Figure 3 shows several of the more common approaches used to structure rewards (or penalties when expected standards

Table 3. Organizational Incentives

► Utilitarian
　　Funding-financial
　　In-kind goods and services
　　Special privileges
► Normative
　　Organizational status
　　Obligations to provide services
　　Public relations
► Affective
　　Collaboration in the service delivery network
　　Interorganizational decision-making process

---

of performance are not met) (Pace, 1970). For the most part, the structures and examples that follow relate to utilitarian incentives, but they may also stimulate suggestions for the application of other incentives, as discussed previously.

Example A in Figure 3 depicts a linear structure of incentives that provides for a graduated reward or penalty that is based on measures of success in achieving or exceeding the standards of performance. For example, for a service whose aim is to enhance the self-esteem of a group of clients, the reward or penalty could be matched to the clients' scores on a measure that reveals the degree of their enhanced self-esteem. Thus, a reward of $10 to the contractor could be keyed to each documented increment of improvement in a client's self-esteem. By contrast, if the measure revealed a drop in self-esteem, the payoff to the contractor could be reduced by the same proportion. A maximum reward or penalty is usually specified in this structure.

Application of the linear performance structure implies the use of agreed-on valid and reliable measures to gauge performance, a problem for many areas of the human services in which such measures may be questioned. Social programs that have an educational component and standardized measures of success appear most applicable for this performance structure. Examples of how the linear structure for performance contracting has been applied in the field of education are presented in *The School Executive's Guide to Performance Contracting* (American Association of School Administrators, 1972).

In the step structure (example B of Figure 3), less reliance on discrete measurement increments is possible. The steps can, however, be structured in fine or more global categories, depending on the application. Following the example presented for the linear method, a structure could be developed to provide a reward or penalty of $50 for each 10 percentage points of change revealed in clients' self-esteem.

Figure 3. Structures for Incentives in Contract Performance

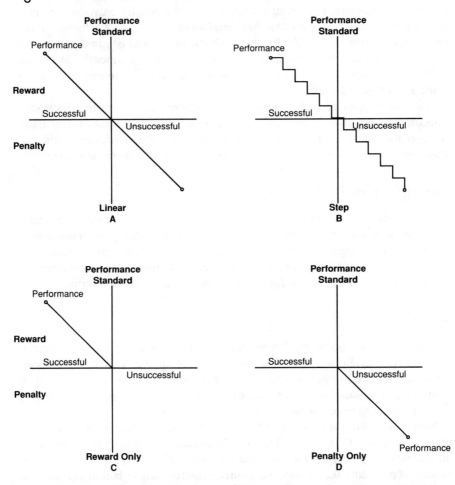

SOURCE: Adapted from D. F. Pace, *Negotiation and Management of Defense Contracts* (New York: John Wiley & Sons, 1970), p. 257. Used by permission of author.

The "reward-only" structure (example C of Figure 3), in its most simple application, provides for a set reward only when a specified standard of service is achieved. For instance, a reward could be offered to the contractor for exceeding the standard time for returning an institutionalized client to his or her home or to an appropriate alternative setting. If the standard time is two months, the contractor could be rewarded $100 for each client who is successfully placed out of the institution in fewer than two months.

A "penalty-only" structure (example D of Figure 3) works the reverse of the reward-only structure. In its simplest application, the penalty-only structure provides for a set penalty when a specified standard of service is not achieved. Thus, for example, a penalty of $100 less in reimbursement could be imposed for each client who is not successfully placed out of the institution in two months. Miller and Wilson (1981) reported on one state's use of penalties for performance contracting in the area of mental health.

The written contract is the centerpiece of performance contracting because it embodies the expectations and rewards (or penalties) that will result. Taken alone, however, the contractual document misses the full process of performance contracting. Therefore, critical issues in managing performance contracts are considered next.

Managing for Performance

This chapter relies heavily on the planning function to put into place the structural aspects or parameters required to enter into performance contracts. Attention should be given to the managerial functions that are also necessary to design and implement successful contracts for performance. Two areas of human services management that are particularly applicable for POSC are negotiation and monitoring.

Negotiation

Negotiation may occur at different stages in the life of a performance contract. The contract may, in fact, be the result of negotiations to provide specific services. In the case of POSC, however, the process is more likely to begin with a competitive request for proposals. Once a contractor is chosen through competitive bidding, it is still possible to negotiate the fine points of the contract.

Negotiation skills are important for the contract manager at each stage of the process (Hirsch, 1986). To be effective, these managerial skills must be based on an understanding of organizational dynamics, the clarification of roles, the identification of problems, the resolution of conflicts, and consensus building (Gibelman & Demone, 1989). Beyond the acquisition of knowledge and skills in this area, human services managers who are involved in POSC are challenged to consider the overall purpose of their deliberations. Negotiation in POSC is more than simply trying to "win all you can," as the popular literature sometimes implies. In the context of POSC, an integrative bargaining approach is generally needed, with both the governmental sponsor and the provider of the service setting priorities for the provision of good-quality services to clients, as opposed to negotiating the lowest or highest possible price for services (Kettner & Martin, 1987). Popple (1984) summarized the key management literature on negotiation and offered advice on how human services managers may apply critical negotiation skills. Managing performance contracts offers a fertile field for applying these skills.

Monitoring

Monitoring assumes special importance in performance contracting. It is a way to document whether standards of performance are being met and the basis for appropriate reimbursements to the providers of services. Human services managers may be involved in monitoring in a variety of situations, each calling for different skills. Critical mediating variables in monitoring performance contracts are (1) requirements of the system (designating which organization will carry out the monitoring), (2) timing (day to day or periodic), and (3) technology (behavioral tests and measurements).

Litzler

"The government contract!? Heck no, this is just their proposal specifications and guidelines."

Considerable attention has been given to the knowledge and skills required for monitoring contracts (Hirsch, 1986; Jansson, 1989; Kettner & Martin, 1986; Rehfuss, 1989; Tatara & Pettiford, 1989; Wedel & Chess, 1989). As in the case of negotiation, variations in the system substantially mediate the role that a given human services manager may play in the monitoring process.

Some governmental sponsors designate a central unit to monitor functions for a range of human services that are contracted out. Human services managers who work under this organizational arrangement become full-time monitors, for which program-evaluation skills are central. Others use a decentralized system, in which contract managers in discrete service areas monitor the performance as part of a diversified job (that may even include negotiation on matters pertaining to contracting). In some cases, the contractor who is providing the service monitors the performance, using guidelines adopted in conjunction with the governmental sponsor. Finally, some arrangements involve independent "third-party" monitors. No matter which plan is used, human services managers and contract managers representing either party to the contract should have a solid understanding of monitoring and the skills to effect positive changes in the process.

The application and monitoring of performance contracts is still limited by the technology for measuring the attributes of performance, despite the attention that has been paid to measuring the outcomes of services, such as child welfare services (Magura & Moses, 1986). Nevertheless, performance contracting generally calls for a realistic turnaround time for reimbursing providers of services. Although performance can be determined reasonably quickly in some cases (such as the rate of success in placing clients), in other cases, true performance (such as the rate of success of these placements in a reasonable period) may not be evident for some time after the service is delivered. The message is that faulty planning for performance contracting early in the process can show up dramatically in the monitoring stage. As a general rule, human services managers are advised to look carefully at the matter of performance measurement, not only in the initial planning stages, but throughout the contracting process.

Controversies in Performance Contracting

The concerns about POSC that have been raised involve organizational management and broader social policy issues about the appropriate roles in this society for the governmental and private sectors. Since these concerns have appeared in the literature on social work and on management, they will not be repeated here. Rather, this section considers how the application of performance contracting in the human services could influence them.

Performance contracting suggests a comfortable fit with past and current efforts to streamline the administration of the government, save costs, improve the quality of services, and ensure greater control of and accountability for services that are rendered. In essence, performance contracting epitomizes the "rational goal model" (Quinn, 1988) of organizational management. Both for governmental sponsors and contractors, there appears to be a reasonable potential for enhancing productivity and maximizing output. What remains to be seen, however, is under what circumstances these benefits can reasonably be expected. When should performance contracting be applied, and when is it inappropriate? This chapter has attempted to advance the criteria to be considered and to stimulate further empirical testing of the practice in the human services.

A specific problem for performance contracting is the naturally occurring changes in contractor organizations and the complexity of organizational incentives. Thus, although one set of incentives may motivate an organization during the formative stages of the process, a different set may be needed later.

Furthermore, organizations that share certain attributes (a stake in the human services market, members, resources, and so on) tend to compete with one another. When the incentives are economic, the competition is more or less impersonal. When the stakes are intangible, however, the competition is often more personal and more intensely felt. It is difficult to maintain genial relationships when the stakes are either endowed with a moral or sacrosanct quality (as with some purposes) or are an attribute of personality and reputation (as with prestige, status, honor, conviviality, and so forth) (Clark & Wilson, 1961). Although there has been little evidence of such problems in community social welfare efforts when performance contracts contain intangible incentives, such competition should be carefully considered in planning and evaluating the results that are obtained.

At the broader policy levels, performance contracting may stimulate entrepreneurship and further involve the private profit-making sector in the human services—a trend that has been evident for some time (MAXIMUS, 1986). Performance contracting also encourages nonprofit organizations to explore profit-making ventures. At the same time, the old fears about the further erosion of the value base of the voluntary nonprofit sector of the human services in the United States are raised by the use of contracts focused narrowly on marketplace (economic) incentives (Lewis, 1989; Perlmutter & Adams, 1990). Finally, the routine reporting by the mass media of cost overruns, shoddy quality, and even fraudulent practices in other areas of performance contracting raises serious questions about what may become of the social welfare sector if large-scale performance contracting becomes common.

Another issue concerns assumptions about the context of the marketplace in which POSC operates. Kettner and Martin (1986, 1987, 1990) conceptualized alternative approaches to POSC as a partnership model and a market model. Although contracting may be viewed as enhancing pure competition for human services, there are often extenuating circumstances that bias the marketplace: a limited number of potential contractors, matching requirements that influence "true-cost" proposals for services, insufficient information on bidding or requests for proposals, and the like. Results of the imperfections in the POSC marketplace may be seen when "different segments of government tend to be co-opted, controlled, or changed by those interests which are most successful in organizing and articulating their interests" (DeHoog, 1985, p. 25). A special concern is that individual contractors (those with the most power and influence) systematically try to exclude competition by using their influence with governmental bureaucrats and policymakers, for example. The human services have generally escaped serious incidents or charges of this concern. Whether performance contracting in POSC will further promote the long-held partnership model between the public and private sectors or lead to imperfections in the marketplace is still to be seen.

Performance contracting has had mixed results, with some participants reacting positively and some negatively and some lamenting that it requires sophisticated personnel (both buyers and sellers of services) (Hatry & Durman, 1985). Further field testing with empirically based evaluations should provide additional information on the potential application of performance contracting in the social services and present new knowledge on how and when it works best.

Summary

This chapter has explored the concepts and issues related to performance contracting in government-sponsored and funded services delivered by nongovernmental service providers. The main concern has been to stimulate thinking about performance in POSC and the use of incentives to structure performance contracting when it can be considered viable. Limitations to applying performance contracting and the controversies about the practice have been included. It should be clear from the discussion that in some instances, performance contracting may be a viable POSC modality, and in others (perhaps most) it is not feasible. However, attention to incentives (and disincentives) in POSC contracts is important for human services managers. To promote thinking about the knowledge and skills that are required in this area, the following skills-application exercise provides the opportunity to apply these ideas conceptually.

SKILLS-APPLICATION EXERCISE

Consider the values involved in the following case example of a state department of social services (SDSS) that is contracting for the placement of troubled children.

The governmental sponsor, SDSS, is mandated by state statute to provide care and treatment for troubled children in the department's custody. Currently, SDSS contracts out most of these services to the private nonprofit sector

continued

through fixed-price contracts. A system of classifying levels of care and service has been developed as follows:

▶ A level A facility provides services to youths who are considered a low risk to themselves or others, and 24-hour awake coverage is not required.

▶ A level B facility provides for youths with demonstrated behavioral problems and the need for a structured community-based setting that requires 24-hour awake supervision to respond to crises.

▶ A level C facility provides for youths who display emotional disturbances or extreme antisocial and aggressive behavior and who require a highly structured setting and 24-hour crisis intervention. In level C contracts, the contractor agrees to "no right of refusal" of clients referred to the contractor.

SDSS assesses the provider agencies annually to ensure that the providers are meeting the designated requirements for each level. Also, when a youth enters the system, he or she is evaluated to determine the appropriate level of care and services case by case.

Required legal clauses and provisions are included in the body of the contract. In the interests of brevity, only a general outline of the contract is presented here:

▶ Introduction, including identification of SDSS and the provider that is entering into the contractual agreement.

▶ Part 1: Terms of the contract, including beginning and ending dates.

▶ Part 2: Level-of-care-assessment, including the date of the assessment by SDSS.

▶ Part 3: Services to be provided, including an assessment of and treatment plan for each resident within 30 days of admission, with input from SDSS staff. The services specified in the body of the contract include case management, psychological and counseling services, recreational services, educational services, crisis behavior management, training in independent living skills, employment services, and a host of general child care services.

▶ Part 4: Basis for payments, financial cap or maximum reimbursement possible, procedure for documenting the residents served and the services provided, and the time frame for filing claims for reimbursement and receiving payments.

▶ Part 5: Minimal qualifications for the child care staff, including training records, consultation, and the orientation of new staff.

▶ Part 6: Characteristics of residents, including descriptive characteristics.

▶ Part 7: Miscellaneous requirements, including provisions against corporal punishment and referral for specialized services.

▶ Part 8: General provisions, including agency reporting, audit requirements, compliance with the law, and so on.

The concern in this exercise is primarily with three provisions of the contract: Parts 3, 4, and 8.

continued

Assume that contractors are often reluctant to accept Level A and Level B clients for treatment. Remember, the Level C contracts stipulate "no right of refusal" of referrals. It is perceived that the SDSS clients are often troubled and difficult youths. When SDSS cannot make immediate placement in a contract provider's facility, these youths have to wait in shelters, detention facilities, or hospitals.

How could you write a contract that would offer incentives to overcome this kind of problem? Specify the basis for reimbursing the contractor for the incentives you have chosen. Specify the means to monitor the contractor's performance in the area of the incentives you have chosen.

References

American Association of School Administrators. (1972). *The school executive's guide to performance contracting*. Washington, DC: Author.

Clark, P. B., & Wilson, J. Q. (1961). Incentive systems: A theory of organizations. *Administration Science Quarterly, 6*, 129–166.

DeHoog, R. H. (1985). *Contracting out for human services: Economic, political, and organizational perspectives*. Albany: State University of New York Press.

DeMong, R. F. (1978). The effectiveness of incentive contracts: What research tells us. *National Contract Management Quarterly Journal, 12*, 12–22.

DeMong, R. F., & Strayer, D. E. (1981). The underlying theory of incentive contracting. *Defense Management Journal, 17*, 45–51.

Fisher, I. N. (1969). An evaluation of incentive contracting experience. *Naval Research Logistics Quarterly, 16*, 63–83.

Fox, J. R. (1974). *Arming America: How the U.S. buys weapons*. Cambridge, MA: Harvard University Press.

Gibelman, M., & Demone, H. W. (1989). Negotiating a contract: Practical considerations. In M. Gibelman & H. W. Demone (Eds.), *Services for sale: Purchasing health and human services* (pp. 131–148). New Brunswick, NJ: Rutgers University Press.

Hasler, B. S. (1985). *Evaluation of performance based contracting in aging programs*. Washington, DC: Urban Systems Research and Engineering.

Hatry, H. P., & Durman, E. (1985). *Issues in competitive contracting for social services*. Falls Church, VA: National Institute of Governmental Purchasing.

Hirsch, W. J. (1986). *The contracts management deskbook*. New York: American Management Association.

Hunt, R. G. (1971). *Extracontractual influence in government contracting*. Buffalo: State University of New York.

Hunt, R. G. (1984). Cross-purposes in the federal contract procurement system: Military R & D and beyond. *Public Administration Review, 44*, 247–256.

Jansson, B. S. (1989). The political economy of monitoring: A contingency perspective. In M. Gibelman & H. W. Demone (Eds.), *Services for sale: Purchasing health and human services* (pp. 343–359). New Brunswick, NJ: Rutgers University Press.

Kettner, P. M., & Martin, L. L. (1986). Making decisions about purchase of service contracting. *Public Welfare, 44*, 303–337.

Kettner, P. M., & Martin, L. L. (1987). *Purchase of service contracting*. Newbury Park, CA: Sage.

Kettner, P. M., & Martin, L. L. (1990). Purchase of service contracting: Two models. *Administration in Social Work, 14*, 15–30.

Knoke, D., & Prensky, D. (1984). What relevance do organization theories have for voluntary associations? *Social Science Quarterly, 65*, 3–20.

Lewis, H. (1989). Ethics and the private non-profit human service organizations. *Administration in Social Work, 13*, 1–14.

Magura, S., & Moses, B. S. (1986). *Outcome measures for child welfare services: Theory and applications*. Washington, DC: Child Welfare League of America.

Malka, S. M. (1990). Contracting for human services: The case of Pennsylvania's subsidized child day care program—policy limitations and prospects. *Administration in Social Work, 14*, 31–46.

Massachusetts Taxpayers Foundation. (1980). *Purchase of service: Can state government gain control?* Boston: Author.

MAXIMUS. (1986). *Final report of the findings of an evaluability assessment regarding the practice of contracting with for-profit social and health service firms*. McLean, VA: Author.

Miller, S., & Wilson, N. (1981). The case for performance contracting. *Administration in Mental Health, 8*, 185–193.

Nolan, A. J. (1980). Incentive contracting in the aerospace industry. *National Contract Management Journal, 14*, 35–40, 41–54.

Pace, D. F. (1970). *Negotiation and management of defense contracts*. New York: John Wiley & Sons.

Perlmutter, F. D., & Adams, C. T. (1990). The voluntary sector and for-profit ventures: The transformation of American social welfare? *Administration in Social Work, 14*, 1–13.

Popple, P. R. (1984). Negotiation: A critical skill for social work administrators. *Administration in Social Work, 8*, 1–11.

Quinn, R. E. (1988). *Beyond rational management: Mastering the paradoxes and competing demands of high performance*. San Francisco: Jossey-Bass.

Rehfuss, J. A. (1989). *Contracting out in government: A guide to working with outside contractors to supply public services*. San Francisco: Jossey-Bass.

Riemer, W. H. (1968). *Handbook of government contract administration*. Englewood Cliffs, NJ: Prentice Hall.

Scherer, F. M. (1964). *The weapons acquisition process: Economic incentives*. Cambridge, MA: Harvard University Press.

Tatara, T., & Pettiford, E. K. (1989). Purchase of service monitoring and evaluation policies and practices. In M. Gibelman & H. W. Demone (Eds.), *Service for sale: Purchasing health and human services* (pp. 331–342). New Brunswick, NJ: Rutgers University Press.

U.S. Department of Health and Human Services, Administration on Aging. (1982, May 24). *AoA-Im-82-25 Model performance-based contracting system*. Washington, DC: Author.

Wedel, K. R., & Chess, N. (1989). Monitoring strategies in purchase of service contracting. In M. Gibelman & H. W. Demone (Eds.), *Service for sale: Purchasing health and human services* (pp. 360–370). New Brunswick, NJ: Rutgers University Press.

Wedel, K. R., & Colston, S. W. (1988). Performance contracting for human services: Issues and suggestions. *Administration in Social Work, 12*, 73–87.

CHAPTER

22

Managing Mergers and Consolidations

John A. Yankey and Mark I. Singer

Nonprofit organizations underwent much restructuring during the 1980s. In an effort to increase efficiency, achieve economies of scale, diversify services or products, or meet other organizational needs, many nonprofit organizations actively pursued a variety of alternative strategies, the most important of which were mergers and consolidations. Managers were challenged to work with their organizations' governing bodies to determine if they should consider merging or consolidating and, if so, how they should pursue it. Although the scope of this unifying activity among nonprofit organizations in the United States is unknown, ample experience exists to provide managerial guidelines for initiating and concluding successful restructuring through these strategies.

Merger and Consolidation: Definitions

In its purest form, a *merger* is the complete absorption of one or more organizations by another organization whose corporate existence is preserved. The body (or bodies) being absorbed dissolves and loses its corporate existence. The American Hospital Association (1989, p. 4) defined a merger as

> a statutorily defined corporate transaction in which two similar corporations come together permanently, leaving a single survivor corporation and the other extinguished. Assets do not have to be transferred, since this happens by operation of law, with the surviving corporation owning all the assets and liabilities of both parties.

A *consolidation* occurs when each nonprofit organization involved dissolves and a new, single corporate entity is formed. The assets, liabilities, and operations are combined into one. Again, the American Hospital Association's (1989) definition is instructive:

> the process by which two usually not-for-profit corporations come together to form a third corporation, resulting in the extinguishment of the original two. Less technically, a consolidation is virtually any legal transaction by which the assets and operations of two organizations are combined into one.

These definitions underscore the substantial differences between these two strategic approaches to restructuring nonprofit organizations. But although they result in different structural outcomes, managerial activity in considering their appropriateness for any nonprofit organization is much the same. Managers need to work with their governing bodies to (1) decide to explore a merger or consolidation, (2) determine a potential partner, (3) plan for implementing the unification, and (4) implement the new structural arrangement.

Deciding to Explore a Merger or Consolidation

The restructuring of nonprofit organizations requires a significant commitment of resources from all the organizations involved. In their study of mergers and consolidations of nonprofit organizations, Singer and Yankey (in press) concluded that two years is the average time required for exploring, deciding, planning, and implementing a unification. Given the significant commitment of human resources that is required, it is imperative that managers carefully determine if their nonprofit organizations should formally explore this option.

Managers and boards of trustees can be guided in making this decision by answering some key questions ("Consolidation," 1989; Greater New York Fund–United Way, 1981) about their organizations and programs:

▶ Is the organization providing only one service?

▶ Is the need for this service declining in the community?

▶ Is another agency providing this or a similar service to the same population?

▶ Could the organization deliver its services more efficiently or effectively in conjunction with another organization?

▶ Could the organization achieve economies of scale in conjunction with another organization?

▶ Has the organization's director recently retired (or is he or she going to retire within the next year)?

▶ Are the knowledge and skills of organizational personnel being used effectively or creatively?

▶ Is the organization experiencing instability or a lack of responsiveness among members of its governing bodies?

▶ Is the organization experiencing declining financial stability?

▶ Is the organization dependent upon a source of funds that is eroding or being eliminated?

▶ Is the organization's fundraising capacity limited?

Although this list is not all-inclusive, a yes response to a number of these questions strongly suggests that managers and governing bodies should give serious consideration to exploring the appropriateness of unification.

Deciding about a Partner

Three approaches are used to initiate discussions with nonprofit organizations about their interest in a merger or consolidation: executive to executive, board leadership to board leadership, and third party.

In the direct executive-to-executive approach, at least one executive has made a preliminary decision that exploration is worthwhile. For it to work, the executives must respect each other; they cannot be competitive or have personality conflicts. The discussion of a potential partnership usually begins with a series of informal meetings of the executives during which these issues are explored:

▶ The personal and professional interests or desires of each executive regarding his or her future

▶ The respective organizational missions and programs

▶ The management and operations of the respective organizations

▶ Potential staffing patterns

▶ The financial status of each organization

▶ The executives' perceptions of the strengths and weaknesses of each organization.

If these discussions conclude with both executives desiring to proceed with more formal conversations with the leadership of their respective governing bodies, the executives' next steps include the following:

▶ Identifying the steps in the formal exploration

▶ Anticipating their respective governing bodies' concerns and expectations

▶ Determining whether to recommend a neutral facilitator to guide and assist in the decision-making phase

▶ Deciding on an appropriate timetable by which to enter the formal decision-making process

▶ Planning how to present the recommendation to explore unification to the governing bodies.

The board leadership–to–board leadership approach is also direct, but involves none of the executives of the organizations. In this approach, two or three members of the governing bodies of each organization meet informally to discuss the same issues as those discussed in the executive-to-executive approach. However, these initial conversations often include preliminary discussions of future arrangements for governance in any type of partnership. If these discussions conclude with a desire to proceed with the formal exploration of a merger or consolidation, the next steps are the same as those suggested in the executive-to-executive approach.

The third-party approach encompasses two scenarios. In the first, someone is selected by one organization to approach a targeted organization to determine if it is interested in formally exploring the potential of unification. This person should be familiar with the two groups, be (and be perceived as being) neutral, and consider the approach a confidential matter. The major issues that are addressed are whether the organization being approached is interested in a more formal exploration and how to make the transition to such formal deliberations. Usually, the third party is not involved in the early exploration of the issues indicated as appropriate in the two direct approaches.

In the other third-party approach, the third party—a funding body such as the United Way or a foundation—influences externally and may or may not be neutral. The initial approach is usually to the respective organizations separately. This form of third-party involvement is likely to be with the organization's governing bodies. Although there may be some substantive discussion of issues, the major purpose of this type of approach is to encourage the respective governing bodies to engage in a formal exploration of the potential for unification. Meetings often are on neutral sites, and efforts are made to keep the discussions confidential. The major outcome sought is a formal recommendation made to the respective governing bodies to begin a formal process to explore the unification of the organizations.

Once a decision is reached to explore formally a merger or consolidation, a nonprofit organization frequently forms a work group to do the following:

▶ Obtain an agreement in principle to explore in depth a specific potential partner

▶ Develop a specific plan and timetable for conducting an in-depth exploration

▶ Determine the feasibility of the organization's entrance into a partnership with another specific organization

"It isn't your 'desire' to buy Park Place or Boardwalk that concerns me. . . .
It's your 'motivation.' "

▶ Develop and present a report to the respective governing bodies of the organizations involved.

The numerous "membership models" for this work group include the executive and key members of the governing body of one organization; the executive, key members of the governing body, and staff of one organization; the executive, key members of the governing body, staff, and clientele of one organization; the executive, key members of the governing body, staff, and clientele of one organization, as well as funding bodies and community leaders; or any of the foregoing but including members of both organizations. Members who are asked to serve on a work group should be articulate and influential and should include those who harbor reservations about unification. The chairperson of the group should have the requisite leadership skills, have cross-organizational and community credibility, and be mutually acceptable to all organizations involved in the exploration. Co-chairs help share the leadership among participating organizations.

The use of consultants is a key issue in structuring and facilitating the exploration. Increasingly, nonprofit organizations are discovering that consultants can be vital contributors to the success of deliberations. Depending on the contextual "state of affairs" in which this exploration occurs, a process consultant can be most helpful in shaping and facilitating the activities. In addition, legal and financial consultants often are required for special expertise.

The major product of the work group's activity is a feasibility study. This study entails an organization-by-organization analysis that generates comparative profiles. The elements of these profiles include the organization's mission and philosophy, organizational culture, governance, management, programs (services and markets), human resources (paid personnel and volunteers), facilities (buildings), equipment, land, legal status, finances, revenue generation (fundraising), and community relations. In addition to this information, the work group may collect background information on comparable unification situations in the community or the industry; review the state's laws on nonprofit corporations and the regulations of the Internal Revenue Service; assess the views of others, such as funding bodies, donors, and the community, about the potential partnership; and evaluate the groups' readiness for change.

Following the development of comparative profiles, the collection of supplemental information, and the discussion of the issues that have been identified, the work group will develop its report for distribution to the governing bodies of the organizations that are involved. The report must provide enough detail to allow the respective governing bodies to decide whether to accept or reject the recommended actions. If the recommendation is to proceed with unification and the governing bodies approve, the approval should be formalized and documented by a vote. In addition, decisions are necessary regarding the mechanism and process for planning the unification, leadership for the planning activities, use of consultants, time schedules, communication of the merger or consolidation (internally and externally), and transitional budgets.

Planning to Implement the Merger or Consolidation

The previous decisions about the leadership for and structure of the planning process, utilization of consultants, and time schedules will help determine the time required for this phase of planning. The planning probably will take four to six months. The most suitable vehicle for carrying it out is a planning committee. Although the committee could include some members from the earlier work group, the tasks will require a larger group of up to 30 carefully selected individuals. It should include representatives of the professional and volunteer leadership of all the organizations that are involved, especially those whose expertise is in the areas to be discussed.

A series of subcommittees can do the in-depth planning. Some subcommittees may work on unique situations, whereas generic subcommittees might work on the corporate structure and bylaws, programs and services, human resources, office facilities and services, financial management, fund development, and public relations and community relations.

The feasibility study produced in the decision-making phase will be an essential element of the in-depth planning. The comparative organizational profiles will be especially useful in planning the implementation. Some of the most important planning activities will include these:

▶ Compiling a list of stakeholders whose receptivity to the union must be determined and who must be effectively and consistently communicated with throughout the planning and implementation phases

▶ Finalizing (or designing the process and mechanism for finalizing) the choice of the executive director for the new organization

▶ Selecting (or designing the process and mechanism for selecting) the name of the new organization

▶ Establishing (or designing the process and mechanism for establishing) the transitional volunteer leadership for the new organization

▶ Initiating any required advance notifications of or clearances for unification

▶ Developing agreements on the source, timing, and mechanisms for public statements about the unification

▶ Completing the implementation plan

▶ Presenting the implementation plan to the respective governing bodies, management, and staff of the involved organizations.

Following approval of the implementation plan, the planning phase should conclude with opportunities for both mourning the end of the separate organizations and celebrating the beginning of the new one.

Implementing the "New" Structural Arrangement

As Pritchett (1989, p. i) stated, "making the deal is just a warmup . . . the real job is making it work." Many details need to be handled in implementing a merger or consolidation, such as finalizing the required changes in the bylaws; submitting necessary forms to appropriate regulatory and governmental agencies; ensuring that funding bodies, banks, insurers, and the like are informed of the new organization's name; communicating the unification to clientele and the community; developing printed materials that include the new name and corporate identity; reviewing and revising insurance policies, leases, and so on and integrating personnel policies and practices; establishing a comprehensive record-keeping system; implementing a "common" financial management system; and arranging office facilities and equipment to support the new structural arrangements.

In research conducted on 40 mergers (including consolidations and acquisitions) in the for-profit sector, Merrell (1985) discovered that 65 percent of the companies surveyed considered the outcome to be "either disappointing or a total failure." In probing the reasons for such perceptions, Merrell found that human resource issues were considered central to the disappointment or failure. After for-profit mergers, companies often report dysfunctional changes in employees' behavior, lost productivity, high turnover rates among senior managers, leadership struggles among managers, and other personnel problems. Although information about mergers and consolidations in the nonprofit sector is limited, personnel-related issues probably will be especially important to both the short- and long-term success of the new organization.

Employees' feelings of uncertainty and powerlessness during the implementation of a merger or consolidation can lead to many dysfunctional behaviors. It is normal for individual employees to be concerned about how the unification will affect their job responsibilities, salaries, and benefits. Accurate and timely information increases an individual's sense of control, and open and honest communication by managers may increase employees' feelings of individual control at such a time (Davy, Kinicki, Kilroy, & Scheck, 1988).

Furthermore, "newly acquired" employees need to be welcomed into the combined organization through a variety of approaches, including welcome wagons, "buddy" mentor systems, and staff development and training. In addition, the following activities can help make the new organization work well:

▶ The appointment of a manager of the merger or consolidation can prove useful in championing and coordinating the implementation plan.

▶ The new executive team needs to be profiled and made visible to employees throughout the organization.

▶ Managerial emphasis should focus on identifying and solving problems. Employees should be rewarded as identifiers and solvers of problems.

▶ All stakeholders must be given a reason for wanting the unification to work. The top management needs to recognize and communicate its understanding that success will come only if everyone assumes some responsibility for making the new arrangement succeed.

▶ To communicate frequently with both internal and external constituencies, a variety of mechanisms should be used, such as newsletters, surveys, public service announcements, and a speakers bureau.

▶ Systems for monitoring and evaluation should be introduced and put into place to ensure that necessary data will be collected and related to the specific goals and objectives of the unification.

Homes, Inc.: A Case of Merger

In 1987, Homes, Inc., a voluntary, nonprofit (501[c][3]) organization, was a small but well-funded agency whose mission was "to provide and advocate for housing for the homeless in Summit City." With a staff of eight professionals and three support personnel, it provided a series of programs in community development, rehabilitation of housing, and advocacy of housing. The agency, with a budget of $745,000, was funded by an endowment (50 percent), United Way Services (25 percent), grants from the government and foundations (15 percent), and its own varied fundraising activities (10 percent). It was directed by a dynamic female executive who had been with the agency for five years and was held in high esteem in Summit City. The agency's board of trustees consisted of 22 committed, involved persons representing a mix of gender, expertise, ethnic origins, race, geography, and economic means.

Summit City had another voluntary, nonprofit organization that provided services to the homeless in 1987. The mission of this agency, the Summit City Housing Corporation (SCHC), was to "strengthen and promote Summit City's housing for the homeless through counseling, education, and community involvement." With three professional staff members and one full-time and one half-time support person, SCHC had a budget of $175,000 to provide its community education, advocacy, and counseling services.

SCHC's revenues came from United Way Services (65 percent), governmental and foundation grants (30 percent), and individual contributions (5 percent). The executive director had been with the agency since its inception some 10 years earlier, and he was planning to retire in 1988. SCHC's board of trustees numbered 18, but the members' participation was uneven and their performance was perfunctory. However, a major strength of the board was its expertise in housing stock and the financing of housing.

It was in this context that the executive director of Homes, Inc., approached the executive director of SCHC to request an informal discussion of the possibility of a merger of the two groups. SCHC's executive director had made public his plans to retire. The executive director of Homes, Inc., reasoned that the agencies' similar missions and program activities made the merger a natural consideration. SCHC's executive director responded affirmatively to this initiative, perceiving that the joint expertise of the boards of trustees and the professional staff would strengthen the community's ability to respond to the needs of the homeless.

A series of informal meetings between the two heads occurred during a two-month period. As a result, the two reached an informal, tentative agreement regarding several critical issues:

▶ It was clear that the respective missions of the groups were similar.

▶ Homes, Inc., would be the "acquiring" organization whose corporate existence would be preserved.

▶ The programs and services offered by SCHC had merit, and although none could be guaranteed to be part of the merged arrangement, all would receive full consideration in any formal exploration of the merger that grew out of these talks.

▶ All present SCHC personnel would become employees of Homes, Inc., and be incorporated into its better compensation plan.

▶ Homes, Inc., would assume responsibility for an outstanding debt ($55,000) of SCHC.

The two leaders recommended a formal exploration of the merger to their respective boards of trustees, emphasizing the retirement of SCHC's executive, the potential future decline of funding by United Way Services for housing programs, the likelihood that programs would be strengthened if the expertise of the boards and professional staff was merged, and the greater acceptance and support of the community for groups that attempt to achieve economies of scale in operations and to decrease the competition for funding and volunteers. In addition, the executive directors recommended that a professor at a local university who was a recognized expert in mergers and consolidations be used as a consultant to shape and facilitate the process.

Homes, Inc.'s board leadership responded enthusiastically to the recommendation of such an exploration. The response of SCHC's board leadership was somewhat mixed. Although the president of SCHC favored a formal exploration, two other officers, "charter members" of the board, opposed any loss of the agency's identification and visibility. Both expressed reservations about the extent to which the expertise of the current SCHC board would be retained in a merger.

Because of this response, Homes, Inc.'s executive director delayed any effort to pursue the matter with her full board, while SCHC's executive director worked diligently in a series of one-on-one meetings with his several resistant board leaders. After nearly two months, SCHC's director persuaded these board members to allow the recommendation to be brought to the full board by promising to include them in any work groups that would be formed to carry out the formal exploration.

Thus, five months after the initiation of the informal discussions, the two groups approved the formal exploration of a merger. A work group was established to carry out the formal deliberations. This group included the two executives, three members of the respective boards of trustees (including the two "resistant" members of SCHC's board), a member of the professional staff of each agency, a representative of United Way Services, and a program officer from the foundation that funded the programs of both organizations. The professor was employed as a consultant to help plan and facilitate the exploration process.

The work group planned a series of six meetings during the next three months. These meetings were conducted at the offices of the United Way or the foundation, with the consultant facilitating the process. A major responsibility of the group was the development of organizational profiles—the compilation of information about each organization's mission, governance, management, programs, staff, facilities, funding, fundraising, and community relations. These comparative profiles were to be the basis of the feasibility study, the major report to be directed to the respective boards. Several subgroups were established to compile this information, with the executives and staff taking lead roles. Also, one subgroup determined the other key stakeholders' perceptions of the potential merger.

At the scheduled meetings of the work group, the work of the subgroups was reviewed, debated, and finalized for inclusion in the feasibility study. Discussions on many of the issues were prolonged. Negative views about the loss of identity and name, the potential loss of support from donors, and the composition of the board of a merged organization were consistently presented by the resistant two members of the SCHC board. The group-processing skills of the consultant proved invaluable in moving the work along and balancing the discussion of the issues. Nonetheless, two additional months were required to finalize the work.

During this time, numerous efforts were made to keep communication open, especially with the board and staff of both organizations. Monthly progress reports were made to each board. Monthly meetings were held by the executive directors with their staff. The executive director of Homes, Inc., attended some of the staff meetings at SCHC and answered questions about the agency. Each group's newsletter was used to keep the exploration "in front" of these two key stakeholder groups. A public forum was conducted to allow the broader community to express its views about the potential merger. Although it was poorly attended, the dominant reaction expressed at the forum was positive. This reaction was affirmed by the work of the subgroup that dealt with the perceptions of the major stakeholders.

By the end of the fifth month, the comparative profiles were completed and the draft feasibility study was prepared. These two documents were the foci for intense discussions by the work group at a one-and-a-half-day retreat. The consultant facilitated the retreat, mediated the different viewpoints, and provided guidance for completing the task. The retreat was a spirited exchange, with the resistance of the two SCHC board members continuing. In the end, however, these members' arguments were not persuasive. The remaining SCHC board member and the executive director joined the other members of the group in recommending the merger.

The respective boards of the two groups approved the recommendation at specially called meetings. A merger planning committee, comprising 22 members from both organizations, was established and empowered to make planning and operational decisions to ensure the successful implementation of the merger. Using the previously developed organizational profiles and feasibility study, the committee did the following:

▶ Reaffirmed the continuing use of Homes, Inc., as the name for the merged groups

▶ Finalized the selection of the executive of Homes, Inc., as the executive of the new agency

▶ Developed a new organizational structure that provided ongoing visibility for SCHC's programs

▶ Determined a new governance arrangement to include eight of the most active members of the SCHC board

▶ Drafted new bylaws

▶ Incorporated SCHC's personnel into the more financially beneficial compensation plan of Homes, Inc.

▶ Contacted a number of key stakeholders to respond to questions and to keep them apprised of the planning

▶ Continued the monthly meetings with the staffs of both organizations

▶ Coordinated comprehensive public information efforts with clientele of both organizations, as well as with the general public.

As its final action, the planning committee presented the implementation plan at a joint meeting of the two boards. The two boards met together to recognize and highlight the history and achievements of SCHC and to launch the new organization in a celebratory fashion.

A much stronger, revitalized Homes, Inc., emerged as a result of the unification. The implementation plan provided the guidelines and directions needed to move forward, including an excellent framework for annual explorations of the successes and shortcomings of the merger. Although the exploration and planning processes were drawn out, the value of the time invested was abundantly clear in the smooth implementation of the merger. Homes, Inc., was strengthened by the new expertise in the areas of housing stock and financing, and Summit City was in a much stronger position to target its resources to deal with the increasingly challenging problem of homelessness.

Summary

Mergers and consolidations have become an important way for nonprofit organizations to deal with changing environmental conditions. Although not a panacea, these restructuring strategies can offer opportunities for increasing the quality of services, maximizing resources, and responding more effectively to community issues. Timing is critical in exploring and selecting potential partners. Involving key stakeholders in the exploration, planning, and implementation processes and maintaining open communication with them characterize successful unification activities of nonprofit organizations. Comprehensive analytic work can contribute significantly to more informed decision making among the involved groups. The foregoing processes, methods, and guidelines can be employed by managers to explore and, if feasible and desirable, implement mergers and consolidations.

SKILLS-APPLICATION EXERCISE

You have been asked to provide consultation services to two organizations that are interested in exploring and deciding whether to merge or consolidate. The groups have been asked by United Way Services to consider these options, and, at the agencies' request, United Way Services has employed you to facilitate this process. You want to be especially well prepared for this consulting assignment and, therefore, must develop answers to the following questions:

▶ What are the reasons for *any* organization to consider merger or consolidation?

▶ What are the reasons given by *any* organization for not considering a merger or consolidation to be a viable option?

▶ What are some of the known problems with, or reasons given for the failure of, mergers and consolidations?

▶ What alternatives exist for structuring the exploration and decision-making processes of these organizations? What are the advantages and disadvantages of each alternative?

▶ What questions must be addressed to determine a potential partner for a merger or consolidation?

▶ What elements need to be included in developing comparative profiles of the two groups?

▶ What should the format be for reporting the consultation process and outcomes to the respective boards and United Way Services?

References

American Hospital Association. (1989). *Merger guidelines/checklist.* Chicago: Author.

Consolidation: A nonprofit success story. (1989). *Nonprofit World, 7*(2), 20–22.

Davy, J., Kinicki, A., Kilroy, J., & Scheck, C. (1988). After the merger: Dealing with people's uncertainty. *Training and Development Journal, 42* (11), 57–61.

Greater New York Fund–United Way. (1981). *Merger: Another path ahead (a guide to the merger process for voluntary human service agencies).* New York: Author.

Merrell, D. (1985). Playing hardball on a mergers and acquisitions team. *Personnel, 62,* 22–27.

Pritchett, P. (1989). *Smart moves: A crash course on merger integration management.* Dallas, TX: Pritchett & Associates.

Singer, M., & Yankey, J. (in press). Organizational metamorphosis: A study of 18 nonprofit mergers, acquisitions, and consolidations. *Nonprofit Management and Leadership.*

Index

The Editors

Richard L. Edwards, PhD, ACSW, is Dean and Professor at the Mandel School of Applied Social Sciences, Case Western Reserve University, Cleveland, Ohio. He has worked in the human services arena as a clinician, supervisor, and manager. He currently serves on the boards of trustees of several community agencies and frequently consults with nonprofit and government organizations. In June 1991, he completed a two-year term as President of the National Association of Social Workers. He is a frequent contributor to the management literature.

John A. Yankey, PhD, ACSW, is Director of the Ohio Family and Children Services Executive Institute and Professor at the Mandel School of Applied Social Sciences, Case Western Reserve University. He has had a long career in public social services agencies that includes the position of Deputy Commissioner of the West Virginia Department of Public Welfare. He is currently involved in research, teaching, and consulting on strategic planning, marketing, fundraising, and legislative processes. He has also chaired the Legislative Affairs Committee of the National Association of Social Workers.

Contributors

Chauncey A. Alexander, MSW, ACSW, CAE, is Professor Lecturer (part-time) in the Department of Social Work at California State University, Long Beach, and volunteer Chair of the Orange County United Way Health Care Task Force. He has had a distinguished career as a social work practitioner and administrator and was Executive Director of the National Association of Social Workers from 1970 to 1982.

David M. Austin, PhD, ACSW, is the Bert Kruger Smith Centennial Professor at the School of Social Work, University of Texas at Austin. He also chairs the national Task Force on Social Work Research. He has 17 years of professional practice experience in community organization and social planning, as well as a distinguished career in university teaching and research. He is a frequent contributor to the professional literature.

Darlyne Bailey, PhD, ACSW, is Assistant Professor at the Mandel School of Applied Social Sciences, Case Western Reserve University, Cleveland, Ohio. She has a secondary faculty appointment at the Weatherhead School of Management and is a faculty associate with the Mandel Center for Nonprofit Organizations. She has worked in the human services arena for more than a decade as a clinician, administrator, consultant, and trainer. She also serves on several boards of trustees for community agencies.

Dixie L. Benshoff, PhD, is Executive Director of Highland Home Health. She also maintains a private practice in psychology. She is active as a consultant and trainer for nonprofit organizations, private industry, educational institutions, hospitals, and community groups.

Ralph Brody, PhD, ACSW, is Executive Director of the Federation for Community Planning in Cleveland, Ohio. He also serves as an adjunct lecturer at the Mandel School of Applied Social Sciences, Case Western Reserve University. He has served as a management consultant to organizations throughout the United States and in Kenya, Spain, and China.

Claudia J. Coulton, PhD, ACSW, is Professor at the Mandel School of Applied Social Sciences and Director of the Center for Urban Poverty and Social Change, Case Western Reserve University. Her social work practice experience includes work in public welfare, health, and mental health settings. She serves as a consultant to various hospitals and human services agencies and is the author of numerous articles, as well as *Social Work Quality Assurance Programs: A Comparative Analysis*.

Laurie Newman DiPadova, MS, is a doctoral candidate at the Rockefeller College of Public Affairs and Policy, The University at Albany, State University of New York. She was previously a training associate with the Office of Human

Resources Development in the New York State Department of Social Services. She recently coauthored a chapter and wrote the Instructional Guide for the management development text *Becoming a Master Manager: A Competency Framework.*

Douglas C. Eadie, MS, is founder and President of Strategic Development Consulting, Inc., a Shaker Heights, Ohio, firm specializing in the design and implementation of strategic management applications in the nonprofit and public sectors. Prior to establishing his firm, he served as senior manager in a variety of public and nonprofit organizations. He coauthored one of the first books on public and nonprofit strategic planning, *The Game Plan: Governance with Foresight,* and his articles and chapters have appeared in numerous journals and books.

Sue R. Faerman, PhD, is Assistant Professor at the Rockefeller College of Public Affairs and Policy, The University at Albany, State University of New York. Her major research interests are in the areas of managerial transitions and management education and development. She is coauthor of the management development texts *Becoming a Master Manager: A Competency Framework* and *Supervising New York State: A Framework for Excellence,* as well as numerous articles focusing on the evaluation of management development programs.

Perry P. Heath, MSSA, is Director of Resource Development/Campaign for the United Way of Greater Milwaukee, Wisconsin. He also serves on the National Advisory Council, Information Technology Committee, and the Resource Development Committee for United Way of America. He was formerly Executive Director of the United Way organizations in Newark, Ohio, and Carlisle, Pennsylvania. He serves as an adjunct lecturer on computer use at the Mandel School of Applied Social Sciences, Case Western Reserve University.

Clarence Jones is head of Video Consultants, Inc., in Tampa, Florida. He teaches media strategy and on-camera performance to a broad range of professionals and executives in the nonprofit, governmental, and private industry sectors. He was a reporter for 30 years in both the print and electronic media. He published the first edition of *How to Speak TV, Print, and Radio* in 1984 and left the news business to form his consulting firm.

Mary Kay Kantz, JD, is a member of the faculty at the Case Western Reserve University School of Law. Her areas of teaching include legal research, analysis, and writing, as well as persuasive public speaking.

Paul A. Kurzman, PhD, ACSW, is Professor at the Hunter College School of Social Work, City University of New York, where he specializes in organizational theory, risk management, and occupational social work practice. He has been an administrator of public and private human services agencies and is author or editor of four books as well as numerous articles in human services journals.

Kathryn Mercer, MSSA, JD, is a member of the faculty at the Case Western Reserve University School of Law. She teaches courses on family law, law and public policy, alternative dispute resolution, and lawyering skills as well as on legal research analysis and writing.

Elliott Davis Moore, MSW, ACSW, is the President of Hospital Alliance of Tennessee, Inc., a statewide public relations and lobbying organization for not-for-profit hospitals. She was previously Executive Director of the Tennessee Chapter of the National Association of Social Workers and has been involved in legislative advocacy activities for mental health professionals since 1983. She also serves as a member of the Legislative Affairs Committee of the National Association of Social Workers.

Regina Nixon, PhD, is a faculty associate with the Center for Urban Poverty and Social Change at the Mandel School of Applied Social Sciences, Case Western Reserve University. She was formerly a Senior Research Associate at the National Urban League. She has written extensively on career patterns of minorities and women in the corporate and nonprofit sectors.

Peter J. Pecora, PhD, holds a joint appointment as Manager of Research at The Casey Family Program and Associate Professor at the School of Social Work, University of Washington, Seattle. His research and writing have focused on personnel management in the human services, evaluation of Intensive Family Preservation Services, risk assessment in child protective services, long-term foster care, and in-service training for child welfare staff. He has served on NASW's Commission on Families.

Robert F. Rivas, MSW, ACSW, is Associate Professor and head of the Social Work Department at Sienna College in Loudonville, New York. He has social work practice experience in the fields of family and child welfare and in residential treatment of children. His research and publications have focused on social work education, management, and social group work. He is coauthor of *Introduction to Group Work Practice.*

Mark I. Singer, PhD, ACSW, is Associate Professor at the Mandel School of Applied Social Sciences, Case Western Reserve University. He also maintains a private clinical social work practice. He has worked in hospital administration and mental health program development. He has published extensively on adolescent mental health and substance abuse issues and is involved in research related to nonprofit mergers, acquisitions, and consolidations.

Margaret Spearmon, MSW, is Assistant Director of Field Education and an instructor at the Mandel School of Applied Social Sciences, Case Western Reserve University, Cleveland, Ohio. She was previously a senior planner at United Way Services of Cleveland. For more than 15 years, she has been involved in developing training curricula and providing training on human relations and minority issues.

Kenneth R. Wedel, PhD, is Professor at the University of Oklahoma School of Social Work, Norman. He previously served there as Director and was Associate Dean of the School of Social Welfare at the University of Kansas. His major areas of research and teaching include social policy, program planning, and evaluation, with a particular focus on governmental funding of nongovernment organizations. He is coauthor of a forthcoming book entitled *Evaluating Social Programs.*

Myron E. Weiner, MGA, is Professor and Chair of the Administration Sequence at the University of Connecticut School of Social Work, West Hartford. Prior to assuming his faculty position, he served in a number of state and local government management positions. He has also served as a management and professional development consultant for numerous public and private human services organizations throughout the nation. He is a frequent contributor to the management literature and is the author of *Human Services Management: Analysis and Application.*

Dennis R. Young, PhD, is Director of the Mandel Center for Nonprofit Organizations and Mandel Professor of Nonprofit Management at Case Western Reserve University. He is the author of numerous articles on nonprofit organizations and public services and has written or edited several books, including *Educating Managers of Nonprofit Organizations* (with Michael O'Neill), *Casebook of Management for Nonprofit Organizations,* and *If Not For Profit, For What? A Behavioral Theory of the Nonprofit Sector Based on Entrepreneurship.* He is also Editor of the journal *Nonprofit Management and Leadership.*